Sarah Raven

good

Recipes to help you look, feel and live well

good

Photography by Jonathan Buckley

food

**For Jonathan Buckley
In gratitude for all the happy
times and beautiful pictures**

BLOOMSBURY
LONDON • OXFORD • NEW YORK • NEW DELHI • SYDNEY

Introduction

I WANT EVERY dish I eat to look good, be good to eat and do me good. If you go about it the right way, you can eat wonderful food which also has a positive effect on your health, and makes you live longer and feel better.

With our greater life expectancy these days, it's more important than ever that we keep ourselves in good shape physically (as well as mentally), both through exercise, and eating sensibly and well. But 'sensible' or 'healthy' dishes can often be too earnest, and either feel heavy or too much like rabbit food. The challenge I set myself when writing this book was for every recipe to be truly tempting and colourful, but also one that I'd be happy to eat regularly, without feeling the hair-shirt was on. That way each recipe would be likely to enter the everyday food repertoire – and that has to be the aim.

In my early years here in Sussex, until 1996, I was a medical doctor. When I was not on the wards, I was a doctor who cooked – I have been passionate about cooking since I was a teenager – and I became increasingly fascinated by the amount of evidence showing how health is utterly entwined with diet. My cooking began to reflect these ideas. I moved away from processed to whole grains and, even in winter, ate more salads, used only the best cold-pressed oils, cooked and ate more soups, and decreased my reliance on dairy. So, as you can appreciate, the book you're holding is one that's been at the back of my mind for a long time.

And, for more than 20 years now, I've grown my own food at Perch Hill, and everything I've cooked has revolved around the wonderful things the garden has given me. Fruit and veg have become even more the centrepiece of what I eat – and they are also at the heart of the recipes in this book. If you grow your own foods, whether in the garden or allotment, you can ensure that they are grown organically, without being sprayed with insecticides or chemical fertilisers, and you can pick them when they are at their seasonal peak. If you aren't fortunate enough to be able to grow your own, choose your fruit and veg carefully: try to buy seasonally (when everything is at its best), locally (so it is very fresh) and organic. You must be aware of the provenance of the food you are eating – it's central to *Good Good Food*.

Another insight into the intimate relationship between health and diet came about through my visits to Crete, where I became gripped by statistics about Cretan longevity. Cretans live substantially longer than the rest of us, and significantly longer even than Greeks on the mainland only a few miles away. Many people from places and communities similarly renowned for their longevity – such as Sardinia, the Okinawa Islands of Japan and the south coast of Nova Scotia live to be around 100 years old. And when I say live, I mean that they live very long lives, in a healthy, integrated and active way. They may be old, but they are not crippled by the illnesses and afflictions of our elderly population: dementia, depression, disabling cardiovascular disease or cancer. Such diseases are rare in these communities, and there are several reasons why this is so. One is that, on

the whole, they are more physically active, but it's also important that in their traditional diet they tend not to eat processed foods; nor do they over-eat, as we tend to do in more industrialised countries; and they have a lifestyle in which they eat sociably, with food and meals bringing people together. It is very difficult to quantify, but I believe this is a major factor in eating for health and longevity.

Healthy eating is a vast subject, made ever more complicated by the increasing problem of obesity in western cultures. There is so much information drip-fed to us through newspapers and television, books and social media, that it's hard to know what we should believe and which path to follow. The ideas on the following pages and throughout this book should help you re-think your ways of buying, cooking and eating. But do remember, none of this is meant to be a punishment. It's a way of enhancing your life, not diminishing it. A lot of it is fun, and many of the recipes bring smiles to the faces of the people who are eating them.

So let's get started. It's time to begin a new campaign to make tasty food which is positively good for you too. Take it at your own pace – none of us can change the habits of a lifetime overnight – but whether it's a midweek supper or a weekend lunch, aim to make something that is simply *Good Good Food*.

Sarah Raven
November 2015

Eat yourself healthy

THE WORLD WE live in has been transformed in the last century or so. We have seen massive dietary and lifestyle changes in a relatively short time, changes that have come about much faster than our genetic make-up. Environmental and personal stresses have increased exponentially, and our bodies can no longer cope.

These changes are particularly true in the food we eat. Many of us have been pushed towards sweet, nutrient-sparse, but calorie-dense, fatty foods, leaving us over-fed, but counter-intuitively undernourished. Our bodies are increasingly intoxicated by the vast array of chemicals we are presented with on a daily basis; they're stressed from fluctuating blood-sugar levels, due largely to the excess of refined food, caffeine and alcohol many of us consume; and they're in a state of chronic inflammation, setting us on the road to almost inevitable ill health.

We may be living longer, but that's not because we're looking after ourselves better. It's largely down to improvements in medical care and sanitation. We are dying of different things from our great-grandparents and even our grandparents. At the beginning of the twentieth century, over 60 per cent of deaths were due to infectious and transmissible diseases. Now, in the early twenty-first century, more than 60 per cent are due to chronic diseases such as Alzheimer's, atherosclerosis (clogging of the arteries), type 2 diabetes, cancer, cardiovascular disease, stroke and obesity-related conditions. They're our killers, and we are actively encouraging them with our diet and lifestyle choices.

It used to be thought that some inevitable biological clock was ticking – that's what made us old – but it is now understood that ageing can be due to the cumulative damage done to our bodies at a cellular level and the increasing inability of our cells to respond to lifestyle, diet and environmental challenges that can lead to disease. So if we can find ways of *reducing* the rate of damage, or *increasing* the effectiveness of repair mechanisms, we might be able to delay the onset of disease and have a healthier, fitter old age.

This book is about exactly that: first choosing the best, non-faddy superfoods that can really make a difference to your health, including many that we ought to be eating day to day; and then offering you my best ideas on how to eat them. I've highlighted over 100 healthy ingredients here, and have included for each of them a mini food 'biography'. Gathering information from nutritionists, medical journals and research centres, such as The Institute of Food Research (IFR) and the John Innes Centre, these outline the latest evidence on the healthiness of all these special foods, with technical terms in bold type explained in the glossary. There are some 250 recipes which feature these wholesome ingredients, nearly all of which signal their goodness through bright colours and strong flavours, dimensions of the healthy elements they contain.

Coming up with these recipes and exploring a new way of eating has given my daily menu a huge boost. This way of cooking involves new ingredients, such as black rice, quinoa, seaweeds

and coconut oil – things I'd hardly heard of, let alone cooked, a few years ago – as well as traditional foods such as kale and beetroot, vegetables often served in a pretty tedious, run-of-the-mill, boiled or steamed way. I hope to give each of them a new lease of life – as well as a regular new place in your diet – so you'll be rushing out to grow and pick or stock up on them, creating meals including at least one of them every day.

What to eat and drink

We're getting ill nowadays because we are no longer eating the right foods in the correct proportions and volume. How can we remedy this to keep our bodies feeling good? Here are some basic rules as to what you should eat and drink.

Eat more vegetables and fruit. Both veg and fruit help protect us against chronic disease. In general they contain many of the natural 'anti-stress' nutrients like magnesium and the B vitamins, as well as essential immune-supporting, disease-fighting, age-delaying, health-boosting antioxidants and phytonutrients. You can't get too much of any of these, yet the latest figures from the 2014 National Diet and Nutrition Survey show that fewer than 40 per cent of adults achieve the 'five-a-day' recommendation; and more worryingly only 10 per cent of boys and 7 per cent of girls aged 11 to 18 manage it. That's why almost every recipe in this book includes a pile of veg or fruit.

Enjoy a 'rainbow' of veg. Dark-green and brightly coloured vegetables such as kale, tomatoes, beetroot, carrots and sweet potatoes are especially rich in nutrients. Their different pigments, such as lycopene (red, purple and blue), anthocyanin (red, black and blue), lutein (yellow), beta-carotene (orange), and chlorophyll (green), to name but a few, are all important antioxidants which play different roles, so your ideal diet needs to include a good colour range. Scientists have recently discovered that orange and red pigments derived from beta-carotene in fish and plankton are used by seabirds as signals of good health when choosing a mate. A bright orange beak and legs on a puffin means it's been eating the right things and will make a healthy partner.

Eat some of your veg raw. Cooking can denature the goodness of many vegetables, so be sure to eat a mix of raw and cooked, and then you'll be guaranteed a wide array of micronutrients. Vitamin C for example – crucial for a healthy immune system – breaks down on cooking, as does chlorophyll, which makes leaves bright green. The chlorophyll contained in raw green leaves is thought to be detoxifying, possibly helping to cleanse the blood and also support the immune system.

Choose organic veg if possible. Organic food tends to be raised more slowly, less intensively, and may have more nutrients in it. You also avoid the danger of chemical residues. And, if you do manage to buy organic, don't peel your veg. The highest concentration of antioxidants is nearest the skin, where they can best protect the plant from pests and diseases. We benefit from these antioxidants too, so keep the skin on if possible, or if the skin looks unappetising, scrape veg and fruit as finely as you can.

Include fermented vegetables in your diet. Fermenting not only preserves vegetables, but also enhances taste and the availability of nutrients. By preserving the veg in their raw state, the availability of vitamin C and other vitamins like folate is increased, and other nutrients are broken down into more easily digestible forms. Even for those in good general health, a fermented vegetable or fruit makes a tip-top superfood.

Fermented food is also powerfully beneficial for anyone with digestive problems. It contains lots of 'good' bacteria such as *lactobacillus*, and makes a strong natural probiotic that helps to restore the correct balance to our gut flora. It can work to improve an imbalance associated with chronic illnesses such as IBS, Crohn's and even mental health problems such as depression. In Germany, they're so hooked on it, they sell the fermented juice of sauerkraut separately to drink as a tonic. Fermented veg and drinks such as sauerkraut, kimchi and kombucha are available at good health-food shops, or you can make your own – recipes for sauerkraut and kombucha are included here.

Eat plenty of berries. Blueberries, raspberries and strawberries are particularly good for you, and don't forget old favourites like the top-ranking superfood, blackcurrants, choosing very fresh or frozen. Berries all have a low sugar content – a fraction of that found in pineapple, mango or apples. They are also low in calories, high in fibre, vitamins and minerals, and super-high in antioxidants. They're in the stratospheric superfood crew.

Prioritise *good* proteins, including eggs. Every cell in the body is made from protein and it's associated with muscle strength and stamina, cell repair and replication – all essential when fending off, or recovering from illness. Fish and poultry, lean cuts of organic grass-fed red meat and game or, for vegetarians, nuts, seeds, tofu, lentils and legumes are all good news. In general try to include protein with each meal and snack, as this also helps balance blood sugar. With protein, a good-sized portion should just fill the palm of your hand.

And don't forget the protein in eggs. There has been a swathe of misinformation flying around about eggs, but you can now be certain: they're a brilliant and healthy food.

Choose whole grains and pulses. For energy and fibre, we need carbohydrates, but you must go for the complex sort. Whole grains – such as oats, freekeh, buckwheat, black, red and brown rice – have all three elements of the grain intact. The coarse outer layer – the bran – contains the most fibre; the endosperm, the large bit in the middle, is the main energy source with most of the carbohydrate; and

the germ, right down at the base, is the embryo in its early stages. That's the smallest part, and it's packed with nutrients.

Milled wheat and rice have had everything but the endosperm stripped away, leaving them with less fibre and fewer vitamins, minerals, antioxidants and other nutrients. Although the bran and germ make up about an eighth of the wheat grain's weight, they contain four-fifths of its valuable nutrients. Without them, the grain is just less good for you. Refined carbohydrates also give you a steep blood-sugar rise as they quickly break down into glucose, and if this is not used as energy, it is stored in the body as fat.

Know the difference between good and bad fats. We need fat in our diet, but we should aim to eat good fats. Good fats include the heart-friendly and anti-inflammatory omega-3 and omega-6 essential

they clog the arteries, raise your blood pressure and can contribute to heart disease.

And finally, there are the downright very bad fats, the disease-inducing, man-made 'trans' fats. Used to make food taste good and provide a longer shelf-life, they have been banned in America, but are still in tons of food in Europe. These processed unsaturated fats are particularly detrimental to our health, raising bad cholesterol levels, but also lowering the good cholesterol that protects us against heart disease. They are rare in nature but are common in industrially produced vegetable oils, with a widespread use in processed foods such as biscuits, pies and cakes, margarine, fried foods and average takeaways. The rule is simple with these: read the labels and avoid foods that include hydrogenated or partially hydrogenated vegetable oils.

Balance your intake of omega-3s and omega-6s. As well as having plenty of the good fats, and reducing the bad and very bad fats, it's crucial to have the right *balance* of omega-3 to omega-6 essential fatty acids. Even though they're healthy, omega-6 fatty acids compete with omega-3s for use in the body, and so excessive intake of omega-6s means that we're unable to reap the benefits of the anti-inflammatory omega-3s. Ideally the ratio should be between 1:1 and 1:4, omega-3: omega-6, but with most people, it's between 1:10 and 1:25, which is way out of kilter. This imbalance is mainly due to our increased reliance on processed foods and oils.

With a low-fat diet, minimal processed foods and lots of oily fish (sardines, mackerel, salmon, trout and herring), you're on the right track, but to rely on this alone would mean eating *a lot* of oily fish and hugely more than most of us consume. Flaxseed oil and ground flaxseeds are particularly good choices to meet your needs for omega-3s. Upping your intake is surprisingly easy: one teaspoon of flaxseed oil or one tablespoon of ground flaxseeds will supply the daily requirement and will also give you enough omega-6 to make sure you're meeting your daily requirement. Many of the recipes here include flaxseeds or their oil.

fatty acids. These are essential because we can't make them in our bodies, so need to eat them. For healthy sources of high omega-3s, think oily fish, flaxseed oil, chia and flaxseeds, walnuts and leafy green vegetables; for high omega-6s, think nuts, seeds and avocados, rapeseed oil, game and poultry. Then there is olive oil, which contains oleic acid, thought to protect the heart and to lower cancer risk. Your average Cretan consumes 31 litres a year, or 750ml a week. This is five times the British rate. As more of us are living longer, dementia is becoming more and more common in our more northerly societies, yet it is an almost non-existent disease in Crete. This is thought to be partially due to the super-good qualities of olive oil.

The bad fats are the saturated fats, such as those in meat, processed meats like bacon, fried food, animal-based foods – lard, butter, hard cheese and cream. It's best to limit these because

Eat yourself healthy

Drink plenty of liquid. Increase the healthy hydrating liquids you drink such as water, herbal and green tea; and cut back on the ones that dehydrate, such as alcohol and coffee. If you consume around 2 litres of water – or other healthy liquid – a day, this will help with weight loss and general health.

What not to eat

As well as knowing what to eat to help protect us against illness, it's worth knowing the things which are best avoided or reduced in your daily diet. Here's a list of those too.

Banish processed sugars. Refined sugar is very calorific and causes the body to store fat. It comes from sugar beet or sugar cane, but is so highly processed, it's left with no plant nutrients, thus zero goodness. Sugar consumption causes spikes in blood-sugar levels, and continual over-consumption can lead to type 2 diabetes. Sugar can also switch off mechanisms that make us feel full, as well as having the potential to damage the heart and cause cancers.

If you have a sweet tooth, do not replace sugar with artificial sweeteners as these can play havoc with our bodies' systems. There are some natural sweeteners, which are better for you, but you want to limit these too. Maple syrup, for instance, has a third fewer calories than table sugar, and is a little sweeter, so you can use less; and a top-quality maple syrup is not a nutritional void. Dates and any dried fruit are also good as natural sweeteners. *But* don't add any of these willy-nilly. They're packed with sugar too. The aim should be to cut down on sugars and re-educate our taste-buds to less sweet flavours.

Avoid processed and packaged foods. These tend to be full of fat, salt and sugar – and sugar is included in an astonishing number of *savoury* foods (such as baked beans, most ready meals, tomato ketchup, savoury pies and fish fingers, tinned soups, and many low-fat products). The ingredients are listed in descending order of importance, and sugar is often horrifyingly high on that list.

Interestingly, fat and sugar are even *worse in combination* than when eaten on their own. Mixed together, they are tasty, encourage us to over-eat and some studies show they can make our weight balloon. Most pre-made biscuits, cakes and sweets contain this dangerous fat and sugar combination in spades. They often also contain hydrogenated fats. You're better off cooking your own puddings and sweet things – then you can control what you're putting in.

Watch your salt intake. Salt is essential for life in animals and humans: it helps electrical impulses sent from the brain to communicate with nerves around the body. However, we don't need too much of it. Most processed foods rely on added salt for their taste, and that's one of the reasons they're best avoided.

The type of salt you use is also important for health. There are three basic salts: sea, rock and table salt. Table salt is highly refined, 97% sodium chloride, with most of the impurities and trace minerals removed. It is bleached to give the white colour rather than a natural yellow, and is best avoided. Instead, choose sea or rock salt. Sea salt, made by evaporating sea water, contains small amounts of trace minerals such as potassium, calcium and magnesium which work synergistically with sodium to regulate water balance in the body. It has a less bitter flavour than table salt and is milder. Unrefined sea salts often have a pink, off white or grey tinge, hinting at the trace mineral content.

Rock salt such as pink Himalayan salt, from the Khewra salt mine in Pakistan, is a pure salt which is uncontaminated and free from toxins or pollutants. The pink colour is due to the presence of iron oxide. It contains the same trace minerals as above, and slightly lower amounts of sodium than regular salt.

How to eat and cook

As well as knowing what to eat – and what to avoid – it's good to have an idea of when to eat, as well as some guidelines on the healthiest ways to prepare and cook your food.

Always eat breakfast. Food is energy, so you want to fill yourself with fuel at the start of the day.

Don't eat too much, and spread what you eat throughout the day. There's plenty of evidence that eating three small meals and a couple of small snacks a day is a healthy way to eat and it is much better for you than a major blow-out, particularly in the evening.

Cook sensibly. How we cook things is important, and steaming is at the top of the list. Steaming is low-fat and, rather than washing nutrients away, keeps most of them available for us. Boiling diminishes the nutrient content of food, with valuable things lost into the water. Roasting and frying almost always involve fats and oils. With either, but especially when frying, it's important to use high smoke-point oils/fats such as cold-pressed rapeseed oil (not canola), hempseed, coconut or avocado oils, or ghee. These oils won't degrade to unhealthy fats when exposed to high heat (each has a different smoke point), so this makes them better for us than the more traditional choice of olive or sunflower oil or butter.

Make soup part of your weekly menu. When you're deciding what to eat, regularly choose soup for lunch or dinner, as soup immediately ups your consumption of veg and it is excellent for weight control. Soup is processed more slowly than the same ingredients plus water, as the water is combined with the ingredients and is not passed straight through the stomach. This makes you feel full for longer. There are lots of soup recipes here – and good things to eat with soup to make it into a meal.

Eat more slowly, and chew! Most of us eat far too quickly, and most of us do not chew food for long enough to properly start the digestive process. Nutritionists tell you to chew every mouthful twenty times before you swallow it. This gives the body time to realise what it's eaten, start the digestion process and for the 'I'm satisfied' hormones to be released, so you'll feel full with less.

Fast every now and again. There is increasing evidence that periodic fasting – perhaps a day a week or fortnight – is good for everyone, and that fasting for two days each week can really help those who need to control their weight. Occasional fasting helps correct insulin secretion, sugar cravings and over-eating, as well as re-setting expectations about what it's sensible to eat. We all know how after Christmas or a good holiday, when portions can be excessive, you want to go on eating too much, and the odd day of fasting or light eating keeps this on track. There are calorie counts at the end of every recipe to help you on your way.

How to cope with food intolerance. If you have a diagnosed food allergy or an intolerance – perhaps to gluten or lactose – there are plenty of recipes designed for you here. The index flags gluten-free and dairy-free recipes, to help you find the ones suited to your needs.

Share your food with others. In the places where people live long and healthy lives there tends to be a pattern of sharing food with family or friends at least a few times a week, if not every day. Offering an array of dishes and sharing our meals with others seems to be good for our state of mind and our health.

If you follow these key principles it will give you a really sure foundation for a healthy way of eating.

Eat yourself healthy

Breakfast

BREAKFAST IS THE easiest meal to skip when you're running late and rushing out of the door. Many of us do just that, but studies show the old cliché is true: to fire on all cylinders, you should 'breakfast like a king, lunch like a prince and dine like a pauper'.

Food is energy, so fill yourself with fuel at the start of the day. The space between last night's dinner and the morning's breakfast is the longest time our bodies go without food, and extending the fast is not a good idea. Countless tests have shown that increasing glucose concentration and the nutrient supply to the brain by eating breakfast makes us quicker and sharper. It improves cognitive function and short-term memory.

Lack of food releases stress hormones, which in turn propel sugars into the blood to correct the balance. That keeps you going, but cortisol, adrenalin and noradrenalin – the stress hormones – have other effects on the body too. When they're not needed for fight or flight, they don't do you any good. They make the body feel jangly and un-relaxed, and lead to storage, not usage, of fat. Acute stress is OK, because it's finite, but if you run too long on adrenalin then your body stops responding in a healthy way and you become, in effect, a stress addict.

So, you need some food at the start of the day, and what you choose is important. If you have minimal or no breakfast, you will almost always blow it and go for fatty or sugary things by mid morning when you're starving. You might think that as glucose is needed for energy, then eating something sugary would be the perfect solution. However, too much glucose – as well as too little – impairs rather than enhances brain function. Lots of sugar also makes you slow. It offers you a quick fix of energy and a feeling of being full, but drops just as quickly as it peaks, leaving you lower than where you started.

You might reach for low-fat fruit yoghurt thinking it's a healthy option, but lots of these are jam-packed with sugar as a replacement for fat. An extreme case is one of those apparently child-friendly yoghurt pots with chocolate cereal hoops on the side – they contain over 25g of sugar in a 135g pot. That's over six teaspoons of sugar; the equivalent of the World Health Organisation's total recommended daily allowance for an adult in one hit. Recently – in order to contain the current diabetes and obesity epidemic – scientists at University College London have called for the recommended daily sugar intake to be slashed to 15g, just under four teaspoons, so with that pot of yoghurt, you're already well over. With any fruit yoghurt, make sure to check the label for sugar content before you buy it or, better still, make your own. There are several recipes here (see pages 45, 46 and 50).

This glucose hit doesn't just apply to sugar. You'll also get it with highly processed carbohydrates such as white bread and most packaged cereals. These contain little or no nutrition and are broken down to sugars very quickly by the body. Don't make these your easy breakfast option, but choose carbs which are

whole grains: oats, rye, millet, barley, quinoa, spelt or buckwheat. Cut, rolled or pearled, many make good porridge and are also ideal bases for granolas and mueslis. These complex carbs will sustain you for longer, and have more good stuff in them than processed grains.

If you're trying to improve your body's handling of blood sugar, or lose weight, it's best to have your carbs in the morning and don't make them all you eat. With both these scenarios, in the short term, you may want to cut back the carbs, eliminate fruit and, even at breakfast, stick to protein, healthy fats and vegetables (for some ideas, see pages 54 and 55).

Protein is good for us all at breakfast. It's a key building-block to health and is sustaining. It helps to stabilise your blood sugar, keeps you full for longer and maintains energy levels well. Eat a few nuts in your muesli; discover protein-rich quinoa porridge; add some natural yoghurt or seeds to granola; put tofu in your smoothies to give them a creamy texture; have a couple of eggs, or even some fish – but smoked fish only occasionally, since it contains a lot of salt and sometimes also chemicals from the smoking process.

Milled organic flaxseeds (also known as linseeds) are a good addition to breakfast. They up the protein content and are rich in valuable omega-3 fatty acids. These can go into your muesli, granola, porridge, bread and smoothies. You'll find flaxseeds in many of the breakfast recipes here.

It's worth thinking carefully about what you drink at breakfast, too. Fruit juices are not a good idea for every day, even if they are freshly juiced. They can contain high amounts of sugar (albeit natural sugar), and don't provide the fibre that you would get from eating the fruit whole. Smoothies or breakfast gazpachos on the other hand – where you include the whole parts of the fruit or veg that you would usually eat, just blitzed raw – are good. They contribute to your all-important quota of fruit and veg per day. However, there is more sugar in a fruit smoothie than in a veg one, so ideally make them with two parts fruit to three parts veg or 1:2. Look for recipes for these in the drinks chapter.

Caffeine in the morning seems to wake you up and give you a boost. It increases neuron activity and sparks off the stress hormones, which then release sugar stores into the bloodstream. That explains the extra energy and the bright and zingy brain, but at the same time caffeine can increase anxiety and make you clumsy; and too much in the system leads to headaches and – as we all know – insomnia. None of that does any good for overall energy levels or cognitive function in the longer term. Caffeine also bounces blood-sugar levels up and down, creating sugar cravings and again spurring you on to reach for quick-fix, high-sugar food. If you fancy a zippy espresso in the morning, make sure to have it with or after food, not on an empty stomach. Also think of moving to one of the less caffeine-rich teas: a cup of weak Earl Grey or Lapsang Souchong contains less than a third of the caffeine in one espresso.

Lemon in hot water as you get out of bed is the best drink of all – it helps refresh your system. But ideally rinse your mouth with water or clean your teeth afterwards to protect your tooth enamel. Also try to acquire a taste for antioxidant-rich green tea. It contains caffeine, but tons of goodness too.

So what are the guidelines for an ideal breakfast?

» Include good-quality protein.
» When choosing carbs, always use whole grains.
» Don't kick off breakfast with a double espresso. Caffeine-free or low-caffeine drinks are the way to go, at least at the beginning of the day.
» Start your veg consumption early in the day with a smoothie, and move to these instead of fruit juice.
» Above all, make sure you've got a few healthy and delicious breakfast options in the cupboard or fridge. Most of us – even keen cooks – think about what's for dinner, but don't bother to stock up with the ingredients for good breakfasts.
» Remember a good old, easy-to-prepare egg or two makes an excellent breakfast.

If you want to be brainy, scintillating and slim, breakfast is key.

Bircher muesli

This authentic recipe from a Swiss friend is the ideal start to the day. It is oat-based, and oats are rich in protein and slow-release carbohydrates. With added nuts and seeds, this makes a high-protein breakfast to sustain you until lunchtime. If it feels like too much of a faff to make every morning, prepare a double portion and keep half in the fridge for the following day. You can also make it the night before.

Quark is a fresh, soft, creamy cheese popular in Scandinavia and Switzerland. It's like yoghurt in consistency, but without the sour taste, which means you don't need to add maple syrup or honey to make it delicious. If you can't find quark, use live Greek yoghurt or even full-fat milk. I sometimes add a little ground cinnamon – which has been shown to be beneficial to blood-sugar levels and is naturally sweet (see page 22).

Blood oranges, and their juice, are good to use when they're available. You can add whatever you fancy – orange segments, strawberries, raspberries, peaches, pomegranate seeds or cranberries – depending on the season.

For 2:
Juice of 1 orange
Good handful of rolled oats
½ apple, skin left on
2 tbsp almonds or hazelnuts, chopped into
    2–3mm pieces
1 tbsp pumpkin seeds
1 tbsp sunflower seeds
1 tbsp milled organic flaxseeds
1 tbsp currants
1–2 tbsp quark (or live Greek yoghurt)

Stir the orange juice into the oats until well mixed. Finely grate the apple into the mixture (use a Microplane if possible – the finer the grate, the gentler and less acidic the taste). Stir, then add the nuts, seeds and currants. Finally, add the quark (or live Greek yoghurt) and stir well to combine.

» 350 calories per serving

More on » oranges p49 » oats p25 » apples p288 » almonds p347 » hazelnuts p50 » pumpkin seeds p105 » flaxseeds p30 » yoghurt p44

Variations
Apple Bircher muesli To vary the flavour, use a little cloudy apple juice instead of the orange juice. The opaqueness of cloudy juice is due to the higher levels of pulp, including fibre, so always choose that over clear and, ideally, freshly juice your own.
» 350 calories per serving
Low-lactose Bircher muesli If you are lactose-intolerant, try sheep's or goats' yoghurt (instead of quark or live Greek yoghurt), which are both lower in lactose.
» Sheep's yoghurt, 350 calories per serving,
    goats' yoghurt, 352
Dairy-free Bircher muesli For a dairy-free version, use coconut milk yoghurt; this is lactose-free.
» 364 calories per serving

Breakfast

Frank's granola

There are four whole grains in this recipe from a friend of mine – oats, plus rolled flakes of millet, rye and barley. You can finish the granola off with dried fruit, and it's also lovely with fresh fruit and live Greek yoghurt. The recipe includes Brazil nuts which – like walnuts – are very nutritious, but go off more quickly than other nuts, particularly when chopped, so don't make this in super-size quantities. That's why you'll often find whole Brazils in shop-bought muesli, which feel out of scale in the bowl.

Fills 2 x 1 litre Kilner jars:
500g jumbo oats
200g millet flakes
200g rye flakes
200g barley flakes
100g pumpkin seeds, whole or roughly chopped
100g sunflower seeds
100g milled organic flaxseeds
100g sesame seeds
100g Brazil nuts, chopped
100g chopped or flaked almonds

For the coating
150ml maple syrup or clear honey
100ml warm water
100ml cold-pressed rapeseed oil or 4 tbsp set coconut oil

To finish
Dried fruit (goji berries, blueberries, cranberries, apricots, sour cherries or raisins), roughly chopped

Preheat the oven to 180–200°C/gas mark 4–6 (i.e. quite hot).

Mix the oats, flakes, seeds and nuts on a baking tray. Mix the maple syrup or honey with the warm water and oil. Add this liquid to the dry ingredients and mix thoroughly, so that they are well coated.

Place in the oven and bake for about 20 minutes, stirring through at regular intervals: start with 4-minute intervals and as the ingredients warm up, change to 2-minute intervals. Don't get distracted – the granola will burn easily. Remove from the oven and allow to cool. Store in clean Kilner jars for up to a month or so.

Serve with full-fat cows' milk, soya or almond milk or yoghurt, and add whichever dried fruit you choose.

» 206 calories per 50g serving (not including the dried fruit addition, or milk or yoghurt to serve)

More on » oats *p25* » pumpkin seeds *p105* » flaxseeds *p30* » sesame seeds *p164* » Brazil nuts *p170* » almonds *p347* » maple syrup *p27* » honey *p334* » rapeseed oil *p248* » coconut oil *p309* » blueberries *p328* » cranberries *p242*

Goji berries are small red berries, gathered from bushes indigenous to the Tibetan and Mongolian mountains. Usually available here dried, they have a long history of use in traditional Chinese medicine. They're expensive, but with an even greater **antioxidant** content than blueberries, they're famed for their anti-ageing qualities. As they are high in antioxidants, **beta-carotene** and zeaxanthin, they are excellent for nourishing the eyes and skin. Goji berries also boost the immune system and energise the body, and a recent study showed that even eating just a few berries a day was good for brain function, improving scores in neurological and psychological tests. One word of warning, though: organochlorine pesticides are often used in their cultivation, and it's also worth remembering that blueberries, blackberries and blackcurrants have similar effects, are a fraction of the price and can be found pesticide-free.

Judges' muesli

Muesli can be dense, rich and calorific, with too much dried fruit or nuts, and it often contains things you don't like (my husband hates coconut, for example), so you end up picking stuff out of the bowl. Not so with this recipe from our local organic bakery in Hastings which, unlike many shop-bought mueslis, contains no sugar. You can use rye flakes if you want to keep it wheat-free, and to make it gluten-free, replace the wheat or rye with quinoa, amaranth or millet flakes. Oats are naturally gluten-free, but are often processed in mills alongside wheat, so check the label. Use the core recipe as a base, and add the things *you* like, changing them from one day to the next.

For 1.8kg muesli base:
50g hazelnuts
600g whole-wheat (or rye) flakes
500g rolled oats
200g jumbo oats
350g raisins
50g milled organic flaxseeds
30g sunflower seeds
1 tbsp ground cinnamon

For the extras (each morning add any of these)
A few dried goji berries
Flaked coconut
Sesame seeds
Pumpkin seeds
Chopped or flaked almonds
Chopped walnuts
Chopped Brazil nuts

Dry-fry the hazelnuts in a frying pan to lightly toast them. Cool, then roughly chop them if you want to. Dry-fry the wheat (or rye) flakes in the same frying pan (this adds to their taste). Keep them moving until they start to gently colour and a toasty smell comes off the pan, but take care not to burn them.

In a bowl, gently mix the hazelnuts with the rest of the muesli base ingredients, using your hands. Stored in an airtight bag or container, and kept out of the light, the muesli base will keep for up to two months.

Serve with full-fat milk, live natural yoghurt or freshly squeezed orange or home-pressed or cloudy apple juice (see page 19). Add any of the extra ingredients, either raw or gently dry-fried, or fresh berries if you fancy.

» 181 calories per 50g serving of the base muesli

More on » hazelnuts *p50* » oats *p25* » flaxseeds *p30* » goji berries *p21* » sesame seeds *p164* » pumpkin seeds *p105* » almonds *p347* » walnuts *p51* » Brazil nuts *p170*

Cinnamon, a spice from the bark of a tropical tree, adds a delicious warm and sweet flavour and packs a punch in terms of nutrition. The unique health benefits come from the essential oils in the bark. Try to buy Ceylon cinnamon, which will be labelled *Cinnamomum zeylanicum* or *verum*, as supermarkets often sell a related spice, cassia, as cinnamon – but healthwise, they have different properties and most of the research has been done on the Ceylon spice, which is usually grown organically. Results so far indicate that cinnamon slows the rate at which the stomach empties after a meal, reducing the spike in blood-sugar levels after eating. This means that consuming plenty of cinnamon can help with weight loss, and reducing the risk factors associated with type 2 diabetes and cardiovascular disease.

Cinnamon also has **anti-inflammatory**, anti-microbial and **antioxidant** properties, and research is being carried out into its potential as a food preservative. With its naturally sweet flavour, it's also a useful sugar replacement in many recipes.

Classic porridge

You could simply throw some rolled oats into a saucepan, cover them with water and cook them for a few minutes then eat, but this classic porridge recipe is much more delicious. The pinhead oatmeal gives a nutty texture. Use full-fat milk and serve with a protein topping (such as the one on page 29), and/or a handful of fruit. The fat in the milk helps us absorb the fat-soluble vitamin E in the seeds. I sometimes add grated nutmeg.

For 2:
50g pinhead oatmeal
50g medium oatmeal
1 tbsp milled organic flaxseeds
200ml full-fat milk
Small pinch of sea salt
40g sultanas

There's no need to soak the pinhead oatmeal – instead dry-fry both types of oats over a medium heat until fragrant (about 5 minutes, shaking regularly). They're ready when you can smell an oaty aroma coming off the pan. This increases their flavour.

Put them in a medium saucepan along with the flaxseeds, milk, salt and 400ml water and bring slowly to the boil, stirring frequently on a medium heat.

Add the sultanas, turn the heat to low and simmer, stirring very regularly, for about 10 minutes. Cover and allow to sit for 5 minutes.

Serve with a splash of full-fat cold milk and the topping of your choice.

» 342 calories per serving (not including milk to serve)

More on » flaxseeds *p30* » milk *p252*

Variations
Dairy-free porridge For a dairy-free version, cook the oats with water or home-pressed apple juice instead of milk, and use freshly squeezed orange or cloudy apple juice to serve. Or cook and serve with almond milk (for home-made, see page 347).
» With apple juice, 329 calories per serving
» With almond milk, 305 calories per serving
Pear and cinnamon porridge Replace the sultanas with a cored and chopped pear. Add ½ teaspoon ground cinnamon at the point of dry-frying the oats, so the flavour is fully absorbed.
» 318 calories per serving (not including milk to serve)

Oats are a special grain. With wheat, milling removes up to half the nutritional value, but oats emerge intact. There are four main ways of processing oats, and the good news is that nutritionally they vary only slightly.

Whole oats are called groats – you'll only get these in health-food shops. They are best soaked overnight and then cooked for about 45 minutes to give you a hearty, grainy porridge. As a complete grain, these are the slowest to be digested, and so regulate our blood sugar best. If you want a traditional type of thick, nutty porridge that you don't need to start preparing the night before, go for pinhead oatmeal (also called coarse oats, steel-cut oats or Irish oatmeal). These are the whole grains that have been cut into small sections. The second type of processed oats are porridge oats (also called old-fashioned oats or jumbo oats). These are rolled as the whole grain and are the most widely available. They are good for making porridge or muesli.

Then you have fast-cook rolled oats (also called quick oats or oat flakes), which are made by steaming and rolling pinhead oatmeal (i.e. cut), and take only a couple of minutes to cook. Finally there are 'instant' oats, which you get ready-to-eat at fast-food chains. The oats here have been sliced and roasted at a higher temperature and rolled even thinner, so they can be eaten with only boiling water added. More processed, these score higher on the **Glycaemic Index** (a measure of the impact foods have on blood-sugar levels) – coming in at 79, compared to 55 for normal rolled oats – but they still contain all the other nutritional elements of the whole grain.

All oats contain a specific type of soluble **fibre** called beta-glucan. Numerous studies have shown the beneficial effects of this on **cholesterol** levels, reducing the incidence of cardiovascular disease, stroke and type 2 diabetes. As oats make you feel full and stabilise blood-sugar levels, while being quite low in calories, they are good for appetite control.

Oats themselves do not contain **gluten**, but they are often processed in mills with other gluten-containing grains. If you are gluten-intolerant or coeliac, check the label to make sure you're buying gluten-free oats, which are processed in a separate place to avoid cross-contamination.

Esther's spelt and orange porridge

This porridge recipe, from a good friend's daughter, is delicious made with pearled spelt, with its characteristic nutty texture and taste. If you want a gluten-free porridge, substitute the spelt with another nutritious grain or seed such as quinoa, amaranth, millet or buckwheat.

For 1:
75g pearled spelt (or buckwheat)
Juice of 1 orange
4–5 prunes or dried apricots (ideally organic, unsulphured)
1 tbsp milled organic flaxseeds (optional)
½ tsp ground cinnamon
½ tsp ground cardamom
Sprinkling of raspberries or blueberries
1 tbsp mixed nuts and seeds (e.g. pumpkin and
    sunflower seeds and flaked almonds), dry-fried

Rinse the pearled spelt in hot water, then place in a non-stick pan with 450ml water, the orange juice (with some of the nutrient-rich pulp), dried fruit, flaxseeds (if using), cinnamon and cardamom, and bring to the boil on a low heat. Simmer gently for about 20 minutes until soft, stirring occasionally.

Serve, topped with raspberries or blueberries and the nuts and seeds. You may want to add a moat of full-fat milk or a dollop of yoghurt.

» 490 calories with seeds, 360 without

More on » spelt *p32* » oranges *p49* » buckwheat *p226* » flaxseeds *p30* » cinnamon *p22* » raspberries *p326* » blueberries *p328* » pumpkin seeds *p105* » almonds *p347*

Fruity chia pots

Chia seeds are deservedly known as a superfood. They look like large poppy seeds, are gluten-free and hugely nutritious, rich in omega-3s. Chia pots go particularly well with tropical fruit – such as sharon fruit or persimmon, mango, kiwi and pawpaw – as well as with raspberries. You can make this the night before and put it in the fridge so it's ready to eat – fully soaked – the next morning. When soaked, chia seeds form a gel and 'set', almost as if the recipe included a little gelatine.

For 4:
40g chia seeds
320ml hazelnut or almond milk, shop-bought
    or home-made (see p347)
1 tbsp maple syrup
1 tsp vanilla extract
1 heaped tsp ground cinnamon
Grated zest of 1 lemon or lime
2 heaped tbsp desiccated coconut
1 tbsp cashew nut butter (see p36)
Good grating of nutmeg (to taste)

For the fruit topping
125g fresh raspberries
Finely grated zest and juice of ½ lime
1 tbsp maple syrup

Put the chia seeds into a mixing bowl. Put the rest of the chia mix ingredients into a food processor and blend (or mix well together in a bowl). Pour over the chia seeds and stir well to combine.

Allow the chia mixture to sit for 10 minutes, stir again then spoon into four glasses or small bowls. Allow the chia pots to set for an hour or two, or overnight.

When ready to serve, mix together the raspberries, lime zest and juice and maple syrup. Spoon onto the top of the – now set – chia pots.

» 188 calories per serving (if made with hazelnut milk)

More on » cinnamon p22 » lemons p346 » raspberries p326

Variations
Oat pots This recipe can also be made with pinhead oatmeal instead of chia seeds. Rather like Bircher muesli, it makes an excellent summer alternative to porridge.
» 165 calories per serving
Coconut water chia pots For fewer calories (but less flavour), replace the hazelnut or almond milk with coconut water.
» 178 calories per serving

Chia seeds come from a South American plant (*Salvia hispanica*), and are one of the richest sources of **omega-3 fatty acids** – precious, healthy fats we all need more of. The seeds are **gluten**-free, but packed with **antioxidants** and **fibre**; they boost our energy, stabilise blood sugar, aid digestion and may lower **cholesterol**. They are also a great source of magnesium and calcium, essential for strong bones and teeth. Chia seeds can be sprinkled on anything – they have a bland taste – but if you soak them, they expand to many times their original size and form a gel, which makes a good porridge and keeps you feeling full for ages. They are also good for sprouting.

Baked quinoa and coconut porridge

Similar to rice pudding, this is one of my favourite everyday breakfasts – it's dairy- and gluten-free and packed with good protein. It's handy as you can make it in advance and then, in a busy week, heat portions for a quick, healthy and sustaining, protein-laden breakfast. If you want to be sugar-free, leave out the maple syrup.

If berries are not in season, then frozen berries are both delicious and excellent value. Two recent studies have found they have more nutrients than the 'fresh' berries on supermarket shelves, which have often been harvested several days before – but always try to find organic.

For 6–8:
200g white quinoa
200g mixed berries (frozen are fine out of season)
400ml tin of coconut milk
250ml almond milk (see p347)
2 tbsp maple syrup
3 tbsp milled organic flaxseeds
1 dessert apple, cored and chopped
1 tsp ground cinnamon
50g chopped nuts (optional)

Preheat the oven to 180°C/gas mark 4.

Rinse the quinoa well in a sieve under a running tap, then combine with all the ingredients in a baking dish. Bake in the oven for 45 minutes until the quinoa is soft and the mix has set, with the top golden. The deeper your dish, the longer it will take.

Spoon into bowls for eating straightaway, or leave to cool, then place in the fridge. You can then heat individual portions in a small saucepan with a little water or almond milk.

Add any additional toppings you fancy – more berries, a pear, some dry-fried walnuts or maple syrup. This is also good with a splash of full-fat organic milk if you're eating dairy.

» With nuts, 368 calories for 6 servings, 276 for 8
» Without nuts, 318 calories for 6 servings, 239 for 8

More on » quinoa p140 » mixed berries p343 » coconut milk p235 » flaxseeds p30 » apples p288 » cinnamon p22

Maple syrup This natural sweetener is made from the sap of maple trees. It has been used for centuries in North America, where the native Americans valued it for its sweetness and health-giving properties. Over 80 per cent of the world's supply now comes from Canada, where it's made in a natural two-step process. First, you drill a hole in the maple tree and collect the sugary sap, then you boil it down to a thick syrup.

Maple syrup is calorific, but it has two-thirds the calories of sugar and four-fifths that of honey, and it's naturally sweeter, so you need less. It is also more **mineral**-dense than honey and, unlike processed sugar, it contains **polyphenols**, so it has more overall goodness.

Take care to buy 100 per cent pure maple syrup, as some cheaper brands are actually a blend of maple syrup and corn syrup or sugar. It has a long shelf life, but once open should be stored in the fridge.

Quinoa porridge topper

Made from quinoa flakes, berries, nuts and seeds, this protein-rich topping for your porridge is also good on yoghurt and excellent with fresh fruit salad. Eaten at breakfast (a tablespoon is a good serving), it will help to keep you going through the morning, and you can put a few spoonfuls in a jam jar to snack on through the day. Reduce the quantity of maple syrup by half for less sweetness.

For 450g (about 20 servings):
150g quinoa flakes
20g dried goji berries (or add fresh berries at the end)
½ tsp ground cinnamon
20g flaked coconut
15g sesame seeds
20g milled organic flaxseeds
20g pumpkin seeds
30g raisins
30g flaked almonds
30g walnuts, chopped

For the coating
2–3 tbsp maple syrup
2 tbsp water
1 tbsp cold-pressed rapeseed oil

Preheat the oven to 180°C/gas mark 4.

Mix all the dry ingredients together in a bowl. Pour on the coating and mix well. Pour onto a baking tray in a shallow layer and bake for 15 minutes. Keep an eye on it for the last 5 minutes, so it does not burn. Remove, allow to cool and store in an airtight jar. Make in batches to last a couple of weeks, or if you leave the walnuts out, it will last several months.

» 1 tbsp (25g) is 96 calories

More on » quinoa *p140* » goji berries *p21* » cinnamon *p22* » sesame seeds *p164* » flaxseeds *p30* » pumpkin seeds *p105* » almonds *p347* » walnuts *p51* » maple syrup *p27* » rapeseed oil *p248*

Protein porridge topper with pomegranate

This is as simple as it gets, but it's a super-nutritious and sustaining nut and seed topping to scatter over porridge. It lasts for a good month in an airtight jar, and tastes good too, especially with the added pomegranate seeds. This is also excellent served as a topping for natural or home-made fruit yoghurt (see page 44).

Fills a 325g jar (12–15 servings):
25g pumpkin seeds
25g sunflower seeds
25g chia seeds
25g milled organic flaxseeds
25g sesame seeds
100g almonds, roughly chopped
100g walnuts, roughly chopped

For every 2 servings (optional)
Seeds of 1 pomegranate (see p46)
Clear honey or maple syrup (optional)

In a frying pan dry-fry the seeds until they start to pop. Tip into a bowl and allow to cool, then tip into a jar.

In the same pan, toast the almonds separately until golden and fragrant. Tip into a bowl and allow to cool, then add to the seeds. Repeat with the walnuts. Mix well.

Dole out the seeds of a half pomegranate per serving, along with the topper, and drizzle with honey or maple syrup, if you like.

» 1 tbsp (25g) is 152 calories

More on » pumpkin seeds *p105* » chia seeds *p26* » flaxseeds *p30* » sesame seeds *p164* » almonds *p347* » walnuts *p51* » pomegranate *p46* » honey *p334* » maple syrup *p27*

Seeded oatcakes

Adding seeds to your oatcakes gives extra substance and nutrition to an already delicious and healthy classic. Make sure you include super-nutritious chia and flaxseeds. As well as being good for breakfast – I love them with peanut butter – oatcakes make a brilliant and filling mid-morning or afternoon snack. I sometimes push some pumpkin seeds in the top before baking to enrich them more. Also try adding some finely chopped rosemary leaves to make them a perfect accompaniment to cheese.

For 20 small oatcakes:

30g organic unsalted butter or 1½ tbsp set coconut oil
120g rolled oats, plus a few extra for sprinkling
2 tbsp poppy seeds
2 tbsp sesame seeds
2 tbsp sunflower seeds
2 tbsp chia seeds
2 tbsp milled organic flaxseeds
Pinch of sea salt
2 tbsp pumpkin seeds (optional)

Preheat the oven to 180°C/gas mark 4 and line a baking tray with baking parchment.

Put the butter or coconut oil and 4 tablespoons of water in a small saucepan on a medium heat.

Pour the oats into a blender and blitz until mostly ground down, with a few left whole.

Tip the oats and all the seeds into the saucepan with a pinch of salt and stir. Add more water if needed to make a tacky dough. Leave to cool, covered, for half an hour.

Sprinkle a work surface with oats and pat the dough out gently with your hands until it is flattened and about 5mm thick. Cut into small 5cm circles using a cookie cutter. Re-roll the leftover dough and cut again. Place some pumpkin seeds on top of each oatcake, if you like.

Using a fish slice, put the oatcakes on the prepared baking tray and bake for 20 minutes, turning the tray around in the oven halfway through.

Allow to cool completely and harden before eating. These store for a few days in an airtight jar or tin.

» 71 calories per oatcake (not including pumpkin seeds)

More on » butter p104 » coconut oil p309 » oats p25 » sesame seeds p164 » chia seeds p26 » pumpkin seeds p105

Flaxseeds (also called linseeds) come from the beautiful blue-flowered plant *Linum usitatissimum*, which you'll sometimes see filling a field in June, turning it the colour of the sky. It's grown for its cotton-like fibres and its brown, golden or reddish seeds. The difference in colour is down to variety, each requiring slightly different growing conditions. Brown flaxseeds have an earthy flavour and golden and red have a nutty taste. Flaxseeds are famed for their high levels of **antioxidants**, and they give us up to seven times more lignans, cancer-fighting **plant hormones**, than sesame seeds, with research indicating they might play a role in protecting us from hormone-dependent cancers in particular (such as breast and prostate). They're also a good source of the hugely important and healthy **omega-3 fatty acids** as well as **fibre**, **protein**, iron and zinc. Brown flaxseeds have a slightly higher level of omega-3 fatty acids.

Use them in your breakfast granola, in a smoothie, sprinkle them over porridge, or toast them and put in a salad... The key thing is to eat them as often as you can.

Swedish crispbread with crushed avocado

An avocado breakfast is great with toasted pumpernickel when you're short of time, but if you feel like doing some quick and easy baking, then an authentic Swedish crispbread is delicious. Perfect for dipping into the avocado mush for a speedy, healthy and sustaining breakfast, they are also ideal as a snack with hummus or tapenade (see pages 182, 183 and 189) and they are great with runny cheese. I sometimes sprinkle sea salt over them before baking. If you have any left over, then the crispbreads store well in an airtight tin.

In Sweden, this crispbread is often made with a mix of coarse and sifted rye flour.

For 8:
200g wholemeal spelt flour, plus extra for rolling
40g milled organic flaxseeds
40g sunflower seeds
40g sesame seeds
40g pumpkin seeds
40g medium pinhead oatmeal
Good pinch of sea salt
1 level tsp baking powder
1 tbsp cold-pressed rapeseed oil

For the crushed avocado
3 ripe avocados, stoned, peeled and chopped
10 sun-blushed tomatoes, finely chopped
½ red chilli, deseeded and finely chopped (optional)
Grated zest and juice of 1 lime
Small bunch of coriander, roughly chopped

First make the crispbreads. Preheat the oven to 180°C/gas mark 4.

Put all the dry ingredients into a bowl and mix to combine. Stir in 250ml water and the oil and allow to sit for 30 minutes.

Take a small lime-sized piece of dough and roll out between two floured sheets of baking parchment as thinly as possible. Gently pull away the top sheet and put the bottom sheet with the flattened dough on top onto a baking tray. Repeat this process for each crispbread. Bake with the crispbreads still on the baking parchment for 15–20 minutes until golden brown and crisp. Allow to cool on the tray.

To make the crushed avocado, put all the ingredients into a bowl and gently mash with the back of a fork, leaving some bits chunky. Or put in a food processor and briefly pulse.

To eat, dip the crispbread into the avocado.

» 234 calories per crispbread (if 8 made)
» Avocado, 235 calories per serving

More on » flaxseeds p30 » sesame seeds p164 » pumpkin seeds p105 » oats p25 » rapeseed oil p248 » avocado p119 » tomatoes p142 » chillies p93 » coriander p204

Spelt is a naturally occurring hybrid between a wild grass and ancient emmer wheat. It first emerged in the Near East at least 8000 years ago and was used throughout Europe in ancient times. Spelt is available as a whole grain and a whole-grain flour, and you can also find 'pearled' spelt (see Esther's spelt and orange porridge, page 25 and Pearled spelt and broad bean risotto, page 224) with the outer, tough bran layer removed, making a slightly softer grain. The great thing about spelt is that it contains 30 per cent more **protein** than wheat, so it keeps us feeling satisfied. It contains a broad spectrum of nutrients, particularly B vitamins, magnesium, manganese, iron, phosphorus and copper in a form that is easily absorbed by the body. The explorer Sir Ranulph Fiennes and many athletes cite spelt as the best source of slow-release energy – an idea that can be traced back to Roman times, when the Roman army used spelt in its marching bread.

All spelt products contain **gluten**.

Seeded spelt bread

Wholemeal spelt loaves are best made small, as the flour is dense and larger loaves are tricky to cook through. This recipe rises and bakes evenly every time. It makes three small loaves, one to eat straightaway, one to keep for a few days in a plastic bag in the fridge, and one for the freezer.

For 3 x 450g loaves:
A little cold-pressed rapeseed oil
1 tbsp clear or set honey
200ml boiling water
2 tbsp easy-bake dried yeast
1kg wholemeal spelt flour
2 tsp sea salt
50g pinhead oatmeal
30g rolled oats
1 tbsp milled organic flaxseeds
100g mixed seeds (sunflower, pumpkin,
    caraway, sesame), plus extra for the top

Use the oil to lightly grease three 450g non-stick loaf tins.

Dissolve the honey in the boiling water in a large measuring jug. Top it up to 1 litre with tepid water (which cools the water down enough for the yeast). Add the yeast. Leave for about 10 minutes to foam.

Put the flour into a huge mixing bowl, then mix in the salt. Pour in the watery yeast mix and stir to combine. Stir in the oatmeal, oats and the flax and mixed seeds. The mix will be quite sloppy – that's how it's meant to be. Divide the mix between the three loaf tins, smooth it a little with a spatula and sprinkle over some more mixed seeds. Cover the tins with a clean tea towel and leave them somewhere warm for about an hour to rise.

Preheat the oven to 190°C/gas mark 5.

Put the tins in the oven and after 10 minutes, turn the heat down to 180°C/gas mark 4 and bake the loaves for about 40 minutes until they are golden on top. You will know they are ready when a

skewer pushed into the middle comes out clean. You could also tip the loaves out of their tins and tap them: if they sound hollow, they are ready. If not, return to the tins and continue baking.

Take the loaves out of the oven, turn them out (over a tea towel so you don't get seeds everywhere) and put them back in the oven for a further 10 minutes on a baking tray – for a nice all-round crust. Take them out and leave to cool on a wire rack.

» 143 calories per slice (if 10 in loaf)

More on » honey p334 » oats p25 » flaxseeds p30
» pumpkin seeds p105 » sesame seeds p164

Buckwheat pancakes

I love the sharp tang of buckwheat flour, more interesting than bland, plain wheat and, on many counts, better for you. Buckwheat is a nutrient-rich whole grain, and it's gluten-free. Also try this with oat pancakes or Bannocks (see page 57) – usually savoury but also good served sweet.

If you can't find buttermilk, mix 300ml of full-fat milk with 1½ tablespoons of lemon juice (or white wine vinegar). Mix well and allow to stand for 5–10 minutes at room temperature. Then use as you would the buttermilk, including the curdled bits.

For about 12 drop-scone-sized pancakes:
80g buckwheat flour
1 tbsp milled organic flaxseeds
½ tbsp baking powder
½ tsp bicarbonate of soda
½ tsp sea salt
2 tbsp maple syrup (optional)
325ml buttermilk (see above)
40g organic unsalted butter, melted
2 medium eggs
120g blueberries/raspberries or blackcurrants (optional)
A little cold-pressed rapeseed oil or set coconut oil

For the sauce (optional)
50g organic unsalted butter
2–3 tbsp maple syrup

To serve
Live natural yoghurt (see p44)
Handful of blueberries, raspberries or blackcurrants
Walnuts, lightly chopped and fried in a little olive oil
Black sesame seeds

For the pancakes, mix together the dry ingredients in a large bowl. Whisk together the wet ingredients in a separate bowl. Stir the wet ingredients into the dry. Be sure not to over-mix or your pancakes will be tough; it is fine if the batter has some lumps. You are looking for a yoghurt-like consistency. If it is too thick, add a bit more buttermilk or milk, but keep it on the thick side. If it is too thin, add a bit more flour. Gently fold in the fruit (if using) at this stage.

Heat a griddle or heavy-based, non-stick frying pan over a medium heat for a couple of minutes. Using a piece of folded kitchen paper, rub a bit of oil over the surface. Drop 1 tablespoon of batter for each pancake into the pan, to form 8cm circles. Don't pack in too many at one time or they'll merge. Allow to cook until bubbles form on top (about 2 minutes). Flip with a spatula and cook until the other side is done (another minute or two). This batter makes quite a fluffy pancake.

For the sauce, melt the butter and maple syrup together in a small pan and pour into a jug.

Serve the pancakes two or three to a plate, topped with yoghurt, fruit, crushed walnuts and black sesame seeds. Finish with the sauce (if using).

» 100 calories per pancake (110 if including blueberries, 127 if including maple syrup)
» Add 40 calories per pancake if including the sauce

More on » buckwheat p226 » flaxseeds p30
» maple syrup p27 » butter p104 » eggs p61
» blueberries p328 » raspberries p326
» blackcurrants p294 » yoghurt p44
» walnuts p51 » sesame seeds p164

Variation
Dairy-free pancakes To make these pancakes dairy-free, replace the milk with unsweetened or home-made almond milk (see page 347) and replace the butter with 1 tbsp rapeseed oil. Other options, which are expensive but delicious, are hazelnut or cashew milk.
» 86 calories per pancake with unsweetened almond milk and rapeseed oil
» 90 calories per pancake with unsweetened hazelnut milk and rapeseed oil
» 85 calories per pancake with unsweetened cashew milk and rapeseed oil

Roasted peanut butter

Roasted nut and raw nut butters are highly nutritious, packed with protein, vitamins and minerals. They also contain nut oils, which make them calorific, but the oils possess great health benefits. It is well worth making your own – nut butters could not be simpler – as you'll know exactly what's in them. Widely available brands often have oil and completely unnecessary sugar and salt added. Home-made versions keep for at least three months in a jar in the fridge.

Serve your roasted nut butters with oatcakes or, if you're not eating carbohydrates, spread on crunchy slices of apple or celery sticks.

Fills 1 x 500ml Kilner jar:
500g unsalted peanuts

Preheat the oven to 180°C/gas mark 4.

Lay the peanuts in a single layer on a baking tray and roast on the middle shelf of the oven for 20 minutes until golden brown. Tip into a bowl and allow to cool.

Put the peanuts into a food processor and blitz for about 5 minutes. This will leave you with a bit of crunch. Blitz for longer if you like it totally smooth. When you start this off, it's easy to think it's too dry and to add some oil, but you don't need it. Just keep blitzing and the oil will gradually come out from the nuts and emulsify the nut butter. Decant into a sterilised Kilner jar (see right) and chill.

» 1 tbsp (25g) is 142 calories

Variations
Roasted cashew nut butter Replace the peanuts with cashews, but roast for only 15 minutes. Continue as per the method above.
» 1 tbsp (25g) is 146 calories
Roasted almond butter Replace the peanuts with almonds. Follow the method above.
» 1 tbsp (25g) is 161 calories

Breakfast

Raw almond butter

There are two ways of making raw nut butter. Purists would say you need to soak the nuts overnight, which activates various enzymes, making the nutritional components easier to digest and even better for you. It also removes phytic acid, which can prevent the body absorbing certain nutrients properly.

But if soaked, the nuts must then be dried out well in a warm (not hot) oven, so the butter texture will not be too runny. If you use this technique it is worth making the butter in decent-sized batches as it is time-consuming and you need to leave the oven on for a long time.

Personally, I don't bother with the soaking and dehydrating, preferring to process the almonds as they come.

Raw nut butter has a more distinctively 'almond' flavour than the roasted equivalent. Eating the nuts raw rather than roasted has some nutritional advantages too. Enzymes, in particular, are heat-sensitive, as is vitamin C, and some minerals are destroyed at temperatures over about 65°C, so this is packed with nutrients (see also the Cashew hummus on page 183).

If you choose to include the salt in the recipe below, the nut butter will keep for up to four weeks in the fridge, or it can be frozen. Halve this time for the maple syrup one.

Fills 1 x 500ml Kilner jar:
400g raw almonds
1 tbsp extra virgin olive oil or 1 tsp set coconut oil
Pinch of sea salt, or 2 tbsp maple syrup (optional)

Place the raw almonds in a food processor and blitz until you achieve a fine powder. At this point add the oil to help bring the almonds together into a paste.

Keep blitzing until you achieve a really creamy paste, about 20 minutes. Oils from the nuts will be released as they warm so you shouldn't need to add any more oil.

Add salt or maple syrup, blitz briefly again to mix and place in a warm, dry, sterilised Kilner jar (you can sterilise this in a very hot dishwasher or boil it in a pan of water for 10 minutes). Seal and label with a date.

» 1 tbsp (25g) is 170 calories

More on » almonds p347 » olive oil p193 » maple syrup p27

Variations
Purist's raw almond butter Put the almonds in a bowl of cold salted water and leave to soak for 8–12 hours (overnight is ideal).

Drain the almonds, rinse well, and place in a single layer on a lined baking tray or two. Place in the lowest possible oven (no hotter than 65°C) and dehydrate, rather than roast, the nuts. This can take between 12 and 24 hours. (If you have a dehydrator use that: the nuts will dry out in 12–18 hours.) Remove from the oven and leave to cool.

Place the almonds in a food processor and follow the recipe above.
» 1 tbsp (25g) is 170 calories
Other nut and seed butters Try also pistachio (no-soak), sesame seed (8-hour soak), sunflower seed (2-hour soak) or flaxseed (8-hour soak) butter. Any seeds that are soaked will also need the dehydration phase – see the Purist's method above.

Whole strawberry jam

This is a runny French-style jam made with honey not sugar, so it is marginally healthier than a standard jam. It is still high in sugar, though, so this is for a treat on special occasions rather than for every day. Marinating the strawberries in honey overnight sets the fruit, so it stays intact, even on cooking. Have this on spelt toast, oatcakes or a bowl of porridge, and it's great with natural yoghurt. It's also good with Buckwheat pancakes (see page 34). Pepper cuts through the sweetness, but leave it out if you prefer a classic flavour.

This is one step up from fruit compote, but without sugar, it doesn't last like standard jam. If you want more of a set, you could add a little pectin to the mixture before bringing it to the boil, or a handful of redcurrants, which are rich in pectin.

Fills 3 x 250g jars:
800g strawberries (small are best), hulled
450g clear honey
Julienned strands of zest and juice of 1 lemon
Julienned strands of zest and juice of 1 lime
2 tsp Sichuan peppercorns or coarsely ground black
    pepper (optional)

Put the strawberries, honey, zests and juice into a bowl, stir well and put into the fridge, covered, and leave overnight.

Put the marinated strawberries and honey mixture into a preserving pan or large saucepan along with the pepper (if using) over a medium heat. Bring to the boil and cook for 5 minutes. Spoon the fruit and pour the juice into warm, dry, sterilised jars (you can sterilise them in a very hot dishwasher or boil them in a pan of water for 10 minutes). Cover with a wax disc and allow to cool. Seal and label the jars with a date. Store in the fridge and use within 7–10 days.

» 1 tbsp (25g) is 53 calories

More on » mixed berries *p343* » honey *p334*
» lemons *p346*

Blackberry and plum jam

This jam is made using xylitol, a natural sweetener which has half the calories of sugar and is positively good, not bad, for your teeth. It has an indistinguishable taste from cane sugar – so this makes a conventionally delicious, yet lower-calorie and healthier jam.

Fills 4 x 500g jars:
900g blackberries
800g plums, stoned, cut into quarters and
    some into eighths
800g granulated xylitol
Finely grated zest and juice of 1 lemon

Put all the ingredients, plus 200ml water, into a preserving pan, stir gently and leave for 45 minutes–1 hour until the xylitol has dissolved. Bring the mixture to the boil, turn down the heat, and allow the jam to simmer gently for 20 minutes.

Take the jam off the heat and test for setting point. Dip a jam thermometer (or digital thermometer) into the panful of jam: when the temperature gets to 105°C, the jam will have reached setting point. If you don't have a thermometer, then have a chilled saucer ready and test by putting a teaspoonful of jam on the saucer and letting it cool in the fridge. If the jam wrinkles when you push it with your finger after a couple of minutes, it's ready. If the jam has not reached setting point, just repeat this process every 5 minutes, pulling the pan off the heat each time you test.

Allow the jam to cool for 10–15 minutes, stir gently, then spoon into dry, warm, sterilised jars (you can sterilise them in a very hot dishwasher or boil them in a pan of water for 10 minutes). Cover with a wax disc. Seal and label with a date. Store in the fridge and use within a month.

» 1 tbsp (25g) is 61 calories

More on » mixed berries *p343* » lemons *p346*

Coconut sugar marmalade

A wonderful rich, treacly marmalade which is ideal on toast or yoghurt. A tablespoon stirred into a Citrus fruit salad (see page 49) is good, or it can be used as a glaze for Orange and almond cake (see page 309) to give extra depth of flavour.

All marmalade uses a lot of sugar to preserve the fruit. Here it's coconut palm sugar (with pectin) as a healthier alternative: because it's sweeter, you use one quarter less than with caster sugar. Even so, there's still a lot of sugar here, so don't have this on toast for breakfast every day! The skin of citrus fruits has a higher concentration of antioxidants than the flesh, so marmalade, spoon by spoon, gives you a small nutritional bonus.

Fills 5 x 450g jars:
1.5kg blood oranges (or Seville if blood oranges
    are not in season)
2 pink grapefruits
2 lemons
1 tsp sea salt
About 1.5kg coconut palm sugar
400ml liquid pectin

Drop the fruit into boiling water, remove using a slotted spoon, then scrub under cold water to de-wax the skins.

Put the whole fruit into a preserving pan or large saucepan, cover with 3 litres water, so the fruit is submerged, and add the salt. Put a lid on the pan, bring to the boil, then turn down the heat and simmer for about an hour, turning the fruit once halfway through.

Strain, reserving the liquor, and allow the fruit to cool. When cooled, cut the fruit in half and scoop the flesh and pips into a metal sieve set over a bowl. Reserve the rinds.

Using a metal spoon, stir and push the flesh through the sieve into a pan or bowl, to make a fruity pulp. Discard the membrane, pith and pips. Cut the rinds into pieces of the size you want in your marmalade. Add the rind to the pulp and weigh it. For every 450g, mix in 450ml of the cooking liquor (if you don't have enough, make up the amount with water). For every 450ml of this liquid, measure out 350g coconut palm sugar.

Put the mixture back into the pan. Heat slowly, stirring to dissolve the sugar. Add the pectin. Increase the heat and bring to a rapid boil, then continue to boil until it thickens to setting point.

Pull the pan off the heat and test the marmalade for setting point. Dip a jam thermometer (or digital thermometer) into the panful of marmalade: when the temperature gets to 105°C, the marmalade will have reached setting point. If you don't have a thermometer, then have a chilled saucer ready and test by putting a teaspoonful of marmalade on the saucer and letting it cool in the fridge. If the marmalade wrinkles when you push it with your finger after a couple of minutes, it's ready.

When ready, take the marmalade off the heat and allow to rest for 20 minutes.

Stir to distribute the peel evenly before pouring into dry, warm, sterilised jars (you can sterilise them in a very hot dishwasher or boil them in a pan of water for 10 minutes). Cover with a wax disc. Seal and label with a date. The marmalade will keep for at least a year.

» 1 tbsp (25g) is 74 calories

More on » oranges p49 » grapefruit p340
» lemons p346 » coconut palm sugar p316

Super fruit compote

This compote will see you through the winter when there's little fresh, local fruit around. A bowl provides two good portions of fruit, but dried fruit contains a lot of sugar, so don't have this for breakfast every day. Ideally buy organic dried fruit, and check the packs for added hydrogenated oil: this is often added to keep the fruit separate.

For 8:
100g dried apricots (ideally organic, unsulphured)
120g dried mangoes
40g dried cranberries
100g stoned dates
100g prunes
120g dried figs, hard stems removed
100g dried apple rings
4 star anise
2 cinnamon sticks
6 cardamom pods, slightly crushed
750ml freshly squeezed orange juice (about 10 oranges)
   – use blood oranges when in season
Grated zest of 2 oranges
Grated zest and juice of 1 lemon
1 tbsp clear or set honey (optional)
Sprinkling of rosewater

Cut the larger fruit into quarters and place with the other ingredients in a bowl. Soak in the fridge overnight. Pour everything into a large saucepan with 400ml water and poach over a low heat for 10 minutes. Serve the compote warm or cold with yoghurt. It will keep for about a week in the fridge.

» 269 calories per serving

More on » cranberries p242 » figs p307 » cinnamon p22 » oranges p49 » lemons p346 » honey p334

Variation

Tea-soaked fruit compote For a delicious, interesting, smoky taste, soak the fruit overnight (up to 24 hours) in 750ml strong, cooled Earl Grey or Lapsang Souchong tea instead of the orange juice.
» 227 calories per serving

Healthy breakfast 'crumble'

A portion of this light and fruity 'crumble' will provide two of your five-a-day. It is at its best when plums and apples are peaking in August or September, but whenever you find plums which are sweet and juicy, think of making this. I first had this crumble on a raw food week – no parts of it are cooked – and I've loved it ever since: it's ideal as a light and healthy pudding, or for breakfast, to eat over a couple of days. Serve with live natural yoghurt (see page 44). For extra nutrition, you can add a tablespoon or two of flaxseeds to the 'crumble' top.

For 6:
3 small dessert apples, not peeled, but cored and
   cut into small chunks
18 plums (greengages are particularly sweet and
   delicious), stoned and quartered
Grated zest of 1 large orange (keep some strands
   of zest back for serving)
Juice of 2 large oranges
Grated zest and juice of 1 lemon
60g walnut halves (or almonds or hazelnuts)
60g stoned dates
30g desiccated coconut
Few drops of rosewater

Put the apples and plums into a mixing bowl. Add the citrus zest and juice. Stir well and cover, then put in the fridge for 6–8 hours or overnight.

Put the nuts, dates and coconut in a food processor and pulse briefly until you have a coarse mix with a texture similar to that of crumble.

To serve, spoon the nut mixture over the marinated fruit and sprinkle with a little rosewater and the remaining strands of orange zest. It will keep for 48 hours in the fridge.

» 260 calories per serving

More on » apples p288 » oranges p49 » lemons p346 » walnuts p51

Live natural yoghurt

Making yoghurt is simple and satisfying. Like bread, it's ideally left in a place like an airing cupboard with a stable temperature and no draughts. Then the yeasts can work away steadily, giving a good flavour and texture, better than when the temperature fluctuates. When buying your starter yoghurt check the label to make sure it contains 'live active yoghurt cultures' such as *Lactobacillus bulgaricus, L. acidophilus, L. bifidus, L. casei or Streptococcus thermophilus*: these are needed to turn the milk into yoghurt.

You can use skimmed, semi-skimmed or full-fat (whole) milk, preferably organic. Full-fat has twice the calories of skimmed milk but some extra health benefits and more flavour, so it's the best to choose. If you buy rather than make yoghurt, get live and ideally unpasteurised. You can use either (but preferably the home-made) to make one of the flavoured yoghurts on the following pages.

If you're going to make yoghurt often, invest in a cooking thermometer. This will ensure you get a consistent flavour and texture.

For 600g (for 4):
600ml full-fat milk
1 tbsp live natural yoghurt, ideally organic

Heat the milk gently. Bring it up to 84°C. If you have no thermometer, you want it to be steaming, but not yet boiling. Stir the milk gently as it heats to make sure the bottom doesn't scorch and the milk doesn't boil over. (You need this heating step to change the protein structure in the milk so it sets as a solid instead of separating.)

Pour it into an earthenware or ceramic bowl, a similar size to a medium Christmas pudding bowl – this retains the heat for longer than glass or metal and the small size helps too. Allow to cool to 43°C. This is important as the temperature of the milk when added to the live yoghurt has a big effect on flavour. Yoghurt made with too hot or too cold milk will have a slight sourness and a grainy, uneven texture. If you don't have a thermometer, test with your finger (43°C is when you can only just keep your finger immersed to the count of 10).

Take a ladleful of the warm milk and mix it with the yoghurt in a small bowl. Pour this back into the warm milk and mix thoroughly. If a skin has formed, stir this back into the mix.

Cover with a tea towel and put into the airing cupboard or a warm, draught-free place. Depending on the temperature of your cupboard, the yoghurt will be ready in 8–12 hours.

Put into the fridge and serve cold. You can keep the yoghurt covered in the fridge for up to two weeks.

To make another batch, reserve a good spoonful of your home-made yoghurt (which is live) and repeat the process.

» 150g live natural yoghurt is 95 calories

More on » milk *p252*

Yoghurt Live natural yoghurt from grass-fed animals (organic is best) is a nutritional goldmine, full of **probiotics** – healthy **bacteria** – which, when eaten in adequate amounts, benefit the microflora in the intestines and strengthen the immune system. Like milk, yoghurt also provides a good dose of **protein**, **vitamins** and **minerals**, including calcium. Studies have shown positive results for live yoghurt in the prevention and treatment of osteoporosis, high blood pressure and high **cholesterol**. Sheep's and goats' yoghurts have lower levels of lactose than cows' yoghurt, and they are often well tolerated by those who are lactose-intolerant.

Rhubarb, ginger and star anise yoghurt

You may think it's easier to buy flavoured yoghurt than making it yourself, but if it's DIY, you know what's in it. Bought flavoured yoghurts – almost more than any other foods – are covered by the shroud of you-think-this-is-good-for-you-but-how-wrong-can-you-be. Before you buy any low-fat flavoured yoghurt, check the label: most are jam-packed with sugar or artificial sweeteners, which are best avoided. New research also shows that full-fat dairy provides a range of health benefits which are lost in the low-fat options.

Home-flavoured yoghurts are excellent for breakfast, as a mid-morning or afternoon snack or for pudding, perhaps topped with some dry-fried nuts and seeds. Make this rhubarb version through the spring and early summer when there's an abundance of stems. Star anise is complimentary to rhubarb, as are ginger and orange.

For 4:
300g rhubarb
Grated zest and juice of 1 orange
2 star anise
2 tsp stem ginger syrup (see below)
25g (about 1 tbsp) finely chopped stem ginger
  (see below)
500g live natural yoghurt (see opposite)

For the stem ginger (makes 250g, enough for
10 yoghurt batches)
100g fresh root ginger
100g coconut palm sugar
6 cardamom pods, lightly crushed

First make the stem ginger – although you can, of course, use bought. Peel the root ginger with a teaspoon. Slice and cut into little chunks.

Bring a small pan of water to a rolling boil and blanch the ginger for 10 seconds. Drain and repeat (repeat more often for a milder taste, but I prefer it punchy).

In a medium saucepan mix the coconut palm sugar with 100ml water and bring to the boil. Add the blanched ginger and the cardamom pods and simmer for 20 minutes.

Remove from the heat and put into a small dry, warm, sterilised Kilner jar (you can sterilise it in a very hot dishwasher or boil it in a pan of water for 10 minutes). Make sure all the ginger is covered by liquid. Seal, label and store; it will last for up to six months. Once open, it is best kept in the fridge.

Now make the flavoured yoghurt. Preheat the oven to 180°C/gas mark 4.

Cut the rhubarb into 4cm pieces and put it into a baking dish in a single layer. Mix the orange zest and juice, star anise and ginger syrup and pour over the rhubarb.

Put in the oven and cook for 15–20 minutes until the rhubarb is just softened. Add the stem ginger and mix gently with the rhubarb. Allow to cool for an hour, or leave overnight in the fridge. Remove the star anise.

Mix with the natural yoghurt to serve. This will keep in the fridge for at least a week.

» 112 calories per 125g serving

More on » oranges p49 » ginger p200 » coconut palm sugar p316

Saffron, walnut and pomegranate yoghurt

This Greek-inspired yoghurt feels sunny and bright for a summer or autumn morning. It's a beautiful golden colour from the saffron, splotched with deep red from the pomegranate.

For 4:
100g walnut halves
2 tsp clear honey or maple syrup
Pinch of saffron strands
1 tbsp boiling water
1 pomegranate
500g live natural yoghurt (see p44)
Finely grated zest of 1 orange
Juice of ½ orange

Preheat the oven to 180°C/gas mark 4. Line a baking tray with baking parchment.

In a bowl, stir the walnut halves together with the honey or maple syrup until coated. Place on the prepared baking tray and roast in the oven for 7–8 minutes until starting to brown. Keep an eye on them as they burn easily. Allow to cool, then roughly chop.

Meanwhile, in a small bowl, steep the saffron strands in the boiling water for 20–30 minutes.

To extract the pomegranate seeds, gently roll the fruit around a few times on the table, then slice it in half over a bowl to collect the juice. Holding one half of the fruit cut-side down over a bowl, tap the skin with a wooden spoon. The seeds will drop into the bowl without their bitter cream-coloured pith.

Mix most of the caramelised walnuts, almost all the saffron strands (along with their liquid), and most of the pomegranate seeds with the yoghurt, then stir in the orange zest and juice. Spoon into serving bowls. Scatter the remaining pomegranate seeds, walnuts and saffron strands – with a splosh or two of the liquid – on top of each serving. This will keep in the fridge for a few days.

» 288 calories per 125g serving

More on » walnuts *p51* » honey *p334* » maple syrup *p27* » yoghurt *p44* » oranges *p49*

Pomegranates You hardly came across a pomegranate here until a few years ago, but now they're on every supermarket's shelf, hailed as an A-list superfood, containing some of the most powerful **antioxidants** of all fruits. They're rich in potassium, vitamin C and pantothenic acid (vitamin B5), and a glass of pomegranate juice – or a small bowl of seeds – has more antioxidants in it than the same volume of red wine, green tea, blueberries or cranberries. As well as a wide range of antioxidants, they also contain compounds called **punicalagins**, found only in pomegranates, which are responsible for many of the health benefits, with potent anti-cancer and immune-boosting properties. Punicalagins appear to improve **apoptosis**, a process by which our tissues get rid of malfunctioning cells, including cancer cells. Research shows that punicalagins may also prevent oestrogen-responsive breast cells from over-growing, with a similar effect on the prostate, helping to prevent the development of both breast and prostate cancers. Punicalagins are also considered anti-ageing, and are especially good for cardiovascular health.

When selecting fruit, aim for glossy, bright-looking skin and then feel the weight. A fresh pomegranate should feel dense and heavy in the palm of your hand.

Citrus fruit salad

Ideally make this with super-nutritious blood oranges – they're only available in late winter and spring, so snap them up when you can. Some supermarkets call them 'blush' oranges, which is a little deceptive, as the darker the orange flesh – the 'bloodier' it is – the healthier. Blood oranges are delicious peeled and eaten as they are, or juiced for breakfast, but my favourite is this fruit salad, which is bright, tangy and sharp, good with the addition of mint. I also love this with a tablespoon or two of Coconut sugar marmalade (see page 40) stirred into the juice, which gives a real richness of taste.

For 4:
4 blood oranges (or other oranges such as navel)
2 pink grapefruits
Small bunch of mint leaves, plus extra for garnishing
2 tbsp pistachio kernels
2 tbsp flaked almonds
2 passion fruits, halved

First prepare the oranges. Slice off both ends of an orange and then peel as you would an apple: hold the fruit with your non-preferred hand and, with a small serrated knife (held with the blade pointing upwards), make short up-and-down sawing movements, going round and round the fruit until it is completely skinned. Do this holding the orange over a small bowl to collect the juice. There should be no pith left. You can then follow each layer of skin down to the heart to cut the fruit into skinless segments, or slice the whole orange horizontally as thinly as you can, into cartwheels (removing the pithy centre of each segment).

Repeat with the other oranges, and arrange in the serving bowl. Do the same with the pink grapefruits.

Now make the mint syrup. Gently heat the orange and grapefruit juice you have collected while peeling and slicing. Add the mint when the liquid is bubbling. Set aside to cool.

Meanwhile dry-fry the pistachios and flaked almonds in a frying pan, on a gentle heat, until they begin to colour. Take care not to burn them.

Once it has cooled to room temperature, pour the mint syrup over the citrus fruit. Top with the nuts and a few small leaves of mint.

Scoop around the passion fruits with a knife or spoon to dislodge the seeds, so they can then be poured out over the fruit salad as people eat.

Divide the salad between individual plates and place a half passion fruit in the centre of each one.

» 193 calories per serving

More on » grapefruit p340 » mint p326 » almonds p347

Oranges All oranges are good for us, but blood oranges are the best, as they are one of the richest sources of **anthocyanins**, those powerful **antioxidants** of the plant world that help the body defend itself from **free-radical** damage.

Oranges have high levels of vitamin C (one medium blood orange will provide more than 100 per cent of your daily needs). Vitamin C is a key nutrient for helping to heal and repair damaged tissues throughout the body, and it does of course boost the immune system. We all reach for citrus – too late – when we feel we're getting a cold. There are also good levels of potassium, calcium, folate and vitamin A in oranges.

Be aware, though, that drinking lots of orange juice is not a good idea, because it contains too much sugar. You're much better off eating a whole orange, where the **fibre** in the fruit will help to even out the steep sugar spike.

Roasted hazelnut and vanilla yoghurt

A lovely warm-flavoured yoghurt; good, filling and comforting on an autumn or winter's day.

For 4:
100g hazelnuts (skin on to add colour and fibre)
1 tsp vanilla extract
½–1 tbsp maple syrup or clear honey (to taste)
500g live natural yoghurt (see p44)

Preheat the oven to 180°C/gas mark 4.

Put the hazelnuts onto a baking tray in a single layer and roast for 5 minutes or until golden brown, but watch them as they burn easily.

Allow to cool and then blitz in a food processor, keeping a bit of texture. Some crunch is good.

Stir the hazelnuts, vanilla extract and syrup (or honey) into the yoghurt. This will keep in the fridge for a week.

» 249 calories per 125g serving

More on » maple syrup *p27* » honey *p334* » yoghurt *p44*

Hazelnuts are a perfect snack food, filling and highly nutritious. They're packed with **protein** and are rich in important **minerals**, such as calcium, phosphorus, potassium – and particularly magnesium, copper and selenium. Like other nuts they also contain oleic acid, so including hazelnuts in our diet can help to improve the balance of **lipids** in our blood, as well as providing the powerful **antioxidant**, vitamin E. Even though hazelnuts, like other nuts, are full of oil, eating a diet rich in nuts provides healthy fats, **vitamins**, minerals and **phytonutrients**. Their high levels of fat, protein and **fibre** leaves us feeling more satisfied.

Pineapple and mint yoghurt

As pineapples have a high sugar content, most of us won't need added sweetener. The protein-rich almonds and yoghurt here help slow the pineapple's sugar release. Roasting pineapple intensifies its flavour, and its sharp acidity is a good contrast to the creaminess of the yoghurt. Top with some lime zest and toasted almond flakes for a delicious and healthy breakfast.

For 4:
1 medium pineapple, skinned, cored and cut into
    2cm-square chunks
1 tbsp maple syrup (optional)
500g live natural yoghurt (see p44)
2 heaped tbsp chopped mint leaves
4 tbsp dry-fried almonds, to serve

Preheat the oven to 180°C/gas mark 4, and line a baking tray with baking parchment.

Put the pineapple chunks into a mixing bowl and stir in the maple syrup (if using), then put onto the prepared baking tray in a single layer. Roast the pineapple for 20–30 minutes until soft and just starting to caramelise on the edges. Take out of the oven and allow to cool.

Chop the roasted pineapple chunks (or pulse very briefly in a food processor), and stir into the yoghurt along with the chopped mint. Serve topped with the almonds. This will keep in the fridge for a week.

» 202 calories per 125g serving (including maple syrup)

More on » maple syrup *p27* » yoghurt *p44* » mint *p326* » almonds *p347*

Healthy flapjack

There is a huge range of granola and so-called 'superfood' bars on the market – but to be sure what's in them, and how much, it's good to make your own. I love a flapjack, but they're full of sugar. That is not true of these, though, which are ideal if you get up too late and have to skip breakfast, or want something crunchy and sweet mid-morning or mid-afternoon.

Based on oats, seeds and nuts, these flapjacks are rich in protein, and many other good things, including dried goji berries, which are packed with antioxidants, including beta-carotene.

For 12 bars:
60g almonds, roughly chopped
40g walnuts, roughly chopped
140g stoned dates
100ml boiling water
160g rolled oats
80g desiccated coconut
20g sesame seeds
1 heaped tsp ground cinnamon
20g dried goji berries
1 medium egg, beaten
Good pinch of sea salt
1 tsp xanthan gum
2 heaped tbsp set coconut oil, melted
2 tbsp maple syrup

Preheat the oven to 180°C/gas mark 4.

Dry-fry or toast the almonds and walnuts until just starting to colour. Then allow to cool.

Put three-quarters of the dates into a jug with the boiling water and leave to cool. Finely slice the remaining dates. When the dates are cool, pour them and the water into a food processor and blitz to a paste.

Put all the remaining ingredients into a mixing bowl, including the nuts. Add the date paste and mix well to combine.

Line a 24 x 18cm (or similar) baking tray with baking parchment and spoon in the mixture so it covers the bottom of the tray. Push down firmly, ensuring that the thickness is even. Score into 12 bars.

Put the tray in the oven and bake for 15 minutes until the top of the flapjack is golden. Leave to cool in the baking tray. The bars will set as they cool.

Once cooled, cut the slab into bars along your score lines. Store in an airtight tin for up to two weeks (or freeze).

» 226 calories per bar

More on » almonds *p347* » oats *p25* » sesame seeds *p164* » cinnamon *p22* » goji berries *p21* » eggs *p61* » coconut oil *p309* » maple syrup *p27*

Walnuts pack a nutritional punch: of all the nuts, they're uniquely rich in the oh-so-important-and-healthy **omega-3 fatty acids**, which might explain their beneficial effect on cardiovascular disease and brain health. They're also particularly rich in **polyphenols** (90 per cent of which are found in their skins), and a good source of vitamin E. Both of these are valuable anti-cancer compounds, and eating walnuts has been shown to reduce the incidence of certain cancers, including those of the prostate and breast. **Anti-inflammatory** and **antioxidant** properties also makes walnuts a top food for combating metabolic syndrome, a condition which can develop into diabetes.

One thing to bear in mind with walnuts is that they go off quite quickly if they aren't stored in a cool, dark place in an airtight jar or packet, or if the nuts are broken. Ideally, you should aim to eat them within a month. You can buy them more cheaply in large bags, then divide into batches and freeze (a good way to preserve any nut).

Pecan and apricot muffins

Made from sugar and processed white flour, muffins can be nutritionally dubious, but these have great flavour, a lovely chunky texture – from the nuts and dried fruit – *and* they're good for you.

For 12 medium-sized muffins:
230g wholemeal spelt flour
2 level tsp baking powder
1 level tsp bicarbonate of soda
Pinch of sea salt
2 tsp ground cinnamon
2 tbsp maple syrup
3 level tbsp milled organic flaxseeds
60g dried apricots, chopped (ideally organic, unsulphured)
60g pecan nuts, chopped
60g stoned dates, chopped
80g stem ginger, chopped (see p45)
125ml apple juice
200g live natural yoghurt (see p44)
1 tsp vanilla extract
3 large eggs, beaten

Preheat the oven to 180°C/gas mark 4. Arrange 12 medium-sized muffin cases on a baking tray.

Put all the dry ingredients, dried fruits, nuts and ginger into a large mixing bowl and stir with a fork. Add the apple juice, yoghurt and vanilla extract to the beaten eggs and stir to combine. Add to the dry ingredients and mix lightly with a fork (take care not to over-mix). Spoon into the muffin cases to three-quarters-fill them. Put into the middle of the oven and bakc for 25 minutes, until a skewer inserted in the centre of a muffin comes out clean.

When cool enough to handle, push the muffins out of the cases onto a wire rack to cool further. These store for several days, and are best kept in the fridge.

» 197 calories per muffin

More on » spelt *p32* » cinnamon *p22* » maple syrup *p27* » flaxseeds *p30* » ginger *p200* » yoghurt *p44* » eggs *p61*

Apple and coconut macaroons

These are good because they're not too sweet. We serve these for the mid-morning break in the garden and cookery school at Perch Hill, adding different grated fruits and sometimes vegetables such as carrots into the mixture too, and I love them for an on-the-hoof breakfast. (If using carrots instead of apples, finely grate 150g into a sieve, then squeeze to remove excess water.) The xanthan gum is optional, but helps hold the macaroons together.

For 15 macaroons:
2 dessert apples, not peeled, grated
50g dried apple rings, chopped
160g desiccated coconut
100g stoned dates, chopped
100g dried apricots, chopped (ideally organic, unsulphured)
60g pine nuts, dry-fried
40g sesame seeds, dry-fried
2 medium eggs, beaten
1 tsp vanilla extract
Pinch of sea salt
¼ tsp xanthan gum (optional)

Preheat the oven to 180°C/gas mark 4. Lightly grease a couple of baking sheets, or line them with baking parchment or silicone mats.

Put all the ingredients into a large bowl and mix well. Leave to stand for a few minutes. Put dessertspoon-sized dollops of the mixture onto the prepared baking sheets – about seven or eight per sheet. Bake in the preheated oven for 10–12 minutes, or until golden brown.

Transfer to cooling racks with a palette knife. You can keep the macaroons in the fridge, stored in an airtight container, for up to a week.

» 167 calories per macaroon

More on » apples *p288* » sesame seeds *p164* » eggs *p61*

Baked egg with truffled mushroom

Mushrooms and eggs go brilliantly together, and when you have a bit more time at the weekend, this is ideal – and healthy – breakfast or brunch food. Serve with some spelt toast or seeded soda bread (see page 105). Eggs and mushrooms are both protein-rich and filling.

For 1:
1 tbsp truffle oil
Small knob of organic unsalted butter
1 garlic clove, crushed (optional)
150g mix of oyster, chestnut and shiitake mushrooms, sliced if large but kept whole where possible
Sprig of thyme, leaves picked
1 tbsp crème fraîche
½ tbsp finely chopped parsley
Scant squeeze of lemon juice
Sea salt and black pepper
1–2 medium eggs

Preheat the oven to 180°C/gas mark 4.

Heat half the truffle oil in a frying pan with the butter over a gentle heat. Add the garlic, mushrooms and thyme. Cook for 2 minutes until the mushrooms are softened but still retain a bite.

Stir in the crème fraîche and parsley, squeeze in a little lemon juice and season. Scrape the mushroom mixture into a small gratin dish and make a well in the centre. Carefully crack the egg into the mushroom well. Drizzle over the remaining truffle oil.

Cover the dish tightly with foil, place in the oven and cook for 15–20 minutes, until the egg white has set but the yolk is still runny.

» 410 calories (if using 1 egg)

More on » garlic *p82* » mushrooms *p88* » parsley *p136* » eggs *p61*

Spinach is a powerhouse of **vitamins** and **minerals**, and has long been regarded as a great brain tonic. As a good source of iron, it improves the quality of our blood, and it's packed with vitamin K, the bone-protecting vitamin, and the mineral calcium, both of which help to prevent osteoporosis. Its dark green leaves contain high levels of chlorophyll, as well as the **carotenoid** lutein, a **phytochemical** which has **anti-inflammatory** and anti-cancer properties. Lutein is especially important for healthy eyes, helping to prevent macular degeneration, the leading cause of sight loss in older adults. Spinach is also one of the best natural sources of folic acid, which is excellent for preventing heart disease and helping nerve function. A lot of the nutrients in spinach are more available when it is eaten cooked, rather than raw.

There is one downside to spinach: it is high in **oxalates**, so avoid eating large amounts if you have a history of oxalate-containing kidney stones or gall bladder problems.

Spinach is one of the vegetables which appears to carry the highest pesticide load when conventionally grown, so it's advisable to buy organic.

Eggs with shrimps

Shrimps and eggs go well together, with a few stalks of parsley or perhaps some chives. This is excellent eaten with thin crispy toast or Swedish crispbread (see page 32) and a small dollop of warm, wilted spinach. If you want the ultimate take-care-of-your-eyes healthy meal, eat spinach and eggs together. You'll then get the maximum amount of fat-soluble pigments, lutein and zeaxanthin, from the spinach, and the fat from the egg yolks will help your body to absorb them.

For 2–3:
4 eggs, any size
Small bunch of parsley
100g cooked and shelled brown shrimps
  (or small prawns), fresh or frozen
Small knob of organic unsalted butter
Nutmeg, for grating
Sea salt and black pepper

To serve
½ tsp set coconut oil
200g spinach
Nutmeg, for grating
½ tsp olive oil
Thin slices of spelt toast, or rye crispbread

Bring a pan of water to the boil and hard-boil the eggs for 6–7 minutes if large, 5 if small. Drain the eggs, and leave them to cool in a bowl of cold water.

Chop the parsley in the small bowl of a food processor, if you have one. If not, chop finely by hand. Put in a small bowl.

When the eggs are cool, shell them and add to the processor, along with the shrimps. Pulse briefly, or chop together by hand. Mix in the chopped parsley.

Melt a very small knob of butter in a pan over a gentle heat. Grate nutmeg to taste into this, and grind in some black pepper. Put the egg and shrimp mixture into the saucepan and just warm

through for a minute – don't cook it. Season with salt to taste.

In a pan heat the coconut oil, add the spinach and allow it to wilt in the heat. Tip into a sieve and press to remove excess moisture. Dress with the olive oil, grate in the nutmeg and keep warm.

Serve the shrimp mixture in small ramekins or bowls with the toast or crispbread, with a dollop of spinach on the side.

» 276 calories for 2 servings, 184 for 3, not
   including spinach

More on » eggs *p61* » parsley *p136* » shrimps *p215*
» prawns *p212* » spelt *p32*

Variation
Ginger, spinach and shrimp breakfast If you feel you've had enough of eggs, but still want a sustaining, protein-rich breakfast, then this is ideal. For two, stir-fry a 200g bag of organic spinach in some coconut oil, along with some finely sliced or grated ginger. After a minute, add a 100g pack of brown shrimps and a handful of coarsely chopped parsley. Serve with toast or crispbread.
» 104 calories per serving

Bannocks with poached eggs and salmon

Bannocks are like pancakes, but they are made with oats not flour, and so they are more sustaining than a standard drop scone. The oats are soaked in milk for at least an hour (for dairy-free, this could be almond), or you can start this the night before. The classic pairing of eggs and smoked salmon is nutritious, but smoked salmon is not something for every day. They are also good with smoked haddock. Some people will only want to eat one bannock, others two, which is why I've given the topping ingredients list per bannock.

If you want the bannocks sweet, you could sweeten the batter with a teaspoon of coconut palm sugar or xylitol, and top the bannocks with fresh fruit and yoghurt. As with the Buckwheat pancakes (see page 34), I also like these with walnuts, blueberries and maple syrup.

For 12 bannocks (enough for 6):
200g rolled oats
Pinch of sea salt
350ml full-fat milk or almond milk (see p347)
1 medium egg
½ tsp bicarbonate of soda
Cold-pressed rapeseed oil, for greasing the pan

For the topping (per person)
½ tsp set coconut oil
150g spinach, washed and dried
A little olive oil
Nutmeg, for grating
1 medium egg
1 tbsp white wine vinegar
20–30g smoked salmon
Live natural yoghurt or crème fraîche
Juice of ½ lemon
Sea salt and black pepper

First make the bannocks. Mix the oats and salt and add the milk. Stir to amalgamate and leave to soak for an hour or so.

Beat in the egg and bicarbonate of soda, using a wooden spoon. Drop a tablespoon of the bannock mixture at a time into a preheated, lightly greased frying pan. Don't make it too big or it won't cook through. The mixture will spread a little. You can do four bannocks in a 28cm diameter pan. Turn the bannocks over when they are set around the edge and you can see a few bubbles on the top. Cook for a few minutes on the other side until they are set through.

Keep the first bannocks warm by wrapping them in a cloth (or in a very low oven) while making the rest.

Now make the topping. In a pan heat the coconut oil, add the spinach, and allow it to wilt in the heat. Tip into a sieve and press to remove excess moisture. Dress with a little olive oil, grate in some nutmeg and season to taste. Keep warm.

To cook the egg, bring a small saucepan of water, half-filled, to a slow rolling boil. Add the vinegar and reduce to a simmer. Crack each egg into a ramekin or small shallow bowl. Gently, and as close to the water as possible, tip each egg in. Cook for 2½ minutes for a very runny yolk, or 3 for a slightly more set yolk. Remove from the water with a slotted spoon and place on a piece of kitchen paper.

Place some spinach on each bannock and top with a good slice of smoked salmon and a dollop of yoghurt (or crème fraîche if you prefer) on the side. Squeeze over the lemon juice and season with a little salt. Top with a poached egg and serve with a good scattering of freshly ground black pepper.

» 93 calories per bannock
» 293 calories per bannock with salmon topping

More on » oats *p25* » milk *p252* » eggs *p61*
» spinach *p54* » salmon *p125* » yoghurt *p44*
» lemons *p346*

Lighter eggs Benedict

This is breakfast party food, also good for lunch or dinner, and healthier and lower in fat than the traditional version. Bannocks have a similar calorie-count to the traditional muffins used in eggs Benedict, but are made from a whole grain, so they are much more filling and release their sugars and energy slowly.

Prosciutto has 195 calories per 100g compared to 541 calories in bacon, and it also contains less salt. Smoked salmon (see variation) has 170 calories per 100g. You want as much spinach as possible in your diet – it's very good for you.

For 4:
8 bannocks (see p57)
1 recipe hollandaise (see p192)

For the topping
8 slices of prosciutto
½ tbsp set coconut oil
500g spinach
½ tsp olive oil
Nutmeg, for grating
Sea salt and black pepper
8 medium eggs
1 tbsp white wine vinegar
A little Tabasco sauce (optional)

Make the bannocks (see page 57). Then make the hollandaise as described on page 192.

Preheat the oven to 180°C/gas mark 4.

To roast the prosciutto, place a cooling rack on a flat oven tray. Lay the slices on the cooling rack and place in the oven. Cook for 10 minutes until crisp. Keep an eye on it: the prosciutto tastes horrid if burnt.

In a pan heat the coconut oil, add the spinach, and allow it to wilt in the heat. Tip into a sieve and press to remove excess moisture. Dress with the olive oil, grate in some nutmeg, season with salt and pepper and keep warm.

Now poach the eggs in batches, two or three at a time. Bring a small saucepan of water, half-filled, to a slow rolling boil. Add the vinegar and reduce to a simmer. Crack each egg into a ramekin or small shallow bowl. Gently, and as close to the water as possible, tip each egg in. Cook for 2½ minutes for a very runny yolk, or 3 for a slightly more set yolk. Remove from the water with a slotted spoon and place on a piece of kitchen paper.

For each person, place a couple of bannocks on a plate, followed by some spinach and a couple of poached eggs. Spoon over a little hollandaise, and break up the roasted prosciutto – two slices per plate – over the top. I love this with a few splashes of Tabasco.

» 576 calories per serving

More on » coconut oil *p309* » spinach *p54*
» eggs *p61*

Variation
Smoked salmon eggs Benedict For an omega-3-rich alternative to bacon or proscuitto, use smoked salmon glazed with maple syrup. Preheat the oven to 160°C/gas mark 3. Cut the smoked salmon slices into strips and lay out on a baking tray lined with baking parchment. Brush with a little maple syrup and bake for 20 minutes until the edges start to brown. Remove from the oven and allow to cool, whilst following the rest of the recipe as above.
» 570 calories per serving

Breakfast

A more virtuous full English

In this big breakfast, there's only half the sugar and salt that you would find in the traditional full English, and yet the vitamin content and fibre are more than double. You can also roast Portobello or field mushrooms and a slice or two of griddled halloumi for the ultimate vegetarian brunch.

The healthy sweet potato and quinoa hash browns are quick to make, but it's worth doing them in larger batches so you have a stash in the freezer. They cook from frozen in 30 minutes and also make a good simple supper, topped with a couple of poached eggs. The rosemary and harissa baked beans are also delicious on their own, and I love them for lunch or supper with a green salad. Pinto beans are healthy and protein-rich, and also high in fibre. With similar properties to chickpeas (see page 182), they are recommended for good gastro-intestinal and heart health.

For 6:
6 medium eggs
1 tbsp white wine vinegar

For the healthy hash browns
100g white quinoa
450ml good-quality vegetable stock (see p101) or bouillon
250g sweet potato
Sea salt and black pepper
50g leek, finely sliced
½ tbsp olive oil
1 tsp whole-grain mustard
1 medium egg, beaten
4 spring onions, sliced on the diagonal

For the baked beans (enough for 2 breakfasts for 6)
1 onion, finely chopped
2 garlic cloves, crushed
1 tbsp olive oil
Sprig of rosemary
1 tbsp harissa paste (or more, to taste)
1 tbsp tomato purée
6 sun-dried tomatoes, finely sliced
2 x 400g tins of chopped tomatoes (or 1kg fresh tomatoes, whizzed)

400g tin of pinto beans, drained, or 200g dried pinto beans, soaked and boiled until soft (about an hour)
1 tbsp maple syrup
Sea salt and black pepper

First make the hash browns. Rinse the quinoa well in a sieve under a running tap, then put it into a pan with the vegetable stock (if using fresh stock, not bouillon, add a pinch of salt). Bring to the boil, reduce the heat and simmer gently for 10–15 minutes (without a lid), or until all the liquid has evaporated. Keep an eye on it. The cooked seed will have a tiny curly tail and should have a slight bite to it. Take the pan off the heat (do not drain) put the lid on and allow the quinoa to rest in the pan for 5 minutes. Spoon into a large serving bowl, then fork through gently and allow to cool.

Grate the sweet potato (unpeeled if organic) into a bowl and mix in a little fine salt. Leave for 15 minutes and then scrape into a sieve and squeeze out as much water from the grated flesh as you can. Dry between two tea towels, rubbing to remove as much moisture as possible.

Meanwhile, fry the leek in the oil until it is just softened but retains a bite.

Preheat the oven to 180°C/gas mark 4.

Put all the hash brown ingredients into the bowl with the cooked quinoa, and mix thoroughly. Line a baking tray with baking parchment and, using a large tablespoon, dollop on 12 tight mounds of the mixture. Press these down slightly. Put in the oven and bake for 45 minutes.

Meanwhile, make the beans. Fry the onion and garlic in the oil until translucent. Add the rosemary, harissa paste, tomato purée and sun-dried tomatoes. Cook over a gentle heat for 2 minutes until the rawness of the purée has been cooked out. Add the chopped tomatoes and cook over a gentle heat for 20 minutes until reduced.

Add the beans to the reduced sauce and cook for a further 15 minutes. Remove the rosemary, add the maple syrup and season with salt and pepper.

Now poach the eggs in batches, two or three at a time. Bring a small saucepan of water, half-filled, to a slow rolling boil. Add the vinegar and reduce to a simmer. Crack each egg into a ramekin or small shallow bowl. Gently, and as close to the water as possible, tip each egg in. Cook for 2½ minutes for a very runny yolk, or 3 for a slightly more set yolk. Remove from the water with a slotted spoon and place on a piece of kitchen paper.

Serve on individual plates, with the beans alongside the hash browns and the egg on top. (Depending on how hungry you are, you may not want two hash browns each.)

» Hash browns, 192 calories per serving
» Baked beans, 197 calories per serving
» 67 calories per egg
» Total calories per person 456

More on » quinoa *p140* » sweet potato *p72* » onions *p281* » garlic *p82* » olive oil *p193* » tomatoes *p142* » maple syrup *p27*

Eggs are nature's perfect food – abundant, cheap, easy and flexible to cook, as well as being one of the most nutrient-dense foods on the planet. Eggs of all kinds – chicken, duck and quail – are a source of high-quality **protein**. All the B vitamins are found in eggs and they also contain especially high levels of choline, which improves memory, is good for the heart and can reduce the risk of breast cancer.

Eggs also contain the vitamin D and phosphorus that is needed for healthy bones and teeth, as well as selenium and iodine, which are difficult to obtain from other foods.

To get the best out of them, eat the egg whole, poached or boiled. Some nutrients are found in the yolk, others only in the white, so you need both. The best eggs have a deep, rich-coloured yolk – this shows that the laying bird has been fed a healthy and varied diet, foraging for a variety of plants with natural pigments to give the yolk its colouring. Beware, some intensive egg farms now add synthetic colours to their feed to mimic this.

There are various stamps you'll find on an egg shell. The first is a date. The maximum legal 'use-by' date for eggs is 28 days from laying, and eggs must be sold at least seven days before this expiry date. This is important if you're using raw eggs (in mayonnaise, say), as food poisoning bugs multiply over time. And always store eggs below 20°C or in the fridge. You'll also sometimes see a lion stamp on the shell. That means the flock the eggs have come from have been vaccinated against salmonella.

I choose organic eggs (which are always free-range) if I can; however, it's less likely that organic flocks have been vaccinated. Don't let this put you off. The incidence of salmonella is naturally much lower in hens that are less intensively raised.

Some egg brands advertise that they contain higher levels of the healthy **omega-3 fatty acids**, enhanced by feeding the birds on fish oil and/or flaxseeds, but you'll get higher levels of omega-3s anyway in grass-fed, free-range birds than in those that are grain- and soya-fed indoors.

Watercress gazpacho

On a summer morning, why not ring the changes and try a fruit and vegetable 'soup' for breakfast? With the fibre and all the nutrients left in, it's more substantial and sustaining than a freshly made juice. It's made with one third fruit, two thirds vegetables and salad, so you don't get too much of a sugar hit. Watercress is hard to beat in terms of nutrition, and the melon is alkalising, which is particularly important first thing after the body has been detoxing overnight. The gazpacho also tastes delicious: peppery and sweet, it is packed with flavour as well as goodness. Serve with Seeded oatcakes (see page 30).

For 4–5:
400g honeydew melon (about ½ melon),
   peeled and deseeded
450g ripe tomatoes
120g watercress
120g cucumber
2 celery sticks
50g (about 4) spring onions (optional)
½ fresh red chilli, deseeded (optional)
1 tbsp organic apple cider vinegar
2 tsp dried flaked seaweed (dulse or kombu)

Roughly chop the melon and vegetables. Put everything into a blender and blitz thoroughly for 2–3 minutes. Chill and serve.

» 69 calories for 4 servings, 55 for 5

More on » tomatoes p142 » watercress p70 » cucumber p148 » chillies p93 » seaweeds p174

Variation
Tomato and cucumber gazpacho This is one of my favourite summer breakfasts, and is a pared-back version of the traditional gazpacho recipe. For four, in a food processor, blitz 500g tomatoes and ½ cucumber with 2 tablespoons organic apple cider vinegar and the same of extra virgin olive oil for a couple of minutes. Chill and serve.
» 103 calories for 4 servings

Apple cider vinegar Vinegar is made from the **fermentation** of ethanol by certain **bacteria** – and, like many fermented foods, it has valuable health benefits. Wine vinegar is fine, but apple cider vinegar is in a class of its own in terms of nutrition.

For hundreds of years apple cider vinegar has been used as both a food and a medicine. It contains loads of important **minerals**, as well as many trace elements, and is a powerful detoxifier (especially of the liver and kidneys) and supporter of the immune system. Apple cider vinegar is also well known for its ability to dissolve the acid crystal build-up in joints and tissues, and so has long been used as a natural remedy for arthritis, credited with helping to combat swelling of the joints and reducing pain. It also appears to increase insulin sensitivity and thus improve blood-sugar control, and because it increases feelings of satiety, it is useful to include in a weight-loss plan.

Try to find organic, if you can. Just one caveat: apple cider vinegar is best avoided if you have a stomach ulcer.

Soups

SOUP LIES AT the heart of a healthy diet. It's one of the easiest ways of eating several portions of veg in one go – and that's key, because most of us are not consuming our recommended five portions of fruit and vegetables a day. The most recent Department of Health survey shows that, although fruit and vegetable consumption has increased over the last decade, the British diet is falling way below the minimum standard set to avoid illness, with only one in ten children and a third of adults getting their five a day. Among boys and girls aged eleven to eighteen, particularly girls, it's drastically less.

There's plenty of evidence that five a day is not enough for optimal health anyway – we should aim higher. With less sugar than fruit, veg has the health upper-hand, so it is a good idea to go for veg in a big way. Eating it in soup sets us well on track for higher veg consumption: 80g is considered a portion, which equates to one medium-sized tomato (or seven cherry-sized), for example. A good bowl of any of the tomato soups here – with all the other veg included – will score you five in one go. And that's true of lots of the soups in this chapter, which are packed with vegetables.

Should you peel your veg or not? Non-organic vegetables are prone to high pesticide and nitrate residues, with the greatest concentration in the skin and outer layers, so these should, on the whole, be peeled. But as a general rule you want to leave the skin on. The highest concentration of antioxidants in most plants lies nearest the skin, where the plants are most vulnerable to attack from pests and diseases. We benefit from these antioxidants too, so should ideally not remove them. However, if the skin looks unappetising, scrape veg as finely as you can.

With all veg, this gives us a good reason to buy organic whenever possible. As well as the peel, stalks of things like parsley and coriander are packed with nutrients, so you want to use as much as possible of these in your soup, too. Remove the coarser stems of kale as they are super-fibrous, but chard stalks in soup are good and contain valuable nutrients. And the cores of things like carrots and parsnips not only contain most of their sweetness and flavour, they're also packed with minerals and nutrients. So as a general rule, use every bit of your vegetable ingredients, with very little going in the compost.

Another good thing about soup is its high water content. Many of us don't drink enough fluids, but with soup you've got liquid as the base, in addition to the water in the veg, so it's easy to consume a good 500ml in one bowl. Usual guidelines are 1.6 litres of fluid for women and 2 litres for men per day as a minimum (and more if you are exercising), so a generous bowl of soup will easily notch up a third.

Soup also keeps you feeling full, which is excellent if you want to lose weight. A BBC documentary on diet in 2011 studied a group of men in an army platoon. The group was divided in two, with each eating exactly the same meal of chicken and vegetables, but one group had it blended as a soup, the other had it as a normal meal, with a glass of water. Everyone's stomachs

were scanned using ultra-sound straight after eating, and then again after a rigorous military exercise. The soup group's stomachs stayed full for longer. Chopped up finely with the liquid as soup, ingredients are processed by our bodies more slowly. Water drunk on its own passes almost straight through the stomach, and the accompanying chicken and veg are then digested fast, leaving the stomach empty. Smooth soups are better than chunky as the nutrients in the very finely chopped veg are rapidly accessible and emptying of the stomach is slow.

The nutritional value of soup is affected by the fat or oil you use to sweat the onions and veg as you start the soup off. Coconut, rapeseed and avocado oils all have a high smoke point, and will degrade less rapidly when exposed to high heat. As a result, this makes them better than the more traditional choice of olive or sunflower oil.

There are other nifty tricks to make your soups delicious *and* good for you. In some soups you want creaminess, but you don't have to use lashings of cream. Add a tin of coconut milk, slow-roast fennel, aubergine, miso (fermented soy) or cannellini beans instead, which will give you that creamy texture, but in a healthier way; the soy and cannellini beans will up the protein content too. Many soups you want to be rich and thick. As an alternative to the usual carbohydrate culprits, bread or potatoes, try using sweet potato, celeriac, cauliflower, almonds or white haricot beans. You'll have the same rich and thick result, but with greater nutritional value. Or, as you ladle the soup into bowls, put a poached egg on the top. All these things give oomph as well as a nutritional bonus.

For some soups, you might want a certain saltiness, but you don't have to use a highly processed table salt. Himalayan mineral salt or flaky sea salt are more natural, milder and taste better. Adding herbs and spices can also give you plenty of flavour, or use one of the dried and flaked seaweeds – dulse, nori, kombu or wakame. Naturally salty and amongst the healthiest plants on the planet, these seaweeds enhance the healthiness of your bowl of soup.

Some soups benefit from a slightly sweet taste but you don't need to add sugar. A bunch of dill, for instance, gives a lovely grassy sweetness. Or use peas in your soup, which are naturally sweet. You could also drizzle a vegetable – a root veg or fennel – with honey before roasting it, which will give your soup a rich, caramelised taste. You can also try adding a few prunes to give a sweet depth of flavour.

So what are the guidelines with soups?

» Choose vegetable soup as often as you can; and if making meat or fish soups, make sure you include loads of veg as well – really pack them in.
» Counter-intuitively, the more puréed the soup, the longer it takes to leave the stomach. So, if you want to lose weight, puréed soups will help keep hunger at bay.
» If you have people round to eat, think of having soup as a starter. Served in beautiful bowls, no-one's going to complain.
» If it's just you and close family for supper, make soup the main focus sometimes. A good bowl – or two – of one of these vegetable soups does not feel too mean, and can help with shedding extra kilos.

For your general health, weight loss, and sheer enjoyment, soup needs to become central in your diet.

Ribollita

Ribollita is a classic 'meal-in-a-bowl' soup, packed with veg. Borlotti beans make it filling and super-nutritious – and although not traditional, broccoli also enhances the nutrition.

While training to be a doctor nearly thirty years ago, I worked as a waitress at the River Café. We were taught that ribollita should be so thick your spoon could almost stand up in the bowl, and this version is thick and substantial. If you're super-hungry, you can add more Parmesan and/or a poached egg on top.

For 8 as a whole-meal soup:
200g borlotti beans, fresh or dried and soaked overnight, or 2 x 400g tins
500g kale
500g red cabbage
2 tbsp cold-pressed rapeseed oil or 1 tsp set coconut oil
2 onions, finely chopped
2 garlic cloves, finely chopped
4 carrots, coarsely diced
8 stoned prunes, chopped
Large bunch of flat-leaf parsley (about 100g), including stalks, finely chopped
1 celery head (about 400g), sliced into 2cm pieces at an angle
2 fennel bulbs, cut into 1cm slices
2 tbsp sherry vinegar
2.5–2.6 litres vegetable stock (see p101)
300g broccoli, broken into small florets
Grated zest and juice of 2 lemons
Dried flaked seaweed (dulse or kombu), or sea salt and black pepper
2 tbsp extra virgin olive oil

To serve
Extra virgin olive oil
A little flat-leaf parsley, coarsely chopped
Parmesan

Cover the fresh beans with water and cook for about 40 minutes until soft (or for about an hour if using dried, soaked beans). Leave them in their liquid. If using tinned, heat through in their juice.

Prepare the kale and red cabbage, removing the coarser stalks and chopping the leaves into easy-to-eat chunks or strands.

Heat the oil in a large saucepan and sweat the onion, garlic and carrot. Then add the prunes, parsley, celery and fennel and cook gently for about 15 minutes, until they are soft.

Scoop out about half the beans, using a slotted spoon, and add them to the large saucepan along with the kale and cabbage. Add the sherry vinegar to help the cabbage keep its brilliant colour. Cover everything with 2.5 litres of the stock and cook gently for half an hour.

Put the other half of the beans in a food processor and purée them with their cooking liquid. Add the purée to the soup, adding a little more stock if the soup is too thick, but don't drown it.

Add the broccoli to the pan for the last 5 minutes or so, until it is soft, but not mushy. Stir through the lemon juice, and season with seaweed or salt and pepper to taste. Pour the soup into bowls, drizzle on a little extra virgin olive oil and top each one with some lemon zest.

Serve with a bottle of extra virgin olive oil and a bowl of chopped parsley. Have some grated Parmesan in a bowl to add, bit by bit, as you eat.

» 216 calories per serving, or 269 with Parmesan, oil and parsley topping

More on » kale *p117* » rapeseed oil *p248* » coconut oil *p309* » onions *p281* » garlic *p82* » carrots *p121* » parsley *p136* » broccoli *p151* » lemons *p346* » seaweeds *p174* » olive oil *p193*

Watercress soup

This soup is very simple, with the pepperiness of watercress set against the creaminess of coconut milk. It's also versatile: you can add a bunch of parsley, sorrel, mustard leaves, chard or spinach. But the most important thing is not to let the leaves sit and stew. Cooking makes the flavour milder and reduces the level of nutrients in the watercress (and mustards), so add them late in the cooking process. Watercress reduces down by three-quarters when heated. There may seem to be a lot of leaves here, but they fast disappear. Serve with Spiced beetroot soda bread (see page 102) – the colours then really sing.

For 4–6:
2 tbsp cold-pressed rapeseed oil or 1 tsp set coconut oil
3 large shallots, or 1 large onion, finely chopped
1 large leek (about 400g), finely sliced
1 litre vegetable stock (see p101), or a good vegetable
　　bouillon if you don't have time to make your own
400ml tin of coconut milk
800g watercress, roughly chopped, plus extra to serve
Nutmeg, for grating
½ fresh red chilli, deseeded and finely chopped
Sea salt and black pepper

Warm the oil in a large pan, and sweat the shallots and leek over a low heat for about 7–8 minutes, without allowing them to brown. Stir in the stock and coconut milk, bring to a simmer, then carry on simmering gently, uncovered, for 5 minutes.

Take off the heat and allow to cool for 5 minutes. Add the watercress (and other herbs and leaves if using), a very generous grating of nutmeg and the chilli to the pan, and stir.

Pour the whole lot into a liquidiser or food processor and blitz until really smooth. You may need to blitz the soup in two batches, depending on the size of the machine.

Taste and season with a little salt, some black pepper and more nutmeg if necessary. Don't put back on the heat, but serve straightaway with a sprig of watercress and an extra grating of nutmeg, if you like.

» 289 calories for 4 servings, 193 for 6

More on » rapeseed oil *p248* » coconut oil *p309* » onions *p281* » coconut milk *p235* » chillies *p93*

Watercress tops the list of powerhouse fruits and vegetables. A handful (about 50g) contains: 45 times more lutein than tomatoes; as much vitamin C as an orange; four times the **beta-carotene** and fifteen times the vitamin A of an apple; more vitamin E than the same weight of broccoli; the same amount of calcium as a glass of semi-skimmed milk; and similar levels of iron to spinach. Its content of vitamin K – which is essential for blood-clotting and wound healing – is excellent, and 50g of watercress provides over 100 per cent of the recommended daily intake. It also contains **glucosinolates**, bio-active **phytochemicals** which can reduce **DNA** damage and may help protect against cancer. More of the benefits of the glucosinolates become available to us when watercress is chopped or chewed, releasing its peppery taste, so cut it up fine. Myrosinae, the **enzyme** responsible for these benefits is destroyed by cooking – so we need to eat watercress raw (as in the gazpacho on page 63), or just briefly heated in a soup (as above). The flavonoid **antioxidants** in watercress (**carotene**, lutein and zeaxanthin) are also good for our eyes and cardiovascular health. Overall, watercress is hard to beat in terms of nutrition.

Sweet potato, carrot and peanut butter soup

Health credentials apart, this is one of my favourite cold-weather soups, with a rich and distinctive flavour, and it's very filling.

For 6 as a main course, 8–10 as a starter:
2 heaped tbsp peanut butter (see p36)
2 tbsp cold-pressed rapeseed oil or 1 tsp set coconut oil
1 large onion (about 200g), roughly chopped
2 garlic cloves, finely chopped
1 red finger chilli, deseeded and finely chopped
2 lemongrass stalks, outer leaves removed, sliced
5 tbsp grated fresh root ginger
800g sweet potatoes, roughly chopped
3 large carrots (about 300g), roughly chopped
1 litre hot vegetable stock (see p101)
400ml tin of coconut milk
Dried flaked seaweed (dulse or kombu), or sea salt and black pepper

To serve
Handful of coriander leaves, roughly chopped
Handful of roasted unsalted peanuts, roughly chopped
A few lime wedges

If you have time, make the peanut butter: follow the instructions on page 36. If not, have a good look at the label of your jar to check it doesn't contain hydrogenated (trans) fats or sugar.

Now start the soup. Heat the oil over a medium heat in a heavy-based pan. Add the onion, garlic, chilli, lemongrass and ginger, and sauté until the onion is soft. Add the sweet potato, carrots and stock, and bring to the boil. Turn down the heat and simmer gently for 10–15 minutes until the sweet potato is soft. The carrots will be a little firmer. Allow to cool slightly, pour into a food processor and blitz for 10 seconds, keeping some texture to the soup.

Pour the soup into a large pan. Add the coconut milk and peanut butter. Stir over a medium heat to warm through but don't let it boil. Season with seaweed or salt and pepper. Serve in bowls with the coriander leaves, peanuts and lime in separate dishes. This is good served with Garlic flatbread (see page 106).

» 365 calories for 6 servings, 274 for 8, 219 for 10

More on » rapeseed oil p248 » coconut oil p309 » onions p281 » garlic p82 » chillies p93 » ginger p200 » carrots p121 » coconut milk p235 » seaweeds p174 » coriander p204

Sweet potato is a great source of **fibre** and it's full of vitamins C and B6, and the orange-fleshed varieties are stuffed with **beta-carotene**. This aids good night-time vision, is **anti-inflammatory**, and appears to help the immune system. Most importantly of all, a diet rich in **carotenoid**-dense foods (beta-carotene included) can help to prevent cancer. A large-scale study at Harvard University (of nearly 125,000 people) showed a 32 per cent reduction in the risk of lung cancer among those who consumed more carotenoid-rich foods. And another study – conducted by researchers at Women's Healthy Eating and Living – of women who had completed treatment for early-stage breast cancer, found that those with the highest blood concentrations of carotenoids (from a diet generally high in these fruit and vegetables) had the least likelihood of cancer recurrence. Carotenoids are fat-soluble, so always eat your sweet potatoes with a little fat such as olive oil or coconut milk, or combine them with nuts, to aid absorption. Sweet potatoes are also a useful **carbohydrate**-rich food, as their natural sugars are released slowly into the bloodstream. This is particularly helpful for those with type 2 diabetes.

Organically grown sweet potatoes can be eaten whole but it's best to peel conventional ones as they are sometimes treated with dye or wax.

Pea soup with mint and dill

The beauty of this soup is its colour and its nutritional punch: it gives you at least three veg units in a decent-sized bowl. In one portion alone, you'll get nearly half your daily recommended intake of vitamin A, which is very important for healthy eyes. It also takes about 20 minutes from start to finish, and it's fine made with frozen peas instead of fresh. Many pea soups include a little sugar, but the dill here makes the soup sweet enough. The herbs, unlike sugar, add nutrients as well as flavour.

For 4 as a main course, 6 as a starter:
2 tbsp cold-pressed rapeseed oil or 1 tsp set coconut oil
2 onions (about 200g), finely chopped
1 large garlic clove, crushed
1 green chilli, deseeded and finely chopped
500g peas (fresh or frozen)
500ml vegetable or chicken stock (see pp101 and 98)
40g mint leaves
40g dill
Finely grated zest of 1 lemon
Juice of ½ lemon
Pea shoots, to serve (optional)

Warm the oil in a medium pan, and sweat the onion and garlic over a low heat for about 7–8 minutes, without allowing them to brown. Add the chilli and continue to cook for 2 minutes.

Add the peas and stock to the pan, bring to a simmer and cook for 3–4 minutes.

Allow to cool slightly then pour into a food processor, add the mint and dill and blend to a velvety consistency. Add the lemon zest and juice, and ladle into serving bowls.

Serve plain, or with some fresh pea shoots added to each bowl. This soup is good hot or cold.

» 208 calories for 4 servings, 138 for 6

More on » rapeseed oil *p248* » coconut oil *p309* » onions *p281* » garlic *p82* » chillies *p93* » mint *p326* » lemons *p346*

> **Peas,** in the legume group of vegetables, are an excellent, easily digestible source of **protein**, and they're fat-free. They are relatively high in sugar, but that's balanced by their good dose of **fibre**, with 5.5g in a small handful (100g). Coumestrol, a **phytoestrogen** isolated from peas and other legumes, is currently being researched for its anti-cancer effects.

Two-colour gazpacho

You can make this gazpacho in less than 5 minutes. It's simple, pure and healthy, one of my favourite recipes for the summer and early autumn when tomatoes are at their best. If you don't grow your own and can't find yellow or orange tomatoes, just use sweet reds. If you use a mix of tomato varieties rather than just one type, you get a range of sweetness and acidity and a better taste. This is true of any tomato-based recipe, but particularly when you're eating the tomatoes raw. This recipe is not precise, so you don't have to be careful about quantities. Just put everything in a food processor together and whizz. It's good served with the Seeded oatcakes on page 30.

For 4 as a main course, 6 as a starter:

For the red soup
1 small red pepper (about 75–100g), deseeded
   and coarsely chopped
300g red tomatoes, ideally a mix of varieties
½ cucumber (about 150–200g), roughly chopped
½ red chilli, deseeded and roughly chopped
2 garlic cloves
2 spring onions (optional)
2 tbsp organic apple cider vinegar
4 tbsp extra virgin olive oil, plus extra for serving
Sea salt and black pepper

For the yellow soup
1 small yellow pepper (about 75–100g), deseeded
   and coarsely chopped
300g yellow tomatoes
½ cucumber (about 150–200g), roughly chopped
½ red chilli, deseeded and roughly chopped
2 garlic cloves
2 spring onions (optional)
2 tbsp organic apple cider vinegar
4 tbsp extra virgin olive oil, plus extra for serving
Sea salt and black pepper

Put the pepper, tomatoes, cucumber, chilli, garlic and spring onions for the red soup into a food processor. Purée until pretty smooth. Add the vinegar, olive oil, salt and pepper and blitz again. Pour into a jug.

Repeat this method with the yellow soup ingredients.

Pour from the jugs at the same time into each bowl – one on either side. Add a swirl of extra virgin olive oil and serve.

» 341 calories for 4 servings, 227 for 6

More on » tomatoes p142 » cucumber p148 » chillies p93 » garlic p82 » apple cider vinegar p63 » olive oil p193

Roasted tomato soup

An aromatic, warming soup, which is ideal hot in early autumn when the weather starts to turn cold, but it's also good served cold, and it freezes brilliantly. You can make it when there is a glut of tomatoes. Cooked tomatoes in general are better for us than raw as their nutrients become more available. Sun-dried tomatoes are expensive, but it's good to eat as many as we can. They are *very* nutritious and great here for their richness of taste.

For 6 as a main course, 8 as a starter:
1kg ripe tomatoes
2 fennel bulbs (about 400g), roughly chopped
2 large onions, quartered
3 tbsp cold-pressed rapeseed oil
Sea salt and black pepper
3 garlic cloves, crushed
8–10 sun-dried tomatoes, or 12–15 sun-blushed
    tomatoes in oil, roughly chopped, plus extra
    to garnish
2 tbsp (about 40g) grated fresh root ginger
½ small red chilli, deseeded and chopped,
    or 1 dried chilli, crumbled
30g bunch of coriander
300ml tomato juice, or juice of about 300g fresh
    tomatoes
2 x 400ml tins of coconut milk
30g bunch of dill
4 tbsp Thai fish sauce
1 tbsp tamari soy sauce
Finely grated zest and juice of 2 limes
A few strips of fresh coconut (see p212), dry-fried,
    to serve (optional)

Preheat the oven to 180°C/gas mark 4.

Coarsely chop the tomatoes – but don't skin them as the skin is highly nutritious. Place on a baking sheet with the fennel and onion. Drizzle with 2 tablespoons of the rapeseed oil, and season with salt and black pepper. Roast for about 30–40 minutes until slightly browning at the edges.

Meanwhile, heat the remaining rapeseed oil in a large saucepan and gently cook the garlic, sun-dried tomatoes, ginger and chilli for 3–4 minutes. Strip the leaves from the coriander and chop the stalks as well as the root if you have it. (The root has the most flavour, so if you grow your own coriander, use it.) Put the leaves to one side, but add the stalks and root to the garlic pan.

Add the tomato juice and coconut milk to the saucepan, and cook for a few more minutes. Remove from the heat, cover and leave for 10 minutes to allow the flavours to infuse.

Add the roasted tomatoes, fennel and onions to the soup, and then the dill, fish sauce, tamari soy sauce, lime zest and juice and some seasoning. Cover and simmer for a further 10 minutes.

Add the coriander leaves (reserve a handful to decorate the soup at the end if you like) and blend in a food processor until smooth. You want to reduce all the tomato skins right down, so this will take a minute or two.

Serve with sliced sun-dried tomatoes on top and/or coriander. Sometimes I garnish the soup with toasted strips of fresh coconut instead of the coriander. I like this best warm, but you can also serve it cold. It's good with Seeded spelt bread (see page 33).

» 305 calories for 6 servings, 228 for 8

More on » tomatoes *p142* » onions *p281*
» rapeseed oil *p248* » garlic *p82* » ginger *p200*
» chillies *p93* » coriander *p204* » coconut milk
p235 » tamari soy sauce *p97*

Fennel and chickpea soup

This warming soup has a rich texture and taste, with the gentle sweet flavour of fennel. With its chickpeas and peas, it's very filling and highly nutritious. The fennel and its seeds contain nutrients excellent for treating colds and flu, so if you're feeling under the weather, this is the soup for you. It's best made the day before to allow time for all the flavours to develop.

For 8 as a main course:
500g dried chickpeas, or 2 x 400g tins of chickpeas
1.5 litres vegetable stock (see p101)
4 fennel bulbs, tough, stringy outer leaves removed,
    cut into quarters
1 tbsp olive oil or cold-pressed rapeseed oil
Sea salt and black pepper
1 tbsp clear honey (optional)
3 tsp coriander seeds
1 heaped tbsp fennel seeds
2 tbsp cold-pressed rapeseed oil or 1 tsp set coconut oil
2 small onions (about 175g), finely chopped
5 large garlic cloves, finely chopped
1–2 red chillies (depending on the heat you prefer),
    deseeded and chopped
½ tsp ground turmeric
400g frozen peas
Grated zest and juice of 1–2 lemons (or to taste)

To serve
1 fennel bulb
Handful sugarsnap peas

If using dried chickpeas, soak them overnight in plenty of water. Drain the chickpeas and put them in a saucepan, add water to cover, bring to the boil and simmer gently for 5 minutes. Drain and rinse. This decreases the quantities of indigestible starches in pulses such as lentils and chickpeas.

Heat the stock in a saucepan, bring to the boil and add the par-boiled or tinned chickpeas. Cover and simmer gently until soft (about 45 minutes for rehydrated chickpeas, 15 minutes for tinned). Strain, reserving the cooking liquid.

Preheat the oven to 180°C/gas mark 4.

Roast the fennel for 30 minutes with the olive oil and some seasoning until soft and the edges are just beginning to char. You can drizzle honey over them for the last 10 minutes of cooking time to up the sugary, treacly sweetness in the soup if you like. Keep to one side.

Meanwhile, dry-fry the coriander and fennel seeds in a frying pan over a medium heat for 2–3 minutes, then crush coarsely with a pestle and mortar.

Put the rapeseed or coconut oil in a large saucepan. Add the onion, garlic, chillies and crushed coriander and fennel seeds and cook gently for 5 minutes. Add the turmeric and cook for another couple of minutes. Remove from the heat, add half of the chickpeas and half the frozen peas (keeping some aside whole) and mix well.

Blitz this mixture in a food processor with the chickpea cooking liquid and the roasted fennel. Return to the cleaned saucepan and add the reserved whole chickpeas and peas. Simmer gently for 10 minutes, thinning with more stock as necessary.

Season with salt and pepper, add the lemon zest and juice to taste, and garnish each bowl with a griddled sliver of fennel and/or a sugarsnap pea sliced in half lengthways.

» 254 calories for 8 servings

More on » chickpeas p182 » olive oil p193 » honey p334 » coriander p204 » rapeseed oil p248 » coconut oil p309 » onions p281 » garlic p82 » chillies p93 » turmeric p87 » peas p74 » lemons p346

Andalusian soup-salad

This is a Raven family recipe, which came originally from a 1970s copy of *Vogue*. I included it in my *Garden Cookbook*, but I am giving it here again, as it is an unmissable summer soup, full of little cubes of healthy raw veg. You can make it with shop-bought tomato juice, but it's even better made from fresh tomatoes, puréed with their skins and seeds. This makes for a thick base, but you can thin it with a little water and/or extra virgin olive oil. The jelly around the seeds and the skin contains the most lycopene, the super-antioxidant compound in tomatoes. Always eat tomatoes – raw or cooked – with a small amount of oil as lycopene is fat-soluble, so you need oil to absorb it efficiently.

This cold tomato soup has egg in it, a good protein, which makes it more sustaining. Start making it at least a couple of hours before you want to eat. It's best eaten really cold and so, once assembled, needs an hour or two in the fridge.

Garlic has long been used as a food and a medicine. It has anti-bacterial and anti-viral qualities, which help to keep common minor infections like colds and flu at bay; and it's good for our circulation, preventing our arteries from getting clogged up and stopping platelets from sticking together, so making strokes and heart attacks less likely. Raw garlic has stronger medicinal effects than cooked. Chopping garlic and letting it sit for 5 minutes increases the concentration of garlic's main active ingredient, intensifying the taste and amplifying the health benefits. If your garlic is fresh and green enough, use the skin too: according to research from Japan, this contains six separate **antioxidants**, which help fight the ageing process and protect the heart. If you're using garlic in a soup that is to be whizzed smooth, and the garlic skin has not yet reached the dry, fibrous stage, you won't even know it's there.

For 4 as a main course, 6 as a starter:

1kg tomatoes or 1 litre tomato juice (1kg tomatoes gives you about 1 litre juice), plus an extra 2–3 tomatoes
4 medium eggs, hard-boiled
1 tsp Dijon mustard
4 tbsp extra virgin olive oil, plus extra for serving
2 tbsp organic apple cider vinegar
3 large garlic cloves, crushed
½ large cucumber (about 150–200g), deseeded and diced
1 red pepper, roasted, peeled, deseeded and chopped, or 1 x 165g bottle Peppadew peppers (hot or sweet), drained and diced
4 spring onions, thinly sliced
1 mild chilli, thinly sliced (exclude if using hot Peppadews above)
Sea salt and black pepper

Coarsely chop the extra tomatoes, but don't skin them. Purée the rest of the tomatoes thoroughly in a food processor, so the seeds and skins are broken down and well integrated.

Shell the hard-boiled eggs and separate the whites from the yolks. Coarsely chop the egg white.

In the bottom of a large bowl, mix the mustard, olive oil, vinegar, garlic and egg yolks to make a paste. Add all the chopped vegetables and then the tomato juice. Stir all together.

Season with plenty of salt and pepper, and add the coarsely chopped egg whites before putting the soup in the fridge to chill.

Serve with a swirl of extra virgin olive oil added to each bowl of soup.

» 312 calories for 4 servings, 208 for 6

More on » tomatoes *p142* » eggs *p61* » olive oil *p193* » apple cider vinegar *p63* » cucumber *p148* » chillies *p93*

Smoky squash and lemon soup

This delicious soup, which uses preserved lemons, was inspired by a dish I had in Morocco a few years ago, and which I have never forgotten. Yellow and orange vegetables have high levels of beta-carotene, which helps to protect us against cancer and is very good for our eyes. You can tell by the colour of their flesh that squashes have a high level, and the deeper the colour, the more beta-carotene they contain.

For 4 as a main course, 6–8 as a starter:
About 1.3kg butternut squash
3 tbsp cold-pressed rapeseed oil or 1 tbsp set coconut oil
1 tsp smoked paprika
2 garlic cloves, unpeeled
Sea salt and black pepper
100g shallots, finely chopped
1–2 preserved lemons, flesh discarded, skin finely chopped
600ml vegetable stock (see p101)

To serve
Handful of flat-leaf parsley, roughly chopped
2–3 tbsp Spiced nuts and seeds (see p170)

Preheat the oven to 190°C/gas mark 5.

Don't bother to peel, but cut the squash in half, remove the seeds, and then cut the flesh into 3cm chunks.

Place the squash chunks in a roasting tray and coat with most of the oil, the smoked paprika, whole garlic cloves and some seasoning. Roast for 45–50 minutes, until the squash pieces are soft and burnished, the edges caramelised.

In a large saucepan, fry the shallots in the remaining oil until translucent.

Add the roasted squash to the shallot, and squeeze in the garlic cloves out of their skins. Stir and then add the chopped skin of 1 preserved lemon. Pour in the stock and simmer for 30 minutes.

Blend until smooth in a food processor and taste to check the 'lemoniness'. Add another ½–1 preserved lemon if necessary. Blitz again. Season.

Serve with a bowl of chopped flat-leaf parsley and a few spiced nuts and seeds to sprinkle on the top.

» 272 calories for 4 servings, 182 for 6, 136 for 8 (without nuts and seeds)

More on » squash *p186* » rapeseed oil *p248* » coconut oil *p309* » garlic *p82* » lemons *p346* » parsley *p136*

Roast beetroot soup with horseradish yoghurt

Beetroot is in a classic trio here with horseradish and orange juice. These flavours are excellent together, always working well. The beetroots are roasted not boiled, so all the goodness ends up in the bowl. The horseradish yoghurt is a contrast in flavour and colour and helps the absorption of fat-soluble vitamins in the veg.

For 6 as a main course, 8–10 as a starter:
1kg beetroots, quartered, peel left on
300g carrots, thickly sliced
3 tbsp cold-pressed rapeseed oil or 1 tbsp set coconut oil
2 tbsp aged balsamic vinegar
1 tbsp caraway seeds
200g shallots (about 8), halved if large
3 garlic cloves, unpeeled
4 sprigs of thyme
1 litre vegetable stock (see p101)
Juice of 1 orange
Sea salt and black pepper
A few sprigs of dill, to garnish

For the horseradish yoghurt
6 tbsp live natural yoghurt (see p44)
1 heaped tbsp grated fresh horseradish
Grated zest of ½ orange

Preheat the oven to 180°C/gas mark 4.

Put the beetroot and carrot on a baking tray with the oil, balsamic and caraway seeds. Mix well and roast in the middle of the oven. After 30 minutes add the shallots, the whole unpeeled garlic cloves and 2 sprigs of thyme. Roast for a further 30 minutes until the root vegetables are soft and the shallots are golden. If necessary, when cool enough, remove the skin from the roast beetroot with your fingers. With young beetroot, the skin is often fine to eat, so leave it on.

Mix together all the horseradish yoghurt ingredients, adding salt and pepper to taste.

Squeeze the sweet roasted garlic out of its skins. Add to a large saucepan, along with the roasted veg, scraping all the seeds and reduced balsamic from the baking tray into the pan. Add the vegetable stock and bring just to the boil. Reduce the heat and simmer for 20 minutes, allowing all the flavours to infuse.

Pick the leaves off the remaining sprigs of thyme and add to the pan, then blitz the soup in a food processor. Add the orange juice and test for seasoning. Serve with a swirl of horseradish yoghurt in the top of each bowl, and a bit of fresh dill.

» 200 calories for 6 servings, 150 for 8, 120 for 10

More on » carrots *p121* » rapeseed oil *p248* » coconut oil *p309* » balsamic vinegar *p189* » garlic *p82* » oranges *p49* » yoghurt *p44* » horseradish *p354*

Beetroot All beetroot contains a stack of **vitamins** and **minerals**, including magnesium, iron, phosphorus, potassium, manganese, folic acid and vitamin C. But it is the natural dietary **nitrate** content, found especially in beetroot juice, that has really excited the scientific world. Nitrate helps our bodies to produce nitric oxide, which dilates (widens) our blood vessels, reducing blood pressure and increasing blood flow to muscles and the brain – this is why sportsmen and women are so keen on beetroot. As well as enhancing stamina, it's thought that beetroot juice may help with altitude sickness; research is being done at high altitudes in Nepal, and also with deep-sea divers, to see if the extra oxygen supply through the blood extends the length of time an oxygen tank can last. The nitrates in beetroot juice are also undergoing clinical trials for the treatment of blood pressure. And the theory that increased blood flow to the brain might improve exam performance? That's currently being researched too...

Spicy cauliflower, turmeric and chickpea soup

This soup has a coarse texture, halfway between a soup and a stew. Turmeric is an intense gold root and in India it's well known for being good for us. It's a perfect and traditional partner to cauliflower, giving good flavour as well as colour. Put it in your soups, your smoothies, your curries; and even – as in Rajasthan – add it to your scrambled eggs.

For 8 as a main course, 12 as a starter:
1 medium cauliflower
1 medium onion, chopped
2.5cm piece of fresh turmeric root, grated,
    or 1 tsp ground turmeric
1 heaped tbsp coriander seeds
Seeds from 14 cardamom pods
1 heaped tsp cumin seeds
1 heaped tsp caraway seeds
2 tbsp cold-pressed rapeseed oil or 1 tsp set coconut oil
4 garlic cloves
5cm piece of fresh root ginger (about 40g), peeled
1 green chilli
400g tin of chopped tomatoes
1 litre vegetable stock (see p101)
3 x 400g tins of chickpeas
Sea salt and black pepper
Small bunch of coriander, to serve

Preheat the oven to 180°C/gas mark 4.

Break and cut the cauliflower into florets and put into a bowl. Add the onion and turmeric.

Dry-fry all the spice seeds in a frying pan for a few minutes, and then grind them into a coarse powder using a blender or a pestle and mortar.

Add the spices and oil to the cauliflower and onion in the bowl and mix very well – your hands are best for this. Place on a baking tray. Roast the cauliflower, onions and spice mix for 30 minutes until the edges of the cauliflower are starting to brown. Meanwhile, in a small food processor or liquidiser, blitz the garlic, ginger and chilli.

Put this garlic mixture into a large saucepan and add the tomatoes. Stir, and cook over a medium heat for 4–5 minutes, then add the stock.

Drain 1 tin of chickpeas then blitz in a food processor until smooth. Add to the soup along with another drained but unblitzed tin of chickpeas.

Bring to the boil, add the roast cauliflower, then cover and simmer for 15 minutes, when everything should be done. Add the final drained tin of chickpeas – just long enough to warm through.

Season with salt and pepper, scatter with coriander leaves and serve.

» 142 calories for 12 servings, 212 for 8

More on » cauliflower *p267* » onions *p281* » coriander *p204* » rapeseed oil *p248* » coconut oil *p309* » garlic *p82* » ginger *p200* » chillies *p93* » tomatoes *p142* » chickpeas *p182*

Turmeric is an intense yellowy-orange coloured rhizome that looks like a slimmer version of ginger. And the more we eat of it, the better: it helps to clear infections and reduce **inflammation**, and ongoing research is examining its potential as a treatment for cancers, including those of the colon, prostate and pancreas. Unusually, its active ingredients can cross the blood-brain barrier, so it may be effective against neurological conditions such as meningitis. Try to find a good source of fresh turmeric (some of the larger supermarkets sell it), or use the powder instead. As a general rule of thumb: 5cm fresh turmeric = 1 tablespoon freshly grated turmeric = 1 teaspoon ground turmeric.

It makes an excellent partner with cauliflower (see here and page 269) and studies have recently shown that they have more health benefits when cooked and eaten together than apart.

Roasted aubergine and mushroom soup

This is a cold-weather creamy soup, yet with no cream in it at all. The richness comes from the roasted aubergine. Aubergines have a certain meatiness to them, which – like cream – adds substance to any dish, yet the vegetables are low in fat and high in fibre. Their slightly earthy taste goes brilliantly with mushrooms, as does the seaweed kombu, which is used here instead of salt.

For 6 as a main course, 8–10 as a starter:
400g mushrooms, quartered (ideally a mix of flat and
    button field mushrooms, plus some shiitake, oyster,
    chestnut etc.)
1 large onion, coarsely chopped
2 large tomatoes (about 200g), roughly chopped
1 large aubergine, roughly chopped into 2cm chunks
2 garlic cloves, unpeeled
2 tbsp cold-pressed rapeseed oil
Sprig of thyme, leaves picked
Pinch of dried marjoram
1 tsp ras-el-hanout
750ml vegetable stock (see p101)
Nutmeg, for grating
Black pepper

To serve (per bowl)
Drizzle of truffle oil
Handful of roughly chopped parsley
Pinch of dried flaked seaweed (dulse or kombu)

Preheat the oven to 190°C/gas mark 5.

Put the mushrooms, onion, tomatoes and aubergine with the garlic in a roasting tin and drizzle with oil. Scatter over the herbs and the ras-el-hanout.

Roast for 40 minutes until the aubergine is soft and blackening around the edges. Squeeze the garlic out of its skins.

Transfer everything to a large saucepan, add the stock and simmer gently for 20 minutes.

Pour the soup into a food processor or blender and blitz until smooth. Pour back into the saucepan and reheat gently. Do not allow to boil.

Grate in plenty of nutmeg and add black pepper to taste. Serve in bowls with a drizzle of truffle oil, and a sprinkle of parsley and dried kombu or dulse.

This is good with the Spiced squash soda bread on page 104.

» 141 calories for 6 servings, 106 for 8, 85 for 10

More on » onions *p281* » tomatoes *p142*
» aubergines *p147* » garlic *p82* » rapeseed oil *p248*
» parsley *p136* » seaweeds *p174*

Mushrooms Rather like seaweed, mushrooms contain many specific **micronutrients**, as well as most general plant nutrients. Their **protein** content makes them filling and yet they're very low in calories, so they're a great food if you want to lose weight. They are brilliant for the immune system as they contain a soluble **fibre** that boosts our body's defence mechanisms and zaps bacteria and viruses. They are also **anti-inflammatory**, and are packed with **vitamins** and **minerals**, including all the B vitamins (especially niacin) and D, as well as the elusive and important zinc and selenium. A deficiency in either or both of these minerals is common in the UK, and has wide-reaching effects, including the suppression of our immune system. Selenium helps support thyroid function and reduces the risk of some cancers.

For the greatest benefit from mushrooms, try to cook with and eat several kinds together, because they each have slightly different health benefits and flavours.

Creamy celeriac soup with chestnuts

Most of the nutrients lie just beneath the skin of celeriac, so for soup, if the celeriac is organic, remove the minimal amount of peel. Top this soup with chestnuts, which are low in fat and calories compared to all other nuts, but still packed with protein and they are filling too. This soup is very rich and creamy, yet it contains no cream or in fact any dairy, with almond milk used in the base instead.

For 2–3 as a main course, 4 as a starter, 10 as a canapé:
2 tbsp cold-pressed rapeseed oil or 1 tsp set coconut oil
1 celeriac (about 1.2kg), diced into 2–3cm cubes
2 shallots, finely chopped
1 garlic clove, crushed
Large sprig of rosemary, leaves finely chopped
700ml good-quality chicken stock (see p98)
500ml almond milk (see p347)
Juice of ½ lemon
Sea salt and black pepper

To serve
Finely chopped rosemary or parsley
100g vacuum-packed chestnuts, sliced
Black pepper

Heat the oil in a heavy-based saucepan. Add the celeriac and cook on a medium heat for 5 minutes, stirring constantly.

Add the shallots and cook for a further 5 minutes until both have softened. Take care not to let them colour. Stir in the garlic and rosemary. Cook for 2 minutes, then add the stock and simmer for 20 minutes. Pour in the almond milk and bring the soup back to a simmer. Blend the soup in a food processor until really smooth.

Pour back into a clean pan and reheat gently. Squeeze in the lemon juice and add plenty of black pepper and some salt if necessary.

Sprinkle over the rosemary or parsley, the chestnuts and a grind of black pepper. This soup is filling, so serve in small bowls, or shot glasses as a canapé at a party.

» 529 calories for 2 servings, 352 for 3, 264 for 4, 105 for 10

More on » rapeseed oil p248 » coconut oil p309 » garlic p82 » lemons p346 » parsley p136 » chestnuts p158

Celeriac This large knobbly root vegetable is much more popular in France, especially when shredded to make a classic rémoulade, but most of us here don't eat it nearly enough. It makes delicious mash, is an excellent alternative to potatoes and it gives a real creaminess to soup. It's low-calorie, with only 27 per 100g of cooked celeriac (compared to 74 for cooked potatoes), has a high **fibre** content, which means its sugars are released slowly into the bloodstream, and it's full of complex **carbohydrates**. All these qualities make it an excellent food for anyone wanting to lose weight and for those with type 2 diabetes.

Tom yum

A classic south-east Asian soup which, served with a bowl of red or black rice, makes a meal. Both these varieties of rice are whole grains, with the husk intact. This means they're rich in the fibre and goodness that has been largely stripped from standard white rice. They make a delicious and nutritious addition here.

For 4:
1 litre vegetable stock (see p101)
1 thumb-length piece of fresh galangal root, peeled
1 lemongrass stalk
1 green Thai chilli, finely sliced
150g shiitake mushrooms, sliced
1 tsp tom yum goong paste (Thai chilli paste with dried shrimps)

1 tbsp Thai fish sauce
180g raw prawns, peeled and de-veined
6 spring onions, finely sliced
12 cherry tomatoes
6 kaffir lime leaves (fresh, frozen or dried)

To serve
30g coriander leaves
Juice of 1 lime
1 lime, cut into quarters
200g red or black rice, cooked (optional)

Heat the vegetable stock to a gentle simmer.

Chop the galangal finely. Prepare the lemongrass by peeling away the outer, tougher layer, retaining only the tender central part of the stalk. Chop this very finely.

Add these and the chilli to the broth. Then add the mushrooms, tom yum paste, fish sauce and prawns. Simmer gently for 3–4 minutes until the prawns are cooked.

Add the spring onions and cherry tomatoes and take off the heat. Allow to cool for a minute and then add the kaffir lime leaves (if fresh, these need to be added at the end or they turn bitter).

Sprinkle with the coriander and lime juice, and serve straightaway with the lime quarters and a bowl of red or black rice (if using) to add in, little by little, as you eat.

» 266 calories per serving

More on » mushrooms *p88* » prawns *p212*
» tomatoes *p142* » coriander *p204* » rice *p224*

Tom kha gai

This Thai soup is similar to tom yum, but uses coconut milk – as well as vegetable stock – as the base, and chicken instead of prawns. This makes the perfect lunch or light supper and takes only about 10 minutes to cook. The red or black rice – served on the side – takes longer to cook, but is delicious, nutty and very nutritious.

For 4:
2 organic chicken breasts (about 320g in total)
500ml chicken or vegetable stock (see pp98 and 101)
400ml tin of coconut milk
1 thumb-length piece of fresh galangal root, peeled
1 lemongrass stalk
1 red chilli, deseeded and finely chopped
150g mushrooms (ideally straw or oyster)
1 tsp tom yum goong paste (Thai chilli paste with dried shrimps)
2 tbsp Thai fish sauce
6 spring onions, finely sliced
Handful of mangetout peas, halved
6 kaffir lime leaves (fresh, frozen or dried)

To serve
30g coriander leaves
Juice of 1 lime
200g red or black rice, cooked (optional)

To tenderise it and make its cooking super-quick, slice each chicken breast into three sections and beat them out gently between two layers of clingfilm or in a plastic bag until each section is just a thin layer. Slice into small, bite-sized pieces.

In a large saucepan, gently heat the stock and coconut milk to a simmer.

Chop the galangal finely. Prepare the lemongrass by peeling off the outer, tougher layer, retaining only the tender central part of the stalk. Chop this very finely.

Add these and the chilli to the stock and coconut milk. Then add the mushrooms, tom yum paste, fish sauce and chicken. Simmer gently for 3–4 minutes until the chicken pieces are cooked.

Add the spring onions and mangetouts and take off the heat. Allow to cool for a minute and add the kaffir lime leaves (if fresh, these need to be added at the end or they turn bitter).

Sprinkle with the coriander and lime juice, and serve straightaway with a bowl of red or black rice (if using) to add in, little by little, as you eat.

» 493 calories per serving

More on » chicken *p260* » coconut milk *p235*
» mushrooms *p88* » peas *p74* » coriander *p204*
» rice *p224*

Chillies contain good amounts of vitamins C, K and folate, and they also contain a **phytonutrient** called capsaicin, which gives them their heat, as well as their **anti-inflammatory** properties. It is thought that capsaicin may relieve migraines and other headaches, and it is used to manage chronic pain; its heat causes eyes to water and noses to run and thus can clear congestion! Chillies have also been shown to boost the metabolism, possibly helping to control weight. Intriguingly, a recent seven-year study of adults in China correlated regular consumption of spicy foods, such as chilli peppers, with a 14 per cent reduced risk of death from all causes.

Thai-style vegetable broth
with soba noodles

Use the Thai broth recipe here as a simple base for your soup and then choose what you want to add. The broth is good as it is with the mix of vegetables, or you can add prawns, salmon or chicken. The stars of the show, though, are the super-nutritious buckwheat noodles (also called soba). These are made with wholegrain buckwheat and contain lots of fibre and protein – a great combination, and one which will fill you up for ages.

To be authentic, you would use at least 10 cloves of garlic, but however healthy this is, I find the taste a little overwhelming.

You can vary this broth by using a garlic garnish and its oil, and a chilli garnish, served in separate bowls (see right).

For 6 as a main course, 8–10 as a starter:

For the Thai broth
2 litres good-quality vegetable stock (see p101)
4 garlic cloves, finely chopped
3 lemongrass stalks, tough outer leaves removed, finely sliced
1 tbsp coconut palm sugar (optional)
30g bunch of dill
6 spring onions, finely chopped (reserve some for garnish)
Sea salt and black pepper

For the noodles and vegetables
100g buckwheat noodles
800g mixed vegetables (courgettes, carrots, pak choi, green beans, runner beans and chard), finely sliced
2 tbsp tamari soy sauce
2 tbsp Thai fish sauce
1 tsp Chinese five-spice powder
Small bunch of mint, leaves coarsely chopped
60g coriander leaves, coarsely chopped (reserve some to garnish)

Put the stock into a large saucepan over a medium heat and add the garlic and lemongrass. Put the sugar, dill and spring onion into the pan, season with salt, stir and leave to cook for 2–3 minutes.

Check the cooking instructions for the noodles. Add to the simmering stock. Cook and add the vegetables for the last 3 minutes of the noodle cooking time (don't overcook as the veg need to retain freshness and bite).

Mix in the tamari and fish sauce. Season with five-spice and black pepper. Add the mint leaves and most of the coriander and take off the heat.

Serve in bowls and top each portion with the remaining chopped spring onion, fresh coriander and/or some of the garnishes below.

» 152 calories for 6 servings, 114 for 8, 91 for 10

More on » garlic *p82* » coconut palm sugar *p316* » buckwheat *p226* » tamari soy sauce *p97* » mint *p326* » coriander *p204*

Variations
Garlic garnish
4 garlic cloves
2 tsp set coconut oil
Finely slice the garlic and fry in the oil until golden brown, but not burnt. Place in a small bowl for people to help themselves.
» 94 calories for the bowl

Chilli garnish
1 fresh red chilli, deseeded (or with seeds if you prefer it hot)
1 tbsp coconut palm sugar
4 tbsp rice wine vinegar
3 tbsp mirin (rice wine)
Crush the chilli and sugar together in a pestle and mortar. Stir in the vinegar and mirin. Pour into a bowl for people to help themselves.
» 181 calories for the bowl

Winter miso soup with sesame and tofu

Fermented foods provide beneficial bacteria for our guts, and we should all aim to have more of them. Miso is made from fermented soya beans. There are three commonly available types of miso: white, red and yellow (see opposite). Any are fine here; once the tub of miso paste is open, store in the fridge.

Miso has a wonderful, rich taste and is surprisingly filling, ideal and warming for winter, all the more so with the added sesame seeds here. The tofu gives more substance, with a lovely texture.

For 4:

For the dashi stock (enough for 2 soups)
4 x 10cm square pieces of kombu seaweed
50g katsuobushi (dried bonito flakes)

For the soup
50g sesame seeds, dry-fried, plus extra to garnish
800ml dashi stock (instant or home-made)
300g silken tofu, drained
3 tbsp miso paste (to taste)
8 spring onions, finely sliced

Tofu, or bean curd, is made by boiling and curdling fresh soya milk, then pressing it into a solid cake. (Soya milk is made by cooking dried soya beans in plenty of water until soft, then straining the solids from the liquid – this liquid is soya milk.) Tofu has similar benefits to soya and edamame beans – it is **protein**-rich and very filling (see page 128 for more on soya beans). Due to the **phytoestrogen** content of soya beans, many women add soya-based foods like tofu to their diet to help relieve symptoms such as hot flushes during the menopause.

Begin by making the dashi stock, if you want to make it yourself. Wash the kombu under cold running water to get rid of excess salt. Put 1.6 litres of water in a large saucepan. Add the kombu to the water, and leave it to soak for 30 minutes.

Place the saucepan on a high heat and lift out the kombu just before the water boils. Add the katsuobushi, bring to the boil and then take off the heat immediately. Allow to stand until all the flakes have sunk to the bottom of the saucepan.

Pour the stock through a fine-mesh sieve. Allow to cool and leave in the fridge for up to 3 days or freeze.

Now make the soup. Grind the dry-fried sesame seeds in a pestle and mortar, or a small food processor, until they become paste-like.

Heat the 800ml dashi stock in a saucepan. Bring to the boil, reduce to just less than a simmer and add the tofu, tearing it into pieces.

Gradually add in the miso paste, stirring until dissolved. You may not need all of it. Miso varies in strength, so taste regularly and add as much as you want depending on how strong or salty it is.

Add the sesame paste to the soup and stir in well. Remove the pan from the heat and add half of the spring onions. Leave to stand for a few minutes and then serve with the remaining spring onions and sesame seeds scattered over the top of each bowl.

» 215 calories per serving

More on » seaweeds p174 » sesame seeds p164

Summer miso soup with konjac noodles

The substance in this summery miso soup comes from konjac (also called shirataki and konnyaku), which are vegetable noodles made from yam. These have a taste and texture similar to rice noodles, but are much more nutritious. Largely composed of water and fibre, they are very low in carbohydrates and calories. You usually buy them wet, packed in liquid, from Asian grocers and some supermarkets. Just pour away the liquid and rinse. As well as noodles, pile in any veg you like, but julienned carrots and daikon (mooli) really add to the flavour.

For 4:
200g konjac noodles (wet weight)
1 tbsp set coconut oil
½ leek
200g free-range chicken, pork or prawns
150g sweet potato, chopped into bite-sized chunks
1 litre dashi stock (see opposite)
30ml sake
4–5 tbsp miso paste
100g carrot, julienned into 5mm batons
200g daikon radish, julienned into 5mm batons
Dried chilli, to garnish

Tear the noodles into smaller pieces and blanch briefly in boiling water to remove any bitterness, then drain.

Heat a little of the oil in a small frying pan. Finely slice the leek into very narrow strips and fry quickly for 1 minute. Set to one side. Thinly slice the chicken, pork or prawns. Heat the remaining oil in a large saucepan and cook the chicken, pork or prawns until cooked through.

Add the sweet potato, noodles, dashi stock and sake. Bring to a simmer, then cook until the sweet potatoes are just tender, about 10 minutes. Gradually add the miso paste, to taste. Miso varies in strength, so taste regularly and add as much as you want depending on how strong or salty it is. Add the carrots and daikon and cook for 2 minutes.

Serve in bowls with the sliced leeks on top and a sprinkling of chilli.

» With chicken, 192 calories per serving, with trimmed pork 245, with prawns 165

More on » coconut oil *p309* » chicken *p260*
» prawns *p212* » sweet potato *p72* » carrots *p121*

Tamari soy sauce and miso Tamari is a thicker, less salty, fermented soy sauce that does not contain wheat. It is a good substitute for salt, and the healthiest of all soy sauces. The soya beans are cooked to a paste, which is then left to slowly ferment. The liquid pressed out of this fermented bean mush (or moromi) is tamari and has valuable immune-boosting benefits.

Miso, a fermented soya paste used as a flavouring, is made from dried soya beans that have been slow-cooked, mashed and then mixed with salt and koji (a live culture that initiates the **fermentation** process). It is then left for many months to ferment. White miso is made from soya beans which have been fermented with a large percentage of rice. It is slightly sweet and is best used in dressings or light sauces. Yellow miso is made from soya beans fermented mainly with barley. It has an earthier taste and is good in soups and marinades. Red miso usually contains more soya beans and sometimes undergoes longer fermentation. With a deep umami flavour, it is very strong but is good in hearty soups and glazes.

Tamari and miso both have strong anti-cancer and **antioxidant** properties, while being rich in **minerals**. The fermentation produces unique **carbohydrates** that help to promote friendly gut **bacteria**.

Restorative chicken broth

Bone broths have been known to be good for us for ever and a day, and they're ideal for when we're feeling under the weather. If you're ill, it is important to eat easily digestible, nutritious meals; and to avoid meat. That's why the chicken here is used only to make a broth. Bone broth can be used to help heal a 'leaky gut' which in turn can reduce our food allergies and intolerances and strengthen our immune systems. There's also a bunch of herbs and spices to flavour the soup, as well as veg that is known to boost our immune system and help ward off colds. If you add a tablespoon of organic apple cider vinegar, it leaches more beneficial minerals from the bones and that's worthwhile too.

This broth stores well for three to four days in the fridge.

For 4:
1.2 litres chicken stock (see below)
2 tbsp cold-pressed rapeseed oil or 1 tsp set coconut oil
2 large onions, finely sliced
4 garlic cloves, crushed
1 tbsp finely chopped fresh root ginger
1 tbsp finely chopped fresh turmeric root,
    or ½ tsp ground turmeric
100–200g fresh shiitake mushrooms,
    or a handful of dried
2 carrots, diced
2 sprigs of thyme
3 bay leaves
1 red chilli, deseeded and finely chopped (optional)
Grated zest and juice of 1 lemon

For the chicken stock (makes 2 litres)
1 raw chicken carcass
2 onions, unpeeled, quartered
2 carrots, scrubbed
2 celery sticks
Good bunch of parsley, including the stalks
2 bay leaves
10 black peppercorns
1 tbsp organic apple cider vinegar

For the stock, break up the carcass and put it in a large saucepan with the vegetables, herbs, seasoning and vinegar. Cover with 2.8 litres cold water and bring to the boil. Simmer gently for 1–2 hours, uncovered. Strain and, if you want a stronger flavour, reduce by boiling in an open saucepan. Cool, and pour into a suitably sized bowl. When cold, remove the layer of fat from the surface, then keep the stock in the fridge or freeze to use later.

Measure out the amount of stock you require for the soup, and heat it in a large saucepan.

Heat the oil in a large pan, and gently fry the onion, garlic, ginger and turmeric until soft, about 7–8 minutes. Add this to the stock, along with the mushrooms, carrots, thyme, bay and chilli (if using), and simmer very gently for 20 minutes until the mushrooms and carrots are cooked.

Take the soup off the heat, add the lemon zest and juice, and serve immediately.

» 148 calories per serving

More on » chicken *p260* » rapeseed oil *p248*
» coconut oil *p309* » onions *p281* » garlic *p82*
» ginger *p200* » turmeric *p87* » mushrooms *p88*
» carrots *p121* » chillies *p93* » lemons *p346*
» parsley *p136* » apple cider vinegar *p63*

Variation
Spinach (or chard) and chicken broth For extra goodness, I sometimes also add 50g spinach or chard as a purée to the final soup. Chop and blanch the spinach or chard leaves by dipping them in and out of boiling water for 30 seconds. Drain and plunge into iced water to stop them cooking. Drain again and purée the leaves in a food processor. This breaks down the cells and releases the chlorophyll. Pour into a jug. Make the soup as above, and add the spinach or chard purée at the end with the lemon zest and juice.
» 12 additional calories per serving

Kamalaya detox vegetable broth

This is a super-nutritious broth I was taught how to make at the Kamalaya health spa in Thailand. It's ideal for when you feel like something clean and healthy, and includes huge amounts of veg for just one portion, but that's the point: it's like getting ten a day in one bowl, with lots of vegetables to produce only a small amount of stock. Make sure you include veg from the super-healthy allium and brassica families, as well as a leafy green like spinach or chard and some seaweed such as wakame. You must cook them over a very gentle heat, with the pan only just steaming, the surface of the liquid not even moving. This technique leaches out the veg's minerals and vitamins, leaving more of these nutrients intact than with intense heat. Think of it like making tea – the longer, the stronger and the better for you.

For 350ml (for 1):
50–60g chard or spinach
20g carrot
1 small onion
1 small leek
10g bok choi or pak choi
10g broccoli
10g kale
10g courgette
10g celery
5g turnip
5g wakame seaweed
2g lemongrass stalks
2g fresh root ginger
2 kaffir lime leaves
Sea salt and black pepper

Chop and blanch the spinach or chard leaves by dipping them in and out of boiling water for 30 seconds. Drain and plunge into iced water to stop them cooking. Drain again and purée the leaves in a food processor. This breaks down the cells and releases the chlorophyll. Pour into a jug.

Chop all the other vegetables into small chunks. Place all the ingredients except the spinach/chard into a large saucepan, along with 350ml water. Heat to steaming (60–65°C), but not simmering, and cook for 30 minutes to extract all the goodness from the veg.

Take off the heat and add the spinach or chard purée. Leave to infuse for 5 minutes.

At this stage, you can do one of three things:
  » Give the whole mix a quick blitz in a food processor, then push through a conical sieve. Season the broth and drink straightaway with a squeeze of lime.
  » Purée the whole thing and eat as a nice hearty soup, fibre and all. This will be more filling and sustaining.
  » Drain without blitzing, and use as a broth to which you can add any mixture of steamed veg you fancy – such as broccoli florets, roast squash cubes, beansprouts with a few diced tomatoes.

» 103 calories (without added veg above)

More on » spinach *p54* » carrots *p121*
» onions *p281* » broccoli *p151* » kale *p117*
» seaweeds *p174* » ginger *p200*

Vegetable stock

Here is a classic vegetable stock, an ideal base for any soup. To pack in the nutrients, there's more veg here than usual in proportion to water. Buy organic veg and don't peel it. Just chop coarsely and add to the pan. The kale or broccoli add to the goodness. If you want to make this super-quick, grate or finely chop the veg and reduce the cooking time to 15 minutes, but don't use intense heat.

Don't add salt to a stock until the end of cooking: if you add salt earlier, as the stock reduces, it becomes ever saltier. (You could also use seaweed instead of salt.)

To make your own stock cubes, reduce the volume by half by simmering very gently after straining. Allow to cool, then pour into ice trays and freeze.

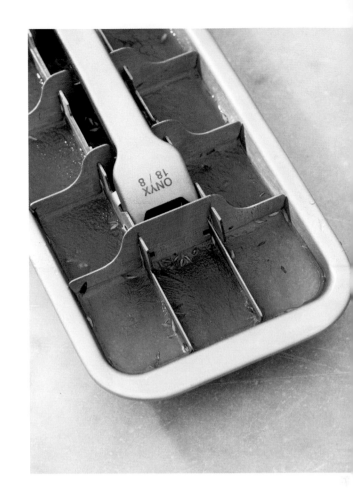

For about 1 litre:
3 carrots, chopped
3 onions, topped and tailed and roughly chopped, but not peeled
3 celery sticks, chopped
100g broccoli or kale, or central stem of calabrese (usually chucked away)
3 garlic cloves, cut in half, unpeeled
2 bay leaves
3 sprigs of thyme
Small bunch of parsley, stalks and all
7 black peppercorns

Put all the ingredients into a large pan with 1.2 litres water, and bring to a simmer over a gentle heat. Simmer with a lid on for 30 minutes and then take the lid off if you want to reduce it and intensify the flavour of the stock.

Allow to cool and strain into a bowl. Keep in the fridge and use within 2–3 days.

» 354 calories

More on » carrots *p121* » onions *p281* » broccoli *p151* » kale *p117* » garlic *p82* » parsley *p136*

Spiced beetroot soda bread

The next few recipes are things to eat with soup. Whole roast beetroot is good for you, and you can include it in this impressive bread, which you can knock up really quickly. We often make this and the following squash version for course lunches at Perch Hill, serving a slice of each – the purple beetroot and the orange squash – to go with almost any soup.

The great thing about soda breads is you don't need to wait for them to rise. Just combine the ingredients and bake in the oven for less than half an hour. Plain soda bread does not last well, but with beetroot, these loaves keep moist for three or four days. You can play around with the spices too.

To add to the loaf's nutrition, you can use wholemeal flour here. This makes for a heavier texture, with less of a rise.

For 2 small loaves (each serves 3–4) or 8 rolls:
400g raw beetroots
Large pinch sea salt and black pepper
2 tsp cumin seeds
2 tsp fennel seeds
10 juniper berries, crushed
3 tbsp olive oil
300g strong white bread flour (or wholemeal bread flour),
    plus a little extra for sprinkling
50g organic unsalted butter, softened
3 level tsp baking powder
4 tbsp sunflower seeds, plus 2 tbsp for sprinkling
    (optional)
100ml buttermilk (see p34 for how to make your own)
1 medium egg

Preheat the oven to 180°C/gas mark 4.

Quarter the beetroot but leave the peel on. Line a baking tray with foil and put the beetroot in. Season with salt and pepper, and sprinkle with the seeds and berries. Add the olive oil and mix well, then cover with foil.

Roast for 50–60 minutes, until the beetroot is soft to the point of a knife. Remove the beetroot, but leave the oven on. Allow the beetroot to cool, then peel with your fingers (or if using young beetroot with very fine skin, leave the skin on).

Purée the roasted beetroot and spices in a food processor. Place the beetroot purée in a bowl with the flour, butter, baking powder, 4 tablespoons of the sunflower seeds and some salt. Stir to combine.

Beat the buttermilk with the egg and add gradually to the flour and beetroot mix to make a dough. Don't be alarmed: it is a rather wet dough, but it produces a fluffy and light bread.

Divide the dough in two, shape the dough into flat rounds, slashing a shallow cross into the top. Place on a greased baking sheet. Sprinkle with extra flour and, if you like, the remaining 2 tablespoons of sunflower seeds.

If making rolls, divide the dough into eight, place on a sheet and sprinkle with extra flour and seeds as for the loaves.

Bake the loaves for 25 minutes in the middle of the oven. The rolls will need about 20 minutes.

Test to see if the loaves are done by inserting a skewer into the centre. If the skewer comes out clean, the bread is done. If not then put back in the oven for a further 5 minutes on the baking sheet. When ready, take them out and cool on a wire rack.

» 438 calories for 6 servings, 329 for 8

More on » beetroot *p85* » olive oil *p193* » butter *p104* » eggs *p61*

Spiced squash soda bread

Squash soda bread makes a good alternative to beetroot, and the texture of this version – a cross between a cake and a bread – is fabulous. You can make it even more nutritious by using 100 per cent wholemeal flour, or a mix of wholemeal and strong white bread flour. You can also scatter over some sunflower or pumpkin seeds.

For 2 small loaves (each serves 3–4) or 8 rolls:

400g squash (onion, butternut, Crown Prince)

3 tbsp olive oil

¼ tsp dried chilli flakes

1 tsp cumin seeds

Sea salt and black pepper

300g strong white bread flour, plus a little extra for sprinkling

50g organic unsalted butter, softened

3 level tsp baking powder

1 tsp chopped sage

1 tsp ground coriander

100ml buttermilk (see p34 for how to make your own)

1 medium egg

Preheat the oven to 180°C/gas mark 4.

Butter contains vitamins A and D, and when made from the milk of grass-fed cows is one of the best sources of vitamin K2. The role of vitamin K2 is just emerging, but the indications are that it is likely to be important for bone health and prevention of heart disease. (In countries where cattle are grass-fed, a high intake of dairy foods is associated with a lower risk of heart disease.) Butter is also a good source of butyrate, a **short-chain fatty acid** that helps to combat **inflammation** and heart disease. Butter does, however, contain some less healthy fats, which have been linked to plaque build-up in the arteries, so buy the best organic unsalted butter and use it in small amounts.

Don't bother to peel the squash, but cut it in half, remove the seeds and then cut the flesh into 3cm chunks. Line a baking tray with foil and add the squash, olive oil, chilli flakes, cumin seeds and some salt and pepper. Mix well and cover with foil. Roast for 40 minutes. Remove the squash, but leave the oven on. Allow the squash mixture to cool.

Leaving the peel on, mash the squash with a potato masher or pulse in a food processor, scooping up as many of the spices from the baking tray as you can, and place in a bowl with the flour, butter, baking powder, sage, ground coriander and 1 teaspoon salt. Stir with a fork to combine.

Beat the buttermilk with the egg and add gradually to the flour and squash mix to make a dough. Don't be alarmed: it is a rather wet dough, but it produces a fluffy and light bread.

Divide the dough in two, shape the dough into flat rounds, slashing a shallow cross into the top. Place on a greased baking sheet. Sprinkle with extra flour. If making rolls, divide the dough into eight, place on a sheet and sprinkle with extra flour as for the loaves.

Bake the loaves for 25 minutes in the middle of the oven. The rolls will need about 20 minutes. Test to see if the loaves are done by inserting a skewer into the centre. If the skewer comes out clean, the bread is done. If not then put back in the oven for a further 5 minutes on the baking sheet.

Turn off the oven and leave the loaves to cool in there for about an hour, or take them out and cool on a wire rack.

» 348 calories for 6 servings, 261 for 8

More on » squash *p186* » olive oil *p193* » chillies *p93* » coriander *p204* » eggs *p61*

Fiona's seeded soda bread

Many whole-grain and seeded breads – when home-made – turn out heavy and brick-like, but there are a few which are easy to make and delicious. This seeded soda bread is very quick and easy, a recipe from a regular visitor to Perch Hill, Fiona Isaacs, who won our Garden Opening loaf competition with this a year or two ago. The pinhead oatmeal adds great crunch and has a high fibre content, which makes the loaf more filling and means its sugars are released slowly into the bloodstream. Try also a mix of white flour with wholemeal spelt, along with the pinhead oatmeal, adding 2 tablespoons each of pumpkin seeds and sunflower seeds to ring the changes.

You can bake the loaf on a baking tray, or a cast-iron pan with the lid on, so you don't even need bread tins. By keeping the lid in place, you turn a cast-iron pan into a mini oven which gives you an all-round crust.

For 1 medium 450g loaf (for 10 slices):
A little cold-pressed rapeseed oil
450g wholemeal bread flour
50g sunflower seeds, plus a few extra for the top
50g pumpkin seeds, plus a few extra for the top
50g pinhead oatmeal
1½ tsp bicarbonate of soda
1 tsp sea salt
400ml buttermilk (see p34 for how to make your own)
30g organic unsalted butter, melted

Preheat the oven to 200°C/gas mark 6.

Lightly oil a 450g loaf tin, baking tray or cast-iron pan that has a lid.

Place all the dry ingredients in a mixing bowl and give them a quick mix using the dough hook on your mixer, or by hand. Working quickly, add the buttermilk and melted butter and continue mixing until the mixture is soft.

Place the bread in the tin, or mould into a circle and put on a baking tray or into a cast-iron pan.

Cut a deep cross on the top to help it rise. Sprinkle the top of the loaf with a few sunflower and pumpkin seeds.

Put the loaf into the oven and bake for up to 45 minutes, but check the bread after 30 minutes. If it's too brown, cover with foil and continue to bake. If using a cast-iron pan, leave the lid on for the first 30 minutes, then remove it to brown the top.

The bread is ready when a skewer pushed into the middle comes out clean. You could also tip the loaf out of its tin and tap it on its base: if it sounds hollow, it is ready. If not, return to the tin and continue baking.

Cool the bread on a rack for at least 1 hour before eating.

» 2,824 calories for the whole loaf, 282 per slice

More on » oats p25

Pumpkin seeds Like other nuts and seeds, pumpkin seeds provide a healthy dose of **protein** and **fibre**, as well as essential fats, **vitamins**, **minerals** and **antioxidants**; they are a great option for a healthy snack as the fats they contain are mostly **unsaturated** and **monounsaturated**. They are nutritional powerhouses, generally supporting gastrointestinal and cardiovascular health, balancing hormones and protecting cells from damage. Pumpkin seeds contain good quantities of magnesium, zinc and iron, amongst other **micronutrients**, and are particularly useful if you want to increase your intake of zinc. Various compounds in pumpkin seed oil have been noted to work synergistically in men to help prevent enlargement of the prostate, and further research into the effectiveness of eating the whole seeds is under way.

Garlic flatbread with coriander

We should be wary of classic garlic bread – the white baguette dripping with butter – but this is fine. It's robust and delicious and ideal to serve with a bowl of soup. Garlic is good for you: it's better raw than cooked, so it's just crushed here, added to warmed oil and then brushed on to wholemeal flat bread. This lets you moderate the amount of garlic you want to add. It is best to crush the garlic 10 minutes before adding to warmed oil to allow the active ingredient, allicin, to be released.

I also like these breads with Baba ghanoush, hummus and tapenade (see pages 182–4 and 189): they make a perfect scoop.

For 16 saucer-sized flatbreads:
500g strong wholemeal flour, plus a little extra
   for dusting
2 tsp sea salt, plus a pinch
4 tsp ground coriander
7g active dried yeast
200ml warm water
200ml coconut milk
50ml cold-pressed rapeseed oil or olive oil
2 garlic cloves, crushed
15g coriander leaves, finely chopped
Nigella or cumin seeds

Put the flour, salt, ground coriander and yeast into a bowl. Add the water and coconut milk and mix well with a fork to form a soft dough.

Bring the dough together with your hands into a ball. Flour a patch of worktop and knead the dough for 8 minutes or so, then place the dough in a lightly oiled bowl. Cover and leave for 2 hours in a warm place.

Meanwhile mix the measured oil with the crushed garlic, chopped coriander and a pinch of salt. Set aside to infuse.

Lightly flour the worktop, and take the dough from the bowl. It will have increased in size. Knock back the dough and divide into passion-fruit-sized balls.

This will make up to 16 individual breads, but you can make larger ones for tearing and sharing.

Once divided, leave the dough balls to sit again, covered on the worktop, for about 20–30 minutes. This makes them easier to shape.

Heat a large frying pan on the hob.

Press the nigella or cumin seeds into the tops of the dough balls and, using a rolling pin, roll out the balls into rough circles, about 5mm thick and the size of a large saucer.

Warm the garlic and coriander oil very gently for a minute or two in a saucepan. Using a pastry brush (silicone is preferable), brush one side of the dough circle with the oil. Carefully flop the oiled side into the hot pan. As it cooks, lightly brush the oil on the upper surface of the dough. Adjust the heat so the flatbread bakes and puffs without burning too much on the base.

Check after a minute: it should be golden with bubbles beginning to form. Use tongs to carefully flip it over and cook the other side for a further minute. Repeat with the remaining dough.

If you like, brush the cooked flatbreads, whilst still warm, with a little more of the coriander and garlic oil for a more intense flavour.

These freeze very well. Allow to cool, wrap and put in the freezer. Reheat – for 10–15 minutes – in a warm oven.

» 238 calories per bread

More on » coconut milk *p235* » rapeseed oil *p248* » olive oil *p193* » garlic *p82* » coriander *p204*

Soups

Salads

EATING RAW VEG on a regular basis is very good for you, and salads are all about rawness. Cooking can denature the enzymes in food, but it is the enzymes that help our digestion. Cooking also breaks down some of the vitamins and minerals, particularly the B vitamins, including folate (B9), as well as vitamin C. The green pigment chlorophyll can also be chemically weakened or destroyed through cooking, so eating a salad raw gives us a valuable supply. Chlorophyll is known to be detoxifying, helping to cleanse the blood and support the immune system.

On the other hand, some micronutrients in certain veg are more available when they are cooked rather than raw. That's true of some of the valuable antioxidants in spinach, kale and tomatoes, but it's still good to have them raw sometimes for their other nutritional content.

The base of a salad is often lettuce, but for extra goodness add the stronger-tasting salad leaves, such as rocket, watercress, the mustards and mizunas. Intense flavour and colour are usually signs that a food is good for you, and these leaves are super-nutritious, invaluable additions to a salad. They are all brassicas, which contain glucosinolates, the antioxidant phytochemicals that make broccoli so good for us. You'll know lots of them are there if you get a good burst of peppery taste when you chew the leaves.

It's worth knowing which raw vegetables have the highest pesticide residue when grown chemically. Celery, cherry tomatoes, cucumber, lettuce and spinach are all in the top ten most contaminated when conventionally grown, even after soaking or scrubbing them with a stiff brush. With these in particular, either grow your own, or try to buy organic.

What you use to dress your salad is important too. Many shop-bought dressings are based on highly processed olive and sunflower oils, which are not nutritionally valuable. What we should be aiming at for all-round good health is a ratio of around 1:1 to 1:4 omega-3 to omega-6 essential fatty acids. A typical western diet has too much emphasis on omega-6s (it can be up to 1:25), which can tip the balance towards producing chemical messengers that encourage a state of inflammation and potential for chronic disease. Our diet usually provides much larger amounts of omega-6s, which are found in vegetable oils (palm, soybean, rapeseed, corn and sunflower) and meat (the balance towards omega-3s is more favourable if cattle are grass- as opposed to grain-fed); omega-6 is also found in processed foods. As a result we want to reduce the omega-6-rich foods and increase the omega-3 sources. Oily fish, as well as flaxseeds (also known as linseeds, see page 30), are the richest sources. Leafy greens, particularly spinach, broccoli, kale and rocket, don't have large amounts of omega-3, but it is the ratio between omega-6 and omega-3 that is important. Leafy greens don't have much omega-6, so their omega-3 content counts. Eat lots of salad and go for walnut or flaxseed oil in your dressings to up your regular intake of omega-3s. The flaxseed oil isn't tasty enough to have as a dressing base on

its own, but is fine when mixed with other good oils. Extra virgin olive oil (see page 193) contains lots of anti-inflammatory fatty acids and polyphenols, and cold-pressed oils contain many phenolic compounds. The less processed, the better.

Most vegetable oils go rancid when exposed to bright light, heat or the air, all of which change the chemical composition and cause the oil to deteriorate and produce damaging free radicals. The changes affect their taste too, so keep your oil in a sealed bottle, in a cool place away from direct sunlight, preferably the fridge.

You may think 'Why not skip the oil altogether if you want to diet?' Oils are calorific, but not only do they enhance flavour, they also help in the absorption of precious nutrients. The leafy greens such as spinach and salad leaves have high levels of beta-carotene, and tomatoes are particularly rich in lycopene. These antioxidants are both fat-soluble, and if you don't have them with oil, you won't absorb them – or much less of them anyway.

What about the vinegar? Organic apple cider vinegar (see page 63) is particularly potent stuff with health-giving properties, and dressings made with it will boost the goodness of your salads. Proper balsamic vinegar (see page 189) is made from fermented concentrated grape juice, left to 'age' for at least ten months to develop its distinctive flavour, and that's been shown to be good for us too. Cheap balsamic is made with harmful sugar syrups, or hugely reduced and very sugar-rich apple juice, and is to be avoided.

We should all eat more seaweeds, and in salads that's simple. You can make almost an entire salad with super-nutritious wakame (see page 174); or use it like crispy bacon or roasted prosciutto for sprinkling over the top of a salad for extra crunch. Or you can add it to the Japanese flavour enhancer, gomashio (see page 164 to make your own), for bonus nutrition and taste.

There are people who live almost entirely on raw food, eaten mostly as juices and salads, and whenever I meet them I'm impressed by how well they look. I ate only raw food for a month a couple of years ago – nightmarish for the family – and even for me that length of time with no hot food

was a challenge. But eating a good leaf salad almost every day is a luxury, not a hardship. It's a life-enhancer in all ways – and very easy to do.

So what are the guidelines with salads?
» Even if it's just mixed leaves, have a salad almost every day. Your health and skin will be better for it.
» Think consciously about the colours of veg in your salad bowl. The wider the range of colour, and different tastes, the wider the range of nutrients.
» As most commercial salad leaves and veg are full of pesticides, either grow your own, or buy organic.
» Wash your salads well to reduce the chance of contamination from things like toxoplasmosis (a parasite carried by cats that may be found on home-grown salads) and other soil pathogens. I pick my salad with elastic bands on my wrist, bunching different varieties as I go, and then submerge the leaves in a sink for two hours to wash and condition them before drying. They wilt more slowly when dressed after this conditioning process.
» Think about adding protein – then your salads become main meals. This will inevitably increase your consumption of raw food and all-important, healthy veg. Add some nuts or seeds, some quinoa, grill some halloumi or hard-boil an egg.
» Vary your dressings, but base them on good oils such as delicious first-pressing extra virgin olive, cold-pressed rapeseed, avocado or hempseed oil. Add a splash of flaxseed or walnut oil to up the omega-3s. Add tahini to some, yoghurt to others – both are excellent sources of protein.
» Always make your own dressing. It only takes a minute. Ready-made bottles often contain sugar and unnecessary preservatives, which are all to be avoided.

With these tips up your sleeve, vow to have at least one raw veg salad at least once a day.

The perfect green salad

The basic rule for a salad is to have at least one thing from five different categories of ingredients. The first is a lettuce to give a gentle flavour and crunch (particularly important in a summer salad) and background bulk to your bowl. Next come the salad leaves to provide strong tastes, powerful nutrition and good splashes of colour. The third addition is one of the salad herbs, just a sprinkling, coarsely chopped or torn, to give a lovely hit of flavour. Then add one or two different salad veg – some radishes, fennel bulb, celery, spring onions or cucumber – to give substance. Finally, add an edible flower for prettiness and colour.

This recipe makes for a good-looking and nutritious bowl. Make a taste-packed dressing and that's it: here are two options – use one or the other.

For 6–8 as a side salad:
3 handfuls of Cos or loose-leaf lettuce
3 handfuls of salad leaves (rocket, mizuna, baby kale, watercress, landcress, any of the mustards, komatsuna – Japanese mustard spinach – and/or pak choi)
1 handful of the mild salad herbs (sorrel, parsley, coriander, sweet cicely, chervil) or ½ handful of the stronger herbs (chives, fennel leaf, tarragon, lovage or mint)
1 bunch of radishes or salad turnips, or 1 fennel bulb, or ½ cucumber, or 3 celery sticks, or a handful of fresh peas or pea shoots
1 small handful of edible flowers (for example, pansy or viola, primrose or polyanthus, the petals of a marigold, dianthus, rose, nasturtium or dahlia)

For the mint and lemon dressing
5 tbsp extra virgin olive oil
1 tbsp flaxseed oil
Sea salt and black pepper
Finely grated zest of ½ lemon
Juice of 1 lemon
1 tbsp chopped mint leaves
1 tsp clear honey
1 tsp Dijon mustard

For the tarragon dressing
5 tbsp extra virgin olive oil
1 tbsp flaxseed oil
Sea salt and black pepper
2 tbsp tarragon vinegar
1 tbsp chopped tarragon leaves
1 tsp clear honey
1 tsp Dijon mustard

Wash and dry the lettuce and tear up any large leaves into a generous salad bowl. Wash and dry the salad leaves and scatter them on the lettuce. Coarsely chop the herbs and add to the bowl.

Using a very sharp knife, or better still a mandolin, slice any veg you can wafer thin, so they don't sink straight to the bottom. You'll then get a taste with almost every bite. Keep a small handful back for scattering on top at the end.

Now make the dressing, whichever one you choose. Put the oils into a small bowl with a pinch of salt and some pepper. Add the lemon juice and zest (or tarragon vinegar) and then the herb (parsley, chives, coriander are also good), honey and mustard. Whisk well to combine. Or put all the ingredients into a jam jar, screw on the lid and shake well.

Dress the salad and toss well – your hands are best for this – to give a light but even coating of dressing over every leaf. Before serving, scatter with flowers and the handful of salad veg kept back.

» 159 calories for 6 servings, 119 for 8

More on » lettuce p114 » mustard leaves and rocket p122 » kale p117 » watercress p70 » parsley p136 » coriander p204 » mint p326 » cucumber p148 » peas p74 » olive oil p193 » flaxseed oil p153 » lemons p346 » honey p334

Warm baby gem lettuce with anchovy, pine nuts and ginger

Heat can destroy nutrients like vitamin C in salads and vegetables, and the longer they're cooked, the more nutrients are lost. The Japanese often cook lettuce and that's delicious, but in this dish you avoid the cooking yet still eat the lettuce warm.

For 4 as a side salad:
3 tbsp olive oil
1 tbsp flaxseed oil
50g tin of anchovies in oil, drained
1–2 garlic cloves, crushed or very finely chopped
2 heaped tbsp (40g) fresh root ginger, peeled and grated
4 tbsp pine nuts
4 small to medium baby gem (or Cos heart) lettuces, cut into quarters or eighths depending on size

In a small saucepan heat the oils with the anchovies and garlic over a very gentle heat until the anchovies have dissolved. Take off the heat, add the grated ginger and leave to infuse for 15 minutes or so. Meanwhile, dry-fry the pine nuts in a frying pan, shaking until golden. Leave to cool.

When ready to serve, arrange the cut lettuce on a platter. Heat the flavoured oil until warm and pour over the lettuce. Toss well. Scatter with pine nuts and serve immediately.

» 284 calories per serving

More on » olive oil *p193* » flaxseed oil *p153* » oily fish *p256* » garlic *p82* » ginger *p200*

Lettuce With only 14 calories per 100g, lettuce famously consists of just short of 95 per cent water. Basically lettuce is vitamin-rich water, full of vitamins A, C and K, along with lots of dietary **fibre** and **minerals**, particularly iron. It's the red and dark green, loose-leaf varieties that are the most nutritious, as well as the crunchy Romaines (or Cos). Icebergs have little goodness (or flavour) – avoid!

Toasted seed and edible flower salad

Here you get substance and protein from the seeds, and then colour and glamour from the flowers. It's surprising how many flowers are edible. All violas, polyanthus and primroses, roses, pinks (dianthus), dahlias and chrysanthemums can be eaten, as well as nasturtiums, courgettes, chives, wild garlic, borage and marigolds. I also love the flowers of runner beans, rocket and dill. Edible flowers don't just look good, there's evidence they add goodness too. Go for it and scatter them willy-nilly.

For 6–8 as a side salad:
8 handfuls of salad (at least 4 varieties, 2 lettuces and 2 salad leaves to vary flavours and colours)
2 handfuls of any soft green herb (mint, parsley, tarragon, coriander or chervil), roughly torn

For the simple dressing
5 tbsp extra virgin olive oil
1 tbsp flaxseed oil
Finely grated zest of ½ lemon
Juice of 1 lemon
Sea salt and black pepper

For the topping
3 heaped tbsp mixed seeds, such as pumpkin, sunflower, poppy and sesame
30 mixed flowers (wild garlic and *Allium cowanii* here)

Scatter the salad leaves and herbs into a generous bowl and mix well. Mix together the dressing ingredients in a screw-top jar, and shake well.

Dry-fry the seeds for the topping in a frying pan for 2–3 minutes. Pour the dressing over the salad and toss together at the last moment, when you want to eat. Your hands are the best tools for the job. Scatter over the seeds and edible flowers and serve.

» 195 calories for 6 servings, 146 for 8

More on » mint *p326* » parsley *p136* » coriander *p204* » olive oil *p193* » flaxseed oil *p153* » lemons *p346* » pumpkin seeds *p105* » sesame seeds *p164*

Wilted kale, avocado and pomegranate salad

I love this salad and, given the chance, would have it several times a week. When cooked, kale loses a proportion of its vitamin C and other antioxidants, so it's good sometimes to eat it raw for an immune boost. For most of us that's a bit of a challenge, but in this recipe, the kale is not cooked, but marinated or wilted, so it's easily digestible. (Chard is another nutritious leaf which you could use in this way.)

I tend to skip the garlic if serving this salad for lunch. It's also good with added slices of grilled halloumi and, to make it portable for lunch, you can stuff it into a pitta, with a garnish of some Healthy chilli jam (see page 188).

For 4 as a main course, 6 as a starter or side salad:
300g kale, any variety (I have used the red curly kale Redbor here)
30g bunch of mint, leaves just torn up a bit

For the dressing
2 tbsp tahini
2 tbsp live natural yoghurt (see p44, optional, to use with the thicker brands of tahini to loosen)
2 tbsp tamari soy sauce
2 tbsp extra virgin olive oil
1 tbsp flaxseed oil
1 garlic clove, very finely chopped (optional)
1 green finger chilli, deseeded and finely chopped (optional)
Finely grated zest and juice of 1 lemon or 2 limes (keep a little juice back for the avocado)
Black pepper

For the topping
1 ripe avocado
Seeds of 1 pomegranate (see p46)
Handful of blueberries (optional)
2 heaped tbsp pumpkin seeds or pine nuts, dry-fried

Put all the dressing ingredients into a large mug or jar and whisk well with a fork, or give it a shake.

Strip the kale off its stalks and tear or slice the leaves into strips or pieces. Place in a large bowl. Pour the dressing over the kale and massage into the kale for 3 to 4 minutes, until the kale is well coated and starts to wilt. Add the mint leaves and mix. Halve, stone and peel the avocados, then chop up the flesh and toss in the reserved lemon or lime juice. Scatter over the kale.

Sprinkle over the pomegranate seeds, blueberries (if using) and the dry-fried pine nuts or pumpkin seeds. Serve before the avocado discolours.

» 329 calories for 4 servings, 219 calories for 6

More on » mint p326 » tahini p184 » yoghurt p44 » tamari soy sauce p97 » olive oil p193 » flaxseed oil p153 » garlic p82 » chillies p93 » lemons p346 » avocado p119 » pomegranate p46 » blueberries p328 » pumpkin seeds p105

Harumi's green beans with a sesame dressing

Harumi Kurihara is the Delia Smith of Japanese cooking and her cookbooks are an inspiration. This simple way of serving beans is one of my favourite ways to eat them. It is also a delicious way of serving steamed baby courgettes, chunks of roasted squash and steamed batons of carrot – the dressing makes an excellent coating for almost any vegetable.

For 6–8 as a side salad:
400g French beans
50g sesame seeds, dry-fried
1 tbsp pickled ginger, chopped
2 tbsp coconut palm sugar
½ tbsp mirin (rice wine)
½–1 tbsp tamari soy sauce
1 tbsp olive oil
1 tbsp flaxseed oil

Top and tail the beans and blanch briefly in a large pan of boiling water. Don't steam the beans, as they would lose their bright colour. Drain and rinse immediately under cold water, but this is best served warm so don't cool the beans completely.

Grind the sesame seeds in a pestle and mortar to make a smooth paste then add the remaining ingredients.

Mix the dressing with the green beans and serve.

» 125 calories per 6 servings, 94 for 8

More on » sesame seeds *p164* » ginger *p200* » coconut palm sugar *p316* » tamari soy sauce *p97* » olive oil *p193* » flaxseed oil *p153*

Kale There is now a ton of evidence that kale (along with broccoli) is one of the healthiest foods we can eat. One measure of the healthiness of a food is its ability to remove certain free-floating molecules – called **free radicals** – from our system. These do all sorts of damage to the body at cell level, and have been implicated in a wide range of diseases, so the more of them we can get rid of the better. **Antioxidants** are compounds in food which switch on the cells' own resources to deal with these free radicals, and kale is an antioxidant superstar. Kale is particularly rich in **glucosinolates**. From research carried out on broccoli, these glucosinolates appear to reset cells to self-cleanse, thus protecting us from a wide array of diseases, including cancer.

Kale is also a rich source of calcium, which helps to prevent osteoporosis, and the leaves contain vitamins K and A, as well as **fibre**. The fibre in kale has recently been proved to bind with bile acids in the gut, thus helping to get rid of them. Bile acids are made from **cholesterol**, and in this way kale reduces overall cholesterol levels (this is far more effective if the kale is steamed for 5 minutes). And finally, as well as helping us to keep young and healthy on the inside, kale keeps us looking good on the outside too, as it's incredibly good for the skin.

Avocado, watercress and blood orange salad

This salad seems to have little to it, but fork-by-fork, it contains a whopping range of good things, and looks lovely too. Serve from one large plate in the middle of the table, or as individual portions. You can put it together in less than 5 minutes. Anyone who has grown coriander will know that, like rocket, it has an annoying habit of running up to flower very quickly in the dry summer months. You can try cutting it back and watering to help prevent this, or harvest the seeds when they're green. Fresh coriander seeds make one of the most delicious salad toppings, and are super-rich in chlorophyll.

For 6 as a starter or side salad:
250g watercress
100g baby spinach
3 oranges (use blood oranges when in season)
2 large avocados
50g macadamia nuts, dry-fried
Pansy or chive flowers, to garnish

For the dressing
1 tsp cumin seeds
1 tsp coriander seeds, fresh if available
5 tbsp extra virgin olive oil
1 tbsp flaxseed oil
Finely grated zest and juice of 1 lemon
1 tsp orange-blossom water
1 tsp clear honey
Sea salt and black pepper

Start by making the dressing. Heat a small frying pan, add the cumin and coriander seeds, and dry-fry for a couple of minutes, being careful not to burn them. (If you grow coriander, use the fresh green seeds instead of dried seeds, and don't dry-fry them.)

Put the toasted seeds into a pestle and mortar and grind briefly, then put into a small bowl. Add the rest of the dressing ingredients except salt and pepper. (If using fresh coriander seeds, crush them roughly and add into the dressing at the end.)

Whisk the dressing with a fork to combine. Taste and season with a little salt and pepper.

When ready to serve the salad, scatter the watercress and baby spinach over a large flat plate. To end up with pith-free segments or slices of orange, follow the instructions on page 49 and catch the juices. Scatter the orange segments over the salad. Cut the avocados in half and remove the stones. Peel off the skin, then thinly slice the avocado halves lengthways, and add to the salad. Add the macadamia nuts as well.

Drizzle over the dressing, mixed with the reserved orange juice from segmenting, and sprinkle with flowers. Serve immediately, before the avocado starts to discolour.

» 358 calories per serving

More on » watercress *p70* » spinach *p54* » oranges *p49* » coriander *p204* » olive oil *p193* » flaxseed oil *p153* » lemons *p346* » honey *p334*

Avocado may be high in fat, but the majority of the fat is **monounsaturated** oleic acid, which is also found in extra virgin olive oil, and is very good for us. Trials have demonstrated that avocados can reduce the risk of heart disease when eaten as part of a healthy diet, and they also have **anti-inflammatory** properties that help to protect us against other diseases such as cancer and diabetes. Avocados also contain vitamin E, a fat-soluble vitamin, and a key nutrient that looks after cell membranes and our all-important **DNA**.

Avocado oil is becoming increasingly available and is good in dressings, as its beneficial balance of oils helps us to absorb all the fat-soluble nutrients found in in salad leaves, leafy greens, carrots and tomatoes, such as vitamin A and **carotenoids**.

Kalette, squash and Parmesan salad

You can make this salad with Brussels sprouts – or the new superfood, kalettes (also called flower sprouts), which have been bred from crossing kale and Brussels sprouts. Kalettes have a slightly sweeter taste than either of the parents, and have incredible health credentials. Like the other brassicas, kalettes are dense with minerals and nutrients, including the powerful antioxidants, glucosinolates, with concentrations many times that found in even kale. Raw kale, sliced into fine ribbons (tough stalks and midribs removed), is a good alternative to the Brussels.

Like coleslaw but fresher, this salad is quite dense, so a little goes a long way.

For 6–8 as a starter or side salad:
400g squash, peeled and deseeded, cut into segments
Grated zest and juice of 1 lemon
Sea salt and black pepper
250g kalettes or Brussels sprouts (I have used a mix here, using the nutty red Brussels sprouts)
2 heaped tbsp pumpkin seeds, dry-fried
3 tbsp grated Parmesan (or 15 slivers)
Extra virgin olive oil

Using a mandolin or swivel-head potato peeler, cut the peeled squash into ribbons, as thinly as possible. Place the ribbons in a bowl with the lemon zest and juice and a pinch of salt, then leave to marinate for a few minutes.

Meanwhile, slice the kalettes or Brussels sprouts as finely as you can. Put in a bowl or on a large, shallow platter. Scatter over the marinated squash ribbons, pumpkin seeds and Parmesan.

Season with plenty of black pepper, add a drizzle of olive oil and toss well before serving.

» 83 calories for 6 servings, 62 for 8

More on » squash *p186* » lemons *p346* » pumpkin seeds *p105* » olive oil *p193*

Salads

Rainbow salad

It's good to be aware of the colour of food. Colours in vegetables represent different pigments and with them, the different vitamins, minerals and phytonutrients. From orange carrots we get beta-carotene and lutein; from red beetroot, blood oranges, pomegranates and red cabbage, anthocyanins; and from green cabbage and parsley, chlorophyll. Red cabbage also has ten times more vitamin A – in the form of carotenoids – than green cabbage, and it contains a different pattern of glucosinolates. Sometimes, think rainbow.

For 6–8 as a starter or side salad:
150g carrot
150g beetroot
150g red cabbage
150g green cabbage
Seeds and juice of 1 pomegranate (see p46)
2 oranges (blood oranges if you can find them)

For the dressing
5 tbsp extra virgin olive oil
1 tbsp flaxseed oil
1 tbsp red wine vinegar
1 tsp Dijon mustard
1 tsp clear honey or maple syrup
1 tsp grated fresh root ginger
1 tsp black sesame seeds
Sea salt and black pepper

To serve
4 tbsp pine nuts, dry-fried
1 tbsp caraway seeds, dry-fried
Large handful of parsley, roughly chopped
Dollop of crème fraîche or live natural yoghurt
  (see p44, optional)

Ideally do not peel the veg, just cut it into chunks that fit into the food processor chute and grate using a coarse grating attachment for the roots and a slicing attachment for the cabbage (or alternatively do by hand). Keep each ingredient apart, as well as the pomegranate seeds, in separate bowls until you are ready to eat. The beetroot juice will otherwise stain everything the same colour. To end up with pith-free segments or slices of orange, see page 49. There should be no pith left on the orange, and catch some of the juices to add to the dressing later. Mix together the dressing ingredients in a screw-top jam jar, adding any pomegranate and orange juices, and shake well.

Combine all the salad ingredients in a large bowl and mix gently. Pour over the dressing and toss together at the last moment, when you want to eat. Scatter with pine nuts, caraway seeds and parsley, and serve with a dollop of crème fraîche or yoghurt on the side if you fancy.

» 199 calories for 6 servings, 150 for 8

More on » beetroot *p85* » pomegranate *p46* » oranges *p49* » olive oil *p193* » flaxseed oil *p153* » honey *p334* » maple syrup *p27* » ginger *p200* » sesame seeds *p164* » parsley *p136* » yoghurt *p44*

Carrots are best known for their rich supply of the antioxidant **beta-carotene**, actually named after them. This is one of the key healthy pigments we should seek out. It helps to protect against various cancers (see also sweet potato, page 72). They are also the source of a wide variety of other **antioxidants** and health-supporting nutrients such as hydroxycinnamic acids, **anthocyanins** and vitamins C and A. The antioxidants are well researched and have been shown to benefit the cardiovascular system and help protect against colon cancer. The **polyacetylenes** in carrots have **anti-inflammatory** properties and help stop platelets sticking together in blood vessels – which, along with their unique mix of antioxidants, is believed to explain the cardiovascular protection offered by carrots. Due to their high vitamin A content, regular consumption of carrots is also beneficial for eye health.

Sweet potato salad with watercress, ginger and soy

Like carrots, orange-fleshed sweet potatoes are stuffed with the orange pigment beta-carotene. The deeper the orange, the greater the density of the pigments, with sweet potatoes having the highest level, equal only to that found in leafy greens like spinach and kale (which, surprisingly, are rich in these orange pigments too). In this recipe, sweet potato slices are steamed and briefly griddled, which is better for our blood-sugar levels than roasting. The oil and dressing here is essential for our bodies' absorption of fat-soluble vitamin A.

For 4 as a main course, 8–10 as a starter:
1kg small sweet potatoes, chopped into 1cm slices
A little cold-pressed rapeseed or set coconut oil
4 large handfuls (about 250g) of mixed peppery salad leaves, such as watercress, mizuna, chicory, rocket or any of the mustards
Large handful of coriander (about 30g), leaves and stems coarsely chopped

For the oriental dressing
4 tbsp tamari soy sauce
4 tbsp extra virgin olive or cold-pressed rapeseed oil
1 tbsp flaxseed oil
1 tbsp Thai fish sauce
Grated zest and juice of 1 lime
1 tbsp pickled ginger, finely chopped
1 level tbsp finely chopped fresh root ginger
1 red finger chilli, deseeded and finely chopped
1 garlic clove, finely chopped
1 tbsp clear honey
Black pepper

To serve
2 heaped tbsp pumpkin seeds, dry-fried
Edible petals (optional)

Preheat the oven to 110°C/gas mark ¼.

Steam the slices of sweet potato for 5–7 minutes, or until just soft to the tip of a knife. Cool.

Whisk all the dressing ingredients together, with black pepper to taste, and put to one side for the flavours to infuse.

Heat a ridged griddle pan or heavy-based frying pan for 3–4 minutes (until you can't reach a count of ten with your hand hovering just above it). Brush on rapeseed or coconut oil and griddle the sweet potato slices in batches for about 3 minutes each side. Keep each batch warm in the low oven while you cook the rest.

Put all the salad leaves and the coriander into a large bowl (keep some back to scatter at the end). Pour over most of the dressing and toss well to coat. Serve on individual plates, with a good handful of salad leaves to each one. Top with griddled sweet potato slices. Finish with an extra drizzle of dressing, the reserved coriander and dry-fried pumpkin seeds, with some edible petals if you fancy (I have used *Carmine dianthus* here).

» 508 calories for 4 servings, 254 for 8, 203 for 10

More on » sweet potato p72 » rapeseed oil p248 » coconut oil p309 » watercress p70 » coriander p204 » tamari soy sauce p97 » olive oil p193 » flaxseed oil p153 » ginger p200 » chillies p93 » garlic p82 » honey p334 » pumpkin seeds p105

Mustard leaves and rocket
These belong to the brassica family, and so are rich in **glucosinolates**, some of the most powerful **antioxidants** in the plant world. From research that has been carried out on broccoli, these glucosinolates appear to re-set cells to self-cleanse, thus protecting us from a wide array of diseases, including cancers. Rocket is also good for the liver, and is a rich source of **beta-carotene**, which is beneficial for eye health. It's also very low in calories. Buy organic if you can.

Roast broccoli and citrus salad with anchovy mayonnaise

You can use the deep-green calabrese, available all year; purple sprouting broccoli, at its best in the spring; and its white, more tender cousin that's hard to find in a greengrocer, but easy to grow from seed. But it's the new Beneforté broccoli (see page 151), which looks like a small-headed calabrese, that has sky-high levels of glucosinolates and we should all use if we can. It's increasingly available in supermarkets.

Swap the anchovies in the mayonnaise for garlic to make an aïoli, or a bunch of punchy-flavoured herbs: parsley, chives, coriander, tarragon or dill. If you whizz these with the eggs at the start, the mayonnaise will be a brilliant green.

For 8 as a starter:
1 lemon
1 orange (blood orange if available)
500g sweet potatoes, peeled and cut into small wedges
3 tbsp cold-pressed rapeseed oil
Sea salt and black pepper
500g Beneforté or purple sprouting broccoli
3 banana shallots, peeled and finely chopped
30g bunch of mint, leaves chopped

For the anchovy mayonnaise
1 recipe mayonnaise (see p156)
8 tinned anchovy fillets in oil, drained

Preheat the oven to 200°C/gas mark 6.

Make the mayonnaise, following the instructions on page 156, adding the anchovies when you blitz.

Next, prepare the fruit for the salad. To get rid of some of the bitterness of the citrus pith, put the lemon and orange in a pan of cold water, bring up to the boil, then drain. Fill the pan with fresh water and repeat. Slice off the tops and bottoms, cut the fruits in half, remove the pithy core and thinly slice them in half-moons, removing any pips.

Put the sweet potato and fruit slices onto a baking tray and toss to coat with the oil. Sprinkle with salt and black pepper. Roast in the oven for 10 minutes, then stir and roast for another 5 minutes. Add the broccoli and shallots to the baking tray and toss well in the oil, adding a little more if needed. Cook for a further 20 minutes, or until the sweet potato starts to brown at the edges. Transfer everything to a serving plate, scatter with mint and serve immediately with the bowl of anchovy mayonnaise.

» 388 calories for servings

More on » lemons p346 » oranges p49 » sweet potato p72 » rapeseed oil p248 » broccoli p151 » mint p326 » eggs p61 » oily fish p256

Wild salmon tagliata

'Tagliata' usually refers to an Italian salad with marinated and quickly seared beef, but here it's with fish instead. For this recipe, I like the salmon seared quickly, so the outside is cooked with the centre only just warm, but you can cook it more if you prefer. Ideally get a whole piece of salmon from the middle of the fish so the fillet is a similar thickness all through. Also try this recipe with marinated, boned chicken thighs.

For 6 as a main course, 8 as a starter:
600g wild salmon, in a whole piece, skin off
A little cold-pressed rapeseed oil
4 large handfuls of mixed peppery spring salad leaves, such as watercress, mizuna, rocket and any of the mustards

To serve
Oriental dressing (see p122)
Large handful of coriander (about 30g), leaves and stalks coarsely chopped
Quartered limes or lemons

Bring the fish to room temperature. Heat a ridged griddle pan (or a heavy-based frying pan) for 3–4 minutes (until you can't reach a count of ten with your hand hovering just above it). Rub a little oil over the salmon and place on the heated griddle. Over a high heat cook for 3 minutes on each side. (If you like your salmon a little more cooked, cook for an extra minute each side.) Allow the fish to cool a little before slicing. Then, using a sharp knife, cut the salmon into 1cm slices.

Make up the dressing, adding black pepper to taste. Put the salad leaves into a large bowl, drizzle over most of the dressing and toss. Serve on individual plates, with a good handful of salad leaves on each, topped with three or four salmon slices. Finish with an extra drizzle of dressing and a scattering of fresh coriander over the top. Serve with quartered limes or lemons.

» 271 calories for 6 servings, 203 for 8

More on » watercress *p70* » mustard leaves and rocket *p122* » coriander *p204* » lemons *p346*

Salmon is an ideal source of **protein**. New research shows that the bio-active **peptides** from proteins such as salmon are excellent at taking care of joint cartilage, enhancing the effectiveness of insulin and reducing **inflammation** in the digestive system. Salmon is an oily fish, and its oil includes **omega-3 fatty acids**, which help to reduce the widespread low-grade inflammation that is now being implicated in the development of many of our most common diseases such as diabetes, dementia and heart disease.

Try to choose wild salmon (such as Alaskan sockeye salmon), not farmed; and if not wild, organic. Wild salmon feed on krill and shrimps in the ocean, and this is what gives its almost artificial-looking pinky-orange colouring and its huge health credits. Not surprisingly, given this colour, they're rich in carotenoids (especially one called astaxanthin, which has ten times the **antioxidant** activity of **beta-carotene**) as well as vitamins A, B and D. Most farmed salmon are fed grain, not krill, and they are packed with antibiotics to fend off disease in their over-crowded pens; you want to avoid the highly toxic and potentially cancer-causing PCPs (persistent chemical pollutants). Added colouring gives their otherwise almost white flesh the more usual salmon tone. For these reasons, farmed salmon is to be avoided.

Smoked salmon contains high levels of salt, and it may contain polycyclic aromatic hydrocarbons, as a result of sea pollution or from the smoking process. As these are thought to be a predisposing factor in some cancers, much commercially smoked fish is best eaten only every so often.

Asparagus, pea and broad bean salad

A perfect late spring, early summer salad, using the best seasonal veg. With several stages – roasting onions and a basil sauce, as well as the salad – this recipe looks more complicated than it actually is.

For 4 as a main course, 6 as a starter:
160g freshly podded peas (frozen are fine)
200g freshly podded broad beans (frozen are fine)
1 bunch of thin asparagus (about 220g)
1–2 tbsp cold-pressed rapeseed oil
2 tbsp extra virgin olive oil, plus extra for drizzling
Small handful basil or mint leaves
Julienned zest of 2 lemons and juice of 1 lemon
Sea salt and black pepper

For the roasted onions
4 red onions (about 400g)
2 tbsp aged balsamic vinegar
2 tbsp maple syrup
50ml olive oil
Sea salt and black pepper

For the basil sauce
50g bunch of basil
1 garlic clove, peeled
Sea salt and black pepper
150ml extra virgin olive oil

Preheat the oven to 180°C/gas mark 4.

Start with the roasted onions. Peel the onions and slice into rings (about 5mm thick) then spread on a baking tray. Stir in the balsamic vinegar, maple syrup and olive oil. Season with a little salt and black pepper and roast for 30 minutes, stirring halfway through the cooking time.

Meanwhile make the basil sauce. Pull the leaves from the bunch of basil and put in the small bowl of a food processor with the garlic and some seasoning. Process until chopped, then slowly add the olive oil. Or do this in a mortar and pestle. (Any sauce not used will keep for a week in the fridge.)

To make the salad, first blanch the peas, boiling them for 2 minutes, then drain and refresh in cold water. Do the same with the broad beans, then slip off their outer grey-green skins.

Griddle the asparagus until lightly charred. Don't oil the griddle pan. Get it really hot before putting on the asparagus and just brush the spears with a little of the rapeseed oil whilst griddling.

Mix all the vegetables with the fresh basil or mint. Add the lemon juice to taste, drizzle with the extra virgin olive oil and toss.

Arrange the vegetables on a large serving plate, add the roasted onions and drizzle with some of the basil sauce. Finally, sprinkle over the lemon zest.

» Using half the sauce, 548 calories for 4 servings, 365 for 6

More on » peas *p74* » rapeseed oil *p248* » olive oil *p193* » mint *p193* » lemons *p346* » onions *p281* » balsamic vinegar *p189* » maple syrup *p27* » garlic *p82*

Asparagus is low in calories, yet huge in taste. Its spears are packed with **fibre** and a good range of beneficial **minerals**, **vitamins** and **micronutrients**, including folic acid and vitamin C. Although not red or orange like tomatoes or carrots, asparagus contains lycopene and **beta-carotene**. Much of its fibre is the insoluble type called inulin (also found in chicory and Jerusalem artichokes, onions, leeks and garlic). We don't digest the inulin in our stomach. Instead, it acts as a **prebiotic**, feeding our beneficial intestinal bacteria as it passes through the gut. As with the **probiotic** foods – fermented yoghurt, sauerkraut and traditionally prepared olives – this is very good for us and for our whole immune system. Asparagus is not just garden caviar – it's an immune booster too.

Salads

Crushed edamame and pea salad

Edamame and soya beans are an invaluable source of protein, good for all of us, and brilliant for vegetarians. They're also filling and are good for stabilising blood-sugar levels. I sometimes add a tablespoon of sweet chilli dipping sauce to the dressing here, but it does contain a lot of sugar, so is not for every day.

For 6 as a side salad:
400g frozen edamame (or soya) beans
400g frozen peas
30g basil leaves, roughly chopped
125g radishes, finely sliced

For the dressing
5 tbsp extra virgin olive oil
Grated zest and juice of 1 lemon
1 heaped tbsp coarsely grated fresh root ginger
1 tbsp pickled ginger, finely chopped
2 garlic cloves, crushed
1 tbsp maple syrup
Sea salt and black pepper

Bring a large saucepan of water to the boil. Add the beans and peas, bring back up to the boil and cook for 2 minutes. Take the pan off the heat, drain, then plunge the peas and beans into cold water. Allow to cool, then drain.

Make the dressing by putting all the ingredients except the salt and pepper into a small bowl and whisking with a fork to combine. Season to taste.

Put half the peas and beans into a food processor and pulse just twice, keeping a good texture to the vegetables. You don't want a purée. Mix with the other half of the peas and beans left whole. Then add the basil and sliced radish. Pour over the dressing and stir well to combine.

» 277 calories per serving

More on » peas p74 » olive oil p193 » lemons p346 » ginger p200 » garlic p82 » maple syrup p27

Green pawpaw, carrot and cashew salad

This is a classic Thai street-food salad, based on pawpaw at its unripe, green stage when it has a firm, nutty texture (ideal for grating for a salad). Unripe, pawpaw has anti-inflammatory and digestion-aiding properties, but none of the big sugar hit.

For 2 as a main course, 4 as a side salad:
1 medium dark green pawpaw (papaya)
1 large carrot
30g coriander, leaves and stalks, coarsely chopped
Some edible flowers, to garnish

For the dressing
2 garlic cloves
1 green Thai chilli
30g green beans, finely chopped
3 tbsp cashew nuts
3–4 cherry tomatoes
1 tsp coconut palm sugar (to taste)
1–2 tbsp Thai fish sauce (to taste)
Juice of 1–2 limes (to taste)

You need a julienne peeler for this salad (or you can chop the flesh into matchsticks but it is laborious). Peel and grate the pawpaw into fine needles, and then do the same with the carrot.

For the dressing, pulverise the garlic, chilli and beans together using the pulse button on a food processor. Add the cashews and pulse again. Finally add the cherry tomatoes and coconut palm sugar and pulse one last time. Pour into a large bowl and add the fish sauce. Spoon in the grated pawpaw and carrot and finally the lime juice and mix well. Serve in individual plates or bowls with plenty of chopped coriander and an edible flower or two over the top. This stores in the fridge for 24 hours.

» 199 calories for 2 servings, 99 for 4

More on » carrots p121 » coriander p204 » garlic p82 » chillies p93 » tomatoes p142 » coconut palm sugar p316

Salads

Light Waldorf salad

There is a classic mix of nuts and fruit in this famous salad, but no mayonnaise, instead natural yoghurt flavoured with peppery rocket and fresh mint. Cranberries add a good sharpness and, along with apples, have high antioxidant scores.

For 4–6 as a starter or side salad:
40g walnut halves
40g pecan halves
3 celery sticks, finely sliced
1 apple (Granny Smith), cored and chopped
40g dried cranberries
40g raisins
75g rocket
300g live natural yoghurt (see p44)
30g mint leaves, roughly chopped
Sea salt and black pepper

Preheat the oven to 180°C/gas mark 4. Put the nuts onto a baking tray and roast for 5 minutes. Allow to cool. Put all the ingredients into a bowl and mix well to combine. Season with salt and pepper.

» 235 calories for 4 servings, 156 for 6

More on » walnuts *p51* » apples *p288* » cranberries *p242* » rocket *p122* » yoghurt *p44* » mint *p326*

Sprouted seeds and beans are a very young version of the whole plant – the root, stem and shoot – which makes them super-nutritious. Broccoli sprouts have been recorded as having thirty to fifty times the amount of the super-healthy **glucosinolates** as the full-grown plant; and alfalfa sprouts are just as good. The roots of the fully-grown plant, from which the seeds are harvested, are known to burrow metres into the ground, extracting valuable trace **minerals** from the soil. When these seeds are sprouted, the minerals are converted into a form that's easy for us to absorb. You can sprout them at home or buy them at a health-food shop (you'll find them in the fridge).

Carrot and sprouted alfalfa/broccoli salad

We make this salad at the cookery school for lunch all the time: simple grated carrot and poppy seeds, with bouncy alfalfa and broccoli sprouts threaded through. It's also good to add the colour of red amaranth sprouts. The mix of sprouts lightens up the dense texture of the carrot and adds bumper nutrition. Carrots – raw – are an excellent source of vitamin A, and they're high in fibre and low in calories. On their own, they make a good salad, but with the sprouted seeds, you have a blockbuster. You can add a teaspoon or so of honey to the dressing if you like.

For 10 as a side salad:
1kg carrots, coarsely grated (only peel if not organic)
100g sunflower seeds (or a mix of sunflower and pumpkin), dry-fried
1 tbsp poppy seeds, dry-fried
100g alfalfa sprouts, broccoli sprouts, pea shoots or red amaranth for a great colour (or a mixture)
60g coriander, stems and leaves, chopped (or flat-leaf parsley or mint)

For the dressing
Grated zest and juice of 1 lemon
3 tbsp extra virgin olive oil
1 tbsp flaxseed oil
Sea salt and black pepper

Make the dressing by putting all the ingredients into a bowl and whisking with a fork to combine.

Put all the salad ingredients into a large salad bowl. Add the dressing and mix well to combine. This salad stores well in the fridge for 24 hours.

» 168 calories per serving

More on » carrots *p121* » pumpkin seeds *p105* » coriander *p204* » parsley *p136* » mint *p326* » lemons *p346* » olive oil *p193* » flaxseed oil *p153*

Warm Asian vegetable 'noodle' salad

I love this warm Asian salad, which you can make in large batches and reheat the next day. It will lose its crunch, but is still delicious. It's a sort of quick, easy, no-carbohydrate nasi goreng, using spiralised courgette and carrot instead of noodles.

For 4 as a main course:
1 tbsp set coconut oil
4 boned and skinned chicken thighs or chicken breasts, preferably organic, sliced into 1cm strips
3 shallots, finely sliced lengthways
240g raw prawns, peeled and de-veined
1 red pepper, deseeded and finely sliced lengthways
150g beansprouts

For the paste
1 garlic clove
3cm piece of fresh root ginger, peeled
1 tsp shrimp paste
4 tbsp unsalted peanuts
1 red chilli, seeds kept in if you like it fiery
1 shallot, finely diced
1 tsp clear honey

For the 'noodles'
3 large courgettes
2 large carrots, peeled

For the sauce
1 tsp clear honey
Splash of Thai fish sauce
Grated zest and juice of 2 limes

To serve
30g bunch of coriander, roughly chopped
4 tbsp peanuts, dry-fried, roughly chopped
Pinch of salt or 1–2 tsp gomashio (see p164)

Begin by making the paste. Blitz all the ingredients together in a food processor until a coarse paste is formed.

Melt the coconut oil in a wok or large frying pan. Add the chicken strips and shallots and fry for about 5 minutes until cooked through. Then add the paste and cook for 2 minutes, until the chicken is well coated. Add the prawns to the peanutty chicken and, stirring constantly, cook until the prawns have just turned pink (3–4 minutes). Add the pepper and cook for 2 minutes. Put the chicken and prawn mix into a bowl and put to one side.

Using a spiraliser or a julienne peeler, make the vegetable noodles (or you can cut the courgette into very thin slices and then into strips). Put in a separate bowl to the chicken.

For the sauce, in a small jug whisk the honey, fish sauce, lime zest and juice. Pour over the vegetable noodles, add the beansprouts, mix well and leave to 'cook' the vegetables for a couple of minutes.

Just before serving, mix the peanutty prawn and chicken with the noodles.

Scatter over the coriander, peanuts and gomashio (or a pinch of salt) to serve. This salad stores quite well in the fridge for 24 hours.

» 483 calories per serving

More on » coconut oil p309 » chicken p260 » prawns p212 » garlic p82 » ginger p200 » chillies p93 » honey p334 » carrots p121 » coriander p204

Beansprouts (usually of mung beans) have the health benefits of the beans, but the germination process means that their **protein** is more easily digested. The **vitamin** and essential fatty acid concentration also increases dramatically as the beans sprout, and their **mineral** content becomes more available to us. The combination of vitamin C and iron in beansprouts is brilliant for preventing and treating anaemia. For maximum benefit, eat beansprouts raw, quickly stir-fried or blanched, and try to buy organic.

Roast roots with walnut oil dressing

A simple beetroot and carrot salad, with the roots roasted to concentrate their flavour and nutrition. Here they're served with walnuts, in a dressing using walnut oil and super-nutritious organic cider vinegar. Keep walnuts only for quite a short time, in a sealed bag, or freeze them. They go off quickly, as does the oil, so keep your bottle in the fridge.

For 4 as a starter or side salad:
400g raw beetroots, peeled, washed and cut into large dice
300g small Chantenay carrots, halved lengthways, or larger carrots (not peeled if organic), cut into 2.5cm lengths
30g flat-leaf parsley, coarsely chopped

For the dressing
25g walnut pieces, dry-fried
1 tbsp organic apple cider vinegar
1 tsp Dijon mustard
1 tbsp walnut oil
2 tbsp cold-pressed rapeseed oil

Preheat the oven to 200°C/gas mark 6.

Put the beetroot cubes into a roasting tin, cover with foil and roast for 20 minutes. Then add the carrots to the beetroot cubes, stir in, cover again with the foil and roast for a further 20–25 minutes.

Meanwhile make the dressing. Put all the ingredients into a bowl and whisk with a fork to combine. Pour half the dressing over the beetroot and carrots as soon as they come out of the oven and mix well. Allow to cool for 10 minutes.

Toss with the flat-leaf parsley and drizzle over the rest of the dressing. Serve warm.

» 204 calories per serving

More on » beetroot *p85* » carrots *p121* » parsley *p136* » walnuts *p51* » apple cider vinegar *p63* » rapeseed oil *p248*

Roast beetroot, yoghurt and hazelnut salad

A simple Greek salad, which uses beetroot boiled in their skins. Some of the goodness will leach out in the boiling, but this makes sure the roots are truly tender. That's important in this salad and makes a good contrast to the shards of crunchy hazelnut. In early summer – when beetroots are still small and the leaves young and tender – this is traditionally served with the beetroot and yoghurt salad in the centre of the plate, surrounded by a circle of boiled beetroot leaves dressed simply in lemon juice and olive oil.

For 6 as a starter or side salad:
1.2kg small or medium beetroots, with their leaves
3 tbsp extra virgin olive oil
Juice of 1 lemon
Sea salt and black pepper
1 tbsp white wine vinegar
1 garlic clove, crushed

For the dressing and garnish
100g whole hazelnuts, roasted or dry-fried
Plenty of nutmeg, freshly grated, to taste
200g live Greek yoghurt
Grated zest of 1 lemon
20g dill, finely choppcd (keep a little back for serving)
20g chives, finely chopped (keep a little back for serving)

Remove the leaves from the beetroots, slicing just above the top of the root. Wash the leaves, and discard any that are coarse or damaged. Then chop the good leaves quite coarsely, including the stems as well – the stems are a great colour.

Put the beetroots in a pan of boiling water and cook for about 45 minutes (depending on size) until soft. Leave until cool enough to handle (ideally you want them still warm), then rub off the skins and cut into decent-sized chunks.

Meanwhile, cook the chopped beetroot stems and leaves in boiling water for about 5 minutes until tender. Remove from the pan and drain well,

squeezing the liquid out through a colander or sieve. Roughly chop then dress immediately with 2 tablespoons of the olive oil, the lemon juice and a little salt.

Put the cooked chunks of beetroot into a bowl, and pour over 1 tablespoon of oil, the vinegar and garlic. Stir well and allow to cool a little.

Put the hazelnuts into a plastic bag and bash with a rolling pin to break up roughly. Add the nuts (saving some to sprinkle on the top to garnish) to the beetroot along with the nutmeg, yoghurt, lemon zest, chopped dill and chives. Season with salt and black pepper to taste. Stir gently to combine.

Serve in the middle of a platter, scattered with a few extra hazelnuts and herbs. Surround with the dressed wilted leaves. Don't serve this fridge cold; it's better at room temperature.

» 238 calories per serving

More on » beetroot *p85* » olive oil *p193* » lemons *p346* » garlic *p82* » hazelnuts *p50* » yoghurt *p44*

Variation
Tahini and yoghurt beetroot salad Add 2 tablespoons tahini to the yoghurt dressing and use fresh oregano instead of the dill.
» 268 calories per serving

Beetroot, parsley and green mango salad

I had this salad at the Kamalaya health resort in Thailand. It included the super-healthy seaweed wakame and the fragrant herb gotu kola. The latter is used a lot in traditional Ayurvedic medicine and is often added to Thai salads. It's tricky to find in Britain, so here it's replaced by its equally healthy cousin, flat-leaf parsley. The mangoes here, even before they ripen and turn orange, are vitamin- and mineral-rich and yet the sugars have not fully developed. Eating them green, or at least unripe, you avoid a sugar bonanza.

For 4 as a main course, 6 as a side salad:
2 green mangoes, peeled (unripe, but orange mangoes are also OK)
125g raw beetroot, peeled (about 1 large)
10g dried wakame seaweed
1 large shallot, thinly sliced
1 lemongrass stalk, outer leaves removed, very thinly sliced
40g fresh coconut (see p212), cut with a potato peeler into slivers and briefly dry-fried
20g coriander leaves
20g flat-leaf parsley
Lime wedges, to serve

For the dressing
4 tsp tamarind paste
½ tsp chilli powder (or to taste)
Grated zest and juice of 2 limes
Sea salt and black pepper

In a jug mix together all the dressing ingredients, seasoning to taste with salt and pepper.

You need a julienne peeler for this salad (or you can chop into matchsticks but it is laborious). Using the julienne peeler, create matchstick strips of the green mango, keeping going until you hit the stone.

Do the same with the beetroot, placing it in a separate bowl to stop the beetroot bleeding into the delicate green of the mango.

Rehydrate the wakame. Put it in a bowl, with twice the volume of cold water to seaweed, and leave for 10 minutes.

Pour half the dressing into the beetroot and half into the mango. Mix to coat thoroughly.

In a large bowl mix the shallot, lemongrass, coconut and mango. Roughly chop most of the coriander and parsley (saving some for garnish) and then finally the beetroot, folding through gently. Taste for seasoning and tear over the wakame. Sprinkle with the remaining parsley and coriander leaves. Serve with lime wedges.

» 163 calories for 4 servings, 109 for 6

More on » beetroot p85 » seaweeds p174 » coriander p204

Parsley Anti-inflammatory and anti-viral, parsley is a good detoxifying herb, traditionally used for settling the stomach (do you remember Peter Rabbit looking for parsley after he'd stuffed himself on Mr McGregor's vegetables?). Parsley is a good source of iron and vitamin C, and one of the best sources of chlorophyll, which makes it a good blood detoxifier; because it acts as a mild diuretic, it may also help to lower blood pressure. The stems and leaves contain eye-protective lutein and zeaxanthin, as well as **beta-carotene**.

Parsnip, rocket and lentil salad with tapenade dressing

Rocket in a tapenade dressing is a good salad in itself, which you can just top with Parmesan, but to make it into a filling and healthy lunch, add Puy lentils and roast parsnips. This is good on its own, and excellent with fish, or roast chicken.

For 4–6 as a main course, 8 as a side salad:

For the roast veg
3 parsnips (about 1kg), cut into 3–5cm batons
2–3 white or red onions (about 400g), quartered
2–3 sprigs of thyme
1 tbsp juniper berries, crushed
2 tbsp cold-pressed rapeseed oil

For the lentils
200g Puy lentils
1 litre stock (chicken or vegetable, see pp98 and 101)
1 red onion, quartered
1 garlic clove, peeled
2 celery sticks, finely sliced
2–3 sprigs of thyme

For the dressing
5 tbsp extra virgin olive oil
1 heaped tbsp black olive tapenade
Grated zest of ½ lemon
Juice of 1 lemon
Black pepper (to taste; you're unlikely to need salt)

To serve
6 handfuls of rocket, or a mix of rocket and watercress
20g parsley, roughly chopped

Preheat the oven to 180°C/gas mark 4.

Roast the vegetables first. Put the parsnip with the onions onto a baking tray, add the thyme and crushed juniper berries, coat with a little oil and mix well. Roast for 35 minutes. Remove from the oven and place in a large serving dish. Remove the thyme sprigs.

Meanwhile, put the Puy lentils into a saucepan, cover with water and bring to the boil. Boil for 5 minutes, then drain. This removes some of the indigestible starches and makes lentils less flatulence-inducing. Put the par-boiled lentils back in the pan and cover with the stock. Add the onion, garlic, celery and thyme. Bring to the boil, turn down the heat and simmer gently for 15–20 minutes until the lentils are soft, but not collapsing.

Mix together all the dressing ingredients in a jug. Drain the lentils – there will be very little stock, if any, left in the pan – and take out and discard the garlic and woody stems of the thyme. Mix the lentils with the roast veg. Pour on half the dressing and gently mix everything together. Put to one side for the flavours to infuse.

To serve, place the salad leaves in a large serving bowl, pour over the rest of the dressing and toss. Scatter over the lentils, roasted veg and parsley.

» 574 calories for 4 servings, 382 for 6, 287 for 8

More on » onions *p281* » rapeseed oil *p248* » garlic *p82* » olive oil *p193* » lemons *p346* » rocket *p122* » watercress *p70* » parsley *p136*

Lentils are a good **protein** source and high in **fibre**, which makes them a great slow-release **carbohydrate**, as the fibre prevents blood-sugar levels from rocketing after eating. Fibre also helps to lower **cholesterol**, and their fibre, folate and magnesium is very good for cardiovascular health. Loaded with lignans, **plant hormones** which help to naturally balance our hormones, lentils are useful in the diet of menopausal women. They're also a natural appetite-suppressant, so are valuable when trying to lose weight. Lentils can also be sprouted; these retain the health benefits of the pulse, and make the protein more digestible.

Quinoa, courgette and lemon salad

Quinoa is filling, and a little goes a long way. It's lovely with this courgette carpaccio. When summer begins, use a mix of courgette colours – yellow and deep and pale greens. You can add a nice flavour by toasting the quinoa in a dry frying pan for a minute before boiling for 10–15 minutes.

For 6–8 as a side salad:
300g quinoa, white or red
675ml vegetable stock (see p101) or good-quality bouillon
4 small, or 2 medium, courgettes (about 300g)
4 tbsp extra virgin olive oil
Grated zest and juice of 1 lemon
1 garlic clove, crushed (optional)
Sea salt and black pepper
About 60g mixed spring herbs (coriander, with flowers if possible, mint, flat-leaf parsley, chervil and sorrel), roughly chopped (save a few whole coriander and mint leaves for garnish)
30g pumpkin or sunflower seeds, or pine nuts, dry-fried
200g feta, roughly crumbled (optional)

Rinse the quinoa well in a sieve under a running tap then dry fry if you want to. Put it into a pan with the stock (if using fresh stock, not bouillon, add a pinch of salt). Bring to the boil, reduce the heat and simmer gently without a lid for 10–15 minutes, or until all the liquid has evaporated; keep an eye on it. The cooked seed has a tiny curly tail and should have a slight bite to it. Take off the heat (do not drain), put the lid on, and leave to rest in the pan for 5 minutes.

Spoon the quinoa into a large serving bowl, then fork through gently and allow to cool.

Very thinly slice the courgettes into a large mixing bowl (a mandolin is great for this). Pour over the extra virgin olive oil, add the zest and juice of the lemon and the crushed garlic (if using). Season with salt and pepper and give it a gentle stir. Allow to marinate for half an hour, or 15 minutes if you like the courgettes to have more bite. Add the

courgette mixture, herbs and dry-fried seeds to the quinoa. Stir and season with salt and pepper, and possibly a little lemon juice or extra virgin olive oil, to taste. Sprinkle over the feta (if using), and some whole coriander or mint leaves.

» 448 calories for 6 servings, 336 for 8

More on » olive oil p193 » lemons p346 » garlic p82 » coriander p204 » mint p326 » parsley p136 » pumpkin seeds p105 » feta p264

Quinoa is a highly nutritious grain-like seed from a plant native to South America. There are three main types – white, red and black. You can buy it whole or flaked (for baking and making porridge), where the grain is steamed and softened and then rolled. White quinoa is the most commonly available, while red is particularly good for salads, as it holds its shape well after cooking. Black quinoa is earthier and sweeter than the other two, with a harder coat, so it takes more cooking, but to my mind it is a little too like a grain of sand.

Quinoa can sometimes be slightly bitter, but you can reduce this by rubbing the seeds in a sieve as you rinse it under cold water to remove a soapy coating called saponin. Quinoa flakes shouldn't need rinsing, but check the pack.

Quinoa is **gluten**-free, and has numerous health benefits. It is a complete **protein**, containing all nine essential **amino acids** and in particular lysine, which is not found in other grains, making it a valuable protein source for vegetarians. It is rich in anti-inflammatory **phytonutrients**, which make it stand out in the prevention and treatment of disease. It contains almost twice as much **fibre** as other grains, as well as some **omega-3 fatty acids**. Quinoa is also magnesium-rich. Magnesium is involved in the body's mechanism for insulin secretion; by relaxing blood vessels, aiding the heart muscle and helping to regulate blood pressure, it helps to prevent heart attacks and strokes.

Salads

Slow-cooked tomato with feta and basil

Use your oven to 'sun-dry' tomatoes, which then retain their sweetness. The process will also preserve them in the short term. Tomatoes are one of the vegetables which are even better for us cooked: cooking makes their nutrients more available, with up to three times the amount compared with raw (although the vitamin C in them is lost when they are cooked). Leave the skins on, as they have the highest nutrient concentration of any part of the fruit. The main nutrient, lycopene, is fat-soluble, hence the cheese, but just use oil if you want to keep it dairy-free.

For 4 as a starter or side salad:
500g tomatoes (a selection of colours and sizes), halved
6–7 garlic cloves, finely sliced
A few sprigs of thyme, leaves picked, or 1 tsp dried thyme
Extra virgin olive oil
Sea salt and black pepper
Good handful of basil
4 handfuls of salad and other herbs, such as rocket, flat-leaf parsley, tarragon, coriander and sorrel
Juice of ½ lemon
100g feta, crumbled
20g pine nuts, dry-fried

Preheat the oven to 220°C/gas mark 7.

Arrange the tomatoes in a single layer on non-stick or lined baking trays. Put a slice of garlic on each, sprinkle with thyme, add a good drizzle of extra virgin olive oil, and some salt and black pepper. Roast in the hot oven for 10 minutes. Turn the oven down to 120°C/gas mark ½, and continue cooking the tomatoes for 50–60 minutes. If using cherry tomatoes, check them halfway through cooking, as they will be ready sooner. Remove and allow to cool.

Put the salad leaves and herbs into a mixing bowl. Pour over 3 tablespoons of extra virgin olive oil, the lemon juice and add some salt and pepper.

Toss well to combine. Divide the salad leaves and herbs between four plates and add a quarter of the slow-cooked tomatoes to each one. Sprinkle with the feta and pine nuts.

» 245 calories per serving

More on » garlic p82 » olive oil p193 » rocket p122 » parsley p136 » coriander p204 » lemons p346 » feta p264

Tomatoes contain high levels of lycopene, the most powerful **antioxidant** to have been measured in food. It is responsible for the deep red pigment in plants, and is also found in watermelon, pawpaw and rosehip. (Grapefruit, asparagus, parsley and basil – although not red at all – are also rich sources.) Lycopene's anti-cancer benefits have been repeatedly shown, with the evidence being strongest for reducing the incidence of prostate cancer, but they are also linked to a decrease in lung, stomach and breast cancers. In tomatoes, lycopene is concentrated in the skin, and is up to three times more available when the tomatoes have been cooked. So leave the skin on, and use as much tomato paste, tomato purée and sun-dried tomatoes as you can in your day-to-day food. Tinned tomatoes are also full of lycopene, they're just not as good as they don't have their skins. Always eat tomatoes with a small amount of oil, as lycopene is fat-soluble and is more bio-available when eaten this way: make sure you use oil when cooking them in sauces, but also add an oil-based dressing or some avocado to tomato salads.

Tomatoes belong to the *Solanaceae* or nightshade family, which also includes aubergines, peppers and potatoes. For some reason, they have the reputation of causing **inflammation** of the joints, and aggravating or causing arthritis, but the Arthritis Research Council states that there is no evidence for this.

Wheat berry, kale and squash salad with goats' cheese

Wheat berries are the entire wheat kernel, minus only the hull. Ground, this is what's used for wholemeal bread and, like other whole grains, is full of vitamins and fibre. I love wheat berries for their sweet, nutty taste and chewy texture, a little like pearl barley but plumper; and they're excellent in salad. They take a fair amount of cooking (up to 45 minutes or more). The grilled goats' cheese here has less than a third the fat and calories of many creamy cheeses, so if you want cheese in any salad, goats' cheese is ideal.

You don't need to soak wheat berries – it does not make much difference to their cooking time – but it is worth dry-roasting them until their aroma comes off the pan. This increases their delicious nutty taste.

For 4 as a main course:
100g wheat berries
1 x 500g butternut squash
1 red onion
1 tbsp cold-pressed rapeseed oil
1 tbsp fennel seeds
Pinch of chilli flakes
2 garlic cloves, left whole and unpeeled
Grated zest and juice of 2 lemons
1 tbsp extra virgin olive oil
1 tbsp set coconut oil
150g kale, stems removed, torn into bite-sized pieces
1 fennel bulb, very thinly sliced
30g bunch of tarragon, roughly chopped
30g bunch of flat-leaf parsley, roughly chopped
2 x 100g goats' cheese rounds, sliced in half across the equator

Bring a large saucepan of water to the boil and add the wheat berries. Simmer for about 45 minutes (check the packet instructions). When tender, drain and rinse under cold water.

Preheat the oven to 180°C/gas mark 4. Line a baking tray with baking parchment.

Cut the squash in half, remove the seeds, and cut the flesh into 2.5cm cubes (you don't need to peel the squash). Place the squash on the lined baking tray, drizzle with the rapeseed oil and scatter with the fennel seeds and chilli flakes. Toss and bake in the oven for 30 minutes. Peel and cut the onion into thick slices. Add the onion and the garlic to the squash and bake for 20–25 minutes until the squash and onion are just starting to brown around the edges.

When the garlic is cool enough to handle, squeeze the flesh out of the skins into a jug. Add the lemon zest and juice and olive oil. Whisk well.

Heat the coconut oil in a large saucepan. Add the kale and fennel and stir-fry for 2 minutes until the kale is just wilted and the fennel softened.

Put the wheat berries in a bowl with the kale, fennel and roasted squash. Pour over the dressing and scatter in half the tarragon and parsley. Mix well, and divide between four plates.

Place the goats' cheese halves under a hot grill and cook for 4–5 minutes until golden and bubbling. Put one on each mound of salad and scatter with the remaining tarragon and parsley.

» 413 calories per serving

More on » squash *p186* » onions *p281* » rapeseed oil *p248* » garlic *p82* » lemons *p346* » olive oil *p193* » coconut oil *p309* » kale *p117* » parsley *p136* » goats' cheese *p268*

Mixed herb and tomato tabbouleh with halloumi

A proper tabbouleh consists of a light creamy flecking of bulghar through a bowl mainly made up of herbs and veg. However, you almost always see tabbouleh weighed down with bulghar, which is not how it's meant to be. The high proportion of herbs makes this salad tastier and more nutritious than the standard stuff, and it's more authentic, springy and fresh. This salad is also thick with tomatoes, including both raw and sun-dried, one of the richest sources of antioxidants.

For 4 as a main course:

For the bulghar
100g bulghar wheat
60g flat-leaf parsley, finely chopped
60g mint leaves, finely chopped
30g dill, finely chopped
250g cherry tomatoes, roughly chopped (or heirloom tomatoes in different colours, textures and shapes)
6 sun-dried tomatoes in oil, drained and finely chopped

For the halloumi topping
200g halloumi cheese (allow 50g per portion)
About 24 fresh bay or sage leaves (depending on the number of halloumi slices)

For the dressing
4 tbsp extra virgin olive oil
Grated zest and juice of 1 lemon
1 tbsp clear honey or maple syrup
1 level tbsp cumin seeds, dry-fried
Sea salt and black pepper

Put the bulghar wheat into a bowl and barely cover with boiling water. Leave to soak for 12–15 minutes. Then fork through. Meanwhile, rinse the halloumi under cold water and pat dry with kitchen paper (this removes the extra saltiness from the halloumi and gives a better flavour when cooked). Cut the halloumi sparingly into slices, just under 1cm in thickness and put a bay (or sage) leaf on each side of each slice.

Heat a griddle or heavy-based frying pan until you can't reach a count of ten with your hand hovering just above it. Cook the halloumi on each side. This doesn't take long, so keep an eye on the griddle or pan. Remove with the bay (or sage) leaves attached and discard the herbs (their flavours will have been absorbed).

Put all the dressing ingredients, with salt and pepper to taste, into a mixing bowl and whisk well to combine. Add the remaining bulghar ingredients to the wheat in the bowl, pour over the dressing and toss gently until well combined. Serve the tabbouleh on individual plates, topped with three slices of halloumi.

» 463 calories per serving

More on » parsley *p136* » mint *p136* » tomatoes *p142* » olive oil *p193* » lemons *p346* » honey *p334*

Wheat berries and bulghar wheat

Wheat 'berries' are entire wheat kernels (or groats), composed of the bran, germ, and endosperm, while bulghar (or bulgur) is whole wheat that has been partially cooked and then cracked and dried. Both are full of dietary **fibre**, which promotes a healthy colon and helps to balance blood-sugar levels. They are also a good source of manganese, which is vital for nerve health, and magnesium, which supports the bones, muscles and nerves.

Bulghar wheat is quick to prepare, whereas wheat berries take longer to cook (about 45 minutes), depending on the kind of wheat berry, as well as how old it is. Start checking after about 30 minutes of cooking and keep checking every 5 minutes until they reach a tender, yet chewy consistency. Pearled or semi-pearled varieties cook more quickly, so start checking those after 15–20 minutes. All wheat products contain **gluten**.

Spiced aubergine salad with pomegranate raita

An intense-flavoured warm salad made with long-cooked aubergine and tomato, with plenty of fragrant spices.

For 6–8 as a starter or side salad, 4 as a main course:
3 medium-large aubergines (about 1kg)
3 tbsp cold-pressed rapeseed oil
1 large onion, finely chopped
2 tsp cumin seeds
2 tsp coriander seeds
1 tsp allspice berries
2 star anise
1 tsp ground cinnamon
1 tsp paprika
10–12 medium tomatoes, roughly chopped, or 2 x 400g tin of chopped tomatoes
30g coriander, coarsely chopped
20g mint leaves, coarsely chopped

For the pomegranate raita
Seeds of ½ pomegranate (see p46)
250g live Greek yoghurt
Grated zest and juice of 1 lime
Sea salt and black pepper

To serve
Seeds of ½ pomegranate (see p46)
10g mint leaves, roughly torn
Some salad leaves on the side

For the raita, mix the pomegranate seeds with the other raita ingredients in a bowl, seasoning with salt and pepper. Cover and refrigerate until needed.

Preheat the oven to 200°C/gas mark 6.

Dice the aubergines into 3–4cm chunks and place on a baking sheet. Drizzle over 2 tbsp of the rapeseed oil and roast for about 30 minutes. Cook until the edges start to char. Meanwhile, in a large pan, fry the onion gently in the remaining rapeseed oil until glassy and soft. In a separate small pan, dry-fry the cumin and coriander seeds, allspice and star anise for 2 minutes until they begin to smoke. Remove from the heat and grind to a coarse powder in a spice grinder or a pestle and mortar.

Add the ground spices, cinnamon and paprika to the onion in the pan, then add the aubergines and the tomatoes. Stir, then cook the mixture over a gentle heat for 20–30 minutes. Once the tomato juice has reduced until there is very little liquid left, take the pan off the heat and allow to cool for 5 minutes before stirring in the fresh herbs. Sprinkle over the pomegranate seeds and mint, and serve warm with the raita and salad leaves on the side.

» 196 calories for 6 servings, 147 for 8, 294 for 4

More on » rapeseed oil *p248* » onions *p281* » coriander *p204* » cinnamon *p22* » tomatoes *p142* » mint *p326* » pomegranate *p46* » yoghurt *p44*

Aubergines have a certain meatiness to them, which adds substance to any dish, and they also fill you up, because they're super-high in fibre. Low in calories and fat, aubergines are an invaluable addition to your diet if you want to lower your cholesterol and lose weight. They also contain nasunin, an antioxidant anthocyanin that is particularly good for the brain, taking care of brain-cell membranes. Nasunin is what gives aubergines their purple colour, and it is found mostly in the skin, so use that as much as you can.

Aubergines belong to the *Solanaceae* or nightshade family, which also includes peppers, tomatoes and potatoes. For some reason, they have the reputation of causing inflammation of the joints, and aggravating or causing arthritis, but the Arthritis Research Council states that there is no evidence for this. Aubergines do, however, contain significant amounts of oxalates, so avoid eating too many if you have a history of oxalate-containing kidney stones or gall-bladder problems.

Wild salmon tartare with cucumber and dill

Salmon and cucumber make a powerfully nutritious pair. I like the look of this served in small (250ml) Kilner jars, with the cucumber ribbons at the side, but making it in ramekins – if you have them – is fine. Like gravadlax, the salmon stores well in the fridge for several days and it's one of those things that you shouldn't eat straightaway.

For 6 as a main course, 8–10 as a starter:
600g wild salmon fillet, skinned and cut into small cubes
Grated zest and juice of ½ lemon
Sea salt and black pepper
400g hot-smoked salmon fillets, skinned, flesh flaked
3 heaped tbsp chopped dill
1 heaped tbsp dill or fennel seeds, dry-fried
Splash of olive oil
Lime wedges

For the dressing
2 tbsp olive oil
1 tbsp Dijon mustard
1 tbsp clear honey

For the salad
1 large cucumber
100ml rice wine vinegar
1 tbsp clear or set honey
Good bunch of dill, with flowers

For the sweet mustard dressing for the salmon, put all the ingredients into a small bowl and mix.

Place the cubed salmon fillet in a large mixing bowl. Add the mustard dressing, lemon zest and juice, and season with salt and pepper. Stir well to combine. Add the remaining ingredients to the bowl and again stir together gently. Try not to break up the salmon cubes. Check the seasoning and add more lemon juice, lemon zest, olive oil, salt and pepper if needed. Spoon the mixture into Kilner jars, cover and place in the fridge for a couple of hours or even better overnight, to allow the flavours to develop.

To make the salad, slice the cucumber as thinly as possible lengthways, using a vegetable peeler or spiraliser. Put in a sieve over a bowl and leave for a while so that it gives out its liquid.

Heat the vinegar in a small pan over a low heat and stir in the honey until it is dissolved. Allow to cool.

Finely chop the dill, plus its flowers. Mix this and the sweetened vinegar with the drained cucumber ribbons, and leave for at least an hour.

Serve the salmon with the cucumber salad and a lime wedge on each plate.

» 397 calories for 6 servings, 297 for 8, 238 for 10

More on » salmon *p125* » lemons *p346* » olive oil *p193* » honey *p334*

Cucumber is 95 per cent water, so it hydrates the body and helps eliminate toxins. Whole cucumbers – including the skin and seeds – contain most of the **vitamins** our body needs. They are a good source of B vitamins and **electrolytes**, and are therefore a good general pick-me-up, and the skin especially is rich in vitamin C. Lignans, a type of **phytoestrogen** present in cucumber, have been the subject of research into their ability to reduce the risk of cardiovascular disease and oestrogen-related cancers. In addition, a group of compounds known as cucurbitacins that are found in cucumbers and other members of the gourd family, are being actively researched for new anti-cancer drugs. It is best to buy organic cucumbers if possible.

Salads

Smoked mackerel, broccoli and almond salad

I love this salad for a winter lunch or as a starter for dinner. You have the choice of two dressings here, use one or the other.

For 6 as a main course, 8–10 as a starter:
1 red onion, very thinly sliced
2 tbsp capers, plus 1 tbsp vinegar from the jar
Grated zest and juice of 1 lemon
Sea salt and black pepper
300g tenderstem broccoli
300g purple sprouting broccoli
4 smoked mackerel fillets, about 100g each
60g flaked almonds, dry-fried
60g blanched hazelnuts, dry-fried, roughly chopped

For the yoghurt dressing
4 tbsp live natural yoghurt (see p44)
3–4 tbsp extra virgin olive oil
20g chopped herbs (mint, parsley, dill)
Grated zest and juice of 1 lemon

For the apple dressing
100ml olive oil
50ml organic apple cider vinegar
½ apple, peeled, cored and chopped
20g chopped herbs (mint, parsley, dill)
½ tbsp clear honey

In a china or glass dish, mix together the onion, capers, their vinegar, lemon zest and juice and a pinch of salt. Leave to marinate for at least an hour, longer if possible. This gives the onions a more gentle taste.

Blend all the ingredients for either the yoghurt or apple dressing in a small food processor until smooth and well combined.

Steam both types of broccoli for 5–7 minutes until tender. Leave to cool or serve warm. Skin and flake the mackerel into chunky pieces. Toss all the salad ingredients together gently in a large bowl with half of the dressing you've chosen and half of the toasted nuts. Leave in the bowl or arrange on a large flat dish. Drizzle with the rest of the dressing and scatter over the remaining nuts.

» 343 calories for 6 servings, 258 for 8, 206 for 10 without dressing
» Yoghurt dressing, 428 calories for 6 servings
» Apple dressing, 485 calories for 6 servings

More on » onions p281 » lemons p346
» mackerel and oily fish p256 » almonds p347
» hazelnuts p50 » yoghurt p44 » olive oil p193
» mint p326 » parsley p136 » apple cider vinegar p63 » apples p288 » honey p334

Broccoli, like all green vegetables, is high in **fibre**, iron, calcium and zinc; it is also packed with vitamins A, B, C and K. It has long been known as a nutritious vegetable, but broccoli is turning out to be in the superfood league, as its combined nutrients have been found to decrease cancer risk. Recent research has found that, like cauliflower, the florets are full of sulphur-containing compounds called **glucosinolates**. Converted to isothiocyanates when chewed, these are important for many health reasons, including liver detoxification and general cell self-cleansing (see also kale, page 117).

With most broccoli varieties, you'll need to eat lots to gain the benefits, but a new type of broccoli, Beneforté (so-called 'super broccoli') contains over twice the levels of glucosinolates, so eating only two portions a week will help protect against disease. To get the best out of it, roast, juice or steam it with minimal water – and try to use the water, rather than discarding it, so you don't lose any of the goodness. On-going clinical trials with Beneforté are taking place in Norwich, UK, to test the theory that eating this type of broccoli improves our metabolism and reduces the levels of **LDL cholesterol** in our blood, as well as slowing the progression of early-stage prostate cancer.

Lemon chicken and herb salad

Simple yet delicious, this is a wonderfully fresh-tasting salad. Once tried, you can't help but make it again and again, swapping the herbs, nuts and dried fruit each time. We serve this for lunches when we're feeding the five thousand at our summer feasts or garden open days. Shred the chicken with your fingers, rather than cutting it into chunks. Take care to buy traditionally cured – and more expensive – olives, rather than the tasteless eye-ball-like, so-called 'processed' olives you get in brine. Choose 'oil-cured', 'brine-cured', 'water-cured' or 'dry-salted'. This salad stores well in the fridge for at least a couple of days.

For 6 as a main-course salad:
4 skinless chicken breasts (about 650g)
4 fresh or dried bay leaves
Extra virgin olive oil, for drizzling
Sea salt and black pepper
4 tbsp raisins
2 tbsp capers
3 tbsp pine nuts, dry-fried
8 anchovy fillets in oil, drained and roughly chopped
Julienned zest of 2 lemons
30 mixed, good-quality stoned olives
30g flat-leaf parsley leaves
30g mint leaves

For the dressing
Juice of 1 lemon
5 tbsp extra virgin olive oil
1 tbsp flaxseed oil
1 tsp Dijon mustard
1 tsp clear honey

Heat the oven to 180°C/gas mark 4.

Put the chicken breasts onto a baking tray with a bay leaf tucked underneath each one. Drizzle with olive oil and season with salt and pepper. Tightly cover the baking tray with foil, and roast for 20 minutes. Remove the chicken from the oven and leave to rest, covered with the foil, for 15 minutes. Discard the foil and leave the chicken until cool enough to handle – it's easier to pull into shreds when still slightly warm, not fully cooled.

Make the dressing by putting all the ingredients into a bowl and whisking together. Season well with salt and pepper.

Place the chicken in a large serving bowl with the rest of the salad ingredients. If the mint leaves are large, tear them in half. Pour over the lemon dressing and toss well to combine.

» 430 calories per serving

More on » chicken p260 » olivc oil p193 » oily fish p256 » lemons p346 » olives p179 » parsley p136 » mint p326 » honey p334

Flaxseed oil contains **alpha-linolenic acid** (ALA), an essential **omega-3 fatty acid** that research suggests may help to reduce the risk of heart disease, stroke and inflammatory diseases such as rheumatoid arthritis. Flaxseed oil also provides a good balance of omega-3 to **omega-6 fatty acids**, which is needed for optimum health.

Try adding flaxseed oil to salad dressings, smoothies and soups. Many of the salad dressings here contain just a little, mixed with extra virgin olive oil, so you get the delicious olive oil flavour, but with the added bonus of the flaxseed oil's omega-3s. As flaxseed oil has quite a bitter after-taste, I don't recommend adding it in a ratio greater than 1:4 with very good olive oil.

Cucumber and wakame salad

The seaweed wakame is a widely recognised superfood, often used in soups, especially miso, and it is also excellent in salads. It's nutrient-dense, and contains a special sugar molecule which is very good for cellular regeneration and slowing down ageing. The head chef at Kamalaya health spa in Thailand, Edmond Che Hang Kwan, eats it every day and has done so for years: even as he turned fifty, he had not a single wrinkle. This salad is perfect with salmon or almost any other fish and is very low in calories.

For 4–6 as a side salad:
15g dried wakame seaweed
1 large cucumber
2 tsp rice vinegar
1–2 tbsp sesame oil (to taste)
20g finely grated fresh root ginger
1 tbsp pickled ginger, finely chopped
4 spring onions, very finely sliced on the diagonal
3 tbsp gomashio (see p164) or pinch of salt
Handful of coriander leaves, roughly chopped

In a large bowl cover the wakame with cold water and leave to soak for 10 minutes. Drain and squeeze dry. Cut any large pieces into small chunks.

Using a spiraliser, a julienne peeler or a very sharp knife, create long thin strips of cucumber, discarding the seedy centre.

In a jug whisk together the vinegar, sesame oil and grated and pickled ginger.

Mix together the cucumber, wakame and dressing, then add the spring onions, gomashio (or salt) and coriander.

» 101 calories for 4 servings, 67 for 6

More on » seaweeds *p174* » cucumber *p148*
» ginger *p200* » coriander *p204*

Shrimp and summer garden salad

I make this often in July and August when we have plenty of courgettes, tomatoes and basil growing in the garden. It looks and tastes best with mixed-colour courgettes and a variety of different tomatoes – some sweet and some more acid – to give a great range of flavour. The shrimps add plenty of healthy protein and are very sustaining.

For 8 as a main course, 12 as a starter:
A little cold-pressed rapeseed oil for oiling
800g courgettes, ideally mixed colours
1kg tomatoes, ideally mixed colours, chopped into chunks
500g cooked brown shrimps
60g bunch of basil, leaves removed and roughly torn

For the dressing
4 tbsp extra virgin olive oil
1 tbsp flaxseed oil
Finely grated zest and juice of 1 lemon
Sea salt and black pepper

Top and tail and cut the larger courgettes lengthways into 1cm slices. If the courgettes are small with the flower still on, remove the flower and put aside to add at the end (after removing the central stigma). Leave small courgettes whole or cut in half lengthways.

Oil a griddle lightly with rapeseed oil and then heat until you cannot count to ten with your hand hovering just above it. Griddle the courgettes for about 3 minutes on either side, depending on size, and put in a large shallow bowl. Add the tomatoes to the courgettes. Scatter in the shrimps and basil.

For the dressing, mix the oils with lemon zest and juice and season with salt and pepper. Dress the salad, and toss well before serving.

» 204 calories for 8 servings, 136 for 12

More on » rapeseed oil *p248* » tomatoes *p142*
» shrimps *p215* » olive oil *p193* » flaxseed oil *p153*
» lemons *p346*

Smoked chicken, mango and spring herb salad

This is salad as comfort food, with the delicious mix of smoked chicken and mango.

The mayonnaise is lower calorie than usual, with less oil included. You will only need a quarter for the salad here. The rest will keep well for a week in the fridge. Put in lots of different herbs and a variety of veg for crunch and goodness. It's good with sugarsnaps or mangetouts and I also love this with green mangoes, cut into julienne strands (use the special cutters) and mixed in; green mangoes have a lower sugar content too.

For 6 as a main-course salad:
1 whole smoked chicken (about 800g meat)
2 mangoes
200g mangetout or sugarsnap peas (optional)
1 bunch of radishes
100g bunch of spring onions
225g tin of water chestnuts, drained
2 little gem hearts, sliced into strands
4 tbsp mayonnaise (see below)
Grated zest and juice of 1 lime, plus extra to serve
60g bunch of herbs, chopped (mainly coriander, but chervil, baby sorrel leaves, chives, mint and baby lovage leaves are also good in small amounts)

For the mayonnaise
1 medium egg, plus 1 medium egg yolk, at room temperature
2 tbsp lemon juice
1 garlic clove, peeled
½ tsp English mustard powder
Sea salt and black pepper
150ml cold-pressed rapeseed oil or light olive oil
50ml extra virgin olive oil
2 tbsp live natural yoghurt (see p44)

To serve
Drizzle of toasted sesame oil
Couple of handfuls of perfect green salad (see p112)
Lime wedges

Make the mayonnaise. Put the egg and egg yolk in a small food processor and blitz them with the lemon juice, garlic, mustard, and a pinch of salt and black pepper. When the mixture is quite smooth, very slowly add the oil in a stream – first the rapeseed, then the extra virgin olive – while blending continuously, until the oil emulsifies and makes a thick mayonnaise. Scoop the mayonnaise out of the food processor bowl and add more lemon juice to taste (if necessary). Stir in the yoghurt and season a little more if needed.

Skin and chop the chicken. Place in a serving bowl. Prepare the mangoes by slicing the two sides off, either side of the stone. Score these into cubes, and invert the 'cheeks' so that they look like hedgehogs. Slice off the cubes from the skin below. Remove as much flesh as you can from the stone as well. Mix the cubed flesh with the chicken.

If using, blanch the mangetouts or sugarsnaps for a couple of minutes in boiling water, then drain, cool and cut into fine slices. Top and tail the radishes and slice quite finely. Slice the spring onions and water chestnuts. Keep a few spring onions and radishes back for garnish. Add the spring onion, radish, peas (if using) and water chestnuts to the chicken mixture, along with the strands of lettuce.

Mix 4 heaped tablespoons mayonnaise, the lime juice and zest and herbs together, saving some of the herbs and a little lime zest for later. Add this to the mango and chicken and mix well. Scatter the reserved spring onion and radish slices over the salad, drizzle with a little toasted sesame oil, and top with the saved herbs and lime zest strands. Serve with some garden salad and lime wedges.

» 406 calories per serving

More on » chicken *p260* » lettuce *p114* » coriander *p204* » eggs *p61* » lemons *p346* » garlic *p82* » rapeseed oil *p248* » olive oil *p193* » yoghurt *p44*

Guinea fowl salad with pomegranate and chestnuts

A fantastic winter salad, using whole guinea fowl (or a couple of whole pheasants). Both these are lean white meats and provide good protein. I also occasionally make this salad with chicken thighs, cut into bits and marinated overnight in olive oil, garlic, rosemary and lemon juice, and then roasted or grilled.

For 6 as a main course, 8–10 as a starter:
1 large guinea fowl, or 2 small (about 1.4kg in total)
2 large fennel bulbs
2 handfuls of mixed winter leaves, such as the small young tips of cavolo nero, rocket, mizuna and lamb's lettuce
2 heads of Treviso, radicchio or Belgian chicory

For the dressing
5 tbsp extra virgin olive oil
1 tbsp flaxseed oil
Juice of 1 lemon
Sea salt and black pepper

Chestnuts
Mediterranean peasants, in times of famine, were forced to survive on a diet consisting largely of chestnuts. They didn't like it, but it did keep them alive. High in starch, the chestnuts were dried and ground into a flour, which was then made into polenta and bread. We should aim to eat more chestnuts too. Unlike many nuts, chestnuts are low in fat and calories (with roasted chestnuts coming in at only 64 per 28g), less than half the calories of hazelnuts and only a third that of macadamias. Like olive oil, they contain high concentrations of **monounsaturated fat** and oleic acid, which is beneficial to the heart. They are also the only nut to provide vitamin C (72 per cent of our daily requirement per 100g) and are a good source of dietary **fibre**, which helps to encourage a healthy gut and reduce the risk of bowel cancer.

To serve
100g Parmesan, cut into rough slivers
250g (12–15) whole cooked chestnuts (from a vacuum pack)
Seeds of 1 pomegranate (see p46)
3 tbsp aged balsamic vinegar

Preheat the oven to 190°C/gas mark 5.

Place the guinea fowl(s) in a roasting tray. Roast for 1 hour or until cooked through and the juices from the thigh run clear (the cooking time will vary according to the size of the bird). Remove from the roasting tray and allow to cool. Carve or pull the meat off the bird in chunky slices or pieces. It's easiest to do this when the meat is still warm.

Thinly slice the fennel (best done with a mandolin). Put this and the mixed salad leaves in a bowl. Cut the radicchio or chicory heads lengthways down their spine. Add to the bowl.

Make the simple dressing by mixing the olive and flaxseed oils and lemon juice with some salt and pepper.

Toss the salad leaves in the dressing, then add the guinea fowl pieces. Add some Parmesan slivers and chestnuts, broken into bits.

Scatter over a few pomegranate seeds. Drizzle over balsamic vinegar and season again to taste.

» 516 calories for 6 servings, 387 calories for 8, 310 for 10

More on » rocket p122 » lettuce p114 » olive oil p193 » flaxseed oil p153 » lemons p346 » pomegranates p46 » balsamic vinegar p189

Warm pheasant and cavolo nero salad

Pheasant is a very lean meat, low in calories, but their wild, active lifestyle can make the meat tough and stringy, so you need to take care how you cook it. I think it's best done by removing the breasts and cooking them in baking parchment with slices of orange or lemon for added moisture. Roast the rest of the bird whole and use it as a base for stock.

For 4 as a main course or 8 as a starter:
4 pheasant breasts, skin on (about 700g in total)
A little olive oil
1 orange or lemon, sliced
1 level tsp Chinese five-spice powder
Sea salt and black pepper
30g coriander leaves, roughly chopped

For the cavolo nero salad
200g bunch of cavolo nero
1 tbsp set coconut oil
1 red onion (about 100g), finely chopped
1 large garlic clove, finely chopped
½ red finger chilli, deseeded and finely chopped
1 level tbsp coarsely grated fresh root ginger
1 tbsp extra virgin olive oil
1 tbsp tamari soy sauce

Preheat the oven to 180°C/gas mark 4.

Cut a piece of baking parchment into a rectangle approximately 45cm by 34cm. Fold it in half and place the pheasant breasts in the middle of one half. Drizzle over a little olive oil and add the slices of orange or lemon. Sprinkle over the Chinese

five-spice and season with a little salt and pepper. Bring the top of the folded baking parchment over the seasoned pheasant breasts and fold in the edges, making a semi-circular sealed parcel.

Put this parcel onto a baking tray and cook in the oven for 20 minutes. Remove from the oven and allow to rest for 10 minutes.

Meanwhile, prepare the cavolo nero. If the leaves are young and the mid ribs not too woody, chop into bite-sized pieces. If the stalks are woody, cut away the mid ribs and chop up the leaves.

Heat the coconut oil in a wok over a high heat. Add the onion, garlic, chilli and ginger and stir-fry for 30 seconds or so. Add the cavolo nero leaves and stir-fry for a further 3 minutes. Add the olive oil and tamari and cook for a further 1 minute. Spoon the cavolo nero onto four plates.

Pull the skin off the pheasant breasts, discard and slice the breast meat into 1cm slices. Top each plate of cavolo nero with the pheasant slices and sprinkle over some fresh coriander.

» 366 calories for 4 servings, 183 for 8

More on » oranges *p49* » lemons *p346* » coriander *p204* » coconut oil *p309* » onions *p281* » garlic *p82* » chillies *p93* » ginger *p200* » olive oil *p193* » tamari soy sauce *p97*

Pheasant is a good source of **protein**. It's raised in the wild, spending its days – like a free-range chicken – foraging seeds, berries and bugs. Pheasant is a very lean meat, with high levels of selenium, which supports a healthy thyroid; it also plays a part in boosting the immune system, and it may reduce the risk of cancer. Pheasant also provides vitamin B6, iron and zinc, and is a good source of magnesium, which is essential for stress management.

Venison and pickled pear salad

Living partly on the west coast of Scotland, I was brought up on venison and love it, the healthiest of all red meats. The deer spend all their time on the hill, and even if the venison is farmed, they are hugely active. That makes venison very lean, but it can also be tough. You don't have to use the tenderest fillet for this salad, but it is a good idea to marinate the meat first. This softens the muscle fibres and makes it more succulent. Submerge the steaks in a covering of white wine, with a tablespoon of crushed juniper berries, some crushed garlic and a tablespoon of olive oil and leave for one to two days in the fridge.

For 2 as a main course, 4 as a starter:
2 venison steaks (about 250g in total)
Sea salt and black pepper
1–2 tbsp cold-pressed rapeseed oil
50g cobnuts or hazelnuts
150g mixed salad leaves (such as rocket, watercress and red chicory), washed and dried

For the pears and marinade
60ml organic apple cider vinegar
1 cinnamon stick
50g coconut palm sugar
1 tbsp coriander seeds
2 star anise
1 tsp black peppercorns
1–2 pears (depending on plumpness), peeled and cored

For the dressing
2 tbsp aged balsamic vinegar
2 tbsp extra virgin olive oil
4 sprigs of thyme, leaves picked

Put all the marinade ingredients – apart from the pears! – into a pan with 100ml water, and bring to a gentle simmer. Stir until the sugar has dissolved.

Cut the pears into 12 slices and put them in a heatproof dish. Pour the hot marinade through a sieve over them and leave for 20 minutes. Discard the spices or put aside to decorate the salad.

Generously season the venison steaks with plenty of black pepper and some salt. Heat the rapeseed oil in a large frying pan. Place the steaks in the pan and cook for 5–7 minutes on each side, depending on their thickness and how rare you like your venison. Remove from the pan and leave to rest in a warm place.

Combine the dressing ingredients and add a couple of tablespoons of the pear marinade to the dressing to sweeten it.

In a frying pan, dry-fry the cobnuts (or hazelnuts) until golden brown and then coarsely chop.

Divide the salad leaves between the plates. Toss with a little dressing. Drain the pears and divide equally between the plates.

Cut the venison into thick slices and place a few slices on each plate. Scatter with the nuts and drizzle with the remaining dressing.

» 741 calories for 2 servings, 370 for 4

More on » venison p240 » rapeseed oil p248 » hazelnuts p50 » rocket p122 » watercress p70 » apple cider vinegar p63 » cinnamon p22 » coconut palm sugar p316 » coriander p204 » pears p162 » balsamic vinegar p189 » olive oil p193

Perry pears with Parma ham and goats' cheese

This is a sweet and sour salad that looks great on the plate, and is ideal for when you're feeding lots of people. The pears, Parma ham and walnuts can be cooked in advance, and then it's nice and quick to assemble. It's worth knowing that lean Parma ham has about a third of the calories of bacon, and contains less salt. Goats' cheese has a third of the calories of full-fat blue cheese, and pears are low-calorie as well as high in fibre.

For 4 as a substantial starter:
8 slices of Parma ham
4 handfuls of mixed salad leaves and herbs
50g walnut halves, dry-fried
200g soft goats' cheese
Borage flowers (optional)

For the spiced pears
4 pears, peeled but stalks left on, with a small slice removed from their base so they can stand upright
1 litre perry or pear cider
6 cloves
1 cinnamon stick
8 cardamom pods
Small sprig of rosemary
2 tbsp clear honey

For the dressing
1 tsp Dijon mustard
Juice of ½ lemon
5 tbsp extra virgin olive oil
1 tbsp flaxseed oil
5 sprigs of mint, leaves coarsely chopped
Pear juice from above
Sea salt and black pepper

Preheat the oven to 180°C/gas mark 4. Put the pears, cider, spices, rosemary and honey into a heavy-based pan and bring up to the boil. Turn down the heat, put on a lid and simmer gently for 20–30 minutes (depending on the size and ripeness of the pears). The pears should be tender all the way through when pierced with a thin skewer.

Meanwhile, lay the Parma ham slices on a lightly oiled wire rack on a baking tray and roast until golden and crisp, about 3–4 minutes. Keep a close eye on this, as the ham tastes horrid even slightly burnt. Put to one side.

Allow the pears to cool in their juice. Remove them, sieve the juice, then pour it back into the pan and reduce until you have 75ml liquid left. Pour this into a small mixing bowl and put to one side.

To serve, put a handful of salad leaves on each plate, place a pear in the centre of each and share out the Parma ham, walnut halves and goats' cheese between the four plates. To make the dressing, add the Dijon mustard, lemon juice, oils and mint to the reduced pear juice and whisk. Season with salt and black pepper and drizzle the dressing over the pears and salad leaves. Dot each plate with a few borage flowers, if using.

» 752 calories per serving

More on » walnuts p51 » goats' cheese p268 » cinnamon p22 » honey p334 » lemons p346 » olive oil p193 » flaxseed oil p153 » mint p326

Pears are naturally sweet, yet have a low **Glycaemic Index**. They are low in calories as well as high in **fibre**, which supports healthy blood-sugar levels and digestive health. They are a good source of potassium, containing around 200mg, and one medium pear has a hefty 5g of fibre (about a fifth of our daily requirement), as well as eye-supporting lutein and zeaxanthin. The skin of pears contains three to four times the levels of **antioxidants**, anti-inflammatory **flavonoids** and anti-cancer **phytonutrients** as the flesh, and 50 per cent of the fruit's dietary fibre. Pears are often found to have significant chemical residue when conventionally grown, so you'll need to peel them or buy organic.

Gomashio

Gomashio is a combination of ground sesame seeds and salt and has been used for centuries in Japan as a flavouring. 'Goma' means sesame and 'shio' means salt. With a lower sodium content than usual salt it has the added goodness which comes with sesame seeds. The ratio of sesame seeds to salt varies between 5:1 to 15:1. It's in about a 12:1 proportion that I like it best, but play around with the concentrations. You can experiment by adding different flavours and spices to your gomashio to inject interesting tastes to everyday meals.

For 1 x 150ml jar:
10g flaky sea salt
125g white sesame seeds

In a frying pan, heat the salt until it turns grey and then pour it into a mortar. In the same frying pan, add the sesame seeds and cook until they begin to turn a shade darker – about 2–3 minutes. Be careful not to let them burn. Add the seeds to the mortar with the salt and pound with the pestle until they have broken down. You can use a food processor but be careful not to blitz them too far or you will end up with tahini!

» 16 calories per teaspoon, 48 per tablespoon

Sesame seeds The **antioxidant** compounds and other nutrients found in sesame seeds – white or black – are good for our circulatory system. Black seeds have not been hulled, whereas white sesame seeds have had their protective casing removed. Sesame seeds contain a particular range of **amino acids** that are often lacking in a vegetarian diet, and are rich in **minerals**, including calcium, iron, magnesium, copper, phosphorus and manganese, as well as vitamin B1. They are also a good source of **phytosterols**, which have many therapeutic effects, including helping lower **cholesterol**. Black sesame seeds are reputed to help keep hair healthy and dark.

Dulse-flavoured gomashio

Dulse is a strong-tasting seaweed with an iron-rich flavour. This gomashio is delicious with baked mushrooms, roast tomatoes and any fish, including squid.

For 1 x 150ml jar:
10g flaky sea salt
125g mix of white and black sesame seeds
5g dried flaked dulse

Follow the method to the left, adding the flaked dulse once the gomashio is ready and mixing it in well before pouring into a jar.

» 16 calories per teaspoon, 48 per tablespoon

More on » seaweeds *p174*

Spicy orange gomashio

This gomashio is delicious with baked fennel and almost any fish, as well as in a vegetable stir-fry.

For 1 x 150ml jar:
10g flaky sea salt
Finely grated zest of 2 oranges
125g mix of white and black sesame seeds
½ tsp chilli powder
1 tsp cumin seeds

In a frying pan, heat the salt until it turns grey. Place in a mortar. In the same frying pan, add the orange zest and dry-fry for 3–4 minutes until it has dried out. Add to the salt. Add the seeds and spices to the pan and cook until they begin to turn a shade darker, about 2–3 minutes. Be careful not to let them burn. Add to the mortar and pound with a pestle until broken down, or blitz them in a food processor (but take care not to blitz too far).

» 16 calories per teaspoon, 48 per tablespoon

More on » oranges *p49*

Small shared plates

THERE ARE FOUR or five places around the world where people regularly live to over a hundred, and they do so while remaining fit and healthy. In Crete, Sardinia, the Okinawa Islands of Japan and the south coast of Nova Scotia, they expect to live to see not only their grandchildren, but their great-grandchildren. In more industrialised societies, dementia, depression, disabling cardiovascular disease and cancer are the banes of our elderly population, but all of these conditions are rare in these long-lived communities.

What can we do to be more like them? We all know that regular exercise, as well as what we eat and drink, is important for a long and healthy life. Genetics and climate also seem to play their part, but there's another repeated theme in the longevity studies of these communities – and that's how they eat, as well as what's on their plate.

They don't eat alone. They share food, often from a row of dishes laid down the centre of the table. Everyone helps themselves, a little at a time, chatting as they eat over several hours. This may not be every day, but it's a regular practice. A family feast will be prepared on a Saturday and eaten on a Sunday. It will often consist of lots of simple plates, which the family will then continue to eat through much of the rest of the week. These parts of the world provide lots of recipe inspiration.

There's some science on this too. Research in Sardinia has repeatedly found that families embedded in powerful social networks, expressed through the tradition of weekly multi-generational meals, tend to live longer. Recipes like the Squash caponata on page 186 come from there. There are also plenty of recipes for shared plates from the two Greek islands where I've spent lots of time – Crete and Hydra. In both these places, regular eating with extended family is the norm.

Research in Japan has also found this to be true. On the Okinawa Islands, the habit of sharing food – and not too much of it – contributes to long and healthy lives. The longevity of the Okinawans is notably different from other Japanese communities, even close-by, who don't eat together and don't live as long.

It looks like a positive feedback loop. If you share food with the people around you, then the sort of food you'll want to make is the kind of food you will enjoy sharing. What you eat becomes the driver of your sociability. And so your sense of belonging becomes bound up with the sense of your own worth: you're not an old and insignificant person, but a respected part of a community, connected to people who like and admire you and whom you like and admire in return. Food is the mortar of this civilisation.

This is obviously only part of the secret to longevity, but it's a message we can all learn from. You can eat as many antioxidants as you like and know everything there is to know about nutritional science, but that's not the whole story. Sharing a plate of food is one of the keys to a good, long life.

So what are the guidelines for small shared plates?

» It's a given that what we're providing is healthy and delicious, using the most nutritious ingredients, cooked in the best ways.

» Pulses and nuts are good to have plenty of and often, and they suit small shared plates.

» Then of course there are vegetables – we just cannot get enough of those. There are several recipes containing all three of these food groups here; these healthy and tasty dishes can make a light lunch on their own, while others can be combined to make more of a feast. There are several types of hummus and a good range of vegetable-based dips, too.

» After these groups of ingredients, next in priority comes fish and shellfish: squid, cockles and mussels are ideal for small shared plates.

» Start with smaller snacky things served with a drink – perhaps home-made vegetable crisps or flavoured popcorn. Follow with a collection of small plates – mezzes, hors d'oeuvres, tapas – whatever you want to call them. Select three or four small plates, or if there are a number of people eating, and you have more time for cooking, double that. There are lots of recipes here to get the ball rolling.

» Have a big cook-up at the weekend so you have plenty of leftovers for the following week. This sort of batch cooking is typically Mediterranean and it's efficient. Most dishes here will keep in the fridge for a few days, and many of them are even better on the second or third day.

So get on the phone and make a plan to share a meal with some friends, a mcal made up of several small and delicious plates. That's a social and healthy way to eat.

Spiced roasted chickpeas

Roasted chickpeas have a great texture and taste and make an excellent snack, much healthier than the standard packet of crisps. They're quick and easy to toast and, spiced-up, they're partyish enough to feed lots of people. Rich in protein and low in fat, these are also good for having in your bag for when you're on the move.

For 10–15:
500g dried chickpeas, soaked overnight, rinsed, cooked and drained, or 2 x 400g tins, drained and rinsed
1 tsp cumin seeds, dry-fried and ground
1 tsp coriander seeds, dry-fried and ground
Seeds from 15 cardamom pods
Light dusting of paprika
Light dusting of ground turmeric
Sea salt and black pepper
1 tbsp cold-pressed rapeseed oil
Large sprig of rosemary, leaves chopped

Preheat the oven to 180°C/gas mark 4. Put the chickpeas into a roasting tin, add the spices, seasoning, oil and rosemary and toss together, mixing well. Spread them out in a single layer and roast for about 40–45 minutes, stirring halfway through their cooking time, until they become crisp. These store in an airtight container for a week or more.

» 86 calories for 10 servings, 58 for 15

More on » chickpeas *p182* » coriander *p204*
» turmeric *p87* » rapeseed oil *p248*

Brazil nuts are the highest natural source of the **mineral** selenium, an **antioxidant** needed for healthy thyroid function, and also thought to protect against some cancers. British and Irish soils are very low in selenium – as is the produce grown in them – so having a boost is a good idea, and one or two nuts a day is all we need (ideally from Brazil, as there are high levels of selenium in the soil there).

Spiced nuts and seeds

These are jazzed-up nuts and seeds, for serving with a drink, or for spooning into a jam jar for snacking when you're out and about. Use a mix of nuts, including Brazil nuts. Nuts are expensive, so we tend to keep them too long. It's best to buy small amounts regularly from a good source and store in a cool dark place in an airtight jar or packet. Eat them within a month, or even sooner if they aren't whole, or you can freeze them. Play around with the flavours to see which you like best, using ground coriander, fennel seeds, celery salt and tamari soy sauce (instead of Worcestershire sauce here), and swap things about a bit.

For 450g:
450g mixed nuts and seeds, 50/50 (e.g. sunflower and pumpkin seeds, Brazil nuts, walnuts and almonds)
20g organic unsalted butter
½–1 tsp smoked paprika or cayenne pepper
1 tsp ground cumin
1 tbsp Worcestershire sauce
Sea salt

Preheat the oven to 190°C/gas mark 5. If using Brazil nuts, roughly chop some of them first.

Gently heat the butter in a heavy-based pan. Add the nuts and seeds, half the paprika (or cayenne), cumin and Worcestershire sauce. Cook over a moderate heat for a minute or so, and then tip everything into a baking tray in a single, well-spaced layer. Bake for about 12–15 minutes, until just beginning to brown.

Pour onto a thick layer of kitchen paper and then toss into a bowl with the remaining paprika or cayenne and salt to taste. Allow to cool. These store in an airtight container for a month or more.

» 178 calories per 30g serving

More on » pumpkin seeds *p105* » walnuts *p51*
» almonds *p347* » butter *p104*

Sushi popcorn

Popcorn is an excellent fat-free snack, ideal as a substitute for crisps – crunchy and satisfying. It is best to pop the corn in a non-stick pan. The intense heat needed for the popping converts sunflower and olive oils into unhealthy transfats, so cook the corn oil-free and add the oil and other flavours afterwards. The corn is lighter once popped, with 30g kernels yielding 20g of popped corn – but you only need to know that if you want to make a big batch and then dress it with several different flavours. You can also buy plain, pre-popped corn and then flavour it, and you can now buy giant kernel mushroom corn, as well as the standard.

I love all these popcorn flavours, especially the sushi and truffle versions. Anything flavoured with a fruity olive oil has to be good news too; and that's also true of fragrant basil. If you fancy a sweet variety, go for the fennel and honey.

For 1 large bowl, for 3–4:
30g popcorn kernels, or 20g popped corn
20g wasabi peas, plus a handful to serve
2 sheets of nori seaweed
7g fresh root ginger, peeled
1 tsp Thai fish sauce
1 tsp tamari soy sauce

Put the unpopped corn in a non-stick pan with a lid, over a medium heat. As soon as the corn starts to pop, shake it around busily, on and off the heat, for a minute or two until the popping has stopped.

In a food processor, blitz the wasabi peas, nori and ginger until you get a fine sushi mixture.

Pour the sushi mixture on to the popped corn. Add the fish sauce and tamari. Stir gently to coat and taste. Add a little more sauce if needed.

Add the extra wasabi peas and serve. This has to be eaten within a few hours, or it begins to go soft.

» 122 calories for 3 servings, 92 for 4

More on » seaweeds *p174* » ginger *p200* » tamari soy sauce *p97*

Variations
Truffle popcorn The earthy taste of dried flaked dulse seaweed goes brilliantly with truffles. Truffle-flavoured salt is also a good addition. Pop the corn as instructed left, then add 1 tablespoon truffle oil. Finely blitz 10g of dried porcini mushrooms with a pinch of dulse (or salt) and mix in well. Decorate with a slice or two of dried porcini to indicate the flavour.
» 93 calories for 3 servings, 70 for 4
Olive oil and sea salt popcorn Pop the corn as instructed left, then pour into a bowl. While still warm, add a drizzle of extra virgin olive oil and some flaky sea salt and mix well.
» 83 calories for 3 servings, 62 for 4
Basil and lime popcorn Pop the corn as instructed left, then in a food processor blitz a bunch of basil with the zest of 1 lime and a teaspoon of clear honey. Add to the popcorn and mix well.
» 46 calories for 3 servings, 35 for 4
Spiced fennel and honey popcorn Pop the corn as instructed left, then add ½ teaspoon each of dry-fried fennel and cumin seeds, a pinch of chilli flakes and a pinch of ground cinnamon. Drizzle over 2 teaspoons warm clear honey and mix well.
» 54 calories for 3 servings, 41 for 4

Small shared plates

Seaweed and vinegar kale crisps

There are so many ways of cooking kale crisps, and over the years we've tried them all at Perch Hill. This is the easiest, and the result is light and crispy. Rather than using an intense burst of heat, the kale is baked gently, so that many of the leaf's active compounds are left intact; and it lessens the danger of burning, which is oh-so-easy in a hot oven. Unlike with frying, it is healthy to use olive – not rapeseed – oil here, as the kale is baked so gently the oil will not reach its smoke point and convert to unhealthy transfats.

Use nutrient-rich seaweed instead of salt for flavour. Eat as a snack, or make slightly larger crisps and serve with hummus, using the crisps as scoops. I also like kale crisps scattered on the top of a smooth soup to add some crunch.

For 4 as a snack:
200g kale (any variety)
2 tbsp extra virgin olive oil
1 tbsp aged balsamic or sherry vinegar
½ tbsp dried flaked dulse seaweed

Preheat the oven to its lowest setting, usually 110°C/gas mark ¼.

De-rib the kale and tear the leaves into rough pieces. Wash, then dry thoroughly using a salad spinner. Put the kale into a large bowl, add the olive oil and massage it into the leaves for a minute so the leaves begin to soften. Add the vinegar and the flaked seaweed, and mix well with your hands.

Spread the kale in a single, non-overlapping layer on two baking trays lined with silicone sheets or baking parchment to prevent it sticking (or shake the trays a couple of times during cooking).

Bake in the oven for 25–30 minutes, swapping the trays from top to bottom after 15 minutes and checking after 25 minutes as to whether it has crunched up. (If you have a range cooker or Aga, cook it overnight in the coolest part of the oven.)

Remove from the oven and leave until almost cool before serving in bowls. The crisps store in an airtight container for three to four days.

» 89 calories per serving

More on » kale *p117* » olive oil *p193* » balsamic vinegar *p189*

Variations
Salt and vinegar kale crisps Massage the olive oil into the kale as instructed left and then use ½ teaspoon ground pink Himalayan salt with the vinegar instead of dulse. Bake as left.
» 87 calories per serving
Spicy oriental kale crisps Massage the olive oil into the kale as instructed left. Blitz 1 deseeded red chilli, 2 garlic cloves, 1 tablespoon each of sliced fresh root ginger, honey and tamari soy sauce in a food processor with 1 tablespoon water. Then mix well with the kale leaves. Bake as left. Toast 2 tablespoons sesame seeds and finish with a scattering of these.
» 138 calories per serving

Seaweeds such as wakame, dulse, kombu and nori are becoming increasingly popular, as they are low in calories and super-rich in **minerals** and **antioxidants**. When I say rich, I mean rich – with minerals such as iron and copper at higher levels than many other sources, including certain meats and spinach. They can provide minerals that are often absent in our drinking water and food crops grown on mineral-depleted soils – key among these is iodine, which is essential for our metabolism and a healthy functioning thyroid. They are also intensely flavoured and delicious, renowned (along with miso and certain mushrooms and fungi) to be one of the best sources of the fashionable umami flavour.

Small shared plates

Smoky sweet potato crisps

Most root vegetable crisps are very calorific because they're deep-fried, but not these ones. Sliced super-thin with a mandolin (or very sharp vegetable peeler), and baked in a medium oven, they need no fat at all. That makes these veg crisps super-healthy and low-calorie. Bake individual batches of sweet potato, parsnip and beetroot crisps and then mix them up. They are great for a party, either on their own, or dipped into the coriander hummus on page 182. Sweet potatoes have such great flavour, they hardly need adding to. As with all these crisps, large roots are good to use.

For 4:
1 sweet potato
1 tsp smoked paprika

Preheat the oven to 180°C/gas mark 4.

Wash the potato thoroughly, but do not peel it, and dry. (The skin contains a lot of the vitamins and minerals and tastes good.)

On the thinnest setting on the mandolin, slice the potato vertically.

Lay the slices on baking trays lined with baking parchment. Spread them out so that they're not overlapping. You may need to do them in a couple of batches. Sprinkle over the paprika.

Bake for 15–20 minutes until curled up and turning a few shades darker. They will become crisper as they cool.

The crisps will last a couple of days stored in an airtight container, and can be re-crisped by putting in a hot oven for a few minutes.

» 56 calories per serving

More on » sweet potato p72

Beetroot and thyme crisps

For the beetroot crisps, just add thyme. These are packed with flavour, super-low in calories and very good for you!

For 4:
1 large beetroot
Sprig of thyme, leaves finely chopped

Scrub the beetroot and dry. If the beetroot is young, fresh and organic, there's no need to peel. On the thinnest setting on the mandolin, slice the beetroot into circles.

Arrange the circles on lined baking sheets, sprinkle with the thyme leaves, and then bake for about 15–20 minutes as described left.

» 9 calories per serving

More on » beetroot p85

Cheesy parsnip crisps

These are flavoured with nutritional yeast flakes, which give a cheesy taste.

For 4:
1 parsnip
1 tbsp nutritional yeast flakes

Scrub the parsnip and dry. If organic, there's no need to peel. On the thinnest setting on the mandolin, slice the parsnip lengthways until you reach the woody core which you can discard.

Arrange the slices on lined baking sheets, sprinkle with the nutritional yeast and then bake for 15–20 minutes as described left.

» 34 calories per serving

Tomato crisps

These are good news: crisps which are genuinely good for us, and sweet and intensely flavoured. The valuable antioxidants in tomatoes are fat-soluble, so the crisps are cooked very slowly and then drizzled with a little bit of extra virgin olive oil before serving. Leave the skin on, as this has the highest nutrient content.

You have to have the oven on low for ages to do these, so make a decent-sized batch, as here, or even double it. These crisps are perfect, healthy snack food for parties, and they're also delicious in salads and scattered over soups.

For 12:
20 firm tomatoes
Sea salt
Bunch of thyme, leaves finely chopped
A little extra virgin olive oil for drizzling, plus 5 tbsp for storing (optional)

Cut the tomatoes in half. Cut each half into quarters. Place on a baking sheet.

Sprinkle the tomatoes with salt and most of the thyme and let them sit for 15 minutes.

Pat the tomatoes with kitchen paper to soak up any moisture. Then cook the crisps using a conventional oven (or a range cooker), a microwave or a dehydrator, as outlined below.

Once cooked, drizzle with a little olive oil to serve. If not eaten straightaway, store in the 5 tbsp of oil in the fridge and eat within a week. You can then use the delicious tomato-flavoured oil for salad dressings.

Oven
Line a flat baking sheet with greaseproof paper and lay the tomatoes out, not overlapping, scattering the remaining thyme leaves over the top.

Cook for 3 hours at 110°C/gas mark ¼ and then carefully turn the quarters over. Cook for a further 3–4 hours until completely dry and crisp. An Aga (coolest oven, overnight) is perfect for this.

Microwave
Spray a flat, microwaveable plate with olive oil spray. Arrange the tomatoes on the plate, scatter with the remaining thyme leaves and spray with olive oil spray.

Microwave for 5 minutes on the lowest setting. Remove the plate from the microwave, carefully flip the tomatoes and microwave for another minute. Take the tomatoes out and put on a cooling rack.

Dehydrator
Lay the tomatoes out on a dehydrator tray, not overlapping, then scatter the remaining thyme leaves over the top.

Set the dehydrator temperature to 60°C. Leave for 10–12 hours until the tomatoes are crisp and completely dry.

» Without oil, 27 calories per serving

More on » tomatoes *p142* » olive oil *p193*

Small shared plates

Marinated olives

You can just put a bowl of olives on the table – they'll go well with many of these shared plates – but dressing them up like this makes olives fit for a feast. Take care to buy traditionally cured olives rather than the tasteless ones you get in brine. The texture and depth of flavour are incomparable.

For 12–15:
500g large, plump green or black olives, stones in
2 garlic cloves, very finely chopped
2 large shallots, very finely chopped
2 celery sticks, very finely chopped
50ml extra virgin olive oil
30ml organic apple cider vinegar
Pinch of dried chilli flakes (optional)
Grated zest of 1 lemon
Juice of ½ lemon
2 tbsp finely chopped basil leaves
1 tbsp finely chopped chives
1 tbsp finely chopped oregano or marjoram
1 tsp clear honey
Sea salt and black pepper

Mix all the ingredients together in a bowl and stir thoroughly. Cover and leave in the fridge for two days.

Take out of the fridge a couple of hours before serving – olives are always best served at room temperature – and give another good stir.

These olives store well in the fridge for weeks.

» 93 calories for 12 servings, 74 for 15

More on » garlic p82 » olive oil p193 » apple cider vinegar p63 » lemons p346 » honey p334

Olives Many of the health advantages of the Mediterranean diet have been attributed to olives and their oil (see page 193). These therapeutic benefits include reducing the risk of coronary heart disease, prevention of cancers (breast and stomach in particular), and support for the immune system and **inflammatory** responses. The **phytonutrients** in olives also have the potential to prevent bone loss and therefore decrease the risk of osteoporosis.

When first picked from the tree, olives are inedible, containing very bitter compounds that have to be removed by soaking and curing. This traditional **fermentation** of olives is a slow process that produces a healthy food with beneficial active cultures. But a cheaper and much quicker way of making olives edible is to soak them in a lye bath to remove the bitterness and then pack them with salt. These are rubbery in texture and have no depth of flavour, so avoid 'processed' olives, choosing 'oil-cured', 'brine-cured', 'water-cured' or 'dry-salted' instead. You'll also be able to tell which is which by their price. Good-quality olives often have stones left in, so don't let this put you off, as often these are the best and tastiest.

Kale and pumpkin seed pesto

Three superfoods – pistachios, kale and pumpkin seeds – together make a delicious and brilliant green pesto. Serve it as one of your dips with smoky sweet potato or mixed vegetable crisps (see pages 174–8), or with home-made bread, or use it as a topping for chicken breast before it's roasted (just spread it on in a thin layer). For a super-healthy lunch or dinner, I love this stirred through spiralised courgette noodles. You can also thin it down with a squeeze of lemon juice and splash of extra virgin olive oil for a delicious dressing.

For 4–6 mezze-sized servings:
50g kale, stalks removed
Large bunch of basil (about 60g), leaves only
50g pistachio kernels, dry-fried
50g pumpkin seeds, dry-fried
Grated zest and juice of ½ lemon
1 small garlic clove
50ml olive oil
Good pinch of sea salt
1 heaped tbsp nutritional yeast flakes (optional)

Place all the ingredients in a food processor and blitz to a smooth paste.

» 257 calories for 4 servings, 171 for 6

More on » kale *p117* » pumpkin seeds *p105* » lemons *p346* » garlic *p82* » olive oil *p193*

Super-nutritious tzatziki

You can't serve a selection of healthy mezzes without including tzatziki. It's a very common recipe, but it's done slightly differently here, always bearing nutrition in mind. Traditionally you'd bleed the cucumber with a heavy dose of salt, but cucumber juices are very nutritious, and salt – in this sort of quantity – is not ideal, so just skip this stage. Instead, strain your yoghurt to make it rich and creamy, with a better flavour. The cucumber skin especially supplies lots of goodness, so leave this on when you grate. Dill is often used (rather than mint in the summer) for tzatziki in Greece.

For 4–6 mezze-sized servings:
400g live natural yoghurt (see p44)
30g bunch of dill or mint, finely chopped
½ cucumber
1 garlic clove, finely chopped (or 2 if you like strong tzatziki)
2 tbsp extra virgin olive oil
Sea salt and black pepper

Whizz the yoghurt briefly with the chopped dill or mint, or just mix well. Leave to stand for an hour for the flavours to infuse.

Line a sieve with muslin or a double thickness of kitchen paper and spoon in the dill- or mint-flavoured yoghurt. Leave it to drain over a bowl in the fridge for at least 6 hours, but ideally overnight, to effectively make a dill- or mint-flavoured labneh.

Grate the cucumber. Mix this into the labneh along with the garlic and olive oil. Season to taste with salt and pepper.

» 121 calories for 4 servings, 81 for 6

More on » yoghurt *p44* » mint *p326* » cucumber *p148* » garlic *p82* » olive oil *p193*

The best-ever hummus

Hummus makes a perfect lunch or snack, dipped into with celery sticks, slices of a crunchy apple, carrot batons, chicory, or the leaves from the heart of a Cos lettuce, and it's ideal shared food. This variation of Yotam Ottolenghi's hummus recipe from *Jerusalem* is silky smooth, tahini-rich and utterly delicious. We often use it as a starting point for lunches in the cookery school and then add different flavours such as fresh coriander (see right). Tahini is made from hulled sesame seeds, so is a bit more refined, with less fibre than straight sesame seeds, but with the chickpeas, this hummus is still full of goodness. Yotam recommends Arabic tahini (in preference to Greek) as it is runnier, smoother and easier to spoon.

For 4–6 mezze-sized servings:
400g tin of chickpeas, drained
2 garlic cloves, chopped
4 tbsp tahini
Grated zest and juice of 1 lemon
50ml ice-cold water
½ tsp sea salt (to taste)
Drizzle of extra virgin olive oil

Put the chickpeas into a food processor with the garlic. Blitz to a coarse paste. Add the tahini, lemon zest and juice and blitz for 2 minutes.

Slowly trickle in the water over 3–4 minutes, and then leave the processor going for another 2–3 minutes until the mixture is silken in texture.

Add the salt to taste, spoon into your serving dish, and drizzle over the extra virgin olive oil.

» 212 calories for 4 servings, 141 for 6

More on » garlic *p82* » tahini *p184* » lemons *p346* » olive oil *p193*

Coriander hummus and yoghurt dip

A fragrant, coriander-rich hummus which is made a little runnier than a traditional recipe, so is an ideal dip. It's perfect for serving with a selection of raw, organic veg: sugarsnap peas, young carrots, sliced kalettes (flower sprouts), young fennel bulb, chunks of apple, slivers of raw beetroot, or mixed root vegetable crisps (see pages 174–8).

For 4–6 mezze-sized servings:
1 tbsp coriander seeds
25g coriander, leaves and stalks
200g live natural yoghurt (see p44)
½ recipe The best-ever hummus (see left)

Dry-fry the coriander seeds in a pan until fragrant and popping, then lightly crush in a pestle and mortar.

Put the fresh coriander into a food processor with the yoghurt, hummus and crushed coriander seeds. Blitz until combined.

Serve at room temperature.

» 154 calories for 4 servings, 103 for 6

More on » coriander *p204* » yoghurt *p44*

Chickpeas UK cancer and heart health organisations advise us to eat pulses several times a week, and chickpeas are among the best. Rich in **protein** and nutrients, they contain plenty of **fibre** and are low in fat. They also have useful levels of iron, magnesium and folate, whilst being very low in calories. When you combine them with a good quantity of vegetables, you get an extremely healthy meal. Chickpeas – along with other pulses including lentils, adzuki, black and borlotti beans – are an ideal part of our diet.

Small shared plates

Roast carrot and cumin hummus

The sweetness of the carrots, with the tangy, warm flavour of roasted cumin, makes for a delicious hummus. The carrots up the nutrition of an already healthy dip and although the carrots contain quite a bit of sugar, the chickpeas are high in fibre, so lessen the impact of the sugar hit.

For 4–6 mezze-sized servings:
500g organic carrots
1 tbsp olive oil
1 tsp cumin seeds
½ recipe The best-ever hummus (see left)
Sea salt

Preheat the oven to 180°C/gas mark 4.

If they are organic, don't bother to peel the carrots. Cut them into 3cm chunks. Place on a baking tray, drizzle with the olive oil and scatter with the cumin seeds.

Roast for 30–40 minutes until the carrot has softened and is beginning to blacken at the edges. Leave to cool.

Put the cooled roasted carrots and their juices from the baking tray into a food processor and add the hummus. Blitz to combine and season with a little salt to taste.

» 185 calories for 4 servings, 124 for 6

More on » carrots *p121* » olive oil *p193*

Cashew hummus

I first had this on a raw-food retreat, and I've made it regularly ever since: it's super-nutritious with the raw cashews and sesame seeds (in the tahini). It is lighter in texture than a standard chickpea hummus, very creamy and delicious. If you use thick Greek tahini, you may need to add a little more water, or some extra virgin olive oil, to get the right texture. Cashews have a lower fat content than other nuts, but this hummus is still more calorific than one made with chickpeas.

For 4–6 mezze-sized servings:
200g raw cashew nuts
2 tbsp tahini
Juice of 2 lemons
2 garlic cloves, crushed
Pinch of sea salt
1 tsp ground cumin
Pinch cayenne pepper
Extra virgin olive oil (optional)
Chopped parsley, to garnish (optional)

Soak the cashews in a bowl of water for at least 3 hours or overnight. Soaking activates enzymes in the nuts, making the nutritional components easier to digest.

Purée all the ingredients in a food processor until well blended. You may want to add 2 tablespoons of water or extra virgin olive oil, little by little, until the hummus reaches the consistency you like.

Sprinkle the top with freshly chopped parsley before serving if you like.

» 354 calories for 4 servings, 236 for 6

More on » tahini *p184* » lemons *p346* » garlic *p82* » olive oil *p193* » parsley *p136*

Baba ghanoush

It's the smoking of the aubergines in a flame, or under a grill, that gives the distinct taste to baba ghanoush, and you want to leave as much of the aubergines' skin on as possible when you purée it. Apart from the smoky flavour, the skin contains the highest level of antioxidants. Serve with a mix of raw veg, some toasted pitta, garlic flatbreads or as here, with toasted Seeded spelt bread (see page 33) and a tomato and basil or parsley salad.

For 4–6 mezze-sized servings:
2 large aubergines
2 tbsp tahini, plus extra to taste
Juice of 1 lemon, plus extra to taste
1 tbsp aged balsamic vinegar
2 tbsp extra virgin olive oil
1 tbsp cumin seeds, dry-fried and ground in a pestle
      and mortar
Sea salt
4 tbsp black olives, such as Kalamata, stoned
      and chopped

To serve
Sprig of thyme, leaves stripped
Seeds from ½ pomegranate (see p46, optional)

Preheat the oven to 190°C/gas mark 5, and turn on the grill, or light a gas flame on the hob, or your barbecue.

Prick the aubergines with a fork in several places and place on the grill rack 10–13cm from the grill (or place near the gas flame of the hob or on a barbecue). Cook, turning frequently, until the skin blackens and blisters, and the flesh just begins to feel soft. This takes about 10–15 minutes.

Transfer the aubergines to a baking sheet and roast for 15–20 minutes in the preheated oven until they are very soft.

Remove the aubergines from the oven, let cool slightly, and remove the most charred bits of the skin. Roughly chop the aubergines, then put into a sieve and leave to drain for 30 minutes.

Place the aubergines in a bowl and, using a fork, mash to a paste. Or blitz very briefly in a food processor, then remove to a bowl. Add the tahini, lemon juice, vinegar, 1 tablespoon of the oil and the cumin seeds and mix well. Season with salt, then taste and add more tahini and/or lemon juice if needed.

Mix in the olives, then drizzle the remaining olive oil over the top. Sprinkle with the thyme leaves and pomegranate seeds (if using). Serve not fridge-cold, but at room temperature.

» 195 calories for 4 servings, 130 for 6

More on » aubergines *p147* » lemons *p346*
» balsamic vinegar *p189* » olive oil *p193* » olives
p179 » pomegranate *p46*

Tahini is simply a purée of sesame seeds (see page 164) and so contains the same **antioxidant** compounds and other nutrients which are particularly beneficial to our circulatory system. It is also rich in **minerals** such as calcium, iron, magnesium and copper. The purée is usually made from hulled sesame seeds and is therefore a more refined product – with less **fibre** – than straight sesame seeds. It's still full of goodness, and adding tahini to dishes such as hummus will boost its levels of **micronutrients**.

Squash caponata

Caponata is most often made with aubergines, and that's delicious, but I love the richness of this squash version. Caponata is a sweet and sour dish from Sicily, but here raisins replace the traditional sugar, giving the all-important contrast to the sharpness of the vinegar and capers. Sometimes the Sicilians add chocolate to caponata. This adds a depth of flavour. The vinegar preserves the mix of fruit and veg, so it can be kept in a jar in the fridge for at least two weeks.

Serve with hummus (in the photograph here it's hummus with a bit of mashed beetroot added), Baba ghanoush and/or Sun-dried tomato tapenade with Swedish crispbread (see pages 182–3, 184, 189 and 32), some toasted pitta or Wholemeal sesame flatbreads (see page 189).

For 4–6 mezze-sized servings:
700g butternut or onion squash (both have thin and delicious skin, so won't need peeling)
A little cold-pressed rapeseed oil
1 onion, finely chopped
2 garlic cloves, chopped
75ml red wine vinegar
400g tin of chopped tomatoes
25g raisins
12–15 black olives, stoned and roughly chopped
2 tbsp capers
1 tbsp unsweetened cocoa powder or grated dark chocolate, at least 70% cocoa solids (optional)
Bunch of soft green herbs (parsley, chervil, chives), coarsely chopped
Sea salt and black pepper

Preheat the oven to 180°C/gas mark 4.

Cut the squash in two and remove the seeds. Dice the squash – skin and all – into 2–3cm cubes. Roast it in the preheated oven with a little oil for 30 minutes until the flesh is soft and the edges start to char. Remove from the oven.

In a saucepan, sweat the onion and garlic in a little oil until soft and then increase the heat slightly and add the vinegar. Simmer until the vinegar has almost bubbled away. Add the tomatoes, raisins, olives, capers and chocolate (if using). Cook gently for 15–20 minutes until the mixture becomes thick and rich. Add the squash and cook for a few more minutes. Remove from the heat and, when cooled a little, add most of the herbs, stir and season.

Sprinkle with the remaining herbs before serving, ideally warm or at room temperature – the flavours are best not fridge-cold.

» 231 calories for 4 servings, 154 for 6

More on » onions *p281* » garlic *p82* » tomatoes *p142* » olives *p179* » chocolate *p291* » parsley *p136*

Squash Winter squashes – pumpkin, butternut and onion squash etc. – are rich in most of the B vitamins and vitamin C, as well as manganese. They are high in **fibre** too, but it's the **beta-carotene** content that makes them excel in terms of nutrition. You can tell by the colour of the flesh that they're a good source: the richer the colour, the more beta-carotene. It's best to roast squashes, and to only peel them if you must as it's the flesh just below the skin where the carotenoid pigment is at its highest concentration. Squashes also contain high levels of substances called cucurbitacins, named after the gourd family *Cucurbitaceae*, to which they belong. Both these groups of **antioxidants** are part of the plant's natural defence mechanisms, and the same properties that make these substances potentially toxic to some animals and micro-organisms, also make them effective anti-microbial, anti-viral and **anti-inflammatory** agents for us.

Squashes are a valuable low-fat source of **omega-3 fatty acids** and healthy **carbohydrates**. They release their sugars more slowly than the potato, and have other insulin-regulating properties, so they are a great food for diabetics.

Small shared plates

Smoked mackerel pâté with ginger, chilli and lime

This low-fat smoked mackerel pâté, made with only a small amount of cream cheese, has a bright and sparky flavour. Mackerel – fresh or smoked – is a fish we should aim to eat at least once a week. It's a good source of protein, with top levels of omega-3s – a classic food for brain and heart health. Doctors and nutritionists recommend eating about 300g of oily fish a week and a good dollop of this will set you on your way. Serve with oatcakes, Swedish crispbread or toasted Seed and nut protein bread (see pages 32 and 191).

You can replace the cream cheese with cottage cheese to reduce the fat and calories even further. It still tastes good!

For 8–10 mezze-sized servings:
60g fresh root ginger
3 garlic cloves
1 green finger chilli, deseeded and quartered
5 spring onions, roots off, cut into thirds (outer skin removed if tough)
Grated zest and juice of 2 limes
500g smoked mackerel, skinned and boned
100g cream cheese
Black pepper

Scrape the skin off the ginger using a teaspoon. Cut it up into chunks. Put the ginger chunks, the garlic, green chilli, spring onions and lime zest and juice into a food processor and blitz to a paste. Add the smoked mackerel and cream cheese and blend briefly. Taste and season with a little black pepper.

Scoop the mackerel pâté out of the food processor into a serving bowl and put in the fridge for at least an hour before serving.

» 208 calories for 8 servings, 166 for 10

More on » ginger *p200* » garlic *p82* » chillies *p93* » mackerel and oily fish *p256*

Healthy chilli jam

This is an excellent dip or sauce to have with many of these mezzes. It's ideal with Spinach and coriander falafels (see page 204) or Smoked mackerel pâté (see left), served as a canapé on toast with a spoon of this on top. Try it as a dipping sauce for Vietnamese summer rolls (see page 210) and Gomashio and pepper squid (see page 214). In this recipe, the sugar is replaced with coconut palm sugar – which is fractionally more nutritious than cane sugar and sweeter as well, so a quarter less is needed.

Fills 4 x 250g jars:
700g ripe tomatoes
2 garlic cloves
4 red chillies (seeds left in if you want it hot)
25g fresh root ginger
1 tsp Chinese five-spice powder
250g coconut palm sugar
350ml organic apple cider vinegar

Blitz the tomatoes with the garlic, chillies and ginger in a food processor.

Pour into a heavy-based saucepan. Add the Chinese five-spice, coconut palm sugar and vinegar, and bring to the boil, stirring slowly.

Then, reduce the heat and simmer gently for 30–40 minutes, stirring from time to time. The mixture will turn dark and treacly.

Pour into dry, warm, sterilised jars (you can sterilise these in a very hot dishwasher, or boil in a pan of water for 10 minutes). Seal and label with a date. It will store for at least a year.

» 1,234 calories in total

More on » tomatoes *p142* » garlic *p82* » chillies *p93* » ginger *p200* » coconut palm sugar *p316* » apple cider vinegar *p63*

Sun-dried tomato tapenade

Black olive tapenade is delicious, but I love the sweet, rich flavour of this tomato version even more. I first had this in Odette's Café in one of the prettiest parts of Amsterdam, on the Prinsengracht in the canal district. There this tapenade is served on bruschetta. It's also good with a plate of raw veg crudités, and a spoonful makes an excellent addition to a salad dressing, particularly for stronger-tasting leaves like rocket (see page 138).

For 6–8 mezze-sized servings:
12 large sun-dried tomatoes in olive oil
2 tbsp tomato purée
50g good-quality olives (green or black or a mix)
1 garlic clove, chopped
2 sprigs of thyme, leaves picked
15g basil leaves
1 tsp aged balsamic vinegar

De-stone the olives if needed, then place all the ingredients in a food processor and blitz to a coarse paste. Add some of the sun-dried tomato oil (if it is olive) to give you the right consistency.

» 57 calories for 6 servings, 43 for 8

More on » tomatoes *p142* » olives *p179*
» garlic *p82*

> **Balsamic vinegar** Proper balsamic vinegar is made from fermented concentrated grape juice, left to age for at least ten months to develop its distinct flavour – and, like many fermented foods, it has been shown to be good for us. Studies suggest that it can help to prevent clogging of the arteries and the resultant cardiovascular disease. Be aware that many so-called balsamic vinegars on sale are fake and get their sweetness not from grape juice, but from condensed and sugary apple syrup. These won't have the same effect – nor taste the same – so check the label carefully.

Wholemeal sesame flatbreads

These flatbreads are simple and tasty, one of the best things to serve with mezze dishes. You can add different seeds to vary the flavour, using cumin, caraway or fennel seeds in addition to, or instead of, sesame seeds. Try these dipped into Sun-dried tomato tapenade (see left), hummus (see page 182–3) or tzatziki (see page 181), or used as a scoop for Squash caponata (see page 186).

For 12 flatbreads:
350g wholemeal flour, plus extra for dusting
1 tsp sea salt
Cold-pressed rapeseed oil
12 tsp sesame seeds

Put the flour, salt and 225ml water into a large bowl and, with your hands, mix into a soft dough. Place the dough on a floured surface and knead for 5–10 minutes. Put the dough into a lightly oiled bowl, cover with a clean tea towel and leave for 2 hours. The gluten needs time to relax, so leaving it to rest will make the dough easier to work and make the cooked bread more tender.

Lightly flour a work surface. Divide the dough into 12 even-sized portions. Roll each portion into a golf-ball-sized sphere, and flatten slightly with the palm of your hand. Sprinkle a teaspoon of sesame seeds evenly over the top. Then, using a floured rolling pin, roll out thinly.

Heat ½ tablespoon oil over a medium heat in a large heavy-based frying pan. When the oil is hot cook the flatbreads in batches (top up the pan with a little more oil as necessary). Cook for 2 minutes then flip and cook for a further 1 minute. Once cooked, stack them up on a baking tray, cover with foil and keep warm in a low oven until ready to eat.

» 123 calories per bread

More on » rapeseed oil *p248* » sesame seeds *p164*

Seed and nut protein bread

A delicious bread thick with nuts and seeds – and that's pretty much it. There's no flour, which makes it a very low-carbohydrate, high-protein bread; it is extremely high in fibre and very filling. I like this toasted and served with smoked mackerel pâté, and it's good with any of the mezze dips – hummus, tzatziki, tapenade or baba ghanoush (see pages 182–3, 181, 189 and 184). I also like it toasted with honey. You'll find psyllium husks at health food shops.

For 1 large 900g loaf:
135g sunflower seeds
90g milled organic flaxseeds
65g hazelnuts or almonds, roughly chopped
145g rolled oats
2 tbsp chia seeds
4 tbsp psyllium husks (3 tbsp if using psyllium husk powder)
Good pinch of sea salt
1 tbsp maple syrup
3 tbsp set coconut oil, melted

Line with baking parchment, or oil, a 900g loaf tin.

In a mixing bowl, combine all the dry ingredients, mixing well. Whisk the maple syrup, oil and 350ml water together in a jug. Add this to the dry ingredients and mix very well until everything is completely saturated and the dough becomes very thick. If the dough is too thick to stir, gradually add 1–2 teaspoons of water until it's manageable.

Pour the mixture into the loaf tin, and smooth out the top with the back of a spoon.

Let the tin and its contents sit out on the counter for at least 2 hours, or all day, or overnight. This allows the chia seeds and psyllium husks to expand and set and hold the other ingredients. If you have a silicone loaf tin, to check that the dough is ready to bake, pull the sides of the loaf tin away from the edge of the dough. The loaf should retain its shape. If you don't, insert a skewer, which should leave a distinct hole when you remove it, rather than filling back in immediately.

Preheat the oven to 180°C/gas mark 4.

Place the loaf tin in the oven on the middle rack, and bake for 20 minutes. Remove the bread from the tin, place it upside down directly on the rack and bake for another 40–50 minutes. The bread is done when it sounds hollow if tapped. Let it cool completely before slicing.

Store the bread in a tightly sealed container for up to five days. It freezes well too, and you can slice it before freezing for quick and easy toast.

» 1,133 calories for the whole loaf, 113 per slice

More on » flaxseeds *p30* » hazelnuts *p50*
» almonds *p347* » oats *p25* » chia seeds *p26*
» maple syrup *p27* » coconut oil *p309*

Light hollandaise

This hollandaise is made with yoghurt, as well as butter, which is why I can justify calling it 'light'. Butter is fine in small quantities, and the yoghurt lightens the sauce nicely. Hollandaise is wonderful served with a selection of lightly cooked early summer veg: small carrots, broad beans, baby beetroot, mini courgettes and asparagus (see right). Serve the sauce warm in a bowl, placed in the middle of a large flat plate with piles of summer veg arranged around it. Then everyone can dig in. It's also classic in a breakfast eggs Benedict (see page 58).

For 4:
4 tbsp live Greek yoghurt
3 large egg yolks
50g organic unsalted butter, melted
Juice of ½ lemon
1 heaped tsp Dijon mustard
Dash of Tabasco sauce

Use a bain-marie, or boil a little water in a small pan and set a heatproof bowl over the top, ensuring the bottom does not touch the water.

In the bowl over the pan, whisk the yoghurt and egg yolks together until smooth and slightly less frothy. Add the melted butter gradually, whisking constantly. Whisk in the remaining ingredients.

Whisking constantly, cook the hollandaise until thick and creamy, about 6 minutes. It should be thick enough to coat the back of a spoon when it's ready.

You can also make the sauce in advance and gently reheat it using a bain-marie, or pour into and store in a thermos flask. Use the same day.

» 155 calories per serving

More on » yoghurt *p44* » eggs *p61* » butter *p104* » lemons *p346*

Asparagus with light hollandaise

Make this when asparagus is in season in the late spring and early summer. It's ideal as a light supper, or as part of a selection of mezzes. The nutty flavour of the sesame oil and seeds is a perfect match with the asparagus. Serve with some salmon or smoked haddock if you fancy it.

For 4:
1 recipe Light hollandaise (see left)
32–40 asparagus spears, woody ends snapped off
1 tbsp toasted sesame oil
Sea salt and black pepper
A few sesame seeds, dry-fried or toasted

Make the hollandaise as described left.

Boil or griddle the asparagus spears until soft to the point of a knife. If griddling, turn them regularly.

When cooked, drain or remove the asparagus spears from the griddle, lay out on a large flat plate and drizzle with a little toasted sesame oil. Sprinkle with a little salt and pepper and a few sesame seeds, and serve with the bowl of hollandaise.

» 238 calories per serving

More on » asparagus *p126* » sesame seeds *p164*

Small shared plates

Olive oil hollandaise

Butter is not as bad for us as we've all been led to believe, especially if it's organic and unsalted, but olive oil is positively good for us. And being butter-free, this hollandaise is ideal for those with lactose intolerance. It is still calorific – but as with mayonnaise, if you use good olive oil and free-range, ideally organic eggs, it's perfectly healthy in limited quantities. If you use only extra virgin olive oil, the taste can be a little strong, so combine with a lighter olive oil, organic if possible. Serve this version of hollandaise in the same ways as the Light hollandaise opposite.

For 4–6:

Juice of 1 lemon, plus more to taste

1 tsp black peppercorns, crushed

3 medium egg yolks

100ml olive oil, warmed slightly (use a mix of extra virgin and organic light olive oil)

Sea salt

Cayenne pepper

Gently heat the lemon juice and peppercorns in a small saucepan until just warmed through.

Set a heatproof bowl over a pan of hot, but not boiling water. The bottom of the bowl must not touch the water. Add the egg yolks and strain in the warm lemon juice. Whisk until pale and frothy.

Very slowly, trickle in the warmed olive oil and keep whisking until thickened. It should be thick enough to coat the back of a spoon when it's ready.

Remove from the heat and add salt and cayenne to taste, and a little more lemon juice if needed.

» 268 calories for 4 servings, 178 for 6

More on » lemons *p346* » eggs *p61*

Olive oil Good olive oil has a high proportion of oleic acid (which you also find in avocados and many nuts). This is the main ingredient responsible for its wide health benefits – it helps to protect the heart and the brain, and a promising line of research indicates that it is also associated with lower cancer risk. Of course, olive oil is a pillar of the Mediterranean diet and it has been proven to contribute to the renowned Mediterranean longevity, but the olive oil you choose is important. Depending on the type of olives, and the site and soil in which they're grown, as well as the production process, the amount of oleic acid varies from 55 to 85 per cent of the total fat content. Extra virgin olive oils made from the first cold pressing of the finest olives are at the top end. And that's not all – olive oil also contains heart-healthy flavonoid **antioxidants** and vitamin E, with extra virgin olive oil again containing the highest levels. So good olive oils don't just taste nicer, they're better for us too. (For more on the goodness of olives see page 179.)

Sauerkraut

The British are unusual amongst avid vegetable-growing cultures in that they don't have a tradition of fermenting veg, the process of preserving raw vegetables in brine. Traditionally all over Europe and Asia, households will have fermenting pots gently bubbling away. As with jam- and jelly-making, the first few times you're feeling your way, but you'll get used to the process after a few tries and it's well worth it. You can buy sauerkraut in good health-food shops and some delis, but it's even better to get into the rhythm of making your own. Fermenting is a clever and tasty way of storing vegetables, and the results are very nutritious.

This is a northern European recipe for cabbage sauerkraut from the book *Wild Fermentation* by fermentation guru Sandor Katz. You can ferment any brassica – cauliflower, Brussels sprouts, broccoli or cabbage – and all are good with the sharp, intense flavour of juniper. You could also try a mix of equal amounts of cabbage and carrot. The carrot adds a nice sweetness, and the recipe also works brilliantly with apples and peppers, as well as other sweet roots such as beetroot, turnips, Jerusalem artichokes and celeriac. Add whatever herbs and spices you fancy (caraway seeds, dill seeds, celery seeds and juniper berries are all classic flavourings). Experiment and see which are your favourites.

I worried when I first made sauerkraut that the whole thing might go too far and rot, but the saltiness of the brine protects against that in the early stages and favours the growth of the desired strains of bacteria – *lactobacilli* – as time goes on. Once under way, the acidic environment created by the fermentation is inhospitable to harmful bacteria. As with any natural process, though, the results can vary, so if your sauerkraut doesn't smell or taste right, play it safe and discard it.

Serve the sauerkraut in small bowls for people to help themselves – a spoon at a time – as a snack. It's also excellent as an accompaniment to any raw, smoked or cured fish, and is traditionally served with sausages. It's got a really punchy flavour and, as the veg are still raw, a delicious crunch.

The temperature should not drop below 13°C as fermentation will stop, nor rise above 24°C as the correct bacteria won't then thrive and it will go off. Crocks are ceramic jars specifically designed for fermentation with a moat at the top, which you fill with water to create a seal, but you can also use a sterilised glass jar.

For 1 crock (2.5kg) or a large glass jar:
2kg cabbage (a mix of red and white is good, as it gives the kraut a beautiful pink colour), cored
3 tbsp rock salt (it's key this has no additives, which would stop the fermentation)
3 tbsp caraway (or other) seeds

Finely chop or grate the cabbage. Place it in a large bowl as you chop it. Sprinkle the salt on the cabbage as you go and massage it together for about 5 minutes, two or three times as you add. Use more salt in summer and less in winter. It is impossible to make kraut with less salt or with no salt at all.

Add the caraway seeds, then add other vegetables, if you like. Mix the ingredients together and pack into the crock or jar. Pack a bit at a time and tamp down hard with a rolling pin, or your fists. The tamping packs the kraut tight into the crock and helps force more water out of the cabbage. Leave at least 6cm clear between the top of the cabbage and the top of the crock or jar.

Cover the kraut with a plate or some other lid that fits snugly inside the crock. Place a clean weight (e.g. a glass jug filled with water) on the cover. This weight helps force the water out of the cabbage and then keeps the cabbage submerged under the brine. Cover the whole thing with a tea towel to keep out the flies.

Press down on the weight to add pressure to the cabbage and help force water out of it. Continue doing this periodically (as often as you think of it, every few hours), until the brine rises above the cover. This can take up to 24 hours, as the salt draws water out of the cabbage slowly. Some cabbage, particularly if it is old, simply contains less water. If you add onion or carrots, they exude much more liquid straight away. If the brine does not rise above the plate level by the next day, add enough salt water to bring the brine level up to 3cm above the cabbage. Add about 1 tbsp of rock salt to 250ml water and stir until it is completely dissolved. Leave the crock to ferment, making sure the temperature range is correct (see left).

Check the kraut every day or so. The volume reduces as the fermentation proceeds. Sometimes mould appears on the surface. Skim what you can off the surface; it will break up and you probably won't be able to remove all of it. Don't worry about this, it is just a surface phenomenon, as a result of contact with air. The kraut itself is under the anaerobic protection of the brine. Rinse off the plate and the weight. Taste the kraut. Generally it starts to be tangy after a few days, and the taste gets stronger as time passes.

Your sauerkraut is ready between 7–14 days. In the cool temperature of the cellar in winter, kraut can keep improving for months and months. In the summer or in a heated room, its life-cycle is much more rapid. Eventually it becomes soft and the flavour turns less pleasant.

Scoop out a bowl or jarful at a time and keep it in the fridge. Each time you scoop out some kraut, repack carefully, making sure the kraut is packed tight into the crock or jar, the surface is level and covered with the salty juice, and the cover and weight are clean.

Develop a rhythm. Try to start a new batch before the previous batch runs out. Remove the remaining kraut from the crock, repack it with fresh salted cabbage, then pour the old kraut and its juices over the new kraut. This gives the new batch a boost with the active culture starter.

» 14 calories per 50g portion

Fermented vegetables

When you ferment vegetables (as for Korean kimchi, or northern European sauerkraut), you're not cooking but preserving the vegetables in a salty brine in their raw state. This uses the natural process of lacto-fermentation to allow **probiotics** (beneficial **bacteria** and yeasts) to proliferate, while slowing the growth of harmful bacteria. It also maintains the levels of vitamin C in the vegetables, and breaks down many of the **vitamins** and other nutrients into more easily digestible and absorbable forms.

Captain Cook was recognised by the Royal Society for having conquered scurvy among his crew by setting sail with large quantities of citrus fruit and sauerkraut on board. And now, even without the curse of scurvy, there's plenty of evidence for the health benefits of fermented foods. They are full of probiotics, which optimise gut health and boost the immune system, helping us to stave off infections, and may help with allergies. In Germany, they're so hooked on sauerkraut that they sell the fermented juice separately, to be drunk as a tonic.

Some salt is used in fermented food, but much less than is used, for example, in commercially produced bread. It is also vital that you use salt that is good-quality, ideally rock or mineral salt (such as Himalayan) or no-additive sea salt, which has not been processed. The resulting fermented food has many health-giving properties that outweigh any concerns about salt.

Japanese squash with a sesame seed glaze

Even with the added sugar here, you can't get much healthier than a plate of squash and seeds. Have this in a collection of mezzes one day and make it into a salad the next, adding more fresh herbs and perhaps some feta.

For 8–10 mezze-sized servings:
1kg whole butternut or onion squash, or pumpkin
Cold-pressed rapeseed oil, for greasing
40g coconut palm sugar
2 tbsp tamari soy sauce
Sea salt and black pepper
30g sesame seeds
30g bunch of mint or coriander

Preheat the oven to 180°C/gas mark 4.

Cut the squash in half and remove the seeds. Dice the squash – skin and all – into 2–3cm cubes. Roast it in the preheated oven with a little oil for 10 minutes, then remove from the oven.

Mix 300ml water with the coconut palm sugar and tamari in a large pan. Bring to the boil and add the squash. Cook until the squash has absorbed nearly all the liquid and then start stirring pretty constantly to stop the squash from burning. Cook until the cubes are soft to the point of a knife but not mushy (this will take about 25 minutes), adding a little more water if necessary. Remove the squash from the heat and and leave to cool. Season.

Dry-fry the sesame seeds and stir through the squash. Serve at room temperature with chopped mint or coriander sprinkled on top.

» 96 calories for 8 servings, 77 for 10

More on » squash *p186* » coconut palm sugar *p316*
» tamari soy sauce *p97* » sesame seeds *p164*
» mint *p326* » coriander *p204*

Japanese griddled courgettes

This is delicious served very simply with black rice, and it's ideal as a vegetable dish with a selection of mezze plates. Use a mix of courgette colours – yellow, dark green and light green.

For 4:
600g small courgettes
2 tbsp cold-pressed rapeseed oil
2 garlic cloves, finely chopped
Sea salt and black pepper
2 tbsp mirin (rice wine)

Top and tail the courgettes. If they're small, cut in half. If they are larger, cut them into 6–7mm slices lengthways.

Meanwhile, heat a cast-iron griddle pan for 5 minutes until very hot. Pour the oil evenly over the griddle and add the courgettes. Cook for 3–4 minutes.

Turn the courgettes over, then add the garlic and some salt and black pepper. Cook for another 2–3 minutes until the courgettes are just beginning to soften to the tip of a knife.

Remove from the hot griddle, put on a serving plate, and drizzle with mirin. Serve at once.

» 110 calories per serving

More on » rapeseed oil *p248* » garlic *p82*

Small shared plates

Fried peppers Japanese style

This dish of juicy peppers has a barbecue flavour and a bit of tang from the fish flakes. The latter, which are from bonito (a type of tuna) are dried and then cut so finely they are super-light: this means that they flip about in a life-like way when they hit the hot peppers. Ideally use green Japanese Shishito frying peppers, which you'll find in good Asian supermarkets, but Spanish Padron peppers are also fine, as are the widely available red-horn variety. If all else fails, use green peppers, sliced and deseeded before cooking.

For 2–3:
½ tbsp cold-pressed rapeseed oil
Good handful of small frying peppers (see above)
2–3 tbsp tamari soy sauce
1 tbsp katsuobushi (dried bonito flakes)

Heat the oil in a frying pan and add the peppers, whole. Turn regularly with tongs, frying for about 7 minutes until all sides are beginning to blister.

Turn out into a bowl and dress with soy sauce. Scatter the bonito flakes over the top.

» 110 calories for 2 servings, 73 for 3

More on » tamari soy sauce *p97* » seaweeds *p174*

Fried peppers Worton style

Worton is my favourite organic farm shop and café north-west of Oxford, where they serve delicious and original food, mostly grown in their garden and fields. I had this almost instant Mediterranean-style fried pepper dish there. It has a good combination of flavours: the fruitiness of the peppers, with the sweetness of the balsamic vinegar and creamy sharpness of the cheese. Ideally use green Padron peppers, or red Jimmy Nardello, but if you can't find these varieties, go for the red-horn peppers, which you'll find in most supermarkets.

For 2–3:
1 tbsp cold-pressed rapeseed oil
8–10 small frying peppers (see above)
2 tbsp aged balsamic vinegar
Pinch of sea salt
2 tbsp pine nuts, dry-fried
200g fresh soft goats' cheese

Heat the oil in a frying pan and add the peppers, whole. Turn regularly with tongs, frying for about 7 minutes until all sides are beginning to blister.

Add the balsamic vinegar and salt straight into the pan so it sizzles, and then pour out onto a serving dish. Scatter with pine nuts and finally add small pieces of goats' cheese on top. Serve while still warm.

» 588 calories for 2 servings, 392 for 3

More on » rapeseed oil *p193* » balsamic vinegar *p189* » goats' cheese *p268*

Steam-stirred pak choi with ginger and lemongrass

This is a delicious and healthy way of cooking pak choi, but you could cook small courgettes, spinach, chard, broccoli and cauliflower in the same way. You cook the veg in a little stock, just the right amount to be absorbed or evaporated by the time the vegetable is cooked. Unlike with boiling or steaming, you lose zero nutrients into the water. Once removed from the heat, you can add a little tasty and healthy extra virgin olive oil and mix it in. All these veg are excellent served warm, and the spinach and courgettes are also good cold.

For 4:

4 pak choi
100ml vegetable stock (see p101)
1 garlic clove, finely grated
20g fresh root ginger, peeled and cut into long thin strips
1 lemongrass stalk, outer leaves removed, very finely chopped
1 tbsp extra virgin olive oil

To prepare the pak choi, cut a thin slice off the base (save this for stock). Then cut the pak choi right across the bulb in circles, or divide it lengthways into strands.

Heat the stock in a wok or frying pan. Add the garlic, ginger and lemongrass, and cook for 2 minutes, stirring all the time. Add the pak choi and cook for 3–4 minutes, again stirring, until wilted and almost all of the stock has been absorbed.

Transfer to a bowl and stir the olive oil through. Serve immediately.

» 61 calories per serving

More on » garlic *p82* » olive oil *p193*

Ginger, the rhizome of a tropical plant, aids digestion, can boost the immune system and is **anti-inflammatory**, with good effects on cardiovascular health. It is also well known for helping with nausea and sickness, with one study showing that it worked better than the anti-emetic drug Dramamine in warding off seasickness. It's also fantastic for morning sickness during pregnancy, and when you're feeling queasy with a hangover. Ginger has long been known to improve circulation, so if you get cold fingers and toes in winter you should increase your ginger intake: use it in cooking, or add slices to a cup of tea.

Patmos chickpeas

The key to the deliciousness of these Greek-island-inspired chickpeas is plenty of onion and rosemary and, crucially, very slow cooking. The joy of chickpeas is that you can't overcook them: they always keep their shape. You can use tinned chickpeas, but the flavour and texture is not so good.

The dish is even better heated up the next day and so makes an ideal mezze plate – just top with a drizzle of extra virgin olive oil.

For 6–8:
500g dried chickpeas, soaked in cold water overnight, or 2 x 400g tins of chickpeas
4 onions, peeled, 2 left whole, 2 finely chopped
4 tbsp olive oil (Greeks are always generous with the oil!)
3 tbsp finely chopped rosemary
Sprig of bay leaves
Sea salt and black pepper
300ml white wine
1 whole head of garlic

If using dried chickpeas, drain them well, and rinse, then cover with fresh water, bring to the boil for 5 minutes and drain. (This removes some of the indigestible starches and so makes pulses less flatulent.)

Cover the chickpeas with water again, and add the whole onions. Bring to the boil, and as the scum comes to the surface, remove it. Continue simmering the chickpeas gently, for 15 minutes. Strain and season, reserving the onions and the cooking liquid.

Preheat the oven to 150°C/gas mark 2.

In a small frying pan gently fry the finely chopped onion in the olive oil.

Purée one third of the chickpeas with the boiled onions and a couple of ladlefuls of the cooking liquid.

Put the remaining two thirds of the chickpeas with the fried onion in an ovenproof dish with a lid. Add the chickpea and onion purée, the rosemary, bay leaves, salt, pepper and white wine. Mix together.

Take the top off the head of garlic and slide it in at the side of the dish. Cover the dish with its lid, then put into the preheated oven. Cook slowly for about 2 hours. If the dish dries out, then just add a little more of the reserved chickpea cooking juices.

Remove from the oven, squeeze the roasted garlic into the dish, and mix well.

If you're using tinned chickpeas, boil the onions separately for about 30 minutes. Mix with one-third of the chickpeas and follow the instructions as above, but cook them for only half the time.

Eat with a green salad, or a selection of other mezzes. This is also excellent with roast venison.

» 266 calories for 6 servings, 200 for 8

More on » chickpeas p182 » onions p281 » olive oil p193 » garlic p82

Roast cauliflower with sesame dukkah

This looks magnificent, the whole cauliflower coming to the table toasty-brown on the outside, but ivory, creamy and soft in the middle.

For 6–8:
250g live Greek yoghurt
Grated zest of 1 lemon
Sea salt and black pepper
1 large cauliflower, base trimmed flat
    and leaves removed
1 tbsp cold-pressed rapeseed oil
Olive oil, to drizzle

For the sesame dukkah
40g sesame seeds, dry-fried
3 tbsp each of coriander and cumin seeds, dry-fried
75g hazelnuts, plus an extra 2 tbsp to serve, dry-fried

Preheat the oven to 180°C/gas mark 4.

For the dukkah, put the seeds and hazelnuts in a food processor and pulse for 5–10 seconds – you want an irregular texture.

In a wide bowl, mix the yoghurt with 3 tablespoons of the dukkah (store the rest in an airtight jar), the lemon zest, salt and pepper. Put the cauliflower upside down into the bowl and swivel it around in the yoghurt mix. Turn it right-side up and place on a large sheet of baking parchment on a baking tray. Smear the rest of the marinade all over the cauliflower.

Enclose in a baking parchment parcel and roast for 30 minutes. Then unwrap, brush with the rapeseed oil and roast until completely soft and brown on the outside. Drizzle with olive oil and scatter with the extra hazelnuts, roughly chopped.

» 212 calories for 6 servings, 159 for 8

More on » yoghurt p44 » lemons p346
» cauliflower p267 » rapeseed oil p248 » olive oil p193 » sesame seeds p164 » hazelnuts p50

Borlotti bean ratatouille

This is my favourite recipe for borlotti beans, which are rich in protein, fibre and flavour. It's ideal as a mezze and also delicious served with a topping of baked cod. Most bean aficionados prefer reconstituted dried or fresh beans, rather than tinned, which tend to be saltier and less flavourful. Try this recipe also with giant butter beans, and add slices of leek, celery and carrot for 'gigantes', a classic Greek mezze dish.

For 4:
300g dried borlotti beans, or 800g fresh, or 2 x 400g tins
1 large onion, finely chopped
2 garlic cloves, finely chopped
3 tbsp extra virgin olive oil, plus a little extra for drizzling
15 medium tomatoes, skins removed and roughly
    chopped, or 2 x 400g tins of chopped tomatoes
Sea salt and black pepper
60g bunch of coriander, leaves and stalks roughly torn
Fine slivers of Parmesan cheese

Soak the dried borlotti beans overnight. Drain well, and rinse, then cover with fresh water, bring to the boil for 5 minutes, and drain. (This removes some indigestible starches to make them less flatulent.)

Cook the onion and garlic gently in the oil until soft. Add the tomatoes and the beans and stew gently for about 45 minutes if using fresh beans, or about an hour if dried. Stir the mixture every 5 minutes or so, adding a little water if it becomes too dry.

When the beans are tender but not mushy, remove from the heat and leave for 15 minutes to cool a little. Season with salt and black pepper. Just before you eat, add the coriander, a drizzle of olive oil and the slivers of Parmesan.

» 264 calories per serving

More on » onions p281 » garlic p82 » olive oil p193 » tomatoes p142 » coriander p204

Small shared plates

Spinach and coriander falafels

Falafels are usually fried, or even deep-fried, but these are baked in the oven for a lighter, less calorific version. They are the most brilliant green. Serve on their own, or in a pitta with plenty of salad, some tzatziki or coriander hummus and a drizzle of chilli jam (see pages 181, 182 and 188). To ring the changes, experiment by replacing the chickpeas with different beans such as mung beans, black beans or broad beans.

For 12 falafels, to serve 4–6 (2–3 balls each as a mezze):
Cold-pressed rapeseed oil for greasing
4 spring onions, chopped
1 garlic clove, chopped
30g bunch of coriander, leaves and stalks
20g bunch of flat-leaf parsley
1 tsp cumin seeds, dry-fried
1 tsp coriander seeds, dry-fried
Pinch of dried chilli flakes
½ tsp ground cinnamon
1 tsp ground turmeric
100g baby spinach leaves
1 tsp gluten-free baking powder
Grated zest of 2 lemons
400g tin of chickpeas, drained and dried with a tea towel
Drizzle of olive oil (optional)
Sea salt and black pepper
4 tbsp sesame seeds, dry-fried

Preheat the oven to 200°C/gas mark 6. Line a baking sheet with baking parchment, and grease lightly with a little rapeseed oil.

Place all the ingredients, except the chickpeas, olive oil, salt, pepper and sesame seeds, in a food processor. Blitz until medium-fine.

Add the chickpeas and pulse until everything is combined and you have a coarse paste. You may need to drizzle in a touch of olive oil to bring it together. Taste the mix and season with salt and black pepper.

Roll into 12 balls, each slightly smaller than a ping-pong ball. Roll in the sesame seeds and place on the baking sheet. Slightly flatten them with your fingers. Place in the oven and cook for 10 minutes. Then turn the falafels over and cook for a further 10 minutes until crisp on the outside.

» 69 calories per falafel

More on » garlic p82 » parsley p136 » cinnamon p22 » turmeric p87 » spinach p54 » lemons p346 » chickpeas p182 » sesame seeds p164

Variations
Beetroot and mint falafels Replace the spinach with 100g grated raw beetroot, and swap the fresh coriander for fresh mint, leaves only. These two colours sing on the plate.
» 69 calories per falafel
Spinach and coriander falafels with sun-dried tomatoes Add a few sun-dried tomatoes to the basic mix.
» 85 calories per falafel

Coriander seeds have long been known for their anti-diabetic and **anti-inflammatory** properties, and recent research confirms that they do indeed help to lower blood sugar, as well as levels of **LDL** ('bad') **cholesterol**, while increasing HDL ('good') cholesterol levels. Prepared as a tea, steeped in boiling water, the seeds work well for indigestion and nausea. Coriander is exceptionally rich in **phytonutrients**, and the volatile oil in the leaves has anti-bacterial, detoxifying and immune-stimulating properties. The fresh leaf is best added as you serve food, scattered on top, as heat destroys both its taste and health benefits.

Split pea and mint croquettes with minted yoghurt

I make these slightly healthier versions of classic Greek croquettes all the time, using feta cheese made with goats' milk, rather than the traditional but higher-fat hard sheep's cheese. I first had something similar in the White Mountains of Crete where it was served with a mix of other small plates including fennel pies (see Greek herb pies, page 207) and tzatziki, each one healthy, sustaining and absolutely delicious.

For 12–15 croquettes:
340g yellow split peas
3 garlic cloves
2 onions
Olive oil
Cold-pressed rapeseed oil
30g bunch of mint, leaves chopped
40g wholewheat or spelt breadcrumbs
100g feta or hard sheep's cheese, grated
1 medium egg, beaten
1 red finger chilli, deseeded and chopped (optional)
Sea salt and black pepper
Wholemeal flour, for dusting

For the minted yoghurt
200g live natural yoghurt (see p44)
30g bunch of mint, leaves roughly chopped
2 garlic cloves, finely chopped

Put the split peas in a pan with the garlic. Peel and quarter one of the onions, and add, along with a good slurp of olive oil and 750ml water. Cook, stirring occasionally, until the split peas disintegrate into a purée with a bit of texture (about 20–25 minutes). You can add more water if it is too dry, and more olive oil to taste. Leave to cool. You can do this stage the day before. (This purée is often served as a mezze in itself in Greece, topped with some finely chopped red onion and a generous drizzle of extra virgin olive oil, although I find it a little bland.)

Peel and finely chop the remaining onion, and gently fry in a little rapeseed oil for 7–8 minutes until softened. Mix into the cold purée along with the chopped mint, breadcrumbs, cheese, egg, chilli and some salt and pepper. Shape the mixture into 12–15 short and fat, sausage-shaped croquettes. Dust in flour and fry in hot rapeseed oil until golden brown on both sides. Drain on kitchen paper to absorb any excess oil.

To make the minted yoghurt, mix the yoghurt, mint and garlic in a food processor with just enough water (usually about 100ml) to give the consistency you want for the sauce.

Serve the croquettes hot, warm or cold, with the minted yoghurt on the side.

» 109 calories for 12 croquettes, 87 for 15

More on » garlic p82 » onions p281 » olive oil p193 » rapeseed oil p248 » mint p326 » feta p264 » eggs p61 » chillies p93 » yoghurt p44

Courgette 'meatballs'

Inspired by a Gujarati recipe for vegetarian 'meatballs', these have a lovely soft texture and brilliant fragrant taste. They are bound with fibre- and nutrient-rich chickpea flour.

For 7–8 as a mezze, 4–5 as a main course:
1kg courgettes (6–7 medium courgettes), trimmed
1 tsp sea salt
2 medium onions, very finely chopped
1 heaped tsp set coconut oil
2 hot green chillies, finely chopped
1 large thumb-length piece of fresh root ginger, grated
Grated zest and juice of 2 limes
2 tbsp pine nuts, dry-fried and coarsely chopped
30g bunch of coriander, stalks and leaves chopped, or flat-leaf parsley, leaves only chopped
100g gram (chickpea) flour
A little set coconut oil (if frying) or cold-pressed rapeseed oil (if baking)

For the sauce
2 medium onions, finely chopped
1 heaped tsp set coconut oil
½ tsp ground turmeric
1 tsp ground cumin
Cayenne pepper (to taste)
2 tsp ground coriander
400g tin of chopped tomatoes, or 400g fresh tomatoes, chopped
400ml tin of coconut milk
1 tsp garam masala
1 tsp cumin seeds, dry-fried and ground
Sea salt and black pepper

For the balls, grate the courgettes and put them in a colander with the salt. Mix well, put to one side and leave for 30 minutes. This will bleed out some of the moisture and give a nice density to the balls, which then hold together better. You also add the exuded courgette liquid to the sauce.

Gently fry the onion in the coconut oil until soft but not browned (about 7 minutes). When cooked, mix in the chilli and grated ginger, and continue to fry for a couple of minutes. Remove from the heat and add the lime zest and juice, pine nuts and coriander.

Squeeze dry the grated courgette with your hands, saving the liquid for the sauce, and mix the courgette with the onion, chilli, ginger and coriander mix. Sprinkle in the flour and mix again. Chill in the fridge while you make the sauce.

For the sauce, fry the onions in the oil for about 7 minutes, until starting to brown. Add the turmeric, cumin, cayenne and coriander. Stir in the tomatoes and the salty courgette liquid, and bring to the boil. Pour in the coconut milk and simmer for 15–20 minutes to reduce. Sprinkle in the garam masala and ground cumin seeds, seasoning to taste with salt and pepper.

Roll the courgette mixture into 16 little ping-pong-sized balls. You can either fry or bake the courgette balls at this stage. If baking, preheat the oven to 170°C/gas mark 3, and line a baking sheet with greaseproof paper or a silicone sheet. If frying, melt the coconut oil in a frying pan and fry the balls for about 10 minutes, turning them as they brown. If baking, put the balls on the baking sheet, drizzle with a little oil and place in the oven. Cook for 15 minutes, then turn them over and cook for a further 15 minutes until crisp on the outside. Serve with the sauce on the side or poured over. If eating as a main course, serve with black rice.

» 116 calories per ball, with sauce
» 232 calories per 2 balls, with sauce (for mezze)
» 464 calories per 4 balls, with sauce (for main course)

More on » onions *p281* » coconut oil *p309*
» chillies *p93* » ginger *p200* » coriander *p204*
» parsley *p136* » turmeric *p87* » tomatoes *p142*
» coconut milk *p235*

Greek herb pies

These flat herb pies are a standard mezze on the island of Hydra, one of my favourite places in the world. They freeze brilliantly, and can be cooked straight from frozen. There are a couple of different pastries to choose between here: shop-bought, ready-made filo which, rolled thinly, has a texture like a water biscuit, and is a good easy cheat; and a more substantial one, made with wholemeal flour.

For 5 flat pizza-shaped pies, for a starter/mezze for 8–10:
500g spinach or chard
3 tbsp olive oil
500g fennel bulbs (and tops if you have them), finely sliced (a mandolin is good for this)
1 large leek (about 400g), finely sliced
2 garlic cloves, finely chopped
40g flat-leaf parsley, leaves finely chopped
40g dill, finely chopped
2 heaped tbsp chopped mint leaves
1 heaped tsp dried mint
Grated zest and juice of 1 lemon
140g Gruyère, coarsely grated
200g feta, crumbled
Sea salt and black pepper
Set coconut oil

For the filo pastry
Set coconut oil
15 sheets of shop-bought filo pastry

For the wholemeal pastry
500g plain wholemeal flour, plus extra for dusting
½ tsp sea salt
4 tbsp olive oil
250ml lukewarm water

If using wholemeal pastry, put all the ingredients into a bowl and bring together with a fork and then your fingers to form a dough. Shape into a ball and allow to rest for 30 minutes in the fridge.

To make the filling, blanch the spinach in boiling water for 30 seconds, and drain. When cool enough to handle, squeeze it in your hands to get out as much water as possible. Then finely chop and put into a large mixing bowl. Heat the olive oil in a large pan, add the fennel, leek and garlic, and cook gently for 5 minutes, stirring frequently. Add this to the spinach. Add the remaining filling ingredients except the coconut oil to the bowl and mix to combine. Season with salt and pepper.

Cut the wholemeal dough into ten equal-sized portions. On a floured surface roll out two pieces of dough to a circle of about 22cm (frying-pan width) and as thin as you can (1–2mm). Heat a little coconut oil in a frying pan and lay in one piece of the rolled-out dough. Spoon over a fifth of the filling mixture and spread it out evenly, keeping a centimetre or two away from the edge. Fry for 3–4 minutes over a low heat.

In a separate pan, heat a little coconut oil and add the other piece of rolled-out dough, fry for 3 minutes on each side or until golden brown and place on top of the open mixture in the other pan. The cheese provides the glue. Remove with a spatula and transfer to a large platter. Repeat this process for the remaining four pies. They can be kept warm in the oven until ready to serve, or served in batches as and when they are made.

If using the filo pastry, heat a little coconut oil in a frying pan and add two sheets of filo. Spread on a fifth of the mixture, keeping a centimetre or two away from the edge, and fry for 2–3 minutes. Top with one more sheet of filo then turn the pie over and fry for a further 2–3 minutes or until golden brown. Repeat the process for the remaining pies. Cut the pies into wedges, and serve.

» Filo pastry, 416 calories for 8 servings, 333 for 10
» Wholemeal pastry, 501 calories for 8 servings, 400 for 10

More on » spinach *p54* » olive oil *p193* » garlic *p82* » parsley *p136* » mint *p326* » lemon *p346* » feta *p264* » coconut oil *p309*

Vietnamese summer rolls with chilli jam

Fresh, healthy and light, these summer rolls are a way of wrapping up a handful of veg for easy eating without going near a stove. They are incredibly moreish. I love the rolls with prawns, but you can leave these out and just add more veg, particularly avocado; they're also good stuffed with cooked chicken.

For 8 rolls for a mezze for 4:
50g rice vermicelli noodles
Sea salt
8–10 rice-paper wrappers
16 large cooked prawns, cut in half
4 sprigs of mint, leaves picked
4 sprigs of coriander, leaves picked
4 sprigs of Thai basil, leaves picked
1 carrot, grated
¼ cucumber, cut into thin matchsticks
½ avocado, peeled, stoned and thinly sliced
1 soft lettuce, ½ shredded
25g shelled peanuts, dry-fried and crushed

To serve
Chilli jam (see p188)
Gomashio (see p164)

Place the rice noodles in a bowl and cover with boiling water. Add a pinch of salt and leave to cook for 4–5 minutes until soft. Rinse in cold water and drain thoroughly.

Choose a bowl large enough to hold a wrapper and fill with cold water. Place one wrapper in the water and allow to go pliable. Drain and lie flat on a clean, dry chopping board.

Place four prawn halves in a horizontal line in the middle of the wrapper, leaving a couple of centimetres on each side. Top with a line of herb leaves.

Add an eighth of the carrot and a few cucumber sticks, some avocado and then a small cluster of rice vermicelli. Finish with some shredded lettuce and a line of crushed peanuts.

Bring the bottom edge of the wrapper tightly up over the filling, and then fold the sides in over it. Continue to roll up tightly and place on a board, join-side down. Cover the roll with lettuce leaves or a damp tea towel to keep it fresh and moist as you make the rest.

Continue making rolls in the same way until you have used up all the mix.

Serve the rolls with the chilli jam and gomashio in small bowls.

» 123 calories per roll
» Dipped in chilli jam, plus 31 calories per roll

More on » prawns *p212* » mint *p326* » coriander *p204* » carrot *p121* » cucumber *p148* » avocado *p119* » lettuce *p114* » chillies *p93* » sesame seeds *p164*

Variation
Peanut dipping sauce   Make a peanut dipping sauce to replace the chilli jam.
Enough for 8 rolls:
2 tbsp peanut butter (see p36)
2 tbsp tamari soy sauce
1 tbsp rice vinegar
1 tsp grated fresh root ginger
1 garlic clove, grated
1 tsp toasted sesame oil
Grated zest and juice of 1 lime
Splash of Thai fish sauce (optional)
Combine all the ingredients in a bowl and serve.
» 312 calories in total

Mieng kam

These make-your-own prawn and lettuce parcels are inspired by a dish served at the Kamalaya health retreat on the Thai island of Koh Samui, where they use betel leaves instead of lettuce. It is ideal for when you've got quite a few people to feed at a party. Serve in the middle of the table and let everyone make their own using a lettuce leaf as a mini plate. You spoon in small amounts of any ingredient you fancy, add a teaspoon of dressing, wrap and eat. (You can also use beaten-out-thin chicken or beef, or cubes of seared salmon.)

If you can't find fresh coconut, buy a whole one. Make a hole in it using a screwdriver, and drain off the water (drink or use this in a smoothie). Wrap the nut in a tea towel like a cracker and, holding the ends securely, whack it down onto a hard surface, preferably outside. This reveals the white flesh.

For 8 as a mezze or starter:
2 shallots, finely sliced
Juice of 1 lime
80g fresh coconut (see above)
1–2 tsp set coconut oil
250g raw prawns, peeled and de-veined
32 large baby gem lettuce leaves (about 4 lettuces)
40g unsalted peanuts, roasted and roughly chopped
½ mango, peeled and diced
2 generous tbsp sesame seeds, dry-fried
1 generous tbsp poppy seeds, dry-fried
40g bunch of coriander, leaves only
3 limes, quartered, to serve

For the dressing
1 red finger chilli, deseeded and finely chopped
2 lemongrass stalks, outer leaves removed,
    finely chopped
1 shallot, finely chopped
2 tbsp sushi pickled ginger, chopped
2 tbsp mirin (rice wine)
3 tbsp tamari soy sauce
½ tsp toasted sesame oil
1 tbsp Thai fish sauce
3 tbsp coconut palm sugar

Make the dressing first. Put all the ingredients into a small saucepan and cook over a medium heat for about 5 minutes until reduced by about a third and turning syrupy. Keep to one side.

To start the parcels, put the sliced shallots into a bowl with the lime juice and leave to marinate while you prepare everything else. Drain before serving. Using a vegetable peeler, peel the fresh coconut into thin strips, and dry-fry until just starting to brown. Heat a griddle or frying pan and melt the coconut oil. Add the prawns and cook for 2–3 minutes until they start to change colour and are cooked all the way through.

Put all the parcel ingredients into individual serving bowls – drained shallots, coconut, prawns, lettuce leaves, peanuts, mango, sesame and poppy seeds (mixed together), coriander and dressing – and serve in the middle of the table.

» 189 calories per serving

More on » coconut oil *p309* » lettuce *p114* » sesame seeds *p164* » coriander *p204* » chillies *p93* » tamari soy sauce *p97* » coconut palm sugar *p316*

Prawns are lean, rich in nutrients and an excellent source of **protein**. They are high in **omega-3 fatty acids**, which are particularly good for cardiovascular and nervous-system health.

You want to look for tiger, green or white prawns, which are wild. Avoid river prawns, 90 per cent of which are farmed in freshwater mud pools. Too often, these pools are awash with antibiotics and growth hormones. Chemical residues and waste seep down into the soil, and the pool is refilled as each batch of prawn fry goes in, so the levels keep accumulating. With saltwater farmed prawns there is some natural water circulation, and they get a few nutrients from the sea, but wild are still best.

Gomashio and pepper squid

Here is a healthier version of a classic, using gomashio made with sesame seeds flavoured with salt, rather than just pure salt. Gomashio is a good way of decreasing your salt intake. Salt and pepper squid is usually deep-fried, but here it is baked in the oven. Squid is an excellent source of almost fat-free protein and it's good value – we should all eat it more often.

For 6 as a mezze:
2 tbsp gomashio (see p164)
2 tbsp toasted sesame oil
Black pepper
450g baby squid, cleaned and cut into bite-sized pieces

To serve
2 limes
30g bunch of coriander, leaves only
Chilli jam (see p188)

Preheat the oven to 180°C/gas mark 4. Line a flat baking sheet with parchment paper.

In a bowl mix the gomashio, sesame oil, some black pepper and the squid together.

Lay the squid out on the baking sheet, not overlapping. Scatter over any excess gomashio, then bake for 10–15 minutes until the squid tentacles are crisp and the rings tender.

Serve with lime wedges, coriander leaves and chilli jam for dipping.

» 86 calories per serving

More on » sesame seeds *p164* » squid *p246*
» coriander *p204*

Cockles, cider and dulse

James Ferguson from Beagle restaurant in Hoxton sent me this mezze recipe after I had it there one summer. I've always loved cockles, but they're too often doused in cheap vinegar. Here their incredible sweetness makes a great contrast to the slightly truffly taste of the dulse.

For 4 as a mezze:
2 large leeks (about 500g), finely sliced
2 bay leaves
Small bunch of thyme
2 tbsp cold-pressed rapeseed oil
2 garlic cloves, finely sliced
250ml good dry cider
1kg cockles in their shells, washed and grit removed as much as possible
About 250g fresh dulse seaweed, just scored a little with a knife, or 1 level tbsp dried flaked dulse
Knob of organic unsalted butter (optional)
20g parsley leaves, roughly chopped
Squeeze of lemon juice
Black pepper

In a large pan that has a lid, sweat the leeks with the bay leaves and thyme in the rapeseed oil over a low heat without browning. Add the garlic and give it a little time to mingle. Turn up the heat, pour in the cider and let it steam and reduce by about a third. Add the cockles and dulse and stir thoroughly, then place the lid on the pan and steam until the cockles just start to open, about 3–4 minutes. Let them stand for a minute and then remove the cockles, leeks and dulse with a slotted spoon to a serving bowl.

Add the butter (if using) to the liquid remaining in the pan, along with the chopped parsley and a good squeeze of lemon. Season with a bit of pepper, and pour over the cockles, leeks and dulse.

» 132 calories per serving without butter, 160 with

More on » rapeseed oil *p248* » garlic *p82*
» seaweeds *p174* » parsley *p136* » lemons *p346*

Light potted shrimps

Potted shrimps are hard to resist served with slices of thin Melba toast, but this is ten times healthier and a doddle to make. We serve these in a mixed plate of mezzes for our dinners at Perch Hill, and they make an excellent starter. Unlike traditional potted shrimps, these won't have a long shelf life.

For 4:
180g brown shrimps, shelled
1 fennel bulb (about 180g), finely sliced (a mandolin is good for this), then roughly chopped
Grated zest of 1 lemon
Juice of ½ lemon
3 heaped tbsp live natural yoghurt (see p44)
2 heaped tbsp finely chopped dill
Sea salt and black pepper
Pinch of ground mace or freshly grated nutmeg

Put the shrimps, fennel, lemon zest and juice, yoghurt and dill into a large mixing bowl and stir to combine. Taste and season with salt and pepper and mace or nutmeg.

Spoon into ramekins and put into the fridge until ready to serve. These are nicest when not fridge-cold, so take out 20–30 minutes before you want to eat. Serve with Swedish crispbread (see page 32).

» 77 calories per serving

More on » lemons *p346* » yoghurt *p44*

Shrimps are lean, rich in nutrients and an excellent source of **protein**. They are also high in **omega-3 fatty acids**, which are particularly good for cardiovascular and nervous-system health. Recent research has shown the bio-active **peptides** (smaller fragments of proteins) in prawns and shrimps have a role in making us feel full. Like eggs, they contain super-valuable choline and selenium. Shrimps are an excellent source of astaxanthin, a **carotenoid** with **anti-inflammatory** and **antioxidant** properties.

Married sardines

This is a recipe from a taverna in Kamini on Hydra, where it is served several times a week, cooked over the coals of a barbecue. You can make this with sardines of almost any size. I've had it in Greece with mini fish no more than 7–8cm long, but I've made it with sardines twice the size, as a main dish. It's also an excellent way of serving small sea bass. Get your fishmonger to clean and fillet the fish, ideally leaving the fillets joined at the tail.

For 4–8, depending on the size of the fish:
8 small to medium-sized sardines, filleted but left joined at the tail

For the stuffing
Grated zest and juice of 1 lemon, plus 1 lemon, quartered, to serve
3 garlic cloves, finely sliced
1 red chilli, deseeded and finely chopped
30g bunch of dill or fennel tops, chopped (parsley is good too)
2 tbsp capers, chopped, plus a few extra to serve
2 tbsp extra virgin olive oil

Mix all the stuffing ingredients together in a bowl.

Lay one of your 2 fish fillets out flat, skin-side down, and spoon over a teaspoon of the stuffing mixture. Fold over the other fillet to lay on top, skin-side up. Repeat with the remaining fish and stuffing. Place the fish in a fine-gauge metal fish grill and cook over a barbecue, or place them under a grill. Cook for 4–5 minutes on each side until the skin is just beginning to char.

Serve with another teaspoon of the stuffing over the top of each pair of 'married' fish, a few extra capers and the quartered lemon.

» 499 calories for 4 servings, 249 for 8

More on » oily fish *p256* » lemons *p346*
» garlic *p82* » chillies *p93* » olive oil *p193*

Raw herring plate with savoury buckwheat pancakes

This is more a collection of delicious things than a recipe. It is a Dutch plate for sharing, a traditional way to start a big family meal. In the Netherlands from mid-June until the end of August, you'll find stalls selling herring specifically to be eaten like this. Herring is a super-healthy oily fish, and the more we eat the better. In the Netherlands, the fish is often served with sticky black rye bread, rye crispbread or toast, but these buckwheat pancakes are even better, like chunky blinis, a classic northern European accompaniment to raw or cured fish. These pancakes are also good for breakfast with a poached egg, and have added goodness from the seeds. To make them dairy-free, swap the milk for coconut milk or coconut water.

Order the herring from your fishmonger, or ask for super-fresh mackerel, filleted and skinned, backbone removed but the tail left on, with both fillets attached. That's the traditional Dutch way of serving them. Marinating the shallots overnight makes them mild and good to eat raw. In the Netherlands, finely chopped onion is often offered by the fishmonger, alongside the herring – and another classic accompaniment is Dutch gin!

It's worth knowing that live natural yoghurt has a third the calories of soured cream, so that's what the calorie count is based on here.

For 10 as a starter:
5 raw medium-sized herrings, filleted and skinned
200g live natural yoghurt (see p44) or soured cream
400g (2 medium-sized) beetroots, boiled until tender, peeled if needed and cut into wedges lengthways
4 pickled gherkins, cut into wedges lengthways

For the buckwheat pancakes (makes 30)
240g buckwheat flour
80g milled organic flaxseeds
1 tsp sea salt
1 litre full-fat milk
120g pumpkin seeds, chopped and lightly dry-fried
120g sunflower seeds, lightly dry-fried
2–3 tsp set coconut oil

For the marinated shallots
2 shallots, sliced as thinly as possible
3 tbsp red wine vinegar
1 tbsp port or red wine
2 tbsp rosemary leaves
2 bay leaves
1 tsp juniper berries, crushed
Sea salt and black pepper

Start by putting all the ingredients for the marinated shallots into a bowl and leaving to marinate overnight. Drain and transfer to a small bowl.

For the pancakes, mix all the ingredients together – except for the seeds and coconut oil – to make a pancake-like batter (it should be quite runny). Then add the sunflower and pumpkin seeds, mixing them well.

Heat a pancake pan over a low heat for 3 minutes or so, then add a teaspoon of coconut oil. Pour in 1 generous tablespoon of batter for each pancake. Cook for 1 minute, then sprinkle 1 teaspoon of the seed mix on top. Cook for 30 seconds and then flip. Cook for 2–3 minutes more until the pancakes are golden brown. Repeat until all the batter is used up, replenishing the oil as and when it's needed. You should have about 20 pancakes.

Lay everything out on a large plate and serve. People can each take a fillet of fish, and then cut it into bite-sized chunks and add it to a pancake, spread with a spoon of yoghurt. Top with a wedge of beetroot or gherkin and serve with some marinated shallots to the side.

» 536 calories for 10 servings with yoghurt

More on » oily fish *p256* » yoghurt *p44* » beetroot *p85* » buckwheat *p226* » flaxseeds *p30* » milk *p252* » pumpkin seeds *p105* » coconut oil *p309* » red wine *p352*

Large shared plates

THE MEAT-AND-TWO-VEG dinner is fast becoming a thing of the past. In terms of lifestyle and nutrition we've moved on. Besides, going to bed at night on a full stomach is not a great idea, as it can encourage the body to store fat and may cause digestive problems.

In a working week, it's tricky not to have your main meal at night, but try to avoid a major blow-out. Then at the weekend, when you're more likely to be at home, feast at lunch or in the afternoon, rather than just before you go to bed. Getting together in the middle of the day for lots of chatting and leisurely eating is often the norm in cultures with high rates of longevity.

Choose from some of the dishes here, all of which are full of goodness. Put vegetables at the centre of your meal, using lentils, chickpeas and other more unusual pulses like adzuki beans to add substance.

Eat lots of fish too: we all need more omega-3 fatty acids, and oily fish in particular are an excellent source. Sadly this does not include widely available and cheap farmed salmon (see page 125), which are usually fed on grain, not krill, and swim in a soup of their feed and their own excrement; toxins build up in their flesh, so overall are not good for us. Wild salmon and mackerel on the other hand are brilliant, as are anchovies and sardines.

And there are concerns too about mercury in the oceans, which is affecting fish, primarily larger fish like swordfish and tuna. Basically the higher up the food chain the fish is, the more likely it is to contain high levels of mercury, although I fear nearly all fish and shellfish have some level of mercury in them. Mercury accumulates in the brain and central nervous system and thus is especially dangerous to the developing foetus and to young infants. Therefore it is advisable that young infants and pregnant women should avoid large fish like tuna (fresh and tinned) and swordfish. Otherwise, all the fish I have included here are fine.

Go too for shrimps, prawns, mussels, squid and octopus: there are recipes for all of these. Like eggs, seafood has had a bad name in the past few decades because it contains relatively high levels of cholesterol. But in fact, eating the fats found in seafood can actually decrease our 'bad' cholesterol, improve our overall cholesterol profile and reduce our likelihood of developing cardiovascular disease.

If you eat meat, offal such as liver and kidneys are good once a week, because they're so iron-rich and lean. The same is true of game. Active and not overfed, venison, pheasant and pigeon are all low in fat and are an excellent source of protein. And free-range, ideally organic chicken and other meats are also fine, just not every day – and never intensively farmed. Knowing where your meat comes from is a good idea too. There are recipes for all these healthy proteins here.

These meats all contain omega-6 fats, which we need and, along with nuts and seeds, these are a healthy source. However, it is not only important to incorporate good sources of omega-3 and omega-6 in your diet, but also to consume these

fatty acids in the proper ratio (see page 12). Omega-6 fatty acids compete with omega-3 fatty acids for use in the body, and so excessive intake of omega-6s can swamp omega-3s. This can potentially exacerbate any inflammation and the likelihood of the development of chronic diseases such as cardiovascular disease, diabetes and brain diseases such as Alzheimer's. This imbalance is mainly due to over-consumption of processed foods and oils, but a low-fat diet with lots of fish will correct this; grass-fed beef and lamb also contain omega-3s – although at a much lower level.

Most of our notions of a portion are a bit skew-whiff, too. The protein section of a 'main' meal – whether quinoa, lentils, chunk of salmon, chicken breast or two or three eggs – should do no more than fill the palm of your hand. That's an easy measure and of course is bigger for bigger people. Eating over-sized meals will burden your digestive system, particularly when they contain meat, which takes some digesting, often causing bloating and a dip in energy whilst the body struggles to process it. Whopping great meals also cause a rise in blood glucose levels, followed by a dip, in which energy and mood both sink. The bigger the meal, the bigger the rise and the greater the crash. A fall in blood-glucose levels will increase the need for the body to refuel: and our bodies' chosen fuel is glucose, hence our urge for a sweet sugary fix following a large meal.

Many of us eat too much, and we eat too quickly. We need to slow down and chew our food more to start the digestive process. Eating slowly gives the body time to realise what it's eaten and for the 'I'm satisfied' hormones to be released. This takes about twenty minutes. If you eat too quickly, the hormones don't have a chance to kick in and make you feel satisfied until it's too late, so you keep eating until you're over-stuffed, rather than feeling just right. That easily turns into a habit, and then every day you're eating more than you need, which leads to long-term weight gain. Just slowing your eating down will help break this pattern. Nutritionists tell you to chew every mouthful twenty times before you swallow it. It may sound crazy, but the benefits are huge.

So what are the guidelines for large shared plates?

» Try smaller portions. It's a matter of adjusting old habits. After two weeks your expectations and satisfaction levels are likely to be reset.
» If weight is an issue for you, perhaps aim to eat less in the evening.
» Eat slowly. Many of us learn to gobble in childhood and at school. It's a habit that needs to be broken.
» Make at least three-quarters of what you eat for your main meal vegetable-based. That's what's good for us, and for the environment.
» We don't all have to be vegetarians, but we do need to eat less meat, particularly due to population growth. A meat-eater needs up to three times more of the world's surface to live off than a vegetarian.
» Have regular meals based around fish. Fish supplies us with excellent protein.
» Add offal and game into your diet – they're highly nutritious and have lower levels of fat than other red meat. But even with these healthy meats, don't eat them more than a couple of times a week, and make sure the offal is organic or grass-fed.

So slow down, start to eat in the Mediterranean way, with a good lunch and less in the evening, and you're on your way to a healthier, longer life.

Kale, mushroom and lentil pilaf with goats' cheese

This is a vegetarian replacement for one of my favourite dishes, lamb's kidneys and lentils (see variation) – both of them hearty, filling winter food.

For 8:
250g Puy lentils, rinsed
1 red onion, finely chopped
2 garlic cloves, crushed
3 tbsp cold-pressed rapeseed oil
1 red chilli, seeds left in, finely chopped
3 bay leaves
Large sprig of thyme
1 tbsp dried flaked dulse seaweed, plus a little extra
    for serving
250ml red wine (or 400g tin of tomatoes, to give
    necessary acidity)
250ml vegetable stock (see p101), or 1 porcini stock cube
    (found in the special food aisle of the supermarket)
    dissolved in 250ml water
300g kale
500g mix of chestnut, button, oyster and flat field
    mushrooms, quartered or cut into sixths or eighths
60g bunch of flat-leaf parsley, coarsely chopped
150g crème fraîche (optional)
Splash of aged balsamic vinegar
4 x 100g cakes of goats' cheese

Put the lentils in a pan, cover them generously with cold water and bring to the boil. Simmer for 5 minutes, then drain and rinse – this helps to remove the indigestible starches. Set aside.

In a heavy-based pan, sauté the onion and garlic over a gentle heat in 1 tablespoon of the oil until soft. Add the par-cooked lentils, chilli, bay, thyme, and most of the 1 tablespoon dulse, and stir briefly. Pour in the wine (or tomatoes, if using) and stock. Cover and simmer gently for about 20 minutes until the lentils begin to soften but not collapse. Add a little more wine or water if necessary to prevent them from boiling dry, but don't drown them. Remove the thyme.

Remove the stalks from the kale and chop the leaves into strips. Steam them for 5 minutes. Allow to cool a little, then chop a little more finely.

Put the mushrooms in a large frying pan and cook gently in the remaining oil, sprinkled with the remaining dried dulse (to replace salt). Cook, stirring occasionally, for 10–15 minutes until they start to brown. Add them to the lentils. Add most of the parsley and stir in the crème fraîche (if using) loosened with a splash of boiling water, followed by the balsamic vinegar.

Halve the goats' cheeses and grill or bake them for a few minutes until they start to melt and brown. Dust with some extra dulse. Serve the lentils and mushrooms on individual plates, each topped with a warm melting goats' cheese, or present on one large platter, with the cheese arranged on top. Serve, scattered with the remaining parsley.

» With red wine, 364 calories per serving;
    with red wine and crème fraîche, 421
» With tomatoes, 350 calories per serving;
    with tomatoes and crème fraîche, 406

Variation
Lamb's kidney and lentil pilaf For the meat option, add 500g lamb's kidneys fried for 5 minutes in a separate pan with a little cold-pressed rapeseed oil and finely chopped garlic. Follow the recipe above for the lentils, leaving out half the mushrooms and the goats' cheese. Combine the kidneys with the lentils to serve.
» 334 calories per serving

More on » lentils *p138* » onions *p281* » garlic *p82*
» rapeseed oil *p248* » chillies *p93* » seaweeds *p174*
» red wine *p352* » tomatoes *p142* » kale *p117*
» mushrooms *p88* » parsley *p136* » balsamic
vinegar *p189* » goats' cheese *p268*

Pearled spelt and broad bean risotto

This spelt risotto doesn't hold together in a smooth, glossy way like risottos made with rice. You'll want about a third less on the plate than with risotto made with white arborio rice, and fibre-rich spelt is healthier. For extra flavour, add some chargrilled broad beans, cooked in their pods and then shelled straight off the grill or barbecue, on top of each bowl.

For 6:
250g pearled spelt
2 medium shallots, finely chopped
2 garlic cloves, finely chopped
1 red chilli, deseeded and finely chopped
20g organic unsalted butter
1–2 tbsp cold-pressed rapeseed oil
750ml hot chicken or vegetable stock (see pp98 and 101)
30g bunch of tarragon, leaves coarsely chopped
500g podded broad beans (fresh or frozen)
100g sugarsnap and mangetout peas
30g Parmesan, grated, plus 20g for the table
Sea salt and black pepper
6 broad bean shoots, coarsely chopped (good if available, but not essential)
100g pea shoots (optional)
2 tbsp aged balsamic vinegar

Rinse the pearled spelt under cold water and drain.

Melt the butter and oil together in a large saucepan and cook the shallot, garlic and chilli very gently until soft but not coloured.

Add the pearled spelt and pour in enough hot stock to cover. Add the tarragon. Bring to the boil then turn down to a simmer and cook for about 15 minutes, stirring regularly, adding more stock as it's needed. Check the texture as you go. You want it soft, but with a slight bite. Remove from the heat. Meanwhile pod the broad beans (if using fresh) and stir them into the spelt with the peas to cook for 3–4 minutes (still off the heat) before adding the Parmesan. They are nicest al dente, a good contrast to the soft spelt.

Check the seasoning, adding salt and pepper as you need. Add the broad bean and pea shoots (if using) and a swirl of balsamic vinegar over each serving. Put a plate of grated Parmesan on the table so everyone can add more if they wish.

» 273 calories per serving

More on » spelt p32 » garlic p82 » chillies p93
» butter p104 » rapeseed oil p248

Rice There are many varieties of rice – long-grain, short-grain, risotto – and most of them come in brown and white forms. All are **gluten**-free. Brown rice retains the nutritional value of the whole grain, while white rice is milled and polished, which removes the bran, germ and other nutrients, thus offering **carbohydrates** but not much else.

Brown rice is an excellent source of **fibre** (it contains about 20 per cent more fibre than other varieties) and selenium, which has been linked with a possible reduction in cancer risk, particularly of the colon and prostate. Brown rice is also a good source of the B vitamins thiamine (B1), riboflavin (B2) and niacin (B3) – these play an important role in cell metabolism and energy production.

Red rice is grown in the Himalayas and has a nutty, earthy taste and a chewy texture. It has similar benefits to brown rice, but the **anthocyanins** responsible for its colour are an added bonus; it is also richer in zinc, and contains twice the amount of iron and many times the level of **antioxidants**.

Black rice – also known as 'forbidden rice' – is a black-purple colour when cooked. It is the highest in anthocyanins of them all. The bran hull also contains significantly higher amounts of vitamin E, which boosts the immune system and protects from **free-radical** damage. Compared to brown rice, it has a higher amount of **protein** and fibre. It's the one I always choose now.

Large shared plates

Beetroot and black rice risotto with goats' cheese

This is a no-stir risotto, cooked like a pilaf and so very easy to do. It's perfect comfort food, but not packed with calories, and the purple and black look marvellous on the plate. The sweetness of the beetroot is set against the sharpness of the cheese for an overall good, earthy taste. Use organic Nerone black rice which, because it is a whole grain, is fibre-rich and nutritious; it also has a nutty flavour and is supremely delicious.

For 4:
500g (3 medium) beetroots
400g spring onions, finely sliced
A little set coconut oil or cold-pressed rapeseed oil
1 tsp ground allspice
1 tbsp thyme leaves, chopped
150g black rice
500ml vegetable stock (see p101)
100g goats' cheese (or feta)
30g bunch of flat-leaf parsley, leaves coarsely chopped

Grate the beetroot (if the beetroot is young and fresh, you don't need to peel it). In a large pan gently fry the spring onion in the oil for 3–4 minutes. Add the allspice, thyme and rice and stir to coat in the oil. Add the grated beetroot.

Pour over the vegetable stock and cover the pan tightly with the lid. Simmer gently for 50 minutes to an hour, checking every so often towards the end of the time to see whether the rice is cooked – it should still be nutty.

Spoon the risotto onto one serving plate or bowl. Slice or crumble the cheese over (you can toast it under the grill first if you fancy). Scatter with parsley, and serve with a large, crisp green salad.

» 300 calories per serving

More on » beetroot *p85* » goats' cheese *p268*
» feta *p264* » parsley *p136*

Cauliflower couscous

This so-called 'couscous' made from cauliflower is an excellent side dish to have with any curry instead of rice or couscous. Low in carbohydrates, cauliflower is slimming too and, like all the brassica family, high in the super-antioxidant glucosinolates.

For 4–6 as a side dish:
600g cauliflower, chopped into smallish chunks
1 tbsp cold-pressed rapeseed oil
1 red onion, finely chopped
1 garlic clove, crushed
¼ tsp ground turmeric
1–2 pinches of chilli powder
Large sprig of rosemary, leaves fincly chopped
1 tsp cumin seeds, dry-fried
2 tbsp pumpkin seeds, dry-fried
6 large sun-blushed or sun-dried tomatoes in oil, roughly chopped
Handful of roughly chopped mint leaves
Handful of roughly chopped flat-leaf parsley leaves
Sea salt and black pepper

Put the cauliflower into a food processor. Pulse a few times until it has the consistency of couscous. Do not over-blend as it will turn into a purée. Alternatively you can grate the cauliflower.

Heat the oil in a large frying pan. Add the onion and garlic and fry gently until softened. Add the turmeric, chilli powder and rosemary, and cook for a minute or two until sizzling and fragrant. Tip in the cauliflower and stir to coat in the spices. Cook for 2–3 minutes, no more: you want to retain the freshness of the cauliflower whilst removing some of its rawness. Spoon into a bowl and add the remaining ingredients. Stir and season to taste.

» 188 calories for 4 servings, 126 for 6

More on » cauliflower *p267* » rapeseed oil *p248*
» onions *p281* » garlic *p82* » turmeric *p87*
» pumpkin seeds *p105* » tomatoes *p142*
» mint *p326* » parsley *p136*

Summer vegetable stir-fry with peanut and sesame noodles

The key thing with any stir-fry is that the vegetables are fresh and crunchy, so add liquid – such as tamari sauce – only after they're cooked. Once you've done the chopping, this moreish stir-fry takes less than 10 minutes to cook. You can use any noodles. It's good with Chinese egg noodles, but buckwheat soba noodles are the most nutritious. They have a strong flavour and are delicious too.

For 6:

600g summer vegetables (equal amount of carrots, courgettes, purple sprouting or tenderstem broccoli, pea shoots or sugarsnap peas, bright-coloured chard stalks)
4 spring onions, cut thinly on the diagonal
250g noodles (ideally buckwheat)
2 tbsp cold-pressed rapeseed oil
1 red finger chilli, deseeded and finely sliced widthways
1 thumb-length piece of fresh root ginger, peeled and cut into matchsticks
2 lemongrass stalks, outer leaves removed, finely chopped
Sea salt and black pepper
300g beansprouts
30g coriander leaves, chopped

For the dressing

3 tbsp cold-pressed rapeseed oil
2 tbsp toasted sesame oil
1 garlic clove, crushed
2 tbsp peanut butter (see p36)
1 green chilli, deseeded and finely chopped
3 spring onions, finely sliced
3 tbsp sesame seeds, dry-fried, plus extra to serve
4 tbsp tamari soy sauce
Grated zest and juice of 1 lime
50g bunch of coriander, leaves and stalks, chopped

Cut all the vegetables into even-sized pieces, about 6–7cm in length and about 3–4mm wide. Cook the noodles following the instructions on the packet.

For the dressing, mix together the two oils, garlic and peanut butter. Add the chilli, spring onion and sesame seeds. Drain the noodles and transfer to a large warmed serving bowl. Pour over the dressing and toss. Add the tamari, lime zest and juice and coriander, toss again and season to taste.

Heat the rapeseed oil over a high heat in a large wok or the largest frying pan you have. Fry the chilli, ginger and lemongrass for 30 seconds, then add the vegetables except the beansprouts. Season and stir continually over a high heat for 5 minutes to ensure all the vegetables get coated in the oil. They will still have a good crunch. Take the vegetables off the heat and stir through the beansprouts and fresh coriander. Serve immediately with the noodles and a sprinkling of sesame seeds, if you like.

» 432 calories per serving

More on » carrots p121 » broccoli p151 » rapeseed oil p248 » chillies p93 » ginger p200 » beansprouts p132 » coriander p204 » garlic p82 » sesame seeds p164 » tamari soy sauce p97

Buckwheat is a plant that is cultivated for its grain-like seeds. Buckwheat noodles, flour and the whole groats are rich in both soluble and insoluble dietary **fibre**, as well as **protein**. In combination, these help us feel full, control blood sugar and facilitate good digestion. Regular consumption of buckwheat has also been associated with a general reduction in body fat. Like asparagus, apples and citrus fruits, buckwheat is an excellent source of rutin, which belongs to a group of plant compounds called **flavonoids**. Rutin strengthens capillaries and keeps platelets from clotting, which is especially beneficial for people suffering from atherosclerosis (clogging of the arteries), varicose veins and high blood pressure.

Shakshuka with chickpeas

This robust Tunisian chickpea stew is perfect for a summer lunch or supper, ideally eaten outside, and it's also great for brunch. I love this with sausages cooked on a barbecue, but it's healthier and just as tasty with eggs. The dukkah spice mix lifts it too and reduces the need for salt.

This recipe will give you much more dukkah than you need. Store the rest in an airtight jar to roast with veg, scatter over lamb or stir through couscous.

For 2:
1–2 eggs per person

For the sauce
600g ripe tomatoes, blitzed
30g basil leaves
2 tbsp cold-pressed rapeseed oil
1 red onion, thinly sliced
1 tsp ground cumin
1 tsp sweet paprika
Flaky sea salt and black pepper
1–2 mild green chillies, deseeded and sliced on the diagonal (optional)
2 garlic cloves, roughly chopped
400g cooked (or tinned) chickpeas
30g bunch of coriander, leaves and stalks, chopped

For the pistachio dukkah
4 tbsp sesame seeds
3 tbsp coriander seeds
3 tbsp cumin seeds
75g pistachio kernels

For the topping
4 tbsp live natural yoghurt (see p44)
Finely grated zest of 1 lemon
1 mild green chilli, deseeded and sliced on the diagonal (optional)
10g coriander leaves

For the sauce, gently simmer the blitzed tomatoes in a saucepan for 20 minutes, until they have reduced right down. Add the basil leaves, torn up.

In another pan, heat the oil and gently fry the onion with the cumin and paprika, adding a pinch of salt and half the chilli (if using) for 10 minutes, until soft. Add the garlic and fry for a further 3 minutes.

Add the tomato sauce and the chickpeas and simmer for 10 minutes. If the sauce becomes too dry, add a little water. Take off the heat, season with salt and pepper. Allow to cool a little, then stir in the chopped coriander.

Preheat the oven to 180°C/gas mark 4.

Put the chickpea/tomato sauce into a shallow, wide dish or two individual dishes. Make a dimple for each egg in the sauce, and crack in the egg(s).

Cover with foil and bake for 5 minutes for soft yolks and 10 minutes for hard-cooked eggs.

Meanwhile, make the dukkah. Lightly dry-fry the sesame, coriander and cumin seeds. Place in a food processor. Dry-fry the pistachio kernels until they turn a shade darker. Add to the processor with the seeds. Pulse for 5–10 seconds – you want an irregular texture. Set to one side.

To serve, dollop the yoghurt over the chickpeas and eggs, along with the lemon zest, followed by a scattering of dukkah, chopped chilli (if using) and coriander. Place a small bowl of dukkah on the table so you can add extra if you wish.

» 1,107 calories for 2 servings (if using 4 eggs)

More on » eggs *p61* » tomatoes *p142* » rapeseed oil *p248* » onions *p281* » chillies *p93* » garlic *p82* » chickpeas *p182* » coriander *p204* » sesame seeds *p164* » yoghurt *p44* » lemons *p346*

Black bean and chicken burritos

This is a good weekday supper, or a casual weekend lunch with everyone compiling their own individual wraps. The ingredients list is long, but the beans store and freeze well, so you could make a double batch and use them again for another meal. Include whatever you like in the filling, but chicken – smoked, or marinated and grilled – avocado, yoghurt (or soured cream if you prefer), chilli and beans are all classic ingredients, along with a good dash of lime and fresh coriander.

For 4:
2 organic skinless chicken breasts (about 300g)

For the black bean chilli
1 red onion, peeled and chopped
1 tbsp cold-pressed rapeseed oil
½ red chilli, deseeded and chopped
1 heaped tsp smoked paprika
1 large garlic clove, crushed
400g tin of chopped tomatoes, or 6 fresh tomatoes, roughly chopped
100g black beans, soaked overnight and cooked until just tender, or 400g tin of black beans (240g drained weight)
25g best-quality dark chocolate (at least 70% cocoa solids)
Sea salt and black pepper

For the guacamole
2 ripe avocados, peeled, stoned and chopped
10 sun-dried tomatoes, roughly chopped
½ small red onion, finely diced
½ red chilli, deseeded and finely chopped
Finely grated zest and juice of 1 lime
30g bunch of coriander, leaves and stalks, chopped

To serve
4 large (60g) multigrain tortilla wraps
2 tbsp pumpkin seeds, dry-fried
A little coriander, roughly chopped
4 spring onions, thinly sliced on the diagonal
4 tbsp crème fraîche or live natural yoghurt (see p44)
1 red chilli, deseeded and finely sliced
1 lime, quartered

For the black bean chilli, in a medium saucepan gently fry the onion in the oil until translucent. Add the chilli, paprika and garlic and cook for 2 minutes. Add the tomatoes and cook gently for about 20 minutes to reduce down. Stir in the black beans and cook for a further 10 minutes. Grate in the chocolate and stir. Taste and season. Keep warm until ready to serve.

To make the guacamole, put all the ingredients except the coriander into a bowl and gently mash, leaving some bits chunky. Or put in a food processor and pulse briefly. Add the chopped coriander and mix through.

Set a bamboo steamer basket over a pan of boiling water, put in the chicken breasts and cover. Steam for 15 minutes until the chicken is cooked through. Leave to cool for 10 minutes and then shred with two forks.

Take a tortilla and spread a quarter of the guacamole over it, leaving a 5–6cm gap at the edges. Add a good tablespoon of the black beans in the centre, and a quarter of the shredded chicken. Sprinkle with the pumpkin seeds, coriander, spring onions, a dollop of crème fraîche (or yoghurt) and a few slices of chilli. Fold in the edges – left and right – into the centre, securing the filling. Then bring the edges nearest and furthest away from you together. The guacamole should hold it all together. Serve with a quartered lime on the side.

» 709 calories per serving

More on » chicken *p260* » onions *p281* » rapeseed oil *p248* » chillies *p93* » garlic *p82* » tomatoes *p142* » chocolate *p291* » avocados *p119* » coriander *p204* » pumpkin seeds *p105* » yoghurt *p44*

Adzuki bean and root vegetable chilli

This is a fantastic vegetarian chilli, served with red or black rice, or ordinary couscous. As a light, vegetable alternative, you could try the chilli with the Cauliflower couscous on page 225. It has all the flavours of a Moroccan lamb tagine, so much so that committed meat-eaters won't miss the meat. It looks like a lot of ingredients, but this is an excellent one-pot meal, which you can make in a big batch and eat over several days. It also freezes well. Ideally buy organic root veg and do not peel them, just scrub well.

Serve the chilli with some yoghurt (see page 44) or tzatziki (see page 181) on the side.

For 6–8:
200g dried adzuki beans, soaked overnight
2 tbsp cold-pressed rapeseed oil or 1 tsp set coconut oil
1 large onion, finely chopped
2 celery sticks, finely chopped
1 red pepper, deseeded and finely chopped
1–2 red chillies (depending on the heat you want), deseeded and finely chopped
2 garlic cloves, finely chopped
150g celeriac, cut into large chunks
150g carrots, cut into large chunks
150g swede, cut into large chunks
150g parsnip, cut into large chunks
150g sweet potato, cut into large chunks
2 bay leaves
½ tbsp cumin seeds, dry-fried and ground
½ tbsp dried oregano
½ tbsp paprika
1 tbsp ground cinnamon
1 x 400g tin of chopped tomatoes
200g tomato passata
2 tbsp golden sultanas
1 tbsp clear or set honey
500ml vegetable stock (see page 101)
Sea salt and black pepper
30g coriander leaves, roughly chopped

Drain the adzuki beans and rinse. Heat the oil in a large flameproof casserole dish, then add the onion, celery, pepper, chillies and garlic. Cook over a medium heat until soft (about 10 minutes).

Add the root vegetables to the casserole, along with the bay leaves, cumin, oregano, paprika and cinnamon. Stir well, then add the adzuki beans, tomatoes, tomato passata, sultanas and honey. Cover and simmer on top of the stove for 30 minutes, stirring at regular intervals to prevent sticking, or cover and cook in the oven at 160°C/gas mark 2–3 for 1 hour.

Add the vegetable stock and continue cooking for another 30 minutes. Taste, and add salt and pepper if necessary.

When ready to serve, sprinkle with the fresh coriander.

» 241 calories for 6 servings, 181 for 8

More on » rapeseed oil *p248* » coconut oil *p309* » onions *p281* » chillies *p93* » garlic *p82* » carrots *p121* » sweet potato *p72* » cinnamon *p22* » tomatoes *p142* » honey *p334* » coriander *p204*

Adzuki beans Compared to other beans, adzuki beans have very high levels of **protein** and are lower in calories. With a low fat content and only 1.3 calories per gram, they are excellent for weight loss – and you feel fuller for longer because of their high levels of protein. They are also a rich source of the essential nutrients folate, potassium and magnesium, and all this in combination with **fibre** makes them an excellent food for a healthy heart.

Large shared plates

Sweet and sour vegetable curry

I would happily eat this with black or red rice every day, with a good dollop of tzatziki or pomegranate raita, and perhaps some chilli jam (see pages 181, 147 and 188). You need the sourness of the lime to cut through the sweetness of the coconut milk, and the sweet potato and the rich spices helps this too. You will only use half of the spice mix – store the rest in an airtight jar, out of bright light.

For 6:

For the spice mix
1 tbsp coriander seeds
1 tbsp cumin seeds
1 cinnamon stick, about 6cm long
1 tsp ground cloves
1 tsp black peppercorns
1 tsp black mustard seeds
1 tsp fenugreek or caraway seeds

For the curry
2 tbsp cold-pressed rapeseed oil
1 large onion, thinly sliced
4 garlic cloves, finely chopped
1 red chilli, deseeded and finely chopped
400ml tin of coconut milk
1kg sweet potato (or squash), cut into chunks
2 x 400g tins of chickpeas, drained and rinsed
300g spinach, roughly chopped, with stalks
Grated zest and juice of 2 limes
Sea salt and black pepper

To serve
Handful of coriander, leaves and stalks
2 tbsp cashews or hazelnuts, dry-fried and chopped

Dry-fry the spices for the spice mix in a frying pan, then grind to a powder using a mortar and pestle or a spice mill.

To start the curry, heat the oil in a large heavy-based pan or flameproof casserole dish over a medium heat. Add the onion, garlic and chilli and cook until soft, about 5–6 minutes. Add half the spice mix. Pour in the coconut milk, bring to the boil, then turn down the heat to a gentle simmer. Add the sweet potato (or squash), cover and cook for 15 minutes, stirring halfway through.

Add the chickpeas to the coconut milk and sweet potato, cover and cook for 5–10 minutes. Remove the pan from the heat, and add the spinach. Stir to just wilt it in. Add the lime zest and juice, and season with salt and pepper to taste. Divide between bowls and garnish with coriander and the cashews or hazelnuts.

» 460 calories per serving

More on » coriander p204 » cinnamon p22 » rapeseed oil p248 » onions p281 » garlic p82 » chillies p93 » sweet potato p72 » squash p186 » chickpeas p182 » spinach p54 » hazelnuts p50

Large shared plates

Kale and chickpea curry

There are very few repeat recipes from my other cookbooks, but I had to include this, which is one of my most frequently cooked recipes at home in the winter. It's perfect comfort food – quick and easy and packed full of nutritious ingredients. As with the Sweet and sour vegetable curry (see opposite), serve with red rice, or the nutty black variety, and a dollop of tzatziki (see page 181). Like many curries, the flavour improves overnight, so make a big batch and go back to it the following day. You can also make batches of the curry base (up to adding the cavolo nero or kale) and freeze, then add the fresh veg when you eat.

For 8:
1 large onion, finely chopped
3 garlic cloves, finely chopped
1 tsp set coconut oil
1 heaped tbsp medium curry powder
25g fresh root ginger, grated
2 green chillies, or 1 red finger chilli, deseeded
    and finely chopped
2 x 400g tins of chickpeas, drained and rinsed, or
    250g dried chickpeas, soaked overnight and cooked
2 x 400ml tins of coconut milk
250g button mushrooms, halved
Juice of 1 lime
2 lemongrass stalks, outer leaves removed,
    cut into 2cm lengths
15 medium cavolo nero (or any kale) leaves
2 tbsp tamari soy sauce
2 tbsp Thai fish sauce
Sea salt and black pepper
50–60g bunch of coriander, leaves and stalks,
    coarsely chopped

In a large, heavy-based pan or flameproof casserole, fry the onion and garlic gently in the coconut oil over a medium heat until soft. Stir in the curry powder, ginger and chilli and cook for a further couple of minutes.

Next, add the cooked chickpeas, coconut milk, button mushrooms, lime juice and lemongrass, stir well and simmer for 30 minutes.

Remove the stalks from the cavolo nero (or kale) and chop the leaves into strips. Steam them for 5 minutes, then stir into the chickpea mixture. Add the tamari and fish sauce. Taste the curry and then season with salt and black pepper.

Scatter the curry with coarsely chopped coriander (use the stalks too, which are full of flavour).

» 272 calories per serving

More on » onions *p281* » garlic *p82* » coconut oil *p309* » ginger *p200* » chillies *p93* » chickpeas *p182* » mushrooms *p88* » kale *p117* » tamari soy sauce *p97* » coriander *p204*

Coconut milk is highly nutritious and is a rich source of **vitamins** and **minerals**. It is especially suitable for people who are lactose-intolerant. It contains significant amounts of lauric acid, a medium-chain saturated fatty acid that may act as an anti-viral and anti-bacterial in the body, helping prevent infections, colds and flu, as well as maintaining healthy **cholesterol** levels. Coconut milk is high in calories but it is an excellent substitute for cream in many dishes including curries, soups, gratins and even tarts. Calories vary according to brand, but 100ml coconut milk contains about 160 calories (and 100ml light coconut milk contains about 73), compared to 350 calories in double cream. As light coconut milk is just coconut milk with water added, you can – if watching your weight – just buy normal coconut milk and water it down.

Green Thai autumn fish and vegetable curry

The flavour of this is fantastic, with an easy-to-make curry paste and the veg all roasted for extra flavour before being dressed in the sauce. All varieties of squash work well. You can use cod, or the much cheaper but still delicious pollock.

Roasting the squash whole makes it easy to peel off the minimal thickness of skin. That's where there is the highest concentration of antioxidants, so you want to reduce the amount removed and chucked in the bin. With butternut squash, the skin can be left on, and is delicious.

For 4–6:
400ml tin of coconut milk
1 tbsp Thai fish sauce
1 tbsp coconut palm sugar
500g cod or pollock, skinned and cut into 4–5cm chunks
3 tsp sesame seeds, dry-fried
30g bunch of coriander, leaves and stalks, coarsely chopped
2 tbsp green coriander seeds (optional)

For the vegetables
200g squash, deseeded, cut into chunks
200g carrots, cut into medium-sized chunks
1 tbsp cold-pressed rapeseed oil
200g Tenderstem broccoli
200g green beans, tailed and halved

For the green curry paste
3 tsp grated fresh root ginger
2 tsp ground coriander
2 tsp caraway seeds
½ nutmeg, grated
2 good pinches of sea salt
2 good pinches of ground black pepper
Pinch of ground cloves
1 lemongrass stalk, outer leaves removed, finely sliced
2 garlic cloves, roughly chopped
2 small onions, roughly chopped
Grated zest and juice of 2 limes
4 green chillies, deseeded and roughly chopped
1 tbsp set coconut oil

Preheat the oven to 190°C/gas mark 5.

Place the squash and carrot chunks on a roasting tray, drizzle over the oil and roast for 20 minutes. Then add the broccoli and beans, and roast for a further 15–20 minutes until tender.

Put all the ingredients for the green curry paste – except for the coconut oil – into a food processor and whizz until you have a smooth paste.

Heat the coconut oil in a large frying pan and add the curry paste. Cook for 3–4 minutes, stirring frequently. Turn down the heat, then pour in the coconut milk and fish sauce and add the sugar. Cook for a further 6–7 minutes, stirring frequently.

Add the roasted veg to the sauce in the frying pan. Add the chunks of fish to the sauce too. Gently simmer for 5 minutes – no longer or the fish will disintegrate.

Sprinkle with the sesame seeds. Serve with the chopped coriander, green coriander seeds (if using) and basmati, black or red rice.

» 693 calories for 4 servings, 462 for 6

More on » coconut milk *p235* » coconut palm sugar *p316* » sesame seeds *p164* » coriander *p204* » squash *p186* » carrots *p121* » rapeseed oil *p248* » broccoli *p151* » ginger *p200* » garlic *p82* » onions *p281* » chillies *p93* » coconut oil *p309*

Indonesian monkfish curry with aubergine

Monkfish is ideal for curry. It's good and meaty and takes more cooking than most fish as it doesn't disintegrate. I had something similar to this in the Porthminster Café in St Ives, Cornwall, and kept going back to have it again! The curry paste makes three times more than you need. Put the remainder into ice-cube trays and freeze for another day.

For 8:
2 medium-sized sweet potatoes, cut into 2cm slices
2 medium aubergines, cut into 3cm cubes
1 tbsp cold-pressed rapeseed oil
Sea salt and black pepper
2 tbsp sunflower oil
1 tbsp sesame oil
600g cleaned monkfish tail, cut into 4cm cubes
4 tbsp curry paste (see below)
12 raw prawns, peeled and de-veined
About 20 mussels (in their shells), de-bearded and cleaned
250ml fish stock (made from a stock cube)
2 x 400ml tins of coconut milk
4 star anise
4 kaffir lime leaves, fresh or dried
1 tsp tamarind paste
12 cherry tomatoes, cut in half
100g chard, stalks finely sliced and leaves torn
Thai fish sauce, to serve

For the curry paste
4 garlic cloves
¼ tsp shrimp paste
2 red chillies
3 tsp ground turmeric
1 lemongrass stalk, outer leaves removed, sliced
4 spring onions
2 plum tomatoes
1 tsp coriander seeds, dry-fried
1 tsp fennel seeds, dry-fried
½ nutmeg, grated
1 thumb-length piece of fresh root ginger, peeled
4g fresh galangal, peeled (or use more fresh root ginger)
3 tbsp coconut palm sugar
20g bunch of coriander, leaves and stalks

Preheat the oven to 180°C/gas mark 4. Place the sweet potato and aubergine on a baking tray, drizzle with the rapeseed oil and season with salt and pepper. Roast for 30 minutes until both vegetables are soft and coloured. Roughly chop all the relevant curry paste ingredients, then blitz them together in a food processor.

Heat the sunflower and sesame oils in a large frying pan and cook the monkfish on a medium-high heat until golden on all sides. Lower the heat and add 4 tablespoons of the curry paste and cook for 2 minutes. Add the prawns, mussels and stock and cook for 3 minutes. Pour in the coconut milk, and add the star anise, lime leaves and tamarind paste. Cook for 5 minutes on a low heat. Finally stir in the cherry tomatoes and chard, and the baked aubergine and sweet potato. Cook together for 4 minutes.

Serve the curry with black or red rice and a dash of Thai fish sauce, or Jewelled freekeh (see page 242).

» 390 calories per serving

More on » sweet potato p72 » aubergines p147 » rapeseed oil p248 » prawns p212 » coconut milk p235 » tomatoes p142 » garlic p82 » chillies p93 » turmeric p87 » coriander p204 » ginger p200 » coconut palm sugar p316

Mussels Out of all the shellfish, mussels have the highest levels of **omega-3 fatty acids**. These improve brain function and cardiovascular health, and reduce the low-grade **inflammation** thought to predispose us to diseases such as diabetes and dementia. Mussels are an excellent source of vitamin B12 and folic acid, which are vital for a healthy nervous system. The good iodine levels are beneficial for those with an underactive thyroid. They provide vitamin A, selenium, iron and zinc too.

Large shared plates

Valentine's venison and coconut curry

Valentine Warner cooked this for us at one of our cookery demonstrations in the school, and it is fragrant and delicious, with the coconut water (rather than coconut milk) making it almost light. (You can use the coconut water you get in a carton.) Valentine had eaten the curry searingly hot in Sri Lanka, but this is a milder and simpler, slightly Anglicised version.

Serve with black or red rice, Jewelled freekeh (as in the photograph; see page 242) and/or Cauliflower couscous (see page 225).

For vegetarians, this recipe is delicious if you replace the venison with large Portobello mushrooms, sliced into strips, and/or aubergine.

For 4:
1 tbsp set coconut oil
2 small red onions, finely sliced
1 cinnamon stick, about 4cm long
2 star anise
500g venison fillet (or loin), cut into bite-sized strips
300ml coconut water
Grated zest of 1 lime
Juice of ½ lime
2 tbsp desiccated coconut, dry-fried

For the spice paste
2 garlic cloves, peeled
1 large thumb-length piece of fresh root ginger,
    peeled and finely chopped
1 heaped tsp flaky sea salt
4 cloves
1 heaped tsp fennel seeds
1 level tsp hot chilli powder
1 level tsp cumin seeds
1 heaped tsp garam masala
3 heaped tbsp tomato purée

Make the spice paste first. Using a pestle and mortar, crush the garlic, ginger, salt, cloves, fennel seeds, chilli powder, cumin seeds and garam masala into a paste. Add the tomato purée to the spice paste, stirring to combine.

Melt the coconut oil in a wok or large frying pan over a medium heat. Add the onions, cinnamon stick and star anise, and stir and cook until the onions are golden.

Add the spice paste to the onions and fry for 2–3 minutes, stirring often. Add the meat to the spices and briskly sauté for 3–4 minutes to seal.

Add the coconut water, lime zest and lime juice and bring to a rapid simmer for 5 minutes, or until you have a thickish gravy. Venison fillet takes very little cooking when cut into these thin strips, but cook for longer if you use another cut of meat.

Scatter with the dry-fried coconut and stir through before serving.

» 289 calories per serving

More on » coconut oil p309 » onions p281
» cinnamon p22 » coconut water p337 » garlic p82
» ginger p200 » tomatoes p142

Venison As a red meat, venison is in a class of its own, with more **protein** than any other, and therefore it particularly satisfies hunger. The significant levels of iron can prevent anaemia and help boost energy levels. This lean meat has less **saturated fat** and **cholesterol** than beef – and it also contains linoleic acid, which may protect against cancer and heart disease. Venison is a rich source of vitamin B12, which is essential for the normal functioning of the brain and the nervous system.

Jewelled freekeh

The textures, colour and flavour make this an almost stand-alone dish, but it is the perfect accompaniment to dishes with strong flavours, particularly curries. Pronounced 'free-kah', freekeh is unripe green wheat that has been parched and roasted to burn off the husks. This gives it a delicious smoky taste. It's one of my new favourite grains, so much nuttier in texture and taste than boring old white rice. You can replace the freekeh with brown rice or bulghar wheat, topping them all with edible flowers. Here I have used dahlias and the yellow petals of the salad plant mizuna.

For 8:
50g dried cranberries
75g dried apricots (ideally organic, unsulphured)
60g raisins
250g freekeh
2 tbsp cold-pressed rapeseed oil
1 small onion, finely chopped
1 medium (250–300g) fennel bulb, chopped
1 cinnamon stick
10 cardamom pods or 1 tsp cardamom seeds
1 tsp coriander seeds
1 litre hot chicken or vegetable stock (see pp98 and 101)
50g pistachio kernels, dry-fried
Sea salt and black pepper

To serve
Handful of mixed herbs or edible flower petals
Seeds of 1 pomegranate (see p46)

Put the cranberries, apricots and raisins into a jug and pour over enough boiling water to cover. Soak for 20 minutes, then drain. Wash the freekeh in a sieve under the cold tap, and drain.

Put the olive oil into a large saucepan and heat gently. Add the onion and fennel and sauté for 5 minutes. Add the freekeh, cinnamon stick, cardamom and coriander, stirring well to ensure all the grains get coated in the oil. Pour in the stock, bring to the boil, then turn down the heat and cook, simmering gently, with the lid on for 5 minutes. Take the lid off and continue to simmer for 10 minutes, or until all the liquid has been absorbed. Remove the pan from the heat and stir in the drained cranberries, apricots, raisins and the pistachio nuts. Taste, and season with salt and black pepper. Scatter with the herbs or edible flower petals and the pomegranate seeds. Serve warm or cold.

» 282 calories per serving

More on » freekeh *p270* » rapeseed oil *p248* » onions *p281* » cinnamon *p22* » coriander *p204* » pomegranate *p46*

Cranberries
For a fruit, cranberries are low in sugar, making them tart but delicious – and very good for you. As well as providing vitamin C, dietary **fibre** and manganese, they are also an invaluable source of a range of **phytonutrients** that appear to work together synergistically in the whole fruit. These **antioxidant** and **anti-inflammatory** phytonutrients have anti-cancer benefits. Cranberries are known to be helpful in treating urinary tract infections – it has been shown that they prevent bacteria from adhering to the walls of the urinary tract, and new research also points to beneficial effects in other parts of the body. Other components of cranberries, the **proanthocyanidins**, may inhibit the activity of the bacteria responsible for stomach ulcers, and prevent the adhesion of plaque bacteria to the teeth, thus preventing periodontal disease.

Add fresh cranberries to your breakfast bowl of muesli or yoghurt, but don't be tempted to drink too much shop-bought cranberry juice, as it has a lot of added sugar. And before consuming large amounts of cranberries or their juice, check with your doctor for any possible drug interactions.

Dried cranberries are often coated with oil or hydrogenated fat to prevent them sticking together and to plump them up – remove this by soaking the fruit in boiling water for 20 minutes.

Large shared plates

Greek octopus and aubergine with green sauce

This is an excellent dish to cook for a party. Dealing with octopus is a bit intimidating the first time, but it's fun to do. You can use frozen octopus – which you'll get from a good fishmonger – as the freezing starts the tenderising process. It makes for a rich, robust stew, cut through by the tangy sharpness of the green sauce. Use whatever herbs you have handy, but fennel, parsley and dill would be traditional in Greece. I sometimes add lots of peppers for extra sweetness and to pad out the expensive octopus.

For 8:
1.5kg octopus, cleaned and gutted (ask the fishmonger to do this for you)
2 bay leaves
1 tbsp black peppercorns
3 tbsp red wine vinegar
2kg aubergines, cut into bite-sized chunks
4 tbsp cold-pressed rapeseed oil
Sea salt and black pepper
1 onion, finely chopped
2 large fennel bulbs, sliced
1 garlic clove, finely chopped
1 tbsp fennel seeds
3 x 400g tins of tomatoes, or 12 large ripe tomatoes, blitzed
4 sprigs of thyme
4 tbsp aged balsamic vinegar

For the green sauce
Large bunch (50–60g) flat-leaf parsley
Large bunch (50–60g) mixed herbs (such as chives, fennel, chervil, coriander or sorrel)
4 cornichons, rinsed
20–30 small capers, rinsed
250ml olive oil
Juice of ½ lemon

Put the octopus in a large pan with the bay leaves, peppercorns, vinegar and enough water to cover. Put a small plate on top of the octopus to stop it floating up to the surface: this will ensure it cooks evenly. Cook for 45 minutes at a slow simmer, covered. (You can also cook octopus with no water at all – slowly at first – and it makes its own juices. This means that you're retaining every bit of goodness. Just top up with a bit of water if it runs dry. Allow a couple of hours at a very gentle simmer for this cooking method.)

Whilst the octopus cooks, roast the aubergines. Preheat the oven to 180°C/gas mark 4. Put the aubergine chunks in a single layer on a couple of baking sheets. Sprinkle with 2 tablespoons of the oil, and season with salt and pepper. Roast for 30 minutes until soft and colouring at the edges.

Heat the remaining oil in a medium pan and gently fry the onion and fennel until they have softened. Add the garlic and fennel seeds and cook for 2 minutes. Stir in the tomatoes, thyme and balsamic vinegar and simmer for 20 minutes.

Drain the octopus. Cut it in half, remove the shell-like beak and discard. Slice the head into strips and cut the limbs into bite-sized chunks. Cook the octopus for another 10 minutes in the tomato sauce: taste to check it is tender. Add the roasted aubergine to the octopus and cook for a further 10 minutes.

To make the green sauce, coarsely chop the herbs. Mix with the cornichons and capers, oil and lemon juice. Blitz briefly, or chop by hand, for a coarse-textured sauce. Season to taste with salt and pepper. Serve the octopus with the green sauce. It's also good with some black or red rice and roast sweet potatoes or squash.

» 386 calories per serving

More on » aubergines p147 » rapeseed oil p248 » onions p281 » garlic p82 » tomatoes p142 » balsamic vinegar p189 » parsley p136 » olive oil p193 » lemons p346

Provençal squid, new potato, olive and tomato stew

This is a recipe from Ivan, a friend of mine, who is a wonderful cook. There are many versions of squid stew, but this one has a particularly rich flavour. Squid goes brilliantly with tomatoes and together they make excellent heart-healthy food. The sweetness of the squid and tomato here is offset by the sharpness of the olives. It's important to have the best ingredients: very fresh squid, lovely sweet summery tomatoes and small, ideally just-dug new potatoes.

For 4:

1 tbsp cold-pressed rapeseed oil
1 small onion or shallot (about 150g), finely chopped
2 garlic cloves, finely chopped
800g squid, cut into bite-sized pieces
Small sprig of rosemary
3 sprigs of thyme
600g tomatoes, chopped, or 400g tin of chopped tomatoes
200g small waxy new potatoes
8–10 sun-dried tomatoes in oil, roughly chopped
Sea salt and black pepper
100g Kalamata olives
1 tbsp extra virgin olive oil
30g flat-leaf parsley, roughly chopped

Heat the rapeseed oil over a medium heat in a large frying pan or flameproof casserole dish. Add the onion or shallot and cook for 5 minutes. Stir in the garlic and cook for a further 2 minutes until the onion and garlic are slightly softened but not browned.

Add the rosemary and thyme sprigs to the pan, and cook for about 5 minutes.

Add the tomatoes, along with the potatoes and sun-dried tomatoes. If using tinned tomatoes, fill half the tin with water, give it a swirl and add that to the pan as well. Stir and simmer for 20 minutes until the potatoes are cooked. Depending on the age and size of the squid, add it between 5 and 10 minutes from the end of this cooking time. Pour in a splash of water if it looks too dry. Season with salt and pepper to taste.

Stir in the olives and the olive oil. Leave to stand for 5 minutes. Remove the rosemary and thyme twigs.

Sprinkle the stew with parsley and serve with a green side salad.

» 405 calories per serving

More on » rapeseed oil *p248* » onions *p281* » garlic *p82* » tomatoes *p142* » olives *p179* » olive oil *p193* » parsley *p136*

Squid (and octopus) are low in fat and exceptionally low in calories (until you fry them in batter), and rich in potassium and vitamin E, nutrients that protect your heart. Squid is full of the health-boosting **omega-3 essential fatty acids** that lower the risk of heart disease and cancer, and may help to control pain in rheumatoid arthritis. In addition these fatty acids can improve your mood and memory. It also provides several trace **minerals**, such as copper and phosphorus, and important B vitamins. Squid is among the best seafood to eat, as it contains only very low levels of mercury. It's relatively inexpensive – we should all eat it more often.

Courgette and salmon parcels

These are neat-looking parcels of marinated salmon in courgette jackets, which are surprisingly easy and quick to do. You can griddle them singly and serve as a canapé, or thread several onto a skewer to cook under the grill or on a barbecue. The skewer makes them easy to turn and they keep together better. This is good served with stir-fried spinach and ginger, or Steam-stirred pak choi (see page 200), but I like it best with Watercress with a light peanut dressing (see overleaf).

For 4–6 as a main course, 10–12 as a canapé:
600g wild salmon, cut into 4cm x 3cm chunks
3–4 medium courgettes
24 cherry tomatoes
1–2 tsp set coconut oil, melted
1 tbsp sesame seeds, dry-fried, to serve

For the marinade
4 tbsp tamari soy sauce
5 tbsp cold-pressed rapeseed oil
1 tbsp Thai fish sauce
Grated zest and juice of 1 lime
1 level tbsp finely chopped fresh root ginger
1 red finger chilli, deseeded and finely chopped
1 garlic clove, finely chopped
1 tbsp clear honey or maple syrup

Mix the marinade ingredients together and put one third of it aside. Marinate the cubes of salmon in the rest of the mix for 30 minutes or so. With a vegetable peeler, cut slices of courgette lengthways.

Wrap one ribbon of courgette one way around a chunk of salmon, and a second at right angles, to make a parcel.

If using wooden skewers, soak them in water for a few minutes before threading three or four wrapped pieces of fish onto skewers, through the narrowest part, with a cherry tomato between each. Make sure not to pack too tightly so that they all cook through evenly.

Heat a griddle until you cannot hold your hand within 2cm and count to ten. Then it's hot enough.

Brush the skewered parcels with melted coconut oil and place them on the griddle, or cook them under a grill. Griddle for 3–4 minutes on each side. This will leave the middle of the salmon slightly glassy. If you want it cooked more, add another minute each side.

Serve dressed with the reserved marinade. Scatter with the dry-fried sesame seeds.

» 476 calories for 4 servings, 317 for 6, 190 for 10, 159 for 12

More on » salmon p125 » tomatoes p142 » coconut oil p309 » sesame seeds p164 » tamari soy sauce p97 » ginger p200 » chillies p93 » garlic p82 » honey p334 » maple syrup p27

Rapeseed oil contains some **saturated fats** and many **unsaturated fats**, including **omega-3 fatty acids**, as well as a significant amount of vitamin E. The best quality, cold-pressed organic rapeseed oil has the highest level of these healthy fatty acids. Rapeseed oil is often used for high-temperature cooking as it has a high smoke point (the point at which an oil starts to smoke continuously, and substances such as transfats that are detrimental to our body are produced). Transfats are implicated in atherosclerosis (clogging of the arteries), which leads to cardiovascular disease and high blood pressure. Rapeseed oil should not be substituted with canola oil, which largely comes from genetically modified crops.

Linguine allo scoglio

I had this pasta dish in a third-generation, family-run restaurant – Il Delfino – in the port of Lacco Ameno in Ischia, just off the coast of Naples. I would almost travel there just to eat it! The pasta is mainly cooked in the juices of the tomatoes and shellfish, contributing to the intensity of flavour.

For 4:
200g linguine (ideally wholewheat)
2 tbsp olive oil
2 garlic cloves, crushed
200g small squid, cleaned and cut into bite-sized pieces
200g raw prawns, peeled, de-veined and cut into chunks
250ml white wine
500g baby plum or cherry tomatoes, halved
500g mussels, de-bearded and cleaned
500g vongole clams, rinsed
Sea salt and black pepper
25g flat-leaf parsley, roughly chopped

Cook the linguine in a large pan of boiling water for 4 minutes. Drain, reserving the cooking water.

Heat the olive oil in a large frying pan, add the garlic and cook gently for 2 minutes. Stir in the squid and prawns and cook for 2 minutes. Add the pasta, white wine and a couple of tablespoons of the reserved pasta water, and cook for 3 minutes, stirring regularly. Add the tomatoes, mussels and clams. Stir gently and cook for a further 5–6 minutes until the pasta is al dente.

Taste and season with salt and pepper. Serve immediately, scattered with the parsley.

» 619 calories per serving

More on » olive oil *p193* » garlic *p82* » squid *p246* » prawns *p212* » tomatoes *p142* » mussels *p238* » parsley *p136*

Watercress with a light peanut dressing

Watercress is one of those salad plants we should all aim to eat as much of as we can. Leaf by leaf, it has one of the densest concentrations of antioxidants, and it's packed with iron. Raw in a salad, there's a limit to how much one can eat, but just briefly blanched, it retains a bit of structure and crunch, while losing a little of its fieriness. It goes perfectly with nuts and seeds. This is an excellent vegetable dish to have with chicken, seafood or fish.

For 4:
220g watercress
1 tbsp sesame seeds, dry-fried

For the dressing
1 tbsp peanut butter (see p36)
1 tbsp toasted sesame oil
1 tbsp tamari soy sauce
1 tbsp mirin (rice wine)
Juice of 1 lemon

Strip the leaves from the stalks of the watercress and set to one side. Bring a pan of water to the boil and then add the stalks and cook until just soft – for a minute only.

Then add the leaves and cook for an instant. Drain and rinse under cold water. Squeeze dry.

Mix together the dressing ingredients until smooth.

Add the dressing to the watercress and fold through until coated. Top with sesame seeds.

» 108 calories per serving

More on » watercress *p70* » sesame seeds *p164* » tamari soy sauce *p97* » lemons *p346*

Smoked haddock and beetroot gratin

Perfect comfort food that's also healthy – with a smokiness from the haddock, a sweetness from the beetroot and a rich tanginess from the leeks and cheese. To reduce the dairy content, I sometimes make the béchamel sauce with almond milk, and replace the butter with solid coconut oil.

For 6:
600g beetroots
2 tbsp cold-pressed rapeseed oil
Sea salt and black pepper
200g leek, finely chopped
425ml full-fat milk or almond milk (see p347)
300g undyed smoked haddock
50g organic unsalted butter or 1 tbsp set coconut oil
1 tbsp plain flour
Nutmeg, freshly grated (to taste)
1 tbsp English mustard
100g mature Cheddar (or less if you want to reduce calories – in which case, increase the mustard), grated
800g fresh spinach or chard, stalks removed
20g Parmesan, freshly grated

Preheat the oven to 180°C/gas mark 4.

Peel larger beetroot (but not younger, smaller ones) and slice into 3mm discs (you can use a mandolin). Place on a baking sheet, drizzle with half the rapeseed oil and season with a little sea salt and pepper. Roast for 25–30 minutes until it is soft and starting to curl at the edges. Meanwhile, gently heat the remaining oil and fry the leek until soft.

Heat the milk in a medium saucepan and, when just beginning to bubble, add the smoked haddock. Remove from the heat and allow to stand in the hot milk for 5 minutes. Take the haddock out of the pan, put on a plate and remove the skin (if necessary). Set the milk aside.

Melt the butter (or oil) in a saucepan over a medium heat, then stir in the flour until combined. Stir in the poaching milk in a steady stream until it is all incorporated and simmer gently for 2 minutes to cook out the flavour of the flour. Add a grating of nutmeg, the mustard and plenty of black pepper. Stir in the Cheddar and leek. Mix until combined and remove from the heat.

Blanch the spinach or chard and drain. Leave to cool slightly, then squeeze to remove as much water as possible. Roughly chop.

Put a layer of beetroot in the bottom of an ovenproof dish, spoon over some cheese sauce, then add a layer of flaked haddock and spinach. Repeat, finishing with a layer of sauce and a scattering of Parmesan and black pepper. Bake in the oven for 20–30 minutes until golden brown.

» 380 calories per serving

More on » beetroot p85 » rapeseed oil p248 » butter p104 » coconut oil p309 » spinach p54

Milk is an excellent source of vitamins B2, B12 and D, along with iodine, phosphorus, calcium and **protein**, many of which are essential for healthy bone growth. Organic milk is higher in the healthy fats that may help to slow growth of certain cancer cells, and also prevent hardening of the arteries. Sheep's or goats' milk is easier for us to digest and assimilate, as the fat globules are naturally homogenised, and it is less irritating to our gut.

Recent research has questioned the emphasis on reduced-fat dairy products as being better for health: in an attempt to make these more palatable, additives are often used which negate any presumed benefit and may even be detrimental to health. Although full-fat milk and dairy foods have a high proportion of **saturated fats**, the latest evidence seems to show that these do not impact heart health as we have been led to believe – rather, the high calcium content and bio-active **peptides** in milk may actually protect us against cardiovascular disease, diabetes and obesity.

Smoked mackerel and parsnip fishcakes

Using parsnip rather than potato gives these fishcakes a sweetness which is very moreish, balanced by *lots* of ginger. And I mean *lots*.

From a portion of these, you get almost half the recommended 300g of oily fish a week. Serve – as here – with three different beetroot relishes (see opposite), which cut through the rich sweetness of the fishcakes, or with Sweet and sour tomato sauce (also opposite).

For 6:
800g parsnips, roughly chopped, core and all
3 tbsp cold-pressed rapeseed oil
2 medium onions, finely chopped
1 red chilli, deseeded and finely chopped
2 garlic cloves, finely chopped

75–125g piece of fresh root ginger, peeled and finely chopped
Small piece of fresh turmeric root (optional), chopped
3 smoked mackerel (or 6 fillets), about 600g
Grated zest and juice of 1 lemon
Grated zest and juice of 1 lime
Sea salt and black pepper
2 medium eggs, beaten
175g fresh wholemeal or spelt breadcrumbs

Boil the parsnips until soft. Drain and allow to cool.

Heat the oil in a frying pan and gently fry the onion, chilli, garlic, ginger and turmeric (if using) for 10 minutes until softened.

If using whole mackerel, skin and bone them before flaking roughly. If using mackerel fillets from a vacuum pack, just skin and flake roughly.

Put the onion mixture, parsnips and mackerel into a food processor and blitz briefly to combine. Add the lemon and lime zest and juice and season with salt and pepper. Chill in the fridge for 30 minutes.

Preheat the oven to 200°C/gas mark 6, if baking the fishcakes. Shape the mixture into 12 fishcakes, dip into the beaten egg and cover with breadcrumbs. Place on a baking sheet, drizzle with rapeseed oil, and bake for 15 minutes. Or you could fry over a gentle heat in a little rapeseed oil. In both cases you want the fishcakes to be golden brown on both sides and piping hot. If fried, drain on kitchen paper and serve immediately.

» 568 calories per serving of 2 fishcakes

More on » rapeseed oil *p248* » onions *p281*
» chillies *p93* » garlic *p82* » ginger *p200*
» turmeric *p87* » mackerel and oily fish *p256*
» lemons *p346* » eggs *p61*

Three beetroot relishes

These relishes go well with any smoked fish, and they're excellent served with barbecued lamb. If you find three colours of beetroot, flavour each one differently and they'll look as good as they taste. The yellow Golden tends to be the sweetest, so I like it with citrus. Flavour the stripy Chioggia, which fades to pink on cooking, with the seeds; and the classic purple with horseradish.

For 6:
750g beetroots, or 250g each of Golden,
    Chioggia and purple, unpeeled
2 tbsp crème fraîche
1 tbsp horseradish, freshly grated, or from a jar
2 tbsp live natural yoghurt (see p44)
Grated zest and juice of 1 lime or lemon
2 tbsp extra virgin olive oil
1 tsp poppy seeds, dry-fried
1 tsp cumin seeds, dry-fried and crushed

Boil the beetroot until tender – the timing depends on size. Keep the different types separate.

Drain and allow to cool. Peel if the roots are large, but leave the peel on if small. Then coarsely grate or finely chop them, keeping the colours apart. Transfer to three bowls – a separate bowl for each.

Add the crème fraîche and horseradish to one, the natural yoghurt, citrus zest and juice to another, and the olive oil, poppy and crushed cumin seeds to the last.

» 743 calories (for the lot)

More on » beetroot *p85* » horseradish *p354*
» yoghurt *p44* » lemons *p346* » olive oil *p193*

Sweet and sour tomato sauce

A quick and easy sauce that goes with almost everything. It's worth making in big batches and then freezing in small portions to dress up instant meals. This is ideal with Smoked mackerel and parsnip fishcakes (see opposite) and fritters or falafels (see pages 204 and 267). You can leave out the anchovies for vegetarians. I sometimes add a tablespoon or two of crème fraîche to enrich it.

For 5–6:
2 banana shallots (or 6 spring onions), finely chopped
2 heaped tsp thyme leaves
1 tbsp olive oil
400g tin of chopped tomatoes
1 tbsp organic apple cider vinegar
1 tbsp coconut palm sugar
Grated zest and juice of 1 orange (blood orange
    if available)
50g tin of anchovy fillets in oil, drained

Sauté the shallots and thyme leaves very gently in the oil until soft.

Add the tomatoes, vinegar, sugar, orange zest and juice and anchovies.

Simmer to reduce over a low heat for at least 30 minutes, stirring occasionally.

» 95 calories for 5 servings, 79 for 6

More on » olive oil *p193* » tomatoes *p142*
» apple cider vinegar *p63* » coconut palm sugar
p316 » oranges *p49*

Mackerel in fennel-seed oatmeal crust

One of my very favourite things to cook on a barbecue in the summer is juicy mackerel rolled in a crunchy, nutty, fragrant casing. I included this in *Food for Friends and Family*, but it has to appear in my healthy book as it's an unbeatable way of eating very fresh mackerel.

Making shallow slashes on both sides of the fish before cooking will allow it to cook evenly. They will also then remain flat in the pan rather than curling as they start to cook, which could leave the flesh near the head and tail in danger of being undercooked.

For 6:

6 very fresh medium mackerel, cleaned but heads left on
4–5 tbsp medium-grade oatmeal (enough to cover
    a dinner plate)
1 tbsp wholemeal or spelt flour
2 tbsp fennel seeds
Sea salt and black pepper
2 tbsp cold-pressed rapeseed oil

Cut several shallow slashes crossways into the mackerel, down both sides.

Combine the oatmeal, flour, fennel seeds and plenty of salt and pepper, then spread out the mixture on a large flat plate.

Dampen the skin of the mackerel by splashing with a little water, then roll the fish in the oatmeal mixture, encouraging some into the cuts on each side.

Heat a little rapeseed oil in a couple of frying pans and cook the mackerel for about 5–7 minutes on each side (depending on the size of the fish).

Serve with a dollop of beetroot and horseradish relish (see page 255), some new potatoes and a green salad.

» 504 calories per serving

More on » oats *p25* » spelt *p32* » rapeseed oil *p248*

Mackerel and oily fish Oily fish are highly nutritious. The SMASH group of oily fish – salmon (and trout), mackerel, anchovies, sardines and herring – are all a good source of **protein**, as well as containing a wide range of **vitamins** (A, B complex, D, E and K) and **minerals**, all of which help maintain healthy nerve tissue, strong bones and teeth and a good complexion. Oily fish have top-whack levels of **omega-3s**. Over the last century there has been an 80 per cent decrease in the consumption of omega-3 fatty acids and many people are deficient in these important fats. They give us a better balance of blood **lipids**, and reduce the risk of coronary heart disease and stroke. Omega-3 fatty acids help reduce **inflammation** at a cellular level all over the body, and can protect our brain cells, reducing the risk of dementia. They are important for eye health and the parts of the brain used for memory, learning and reasoning, and may also ease arthritis in our joints.

Experts recommend eating two 140g portions of oily fish a week; one medium-sized mackerel fillet is usually about 85g.

Large shared plates

Greens and fish pie

A new twist to a classic fish pie. It looks like a long list of ingredients, but this pie incorporates your side veg dishes and is surprisingly quick to make. It is also really delicious, with a creamy, light yet satisfying topping made with celeriac and cauliflower, without either butter or milk in the mash. You can use almost any fish for this: undyed smoked haddock, cod, coley, prawns, salmon – you name it, it's good here.

For 6–8:
600g fish (use a mix for a variety of flavour and texture)
600ml full-fat milk
2 bay leaves
500g celeriac, peeled and chopped into 4cm cubes
500g cauliflower, chopped into small florets
Sea salt and black pepper
2 tsp whole-grain mustard
1 tbsp set coconut oil
4 shallots, finely chopped
1 large leek, finely sliced
100g spring greens or sweetheart cabbage,
   very finely sliced
250g baby spinach
100g fresh or frozen peas, blanched
100g fine asparagus, chopped into 1cm pieces (optional)
Large bunch of dill, finely chopped
Large bunch of flat-leaf parsley, finely chopped
Small bunch of tarragon, woody stalks removed,
   leaves finely chopped
2½ tbsp cornflour
Grated zest and juice of 1 lemon
2 tbsp crème fraîche (optional)
½ nutmeg, finely grated
60g strong Cheddar or Parmesan, grated

Preheat the oven to 180°C/gas mark 4.

Place the fish in a large saucepan with the milk and bay leaves. Heat to a simmer, then take off the heat and leave the fish to cool in the milk.

In a large saucepan, cover the celeriac with cold water and bring to the boil. Simmer for 8 minutes.

Add the cauliflower to the pan and cook with the celeriac for 5 minutes until softened. Drain well and mash, or even better, use a stick blender or food processor to create a smooth purée. Add some salt and pepper and the mustard.

In a large frying pan, melt the coconut oil and gently fry the shallot and leek for 2 minutes until just softened. Then add the spring greens and cook for a couple of minutes. Throw in the spinach and allow to wilt. Add the peas, the asparagus (if using) and all the herbs, then take off the heat.

Drain the fish, reserving the milk in a jug. Put the fish into a large pie dish and add the wilted greens.

Put 4–5 tablespoons of the milk into a mug and mix well with the cornflour. Pour back into the rest of the milk in a pan on the heat and whisk to combine. Stir in the lemon zest and juice, crème fraîche (if using), half the Cheddar or Parmesan, nutmeg, salt and pepper until thickened.

Pour the sauce over the fish and greens and stir gently to combine. Then top with the celeriac and cauliflower mash and scatter with the remaining cheese. Bake in the oven for 20–30 minutes until bubbling and golden. Allow the pie to rest for 10 minutes for the flavours to be at their best.

» 349 calories for 6 servings, 262 for 8

More on » milk p252 » celeriac p91 » cauliflower p267 » coconut oil p309 » spinach p54 » peas p74 » asparagus p126 » parsley p136 » lemons p346

Pheasant with apple and chestnut

A classic combination for autumn and winter, with the apple helping to prevent the pheasant from drying out. As well as the apples, there are healthy chestnuts here: this is the only nut low in fat and therefore relatively low in calories, about a quarter that of hazelnuts and walnuts. Like olive oil, chestnuts contain high concentrations of the monounsaturated fatty acids (palmitic and oleic acids), which are beneficial to the heart. They are also a good source of dietary fibre, which helps lower blood cholesterol by limiting its absorption in the intestines.

For 4:
2 pheasants
2 tbsp wholemeal flour, seasoned
3 tbsp cold-pressed rapeseed oil
4 onions (about 500g), quartered
2 leeks (about 600g), finely sliced
10g sprigs of thyme, a couple kept back for garnish
200g chestnuts (cooked and vacuum-packed), left whole
200ml chicken stock (see p98)
200ml apple juice, home-pressed or cloudy
2 apples, cored and quartered (not Bramley)
Sea salt and black pepper

Preheat the oven to 180°C/gas mark 4.

Roll the birds in the flour. Heat 2 tablespoons of the oil in a flameproof casserole dish, and gently fry the pheasants until golden brown all over. Take the birds out of the pot and put them to one side.

Add the remaining oil, the onions, leek and most of the thyme, and cook over a gentle heat for 10 minutes. Stir in the chestnuts, and pour in the stock and apple juice.

Place the pheasants breast-side down on top of the onion and leek mixture. Put on the lid, place in the middle of the oven and cook for 45 minutes if using cock pheasant. If using smaller hen pheasant, cook for 30 minutes.

Turn the pheasants breast-side up and add the apples, then cook for a further 45 minutes, with the lid off for the last 15 minutes.

Pull out the thyme stalks. Taste the juices and season with a little salt and pepper. Serve the pheasant sprinkled with the remaining thyme leaves, picked from their stalks.

» 567 calories per serving

More on » pheasant p159 » rapeseed oil p248 » onions p281 » chestnuts p158 » apples p288

Large shared plates

Liver with hazelnut dukkah
on stir-fried winter greens

All offal is low-fat and rich in iron, and it's relatively cheap. Ideally, offal should come from organically raised animals, and shouldn't be eaten more than once a week. Another thing to be aware of is that liver is rich in vitamin A. This is very good for us, but it is stored in our bodies and too much is toxic. Because of this, pregnant women should avoid liver.

With a strong flavour itself, liver is enhanced by punchy tastes such as fragrant spices, and yet it's almost always served plain, or at the most floured with a bit of salt and pepper. Try this version, with nuts and classic dukkah spices, served on a bed of wilted winter leaves.

For 4–6:
360g very fresh lamb's liver, cut into bite-sized strips
Extra virgin olive oil
Juice of ½ lemon
Sea salt and black pepper

For the hazelnut dukkah
40g hazelnuts, dry-fried
1 level tbsp cumin seeds, dry-fried
1 level tbsp caraway seeds, dry-fried
½ level tsp ground cinnamon
Pinch of flaky sea salt

For the wilted greens
3 tbsp cold-pressed rapeseed oil or 1 tbsp set coconut oil
250g leeks, cut into 1cm slices
200g Treviso or Belgian chicory, cut into 1cm slices
100g baby chard leaves, left whole
100g radicchio, leaves torn up
Grated zest of 1 lemon
Sea salt and black pepper

Put all the dukkah ingredients into a blender and blitz to a breadcrumb consistency. Place this in a small mixing bowl.

To start the greens, heat half the rapeseed or coconut oil in a wok over a high heat. Add the leeks and chicory and stir-fry for 2 minutes, stirring constantly. Add the chard and radicchio, and stir-fry for a further 2 minutes. Take off the heat, stir in the lemon zest and season to taste with salt and pepper. Lay the wilted vegetables on a flat serving plate.

Coat the liver with a good sprinkling of the dukkah mix. Using the same wok, heat the remaining rapeseed or coconut oil over a medium to high heat. Add the coated liver to the wok and stir-fry for a couple of minutes or so until the liver is lightly coloured but still pink in the centre.

Tip the stir-fried liver over the wilted vegetables. Serve with a drizzle of extra virgin olive oil, a dash of lemon juice and season to taste.

» 478 calories for 4 servings, 319 for 6

More on » olive oil *p193* » lemons *p346*
» hazelnuts *p50* » cinnamon *p22* » rapeseed oil *p248* » coconut oil *p309*

Chicken puttanesca

Pasta puttanesca is a family staple – there are few better sauces. Use the same sauce with chicken for a rich and comforting dish in the winter, or – with lots of basil – for a bright, sunny dish in summer. This needs only a green salad on the side to make it a meal.

This is also good as a one-pot dish with waxy potatoes (650g), such as Belle de Fontenay, Ratte or Pioneer. Slice these into quarters lengthways and add to the sauce with the chicken.

For 6:
1 tbsp cold-pressed rapeseed oil
12 skin-on boneless chicken thighs
30g bunch of basil, stalks removed

For the puttanesca sauce
4 tbsp extra virgin olive oil
20 anchovy fillets in oil, drained
4 garlic cloves, roughly chopped
600g cherry tomatoes (I use Sungold here to give extra sweetness)
3 tbsp good-quality mixed marinated olives, stoned
2 tbsp capers, rinsed
200ml white wine
Sea salt and black pepper

Preheat the oven to 180°C/gas mark 4.

Make the sauce first. Gently heat the extra virgin olive oil in a heavy-based shallow flameproof casserole dish. Add the anchovies and garlic and gently fry for 2–3 minutes, until the anchovies have melted, but the garlic has not browned.

Add the cherry tomatoes, olives and capers, and turn down the heat to simmer gently.

Meanwhile, heat the rapeseed oil in a large frying pan and cook the chicken for 3–4 minutes on each side until golden brown.

Discard the oil from the pan, and add the chicken and wine to the tomato mixture. Stir well to combine. Cover the casserole and cook in the oven for 15 minutes. Stir so the chicken is well coated in the puttanesca sauce, then return to the oven for 20 minutes.

Allow to cool for a few minutes before stirring in the basil leaves. Taste and season with a little salt and pepper, if required, and serve.

» 603 calories per serving

More on » rapeseed oil *p248* » olive oil *p193* » garlic *p82* » tomatoes *p142* » olives *p179*

Chicken and turkey Chicken and turkey are both lean meats and full of good-quality **protein** which builds muscle, and so they are particularly invaluable for growing children. Their protein richness helps keep post-meal insulin levels within a desirable range and so these are excellent foods for diabetics. They also contain all the B vitamins, which are key to our general metabolism, immune system, cardiovascular health, blood-sugar maintenance and cell growth, plus valuable **minerals**, including selenium, zinc, copper, phosphorus, magnesium, potassium and iron.

To minimise the risk of exposure to antibiotics and synthetic pesticides, buy free-range, organic chicken and turkey. The meat from these birds has increased levels of **omega-3 fatty acids**, and helps to create a favourable ratio of **omega-6s** to omega-3s in our bodies. Despite all these nutritional attributes, it's best not to have meat – even chicken – more than two or three times a week, to help keep this ratio of omega-3s to omega-6s in the correct range.

Large shared plates

Thai turkey burgers

This is a super-quick mid-week supper, prepared, cooked and on the table in less than half an hour. Choose free-range, ideally organic turkey: I avoid turkeys filled with hormones and antibiotics like the plague. Turkey is very lean, so is ideal if you're watching your weight.

Serve with a green salad topped with dry-fried pumpkin seeds and some sliced avocado.

For 4 large burgers:
500g organic turkey mince
1 tbsp Thai green curry paste (bought or home-made, see p236)
1 small egg
30g bunch of coriander, leaves and stalks, coarsely chopped
Sea salt and black pepper
1 tbsp set coconut oil

Mix all the ingredients together – apart from the oil – and shape into rounds.

Heat the oil in a large frying pan – or oil a barbecue grill – and gently cook the burgers for 5 minutes on each side, until they are golden and cooked all the way through.

» 190 calories per burger

More on » turkey *p260* » eggs *p61* » coriander *p204* » coconut oil *p309*

Sangria chicken

This is my version of a Yotam Ottolenghi recipe for marinated roast chicken with clementines. Until she became a vegetarian, it was one of my daughter Molly's favourite meals, with the sweet, yet sharp flavour of citrus, along with fennel and celery. It's all the better with blood oranges. You need to start the marinating the night before.

For 4:
Grated zest and juice of 2 blood oranges
Juice of 1 lemon
1 tbsp dark soft brown sugar
4 tbsp cold-pressed rapeseed oil
150ml fino sherry (or dry white wine)
1 tbsp Dijon mustard
Good pinch of flaky sea salt
1.3kg free-range chicken, jointed into 8 pieces, or equal weight in chicken thighs, bone in and skin on
1 celery head, sliced into 3cm wide diagonal slices
2 fennel bulbs, sliced
2 blood oranges, cut into thin slices
2 tbsp thyme leaves

In a bowl, mix together the orange zest and juice, the lemon juice, sugar, oil, sherry, mustard and sea salt. Put the chicken pieces, celery, fennel, orange slices and thyme into a roasting tray. Pour over the marinade. Mix, then leave overnight in the fridge.

Preheat the oven to 200°C/gas mark 6.

Put the chicken in the oven and cook for 1 hour, basting a few times until the juices run clear and the skin is brown and crisp. Drain off the fat from the tray and pour the cooking liquid into a small pan. Reduce a little if too runny.

Serve the chicken with its gravy, with black or red rice and a green salad.

» 674 calories per serving

More on » oranges *p49* » lemons *p346* » rapeseed oil *p248* » chicken *p260*

Large shared plates

Sweet potato, broccoli, feta and red kale burgers

These non-meat burgers are packed with goodness and flavour, and are excellent served with Sweet and sour tomato sauce (see page 255), or with Healthy chilli jam (see page 188). Any kale variety will do. They are also good cold, for a packed lunch the following day, with a dollop of natural yoghurt to dip them in.

For 4:
600g sweet potatoes, peeled (not peeled if organic) and diced
100g tenderstem broccoli
100g red kale, leaves pulled from stalks
1 medium red onion, finely chopped (about 180g)
2 garlic cloves, finely chopped
1 tbsp finely chopped fresh root ginger
1 red finger chilli, deseeded and finely chopped
3 tbsp cold-pressed rapeseed oil
1 tbsp cumin seeds, dry-fried
1 tbsp coriander seeds, dry-fried and crushed
Grated zest of 1 lime
Juice of ½ lime
200g feta, crumbled
1 medium egg, beaten
30g coriander, leaves and stalks, roughly chopped
Sea salt and black pepper
2 tbsp wholemeal flour, seasoned

Steam the sweet potatoes until soft, then drain and mash. Transfer the mashed sweet potato to a large mixing bowl and allow to cool slightly.

Cook the broccoli and kale in boiling water for 3–4 minutes or until al dente, drain in a colander and allow to cool. Squeeze out any excess water from the kale. Put the broccoli and kale onto a chopping board and roughly chop.

Sauté the onion, garlic, ginger and chilli in 1 tablespoon of the oil until the onion is just starting to turn golden brown.

Add this to the sweet potato in the bowl, along with the broccoli and kale. Add the spices, lime zest and juice, feta, beaten egg and chopped coriander. Season with a little salt and pepper, and stir well to combine. Put the mixture into the fridge for 1 hour.

Dust your hands with seasoned flour and form the mixture into eight even-sized burgers. Heat the remaining oil in a heavy-based frying pan over a medium heat and cook the burgers for 5 minutes on each side, or until golden brown and cooked all the way through. Alternatively, bake in a pre-heated oven at 170°C/gas mark 3 for 15–20 minutes.

Serve hot with some chilli jam (see page 188) and perhaps some broccoli on the side.

» 432 calories per serving

More on » sweet potato *p72* » broccoli *p151* » kale *p117* » onions *p281* » garlic *p82* » ginger *p200* » chillies *p93* » rapeseed oil *p248* » coriander *p204* » eggs *p61*

Feta At 262 calories per 100g, feta cheese is low in fat and calories compared to most other cheese (cream cheese comes in at 439). It's traditionally made from goats' or sheep's milk – try to find either of these, rather than feta made from cows' milk. This has become increasingly common, but cheese made with sheep's or goats' milk is known to be less likely to spark allergies than that made with cows' milk. Feta is an excellent source of vitamin D, but it is also the saltiest variety of cheese. Unpasteurised feta and other soft cheeses have a higher risk of containing Listeria bacteria than other cheeses – so be sure to buy pasteurised feta if you're cooking for a pregnant woman or someone with a compromised immune system.

Broccoli and cauliflower fritters

This makes quite a dry, falafel-like mix, which you can form into rounds (it will make around 30 small falafels), or into flat patties – or fritters – as here (in which case, it will make 10). They are delicious fried, or you can bake them in the oven. Try packing them into a pitta bread with some salad leaves dressed with lemon and olive oil, plus some coriander and mint. If you make the falafels, any leftovers are good cold, ideal for a lunchbox the following day, and they freeze well.

For 5–6 (makes 10 fritters or 30 falafels):
400g broccoli, cut into even-sized small florets
600g cauliflower, cut into even-sized small florets
4 tbsp cold-pressed rapeseed oil, plus a little extra
    for frying
1 heaped tsp ground cumin
1 heaped tsp ground coriander
1 heaped tsp ground turmeric
1 level tsp cardamom seeds
1 heaped tbsp coriander seeds, dry-fried and
    coarsely ground
1 heaped tbsp cumin seeds, dry-fried and
    coarsely ground
2 medium eggs, beaten
40g rice flour
Grated zest of 2 lemons
Grated zest of 1 orange
50g bunch of coriander, leaves and stalks,
    roughly chopped
30g bunch of mint, leaves only, roughly chopped
Sea salt and black pepper

Preheat the oven to 180°C/gas mark 4.

Put the cauliflower and broccoli florets onto a baking tray. Add 2 tablespoons of the oil and all the spices and mix well. Roast in the middle of the oven for 20 minutes.

Put the beaten egg, rice flour, lemon and orange zests, coriander and mint into a large mixing bowl and stir well to combine. Season with salt and pepper.

Remove the roasted spiced broccoli and cauliflower from the oven and allow to cool for 10 minutes.

Put two-thirds of the roasted florets into a food processor and whizz very briefly. Add this to the egg mixture. Chop the remaining third of roasted florets a little by hand: you want this to add texture. Mix into the egg mixture too, and stir well to combine. Put into the fridge for 1 hour.

Shape the mixture into 10 even-sized fritters (or 30 falafels) and fry in a little oil for about 5 minutes on each side until golden brown and cooked all the way through. You could bake them in the oven instead, at the above temperature, for 15 minutes. The cooking times are the same for fritters and falafels.

» 133 calories per fritter, 44 per falafel

More on » broccoli p151 » cauliflower p267 » rapeseed oil p248 » coriander p204 » turmeric p87 » eggs p61 » lemons p346 » oranges p49 » mint p326

Cauliflowers belong to the brassica family and – like broccoli and kale – have high levels of many **antioxidants**, the most powerful of which are in the **glucosinolates** group, which are effective liver detoxifiers and have cancer-prevention properties. Turmeric is a good partner for cauliflower (see page 87), adding flavour as well as colour and, what's more, cauliflower and turmeric seem to work together to have a more powerful effect on our health. In a recent animal study, when curcumin, the active **phytonutrient** found in turmeric, was mixed with glucosinolates in cauliflower, the combination shrank tumours – this did not happen when they were given separately.

Stuffed butternut squash with creamy goats' cheese

The shape, colour, texture and taste of this dish make it a good all-rounder in autumn and winter. It's a perfect mid-week supper, with half a small butternut about the right size for a main-course portion. The skin of butternuts is thin, so once cooked, you can eat this too and then you'll get all the nutrients and antioxidants concentrated just below the skin. I also like small stuffed butternut squash as a side veg, but leave out the cheese.

For 2 as a main course, 4 as a side dish:
1 butternut squash (about 1kg)
1 tbsp cold-pressed rapeseed oil
100g soft goats' cheese, crumbled
About 12 sage leaves, finely shredded
Small bunch of chives, finely chopped
100g hazelnuts, dry-fried and roughly chopped
Sea salt and black pepper

To serve
1 tbsp cold-pressed rapeseed oil
About 20 small sage leaves
30g hazelnuts, dry-fried and roughly chopped

Preheat the oven to 180°C/gas mark 4.

Cut the squash in half lengthways, but leave the seeds in at this stage – they're easier to remove with less flesh attached once cooked. Place on a lined baking tray, cut-side up. Drizzle with the oil.

Roast for 50–60 minutes, or until the flesh is soft when pierced with a sharp knife. Allow to cool for a few minutes.

Using a spoon, scoop out the seeds, then carefully remove the flesh from the squash, leaving a 1cm rim next to the skin. Mash the squash flesh in a bowl with all the rest of the ingredients.

Divide the stuffing between the two squash 'boats', then bake in the oven for 20 minutes or until the filling is turning golden on top.

When ready to serve, heat the oil and gently fry the sage leaves until curling at the edges. Pour the sage leaves and their oil over the cooked squash and scatter over the hazelnuts.

» 984 calories for 2 servings, 492 for 4

More on » squash *p186* » rapeseed oil *p248* » hazelnuts *p50*

Goats' cheese In terms of nutrition, goats' cheese has many advantages over cows' cheese, and is often the healthier option. It contains less lactose and smaller fat globules, making it easier to digest than cows' cheese. Typically, goats' cheese is lower in calories and fat than other cheeses. Look out for the Greek feta traditionally made from goats' or sheep's milk (but remember this is salty, see page 264), and halloumi, which originated in Cyprus. These are both slightly healthier options for the confirmed cheese-lover.

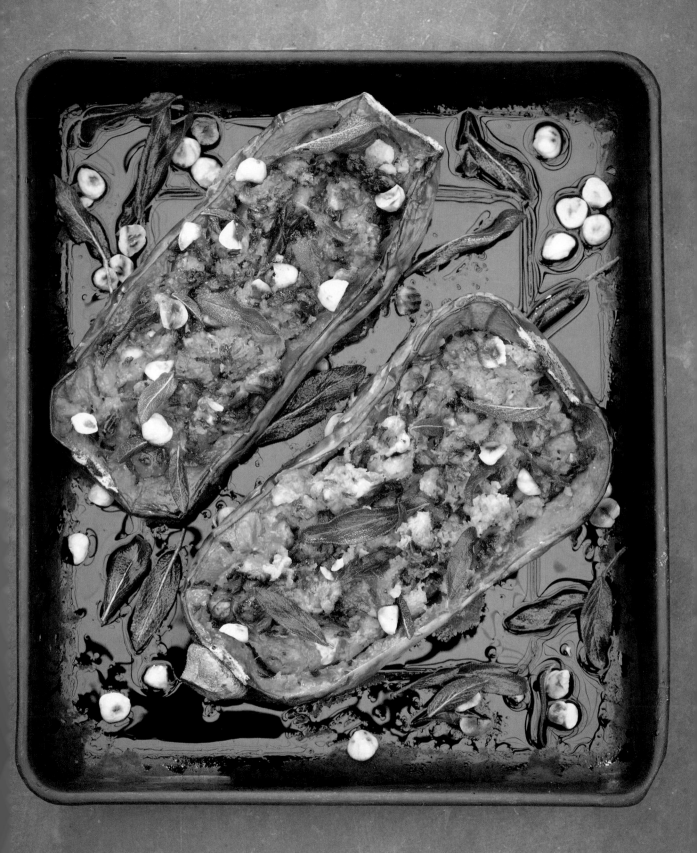

Freekeh-stuffed beefsteak tomatoes

Here, fat, juicy beefsteak tomatoes are stuffed with freekeh, an ancient grain. Unlike rice, this doesn't easily overcook and turn into a mush.

The tomatoes can easily be made a day or two before, refrigerated and reheated at 180°C/gas mark 4 for 10 minutes, or until warmed through. I sometimes add crumbled feta to the mixture too.

For 4 as a main course, 8 as a starter:
160g dried freekeh, or 500g ready-cooked freekeh
2 litres vegetable stock (see p101) or bouillon (made to
    half-strength with 2 tsp powder to 2 litres water)
8 large beefsteak tomatoes
1 large onion, finely chopped
1 tbsp cold-pressed rapeseed oil
2 garlic cloves, crushed
½–1 red chilli, deseeded and finely chopped
2 heaped tsp dried mint
1 heaped tsp ground turmeric
4 tbsp sultanas
2 tbsp capers
Sea salt and black pepper
20g bunch of mint, leaves finely chopped
20g bunch of dill, finely chopped
20g bunch of flat-leaf parsley, leaves finely chopped
4 tbsp pine nuts, dry-fried

Wash the freekeh in a sieve under a cold tap. Cook for 15 minutes in the vegetable stock. Rinse in cold water and leave to drain.

Cut off the top quarter of the tomatoes and scoop out the seeds and inside flesh, being careful to keep the sides quite thick. Set the flesh, seeds and tops to one side. Place the tomatoes on a baking tray lined with baking parchment.

Fry the onion gently in the oil until translucent. Add the garlic, chilli, dried mint and turmeric, and cook for 1 minute. Add the reserved tomato flesh and seeds and the sultanas. Season with salt and pepper. Bring to a boil and then simmer for 20 minutes until reduced.

Preheat the oven to 180°C/gas mark 4.

Stir the cooked freekeh into the sauce and reheat. Add the capers, fresh chopped herbs and pine nuts. Taste for seasoning. Put a good tablespoonful of the mixture into each tomato (but don't overfill as the mixture will expand a little), then put the lid on top.

Cook the tomatoes in the oven for 15 minutes, until they are soft and beginning to colour.

» 250 calories for 4 servings, 125 for 8

More on » tomatoes *p142* » onions *p281*
» rapeseed oil *p248* » garlic *p82* » chillies *p93*
» turmeric *p87* » mint *p326* » parsley *p136*

Freekeh This grain is made from unripe wheat that has been parched and roasted to burn off the husks, giving it a delicious, smoky and nutty taste. It dates back to 2300 BC in the eastern Mediterranean, and has many health advantages similar to quinoa and bulghar wheat. When cooked, it has around four times the **fibre** content of brown rice, and almost as much as quinoa, with a lower **Glycaemic Index** than both. Freekeh contains resistant starch, which is a type of **carbohydrate** that acts like a fibre, making us feel fuller for longer.

The fact that freekeh wheat is harvested while still young gives it its green colour and makes it quicker to cook – about 20 minutes – than wheat berries (see page 145). If you are using a recipe that calls for ready-cooked freekeh, you'll need to start with a third of the amount: a pack of 250g dried freekeh makes 750g cooked freekeh.

All wheat products contain **gluten**.

Sweet potato, coconut and lime 'dauphinoise'

This is a favourite in our family. We might eat it as a main course one day with a green salad, and then often have the leftovers as a side veg the next day, delicious alongside chicken or fish. The dish is good topped with pomegranate seeds for extra crunch and goodness, and it freezes brilliantly. If making double or triple quantities, increase the coconut milk, lime, honey, garlic, ginger and chilli by only 50 per cent to the proportions of the sweet potato – otherwise you'll end up with soup!

For 4–6:
1.5kg (4–5) small to medium sweet potatoes
100g piece of fresh root ginger
1 red chilli, deseeded
3 garlic cloves, crushed
400ml tin of coconut milk
Grated zest and juice of 2 limes
2 heaped tbsp clear honey or maple syrup (optional)
Sea salt and black pepper

Preheat the oven to 180°C/gas mark 4.

Peel the sweet potatoes (unless they're organic), and cut into thin slices. Put in a large bowl. Peel the ginger with a teaspoon. Finely chop it, with the chilli and garlic – I do this in a food processor. Add the coconut milk, lime zest and juice, honey or maple syrup (if using) and blitz briefly. Pour over and mix with the sweet potatoes – your hands are best for this. Season with salt and pepper.

Transfer the mixture to a large round casserole or 21 x 28cm baking dish. Cover with a lid or foil and bake for 1 hour until the potatoes are tender. Uncover and bake for an additional 15–20 minutes until the top is browned.

» 544 calories for 4 servings, 362 for 6

More on » sweet potato p72 » ginger p200
» chillies p93 » garlic p82 » coconut milk p235
» honey p334 » maple syrup p27

Mushroom, leek and silken tofu frittata

This is an ideal dish for a vegetarian, and rich and tasty enough for meat-eaters not to feel deprived. Mushrooms are the 'meatiest' of all veg, and the tofu adds creaminess without the cream.

For 6:
3 medium eggs
300g organic silken tofu
Freshly ground black pepper
750g leeks
2 tbsp cold-pressed rapeseed oil
500g mushrooms, cut into 1cm slices
200g feta, crumbled
40g Parmesan, coarsely grated

Put the eggs and silken tofu into a food processor with a little black pepper and mix well to combine.

Trim the tops and tails of the leeks (keeping as much of the darker part of the leek as possible, as it's full of nutrients and flavour). Peel away the outer leaf layer, then wash and cut the leeks into 1cm slices. Heat the rapeseed oil in a frying pan over a medium heat, and add the leeks in batches, cooking each batch for 5 minutes, stirring them often until softened. Turn up the heat and cook the sliced mushrooms in batches, each for 5 minutes, stirring often. Meanwhile preheat the grill.

Return everything to the pan, increase the heat slightly and sprinkle over the feta. Pour over the egg mixture and stir briefly. Then turn down the heat and cook the frittata without stirring for about 7 minutes or until the edges start to set. Sprinkle over the Parmesan and place the pan under the hot grill (not too close to the element) until golden brown and set in the centre, about 5 minutes.

» 310 calories per serving

More on » eggs p61 » tofu p96 » rapeseed oil p248
» mushrooms p88 » feta p264

Kale, mushroom and sweet potato frittata

Egg, kale, mushrooms and sweet potato – four good things, in one sustaining, protein-rich, super-easy dish. Orange-fleshed sweet potatoes are vitamin A superstars and are one of the highest-rated vegetables on the antioxidant scale. They've also got a low GI (Glycaemic Index) score, which means that their natural sugars are released slowly. Just scrub, don't peel, the sweet potatoes.

For 4:
500g sweet potatoes, cut into 2cm cubes
Sea salt and black pepper
3 tbsp cold-pressed rapeseed oil
200g kale
1 red onion, thinly sliced
2 large garlic cloves, crushed
300g oyster or chestnut mushrooms, sliced
1 red finger chilli, deseeded and finely chopped
½ tsp smoked paprika
2 spring onions, finely sliced
6 medium eggs, beaten
Handful of roughly chopped parsley

Preheat the oven to 180°C/gas mark 4.

Place the sweet potato on a baking sheet and season with salt and black pepper. Drizzle with 1 tablespoon of the oil and roast for about 30 minutes, until caramelised around the edges.

Wash the kale, de-stalk and steam for 5 minutes, then squeeze dry.

Gently fry the onion in the remaining oil in an ovenproof, non-stick frying pan for 5 minutes until soft. Meanwhile preheat the grill.

Add the garlic and mushrooms to the onion and cook for 3 minutes, then add the chilli, paprika and spring onions. Briefly cook, coating the vegetables in the spice. Stir in the kale and sweet potato. Pour in the beaten egg, seasoned with salt and black pepper, and fold through the vegetable mixture.

Cook over a gentle heat for 7–8 minutes, then place the pan under the hot grill (not too close to the element) until golden brown and set in the centre, about 5 minutes.

Turn the frittata out onto a flat plate and then flip it over again. Scatter with plenty of parsley, and serve with a green salad.

» 333 calories per serving

More on » sweet potato *p72* » rapeseed oil *p248* » kale *p117* » onions *p281* » garlic *p82* » mushrooms *p88* » chillies *p93* » eggs *p61* » parsley *p136*

Large shared plates

Courgette filo pie

This is a lighter, healthier version of a Greek classic, *spanakopita*, cutting down on the amount of pastry and cheese, and really piling in the veg between the layers of pastry. You can use a wide range of veg: squash, chard, spinach, leeks and fennel, with a few tomatoes mixed in. You could also add a heaped tablespoon of uncooked rice with any super-juicy veg: this soaks up the liquid so you'll still get a crunchy filo bottom.

A filo pie makes a perfect mid-week supper and is just as nice served hot or cold the next day, even the day after that. It also makes a good packed lunch.

It seems odd not using extra virgin olive oil as the Greeks would do in this dish, but particularly when it comes to oiling the top of the pie, rapeseed oil or butter, both of which have a higher smoke point, are the healthier options.

For 6:
Cold-pressed rapeseed oil or organic unsalted butter, melted
3 medium red onions, finely chopped
500g leeks, finely chopped
2 garlic cloves, finely chopped
600g courgettes, finely chopped
1 red chilli, deseeded and finely chopped (optional)
60g mint, leaves removed from stalks, roughly chopped
60g flat-leaf parsley, leaves removed from stalks, roughly chopped
Sea salt and black pepper
Finely grated zest of 1 lemon
1 tbsp pine nuts, dry-fried
25 Kalamata olives or good-quality mixed olives, stoned
1 heaped tsp dried mint
250g pack of filo sheets (you'll need 9 sheets)
200g feta, crumbled
2 medium eggs, lightly beaten
1 tbsp mix of sesame and poppy seeds

Preheat the oven to 170°C/gas mark 3. Grease the base and sides of a 23cm round cake tin (7cm deep), or a square tin if you prefer, using half a tablespoon of the oil or melted butter.

Put 3 tablespoons of the oil in a large pan set over a medium heat. Add the onions, leeks and garlic and stir well. Turn down the heat to low and cook gently for 10 minutes until softened. Add 2 tablespoons oil, the courgettes, chilli (if using) and herbs, and continue cooking gently over a low heat for a further 15 minutes, stirring occasionally. Season with salt and pepper. Add the lemon zest, pine nuts, olives and dried mint to the courgette mixture, stirring well to combine.

Lay a sheet of filo over the base of the prepared tin and mould it gently into its shape, allowing the ends to fall over the edge of the tin. Brush with a little oil or melted butter. If it breaks up a little, don't worry. Repeat with five more sheets of filo, brushing each one with oil or butter as you go, again letting the pastry hang over the edge.

Now add the layer of rice (if using, see recipe introduction) and then spoon the courgette mixture into the filo-lined tin. Scatter over the feta, then pour in the beaten eggs.

For the top of the pie, layer over three sheets of filo, brushing each one with oil or butter, then fold the hanging edges over the top of the pie, pressing down gently. Brush the top with oil or butter and sprinkle with the poppy and sesame seeds.

Bake the pie in the middle of the oven for 30 minutes until golden.

Cut into wedges (straight from the tin) and serve with a green or tomato salad. Any you don't eat at the first sitting is just as good the next day.

» 532 calories per serving

More on » onions *p281* » garlic *p82* » chillies *p93* » mint *p326* » parsley *p136* » lemons *p346* » olives *p179* » feta *p264* » eggs *p61* » sesame seeds *p164*

Squash, feta and walnut filo parcels

Individual filo parcels are a great way to pack your diet with vegetables. Fill them with squash, or use courgettes, spinach, chard, grated beetroot, fennel, or a mixture of veg.

You can make these filo parcels in batches and freeze them: they are safe cooked straight from the freezer, so you can get one or two out whenever you want an almost instant healthy supper.
You can also use organic unsalted butter, melted, to brush on the filo. Surprisingly, butter has slightly fewer calories than the oil...

For 8 parcels:
1 butternut squash (about 1.3kg)
Cold-pressed rapeseed oil
3 tbsp fennel seeds
Sea salt and black pepper
1 large red onion, finely sliced
1 fennel bulb (about 200g), finely sliced
2 garlic cloves, crushed
1 red chilli, deseeded and finely chopped
8 sage leaves, finely sliced
75g walnuts, dry-fried and chopped
1 tbsp crème fraîche
Small bunch of flat-leaf parsley, leaves removed
    from stalks and finely chopped
200g feta or soft goats' cheese, crumbled
6 sheets of filo pastry

Preheat the oven to 190°C/gas mark 5.

Cut the squash in half, remove the seeds, and then cut the flesh into 2cm chunks (you don't need to peel butternut squash). Place the chunks on a baking tray and sprinkle with 1 tablespoon oil, the fennel seeds, and some salt and pepper. Roast for 30 minutes or until soft and golden at the edges.

Meanwhile, in a large frying pan, fry the onion and fennel in another tablespoon of oil until the onion is translucent and the fennel softened. Add the garlic, chilli and sage and cook for 3 minutes or so. Remove from the heat.

Large shared plates

Put the roasted squash in a bowl and lightly mash with a fork, keeping it chunky. Add the onion mix, along with the walnuts, crème fraîche, parsley and crumbled cheese. Combine and taste for seasoning.

Lay out a sheet of filo pastry. Brush lightly with oil. Add another layer and brush with oil. Repeat once more, so that you have three oiled layers of filo. Cut the pastry into four squares.

Put a rounded tablespoon of squash mix into the centre of each pastry square, then form into a bundle, bringing the corners together and sealing firmly just above the mix. Place on a lined baking tray and brush with a little more oil.

Repeat the last couple of steps, using the remaining pastry and filling.

Bake the filo parcels for 20–30 minutes until golden brown. Serve very simply with a salad on the side.

» 351 calories per parcel

More on » squash *p186* » onions *p281* » garlic *p82* » chillies *p93* » walnuts *p51* » parsley *p136* » feta *p264* » goats' cheese *p268*

Courgette filo parcels

A classic summer version of filo pies that we often make when the garden is open at Perch Hill and we are feeding lots of people.

For 8 parcels:
6–8 courgettes
Sea salt and black pepper
2 leeks, finely chopped
4 tbsp cold-pressed rapeseed oil or organic unsalted
    butter, melted
2 garlic cloves, finely chopped
Grated zest of 2 limes
200g tub of cream cheese
30g mint leaves, finely chopped
2 tbsp pine nuts, dry-fried
6 sheets of filo pastry

Grate the courgettes into a colander set over a plate. Sprinkle with salt, mix and leave for a couple of hours. Squeeze the courgettes, or press them against the base of the colander to remove excess water.

Meanwhile, fry the leeks gently for 5 minutes in a little of the oil or butter. Add the garlic and cook for 3 minutes. Remove from the heat.

Mix the courgettes with the leeks, then add the lime zest, cream cheese, mint, pine nuts and lots of black pepper.

Prepare the filo sheets, cutting them into squares as for the Squash, feta and walnut filo parcels opposite; fill with the courgette filling, then form into parcels and bake in the same way.

» 268 calories per parcel

More on » rapeseed oil *p248* » garlic *p82* » mint *p326*

Asparagus, mint and goats' cheese tart

Asparagus tarts are one of those must-have meals, when asparagus is in season in May and June. Asparagus, like peas and sweetcorn, is best very fresh. Its sugars convert to starch in the spear on storing, losing flavour, so make sure to cook and eat it as soon as possible after picking or buying.

If you don't have time to freeze the pastry (as below), follow instructions for the pastry in the tomato tart recipe on page 282. It may sound unpromising using coconut milk rather than cream for the filling, but with all the strong flavours, you won't notice and it's better for you (see page 235).

For 6–8:

For the wholemeal pastry
200g wholemeal plain flour
Pinch of flaky sea salt
120g cold organic unsalted butter, cut into cubes
1 medium egg yolk

For the filling
600g asparagus spears
1 tsp set coconut oil
50g Parmesan, grated
3 heaped tbsp pine nuts, dry-fried
40g mint, leaves removed from stalks,
    roughly chopped
300g soft goats' cheese, in small pieces
1 tbsp cold-pressed rapeseed oil
4 medium eggs
1 x 400ml tin of coconut milk
Sea salt and black pepper

For the pastry, put the flour and salt into a bowl, then rub in the butter by hand until the mixture resembles breadcrumbs. Alternatively, pulse in a food processor. Add the egg yolk and a little cold water, just enough to bring the pastry together into a ball. Don't overwork it. Roll the pastry into a circle a little larger than a 28cm loose-bottomed tart tin, and line the tin with it. Put it in the freezer for a couple of hours or overnight, leaving the excess draped over the sides to allow for shrinking when the pastry is baked. This freezer technique ensures a flaky pastry tart case.

Preheat the oven to 180°C/gas mark 4 and put a baking sheet inside to heat up. Remove the tart tin from the freezer, line the pastry case in the tin with greaseproof paper and weight down with baking beans or rice. Place on the hot baking sheet and bake from frozen for about 15 minutes. Remove the baking beans and paper. Bake for another 8–10 minutes or until golden and the pastry feels sandy to the touch. Cut the excess pastry away with a sharp knife.

Meanwhile, wash the asparagus, and break off and discard the woody bases. Cut off the spear tips and put to one side, then slice the stalks thinly at an angle, creating long ovals. Place the stalks in a small frying pan with the coconut oil and fry gently until tender (about 3–4 minutes). Scatter the Parmesan inside the pastry case (to absorb any liquid and keep the base crisp). Place the asparagus slices on top and sprinkle over the pine nuts and mint. Scatter over the goats' cheese.

Heat a ridged griddle pan for 3–4 minutes (until you can't count to ten with your hand hovering just above it). Brush the asparagus tips with the rapeseed oil, then griddle for a couple of minutes to char slightly and bring out their sweetness (they might need longer if the tips are thick). Whisk together the eggs and coconut milk. Season with salt and pepper and pour into the pastry case. Arrange the asparagus tips on top. Place on a baking sheet and bake for 30–40 minutes, or until the tart is set and golden. Serve cut into segments, with a crisp green salad.

» 720 calories for 6 servings, 540 for 8

More on » butter *p104* » eggs *p61* » asparagus *p126* » mint *p326* » goats' cheese *p268* » coconut milk *p235*

Onion pissaladière

Here is a classic onion and anchovy tart with an intense, sweet and salty flavour, using a healthy pastry made from whole grains and seeds. This pastry is filling, high in fibre, with a good crunchy texture. A little goes a long way, which makes the tart ideal in mini slivers, served as a canapé. It's great for a picnic lunch, warm or cold.

For 8:

For the pastry
60g quinoa
80g spelt flour
80g rye flour
2 tbsp sunflower seeds
1 tbsp cold-pressed rapeseed oil, plus a little extra
    for greasing
Sea salt

For the filling
4 tbsp cold-pressed rapeseed oil
7 medium onions (900g), finely sliced
3 garlic cloves, finely sliced
2 tbsp sherry vinegar
2 sprigs of rosemary, leaves picked
1 tbsp coconut palm sugar
Dijon mustard
18 anchovy fillets in oil, drained
12–15 stoned black olives

Preheat the oven to 180°C/gas mark 4 and put a baking sheet inside to heat up.

First rinse the quinoa well in a sieve under a running tap. Then combine with all the other pastry ingredients and a good pinch of salt. Add enough water to just bring it together, a tablespoon at a time.

Oil a 28cm loose-bottomed tart tin. Place all the dough into the tin and flatten it with your fingertips. It will be quite crumbly and you will need to patch it up the sides. Put the base in the oven and cook for 20–30 minutes until crisp.

Remove from the oven, but leave the oven on.

Heat the oil in a large saucepan and sweat the onion and garlic on a low heat, stirring often without allowing them to brown, for about 20 minutes until translucent and soft. Add the vinegar, rosemary and sugar and cook for a further 5 minutes until sticky.

Spread a thin layer of Dijon mustard over the base of the cooked pastry, then fill with the onion mixture. Arrange the anchovy fillets in a lattice pattern over the filled tart and then place a stoned black olive in every square.

Put the pissaladière on the hot baking sheet and bake for about 20 minutes.

Remove from the oven, and allow to cool a little. Slice and serve with some green salad.

» 290 calories per serving

More on » quinoa p140 » spelt p32 » rapeseed oil p248 » garlic p82 » coconut palm sugar p316 » olives p179

Onions are rich in anti-bacterial sulphur-containing compounds, which are also responsible for their pungent smell. These **flavonoids** are more concentrated in the outer layers of the bulb, and the main one, quercetin, can help prevent heart disease. Although cooked onions mostly lose their benefits, quercetin can be preserved if the onions are simmered gently to make a soup, the quercetin being retained in the broth (but it is still best to eat onions raw!) Onions provide inulin, a dietary **fibre** known to encourage healthy gut bacteria. Their **anti-inflammatory** and **antioxidant** properties have linked onions with protection against cancer and support for the immune system.

Tomato and poppy seed tart

This is a good summer tart, ideally made with newly ripe, sweet summer tomatoes. You can make these as individual mini tarts, or as one large single. We're used to seeing poppy seeds in bread, but why not in pastry? They're a good source of minerals, as well as healthy fats and omega-6 fatty acids. They also add a delicious nuttiness to the taste.

For 6–8:

For the pastry
140g plain flour
½ tsp sea salt
50g poppy seeds, dry-fried
1 tbsp dark soft brown sugar
100g cold organic unsalted butter, cut into cubes
1–1½ tbsp milk

For the filling
1 large onion, sliced
1 tbsp olive oil
1kg tomatoes, roughly chopped, or 2 x 400g tins
    of chopped tomatoes
8 sun-dried tomatoes, chopped
1 tbsp clear or set honey
1 tbsp red wine vinegar
200g soft goats' cheese
30g basil leaves

Make the pastry. Sift the flour and salt into a bowl, add the poppy seeds and sugar, then rub in the butter by hand until the mixture resembles breadcrumbs. Alternatively, pulse all the ingredients in a food processor. Add enough milk to bring the pastry together into a ball. Wrap in clingfilm and chill in the fridge for an hour or so (or use the freezer technique on page 280 instead).

Preheat the oven to 180°C/gas mark 4 and put a baking sheet inside to heat up.

Line a 28cm loose-bottomed tart tin with the pastry, leaving the excess draped over the sides in case it shrinks. Chill again for half an hour if you

have time. Prick the bottom of the pastry case with a fork, line with greaseproof paper or foil and weigh this down with baking beans or rice.

Put the tart case on the hot baking sheet in the oven and bake for about 15 minutes. Remove the baking beans and paper and bake the case for another 5 minutes. Remove from the oven and trim away the excess pastry with a sharp knife.

Turn up the oven to 190°C/gas mark 5 and reheat the baking sheet.

Meanwhile, sweat the onion very gently in the olive oil until softened. Add all of the tomatoes, the honey and vinegar. Let the mixture bubble away until it has thickened and reduced.

Spread the goats' cheese over the pastry case, then scatter with basil leaves. Cover with the thickened tomato mixture.

Put the tart on the hot baking sheet and bake for 25 minutes. Serve warm with a crisp green salad.

» 456 calories for 6 servings, 342 for 8

More on » butter *p104* » milk *p252* » onions *p281* » olive oil *p193* » tomatoes *p142* » honey *p334* » goats' cheese *p268*

Puddings

THE NOTION OF a healthy pudding seems a bit of a contradiction in terms. However, you can make low-fat and low-sugar but still delicious versions of crumble, jelly, pannacotta, even rice pudding, every once in a while. There are recipes here for these, but for every day, why not try and keep it lighter and simpler? A plate of cinnamon apple crisps will hit that sweet craving on the head, as will fruit leathers, which have intense flavour and lots of goodness.

I also like to finish a meal with a plate of fruit. There's a great Lebanese 'pudding' to be eaten when the weather is boiling hot: frozen grapes, frozen chunks of watermelon and some cubes of feta are laid out on a large dish, and it's healthy and delicious (see page 298). Or simply cut up a selection of seasonal fruit. In Greece and Italy that's a very common way of finishing a meal, with traditional restaurants and tavernas bringing it out 'on the house'. Already roughly chopped into bite-sized portions, the fruit – apples, pears, oranges, peaches or melons – needs nothing more than a squeeze of lemon over it, and perhaps a dusting of cinnamon or nutmeg.

We all know how nice a bowl of strawberries can be, but have you tried strawberries briefly cooked on a barbecue on a sheet of foil? The sugar caramelises within the fruit, adding another level of taste. Quite apart from their flavour, berries are the winners amongst fruit in terms of health. They have a low sugar content (a fraction of that found in pineapple, mango or even apples). They're low in calories, high in fibre, vitamins and minerals, and super-high in antioxidants, which have a huge range of health benefits. Berries can help to prevent clogging of the arteries and lower cholesterol, so helping to protect us against cardiovascular disease. All the highly coloured berries – blueberries, black- and redcurrants, raspberries, strawberries and blackberries – are also firmly established as memory-protecting foods. Their polyphenol (plant antioxidant) content encourages neurons in the brain to communicate with each other better. Just 50g a day, enough to fill one hand, is associated with reduced risk of dementia. You can add them to breakfast, or why not have them for pudding? Changing between one variety on one day, and another on the next, is good too.

One word of warning: fruit cultivation is heavily reliant on chemicals so, if you can, buy organic and, out of season, look for cheaper (but ideally still organic) frozen berries, rather than buying more expensive tasteless imports. Two studies have found that picked and immediately frozen berries have more nutrients than so-called fresh berries harvested several days before.

When eating fruit, avoid lashings of cream. Whether you're having the fruit as it comes, or in ice cream, adding lots of cream is not the only way to make it tasty. Make your 'ice creams' with yoghurt, coconut milk (see page 304) or ricotta instead, or make granitas which don't need any dairy protein at all – and, unlike sorbets, don't require lots of sugar. But the sugar levels of even these mean that they are not for every day.

And, as a general rule, if you have a sweet tooth, there are several better-for-you alternatives to sugar. Using cinnamon is the best of all, as this is a natural sweetener. And then there are maple syrup and honey (see pages 27 and 334), which offer health benefits as well as sweetness. Coconut palm sugar possesses the same calories as table sugar, but it's a little sweeter, so this means you can use less. It's also not a nutritional void. There's some fibre, plant nutrients and minerals in it – as opposed to processed sugar, which has zero goodness. Lacuma is another option, a nutrient-dense fruit from Peru (see page 290). Dates and any dried fruit are also good as sweeteners, but don't go mad, as they're packed with natural sugars. Agave nectar (or syrup) is yet another alternative, but it's not really the answer, as it's normally highly processed and very high in fructose, a sugar we want to restrict.

Sugar on its own is best avoided, but it's fat and sugar together that's the real no-no as a regular part of your diet (see page 13).

Finally, *good* chocolate is good for you. Go for one of the brands with over 70 per cent cocoa solids, and wean yourself off the high-sugar, high-fat, chocolate bars that are light on actual cocoa solids – check the label before you buy. As well as hitting the spot, proper chocolate contains micronutrients that are valuable, so one or two pieces on special occasions is an excellent way to end a meal.

So what are the guidelines for puddings?
  » Keep them small.
  » Keep them light.
  » Promote berries in your diet.
  » An apple a day keeps the doctor away.
  » Use natural unprocessed sweeteners wherever you can, but don't just swap these for sugar.
  » Aim to reduce the number of sweet things you have overall. They easily become addictive.
  » Move away from the idea of having something sweet with every meal.

You don't have to rule everything sweet out of your diet to be healthy, but learn to treat sweet things with respect.

Blackberry and apple fruit leathers

Fruit leathers are a chewy, intensely flavoured snack rather than a pudding, but two or three different leather flavours together on a plate are ideal at the end of a meal. Leathers are made from fruit pastes, not juice: you sieve out a little, but much of the fibre is retained. Apples form the fruit pulp base for all the leathers. For different fruit flavours, try strawberry, raspberry, plum and blackberry, and make them when the fruit is in season, has the best flavour, and is cheaper to buy.

If kept airtight, the high natural sugars and acid content of the leathers mean you can store them for at least a year, so make batches as a range of fruit comes into season; dusted in cornflour, they stay dry and separate.

As you need to have the oven on for such a long time, this recipe makes three trays at once.

For 60 strips:

1.5kg dessert apples, cut into rough chunks, not peeled and pips left in (they help with the set)
500g blackberries
1 tbsp cornflour

Put the fruit – both apples and blackberries – into a large preserving saucepan. Stew the fruit down gently on a low heat, stirring regularly, reducing the fruit to a thick pulp, which takes up to an hour. Put the fruit pulp into a fine sieve and push the flesh through with the back of a wooden spoon into a bowl, discarding the pips and cores.

Preheat the oven to its lowest setting.

Line three 30 x 45cm baking trays with baking parchment. Pour the sieved purée in as thin a layer as possible onto the baking parchment and spread evenly with a spatula.

Transfer to the oven and leave for 10–14 hours until the fruit is completely dry.

Once the leathers are cool, cut them into strips and roll them into scrolls, then serve on a plate. You can also store them: to prevent sticking, dust both sides with cornflour and layer them with baking parchment in between. Store in an airtight tin. To serve, cut into strips and roll as above.

» 15 calories per strip

Apples 'An apple a day keeps the doctor away!' Apples are cheap, widely available and one of the healthiest fruits on the planet. Eat them as they come, eat them chopped with muesli for breakfast, or cooked in healthy puddings – but however you have them, leave the skin on. The skin contains a high concentration of insoluble **fibre**, as well as two to three times more **antioxidants** than apple flesh. Apples contain high levels of **pectin**, a soluble fibre that has the ability to form a gel, binding together water and toxins – this helps to eliminate poisons and excess fatty acids like **cholesterol** from our bodies. Nutritionists use apples when trying to clear the system of heavy metals such as mercury and lead, and they're often recommended after radiotherapy for the same reason. Apples are also useful in the damping down of allergies, and eating two apples a week has been shown to have an inverse relationship with asthma, and possibly other similar immune-based diseases.

Buy organic apples if you can. Fruit cultivation is heavily reliant on chemicals, and conventionally grown apples have a high pesticide residue. Finally, apples last best if kept in the fridge, so if you have a big batch, store them there.

Jane's super-simple fruit bullets

This is a recipe of my sister's for super-quick and easy mouthfuls of sweetness. They're also ideal for a snack on the hoof. Roll them in your favourite nuts – toasted and coarsely chopped – or try them with a coating of flaked, toasted coconut. Ideally, buy organic unsulphured apricots and check they have not been coated with oil or hydrogenated fat to stop them from sticking together.

For 20 walnut-sized balls:
50g raw pistachio kernels, plus extra for rolling (optional)
100g dried apricots (ideally organic, unsulphured)
Grated zest and juice of 1 lime
1 tbsp maple syrup
1 tbsp hazelnuts, dry-fried and finely chopped

Simply blend together all the ingredients except the hazelnuts in a food processor.

Roll into walnut-sized balls and put into the fridge to harden.

Then roll the balls in the finely chopped hazelnuts (or more pistachios). Store in an airtight tin or jar and eat within a couple of weeks.

» 30 calories per bullet

More on » maple syrup *p27* » hazelnuts *p50*

Fruit and seed truffles

These healthy truffles are both filling and satisfying. Rolled in sesame seeds, they taste fantastic and the seeds provide bonus nutrition.

They're sweetened with lacuma, a fruit from Peru, which you should be able to find as a powder in health-food shops (if not, add a few dates instead). It's an excellent sugar alternative with a low Glycaemic Index – and, unlike processed sugar, it also contains fibre, vitamins and minerals, including beta-carotene, niacin (vitamin B3) and iron.

If you feel like something chocolatey, add a tablespoon of cocoa powder.

For 20 walnut-sized balls:
160g dried figs, hard stems removed
30g sesame seeds
80g dried apricots (ideally organic, unsulphured)
80g dried apple rings
100g hazelnuts
80g desiccated coconut
¼ nutmeg, grated
1 tbsp lacuma powder (or 5 or 6 Medjool dates)
1 heaped tsp ground mixed spice
Grated zest of 1 lemon
Juice of ½ lemon

Put the dried figs into a jug and cover with boiling water. Allow to cool, then drain.

Dry-fry the sesame seeds for a minute or two, then tip onto a plate.

Blitz the figs and the remaining ingredients (except the sesame seeds) in a food processor until combined. Roll the mixture into walnut-sized balls, then roll them in the sesame seeds to coat. They will keep for several weeks in an airtight jar or tin.

» 116 calories per truffle

More on » figs *p307* » sesame seeds *p164* » apples *p288* » hazelnuts *p50* » lemons *p346*

Dark chocolate bark

Eating healthily does not mean chocolate goes out of the window. With the right kind, you can enjoy guilt-free nibbling. Here chocolate containing over 70 per cent cocoa solids is spiked with delicious and healthy things, some added into the melted chocolate to flavour it, but most scattered over the top as it sets.

For 1 chocolate bark, about 15 x 30cm:
1 x 100g bar best-quality dark chocolate
   (at least 70% cocoa solids)
Flavouring and/or topping of choice (see below)

Break up the chocolate into small chunks and put into a bowl. Put the bowl over a saucepan of simmering water – the bottom of the bowl must not touch the water – and melt the chocolate.

Add your chosen flavouring and mix in. Take the bowl off the heat and allow to cool for 5 minutes.

Line a 25 x 35cm baking tray with baking parchment and slowly pour the chocolate onto the baking parchment in a vaguely rectangular shape, roughly 15 x 30cm. Smooth it out and scatter over the topping before the chocolate sets.

Allow the chocolate to set. If not serving immediately, break into shards or keep as a whole sheet. Either way, store it in an airtight tin.

Cardamom, orange zest and sesame
1 tbsp cardamom pods, husks removed and seeds
   crushed in a pestle and mortar, to flavour
Finely grated zest of 1 orange, to flavour
1 level tbsp sesame seeds, dry-fried, to top
» 614 calories per bark

Chilli, pink Himalayan salt and lime zest
1–2 pinches of chilli powder, to flavour
Finely grated zest of 2 limes, to top
1–2 pinches of pink Himalayan salt, crushed, to top
» 583 calories per bark

Mixed fruit and seeds
2 heaped tbsp mixed dried fruit and seeds, to top
» 709 calories per bark

Hazelnut
2 heaped tbsp hazelnuts, dry-fried and chopped, to top
» 707 calories per bark

Stem ginger
1–2 tbsp preserved ginger (make your own, see p45),
   finely chopped, to top
» 653 calories per bark

Chocolate is made from the pod-like fruit of the tropical cacao tree, the cocoa bean. Eaten as it is, chocolate is bitter, so sugar is always added, and in the cheaper brands, milk powder, condensed milk, soy, vegetable fat and flavouring might be added as well. The healthiest chocolate is the least processed, with the greatest amount of cocoa solids (these are rich in **flavonoids**). The more cocoa solids a chocolate bar contains, the less sugar and vice versa: a 70 per cent chocolate bar will contain 30 per cent sugar; a 65 per cent bar 35 per cent, and so on. The cocoa bean also gives us cocoa butter, which contains oleic acid, the **monounsaturated fat** that's found in olive oil and is associated with various health benefits, including the ability to lower **cholesterol**.

Dark chocolate is high in **phytonutrients**, including flavonoids, which are beneficial in preventing cardiovascular disease. Studies have shown that eating 50–100g of dark chocolate a day can lower blood pressure, but as little as 15–20g a day is probably enough to provide a good amount of flavonoids. Dark chocolate contains small quantities of caffeine, so you might prefer to avoid eating it in the evening.

Go for organic and fair trade when you're buying chocolate: not only is child labour common in conventional chocolate production, but also lots of pesticides are used in its cultivation.

Strawberry kebabs with basil and balsamic vinegar

All berries are good for you, cooked or raw – but strawberries are the only ones big enough to thread onto skewers. These kebabs work well on a barbecue, and just as well under a grill. The strawberries intensify in flavour as they cook, yet you catch them before they collapse into jam.

This is good made with pineapple chunks too, or a mix of both, but remember that, as fruits go, pineapple is very sugar-rich.

For 4 (2 kebabs each):
32 large strawberries
Drizzle of aged balsamic vinegar
20g bunch of basil, leaves removed and torn into ribbons

You will need 8 wooden skewers, soaked in water.

Hull the strawberries and then roll them in a shallow saucer of balsamic vinegar.

Thread the strawberries onto wooden skewers, four or five on each, packed closely together.

When the barbecue is cooling (or set your grill to a medium-low heat), place the kebabs on a sheet of foil. Cook for 3 minutes on one side and then rotate. But keep an eye on them, as cooking time varies with size and varieties of strawberry.

Serve the kebabs scattered with the basil leaves, or with Frozen basil and ricotta yoghurt (see page 302), or a dollop of live natural yoghurt (see page 44).

» 17 calories per kebab, so 34 per serving
   of 2 kebabs

More on » mixed berries *p343* » balsamic vinegar *p189*

Detox summer fruit salad

This salad involves piling the very healthiest fruits into a big bowl to marinate in honey and lemon verbena. Adding some dried fruit and some toasted seeds makes it even more nutritious and sustaining. The salad is best eaten within 24 hours.

For 4:
500g strawberries
150g blueberries
150g blackcurrants
200g raspberries
1 or 2 dessert apples (not peeled)
4 kiwi fruit, peeled
1 mango, peeled and destoned
Seeds of 1 pomegranate (see p46)
1 tbsp dried apricots (ideally organic, unsulphured)
1 tbsp stoned dates
Sprigs of lemon verbena, to serve

For the syrup
2 tbsp clear honey
15–20 verbena leaves
1–2 tbsp flaked almonds, toasted (optional)

In a small pan, heat the honey, 180ml water and the verbena together until bubbling. Set aside to cool a little – not too much – and allow the flavours to infuse. Remove the verbena leaves.

Prepare the fruit as you like – whole, diced or sliced. Place in a large bowl and pour over the warm syrup. Mix well and leave for another 15 minutes or so for the flavours to deepen.

Serve in individual bowls with a sprig of lemon verbena on each. A bowl of toasted flaked almonds makes a good addition too.

» 285 calories per serving

More on » blueberries *p328* » blackcurrants *p294* » raspberries *p326* » apples *p288* » pomegranates *p46* » honey *p334* » almonds *p347*

Snooker ball nectarines

I love the look of this pudding, which strictly speaking is more like pool than snooker, with its red and black balls. You can add another colour, serving the nectarines with a ball of one of the ice creams or sorbets in the rest of the chapter. It's particularly good with Frozen basil and ricotta yoghurt (see page 302).

Make this when nectarines (or peaches) are at their best in summer, and use white-fleshed if you can find them. You can also use raspberries and blackberries when currants are hard to find – but for the purée, stabilise the juice with a teaspoon of cornflour (redcurrants have a lot of pectin so will form a thick purée).

For 10:
10 ripe nectarines (or peaches)
250g blackcurrants
1–2 tbsp coconut palm sugar (to taste)
250g redcurrants
1 tbsp clear honey

To serve
Frozen grapes
Redcurrants

Peel the nectarines (or peaches) by plunging them into a bowl or pan of just-boiled water for 10 seconds. Remove and peel back the skin with a sharp knife. Cut the peeled fruit in half and remove the stone.

To make the blackcurrant purée, gently simmer the blackcurrants in a pan with only the coconut palm sugar, no water added, over a gentle heat for 3–4 minutes. Allow to cool and then push the flesh through a medium to fine gauge sieve. You are left with a purée which is quite dense.

Next make the redcurrant purée in the same way as the blackcurrant purée, but using honey as the sweetener.

Divide the nectarine halves between two bowls or plates, rounded-side up, and spoon over the currant purée to coat – red over one lot, black over the other – just before you serve. Keep some purée back, pouring it into two jugs to take to the table.

Place the nectarine balls in a serving dish with frozen grapes and redcurrants to decorate, or place half a red and half a black nectarine ball onto each serving plate, rounded-side up. Let everyone help themselves to more currant purée. Eat with a knife and fork, or a fork and spoon.

» 92 calories per serving

More on » coconut palm sugar *p316* » honey *p334* » grapes *p298*

Blackcurrants have an amazing quantity of vitamin C: 100g raw give us 200mg (130mg if cooked); the UK recommended daily amount is 60mg! Vitamin C is excellent for promoting healthy skin and wound healing, and is needed for the metabolism of stress hormones. It is anti-viral and anti-bacterial, helping to fight colds, flu and other viral infections and boosting immunity. Vitamin C is also used in detoxification in the body. The **phytonutrients** in blackcurrants protect against neurological diseases, and studies show they may help prevent Alzheimer's disease and the age-related eye disease of macular degeneration, among other things. Blackcurrants also provide iron and some essential B vitamins.

Cinnamon apple crisps

These are good as a crunchy and delicious pudding or snack, served from a plate or bowl in the middle of the table, just as you would some delicious chocolates. They're best made and eaten pretty much straightaway. Apples – in all ways – are good for us, and so is the classic addition of cinnamon. It's the new super-hero in the nutritional world.

For a medium bowl for 4:
2 dessert apples
A little cold-pressed rapeseed oil
2 tsp ground cinnamon
2 tbsp honey, melted (optional)

Preheat the oven to 170°C/gas mark 3.

Wash and dry the apples, then remove the stalks.

Using the thinnest setting on a mandolin, slice the apples across the core.

Place the slices on a baking tray lined with lightly oiled baking parchment. Do not overlap the apple slices. (If you want to multiply up this quantity, you will need to bake them in several batches.)

Dust with cinnamon and brush with melted honey (if using).

Put the tray in the oven and bake for around 30–40 minutes. Turn halfway through and remove when the slices have curled up like flowers and turned golden.

Leave to cool and crisp up.

» 17 calories per serving (1 apple's worth of crisps is 53), not including honey

More on » apples *p288* » rapeseed oil *p248* » cinnamon *p22* » honey *p334*

Frozen berries with chocolate sauce

A healthier version of the Ivy Restaurant classic dessert of iced berries with hot white chocolate sauce. White chocolate contains only cocoa butter, sugar and usually flavourings, whereas the dark chocolate used here is mainly cocoa solids and comes with plenty of health benefits. Coconut milk is also used here instead of double cream.

For 4:
500g frozen berries (preferably organic)

For the sauce
100g best-quality dark chocolate (at least 70% cocoa solids)
100ml coconut milk
Finely grated zest of 1 unwaxed orange

To make the sauce, break the chocolate into pieces and place in a bowl set over a pan of simmering water. The bottom of the bowl must not touch the water. Melt for 3–5 minutes, stirring every so often.

Once the chocolate has melted, add the coconut milk and orange zest, stir and heat for another couple of minutes.

About 5 minutes before serving, put the frozen berries onto individual plates, or one large plate, and leave at room temperature to lose a little of their chill.

Transfer the hot chocolate sauce to a serving jug and pour over the fruit, or let your guests help themselves.

» 223 calories per serving

More on » mixed berries *p343* » chocolate *p291* » coconut milk *p235* » oranges *p49*

Frozen melon and grapes with feta

Try putting grapes in the freezer on a hot day. It transforms them into mini sorbets – brilliant to take out on a picnic – or flavoured ice-cubes for drinks (see Sangria on page 352). Or mix them with watermelon, made all the more delicious by freezing in mini chunks; both are a good contrast to cold, salty feta.

For 4:
600g watermelon (about ½ small melon)
400g red grapes
200g feta
2 tbsp chopped basil or mint leaves

Skin the watermelon and cut the flesh into bite-sized chunks. Put into a suitable container and place in the freezer.

Put the grapes, left on their stalks, on a plate in the freezer. Leave both overnight, or for at least 12 hours.

When ready to eat, divide the frozen melon and grapes between four plates. Crumble over the feta and scatter with basil or mint.

» 243 calories per serving

More on » feta p264 » mint p326

> **Grapes** – and red grapes most of all – contain hundreds of different **antioxidants**, which are mostly concentrated in the seeds and the skin. These can reduce the damage caused by **free radicals** and slow down the ageing process. They can also help prevent hardening of the arteries and heart disease, and have strong anti-cancer properties. Grapes also protect against metabolic syndrome (which can develop into diabetes) by helping to steady blood-glucose levels.

Blood orange granita

Granitas are the perfect light pudding, and healthy if you avoid the usual vast quantities of sugar. I have used coconut palm sugar to sweeten the juice a little here: it gives a slightly treacly flavour that works well with the blood orange juice. Add a splosh of Campari for a party, either into the granita as you make it, or as you serve a globe or two of the granita in a glass to make a mini moat of the bitter, red drink.

For 6:
Juice of 8 blood oranges
50g coconut palm sugar
Finely grated zest and juice of 1 lemon

Put the orange juice into a saucepan over a low heat. Add the sugar and stir until just dissolved. Do not heat for longer than necessary – it will spoil the flavour of the granita. Take off the heat and allow to cool.

Stir in the lemon zest and juice. Pour the mixture into an ice-cream maker if you have one, freeze/churn for about 20 minutes, then pack into a plastic container and freeze for 2 hours.

If you don't have an ice-cream maker, place the mixture in a shallow plastic container and freeze for 1 hour. Remove and fork through, mixing the frozen edge into the middle to break up the ice crystals. Repeat twice.

Before serving, allow the granita to soften in the fridge for 15 minutes. Spoon into individual glasses.

» 87 calories per serving

More on » oranges p49 » coconut palm sugar p316 » lemons p346

Raspberry and red wine sorbet

This is based on a recipe given to me by Rose Gray of River Café fame, made here with maple syrup and a little live natural yoghurt. It has a wonderful colour and an intense, summery flavour. The recipe includes a large glass of red wine, which in moderation is a jolly good thing, and the slight sourness of the wine cuts through the intensity of the raspberry taste.

For 10:
900g raspberries, plus 300g to serve
250ml Valpolicella (or any good red wine)
100g live natural yoghurt (see p44)
Juice of ½ lemon
2–3 tbsp maple syrup (to taste)
2 egg whites, each one kept separate

In a food processor, pulse-chop the 900g raspberries, the red wine, yoghurt and lemon juice to a liquid. Add 2 tbsp maple syrup, taste for sweetness, then add more if needed. Blitz again, then pack into a plastic container and freeze for 2 hours.

Remove half of the mixure and blitz with 1 egg white in the food processor for 30 seconds. Do the same with the other half and pour all the mixture back into the container. Return to the freezer.

Before serving, allow the sorbet to soften in the fridge for 15 minutes. Serve from wide-bowled glasses, scattered with fresh raspberries.

» 81 calories per serving

More on » raspberries *p326* » red wine *p352* » yoghurt *p44* » lemons *p346* » maple syrup *p27* » eggs *p61*

Strawberry and passion fruit granita

Hardly needing a recipe, this is a super-quick and easy pudding, and it has an amazingly low calorie count. It's best eaten freshly frozen, on the day you make it or soon thereafter.

Strawberries grown conventionally have a high pesticide residue, so try to buy organic.

For 6:
800g strawberries, hulled
2–3 tbsp maple syrup (to taste)
4 passion fruit

To serve
3 passion fruit, halved
175g strawberries, hulled or unhulled

Blitz the strawberries and 2 tbsp maple syrup in a blender.

Put into a bowl and add the passion fruit seeds, flesh and juice. Taste, making sure the mix is slightly over-sweet (when frozen, this dulls a bit, and strawberries vary in sweetness). Add a little more maple syrup if needed.

Pour the mixture into an ice-cream maker if you have one. Freeze/churn for about 20 minutes, then pack into a plastic container and freeze for 2 hours.

If you don't have an ice-cream maker, place the mixture in a shallow plastic container and freeze for 1 hour. Remove and fork through, mixing the frozen edge into the middle to break up the ice crystals. Repeat twice.

Before serving, allow the granita to soften in the fridge for 15 minutes. Place a couple of scoops onto each plate, and serve with a half passion fruit and some strawberries alongside.

» 85 calories per serving

More on » mixed berries *p343* » maple syrup *p27*

Chocolate sorbet

The idea of a chocolate – rather than fruit – sorbet may not necessarily appeal, but do try this; it's wonderfully rich. You can make it with 70, 85 or 99 per cent chocolate.

For 6–8:
80ml maple syrup
35g unsweetened cocoa powder
½ tsp ground cinnamon
85g dark chocolate, broken into pieces
200g raspberries, to serve

In a large saucepan, whisk together 175ml water with the maple syrup, cocoa powder and cinnamon. Bring to a boil, whisking frequently; let it boil, continuing to whisk, for 45 seconds.

Remove from the heat and stir in the chocolate until it's melted, then stir in 75ml more water. Transfer to a bowl or dish, mix well and chill.

Pour the mixture into an ice-cream maker if you have one. Freeze/churn for about 20 minutes, then pack into a plastic container and freeze for 2 hours.

If you don't have an ice-cream maker, place the mixture in a shallow plastic container and freeze for 1 hour. Remove and fork through, mixing the frozen edge into the middle to break up the ice crystals. Repeat twice.

Before serving, allow the sorbet to soften in the fridge for 15 minutes. Serve one good scoop per person with a pile of raspberries.

» 149 calories for 6 servings, 112 for 8

More on » maple syrup *p27* » cinnamon *p22* » chocolate *p291* » raspberries *p326*

Frozen basil and ricotta yoghurt

A wonderful light alternative to standard ice cream, this is best eaten as soon as possible, as the intense fresh flavour of basil will dissipate if it is kept too long in the freezer.

For 8:
250g ricotta
1kg live natural yoghurt (see p44)
100g bunch of basil, leaves only, plus a few extra leaves for decoration
Juice of 1 lemon
150g clear honey

In a bowl, combine the ricotta and yoghurt with a fork until lump-free.

Blitz the basil leaves with a couple of tablespoons of the ricotta and yoghurt mix in a blender or food processor. Add this vivid green purée to the rest of the yoghurt and ricotta. Mix in the lemon juice and honey.

Pour the mixture into an ice-cream maker if you have one. Freeze/churn for about 20 minutes, then pack into a plastic container and freeze for 2 hours.

If you don't have an ice-cream maker, place the mixture in a shallow plastic container and freeze for 1 hour. Remove and fork through, mixing the frozen edge into the middle to break up the ice crystals. Repeat twice.

Before serving, allow the frozen yoghurt to soften in the fridge for 15 minutes.

Divide between individual plates and decorate with basil leaves.

» 205 calories per serving

More on » yoghurt *p44* » lemons *p346* » honey *p334*

Instant banana ice cream

A dairy- and sugar-free ice-cream, as quick to make as the dreaded 1970s Angel Delight but without a preservative or e-number in sight. This is best eaten straightaway.

For 5–6:
8 ripe bananas
100ml coconut milk/full-fat milk/almond milk
1 tsp ground cinnamon
70g hazelnuts, dry-fried and chopped
1 tbsp clear honey, plus extra if needed
1 tbsp dark cocoa powder (optional)

Freeze the bananas in their skins for at least 2 hours. Take them out, peel and cut them into 2.5cm slices.

Put them with the other ingredients into a food processor and blitz until smooth, but not defrosted. Test for sweetness and add more honey if needed.

Ideally eat straightaway, or spoon into an ice-cream maker and churn until smooth and frozen but still soft enough to eat.

» 365 calories for 5 servings, 304 for 6

More on » bananas *p345* » coconut milk *p235*
» milk *p252* » cinnamon *p22* » hazelnuts *p50*
» honey *p334* » chocolate *p291*

Tutti-frutti kulfi

Kulfis are delicately spiced Indian ice creams, traditionally eaten after something fiery. You can cut the calories further by using light coconut milk, but the downside of this option is a more granular texture.

For 6:
400ml tin of coconut milk
¼ tsp cardamom seeds, crushed
2 tbsp desiccated coconut, dry-fried
3 tbsp clear honey
200g live natural yoghurt (see p44)
Finely grated zest of 1 lemon
Seeds of 1 pomegranate (see p46; keep some back
    for serving)
70g pistachio nuts, dry-fried and roughly chopped
    (keep some back for serving)
Rose or dianthus petals, to serve (optional)

Put all the ingredients except the flower petals into a bowl and mix well.

Pour the mixture into an ice-cream maker if you have one and churn for 20–25 minutes. When almost solid, spoon into six containers (dariole moulds are good) and freeze.

If you don't have an ice-cream maker, pour the mixture into a plastic container and freeze for 1 hour. Remove and fork through, mixing the frozen edge into the middle to break up the ice crystals. Repeat, then spoon into the moulds. Freeze until ready to serve.

Allow the kulfi to soften in the fridge for 20 minutes before serving, then turn out onto individual plates. Decorate with the reserved pistachio nuts and pomegranate seeds, and the flower petals.

» 250 calories per serving

More on » coconut milk *p235* » honey *p334*
» yoghurt *p44* » lemons *p346* » pomegranate *p46*

Frozen stem ginger and cardamom yoghurt with grilled figs

This is the perfect late summer and autumn party pudding, when figs are plentiful, cheap and sweet. It does contain a lot of sugar, so have it as a treat.

You could serve grilled figs with a dollop of normal yoghurt, but I love them with the frozen kind. Although the standard shop-bought varieties may be lower in fat than ice cream, they can be jam-packed with sugar, so it's better to make your own. You can also make a dairy-free version using coconut yoghurt. (And unlike commercial stem ginger, the home-made kind isn't swimming in sugar syrup.)

For 8:
2 tbsp chopped stem ginger, plus 1–2 tbsp of the
    syrup (see p45)
1.5kg live natural yoghurt (see p44)
4 tbsp maple syrup
15 cardamom pods, crushed and seeds released

For the grilled figs
8 ripe figs, cut in half
3 tbsp pomegranate molasses
1 tbsp lemon juice
3 tbsp coconut palm sugar or clear honey
4 sprigs of thyme, 2 whole, 2 leaves picked
Zest of 1 orange, half in pared strips, half finely grated

Make the stem ginger, at least 1 day before it's going to be used, following the recipe on page 45. (The recipe makes 250g, so you will have some left over.)

For the frozen yoghurt, mix the yoghurt and maple syrup in a bowl. Stir in the cardamom seeds, the chopped stem ginger and the ginger syrup. Taste, and add more ginger if the flavour is not gingery enough for you.

Pour the mixture into an ice-cream maker if you have one. Freeze/churn for about 20 minutes, then pack into a plastic container and freeze for at least 2 hours before serving.

Puddings

If you don't have an ice-cream maker, pour into a plastic container and freeze for 1 hour. Remove and fork through, mixing the frozen edge into the middle to break up the ice crystals. Repeat twice.

Before serving, allow to soften in the fridge for 15 minutes.

Meanwhile, marinate and grill the figs. Place the figs, pomegranate molasses, lemon juice, 1 tablespoon of the sugar, all the thyme (leaves and sprigs), the pared and grated zest of the orange, and 1 tablespoon water in a bowl. Mix to dissolve the sugar. Add the figs and leave to marinate for 30 minutes.

Preheat the grill. Remove the figs from the bowl (keep the marinade) and arrange them, cut-side up, snugly in a baking dish/pan.

Sprinkle with the remaining sugar and place under the hot grill – not too high up – for 10 minutes, so that the sugar caramelises and the figs are softened.

Pour the marinade into a small pan, bring to the boil, and boil to reduce by half until it has the consistency of clear honey. Remove the thyme sprigs. Pour this sauce over the figs, and serve with the frozen yoghurt.

» 262 calories per serving

More on » ginger *p200* » yoghurt *p44* » maple syrup *p27* » pomegranates *p46* » lemons *p346* » coconut palm sugar *p316* » honey *p334* » oranges *p49*

Variations
Frozen lemon and poppy seed yoghurt Swap the stem ginger and cardamom for 4 teaspoons toasted poppy seeds and the juice and finely grated zest of 2 lemons.
» 203 calories per serving

Frozen toasted hazelnut yoghurt Swap the stem ginger and cardamom for 2 tablespoons finely chopped and 1 tablespoon roughly chopped toasted hazelnuts.
» 211 calories per serving

Figs are a famously good source of dietary **fibre**, and they're also rich in potassium, which helps to control blood pressure. A diet high in fruit and vegetables supplies adequate potassium, but people who consume salt-laden processed foods can be deficient. The body needs a healthy balance of these two **minerals**, and a low intake of potassium-rich foods, especially when linked with a high intake of sodium, can lead to hypertension and contribute to poor bone health. Eating figs regularly – fresh or dried – is one of the things you can do to help correct this.

Frozen apricot and mango mousse

A delicious half ice cream, half mousse that's good at any time of year. The sweetness comes from the dried fruit, which needs soaking overnight in apple juice. Use organic dried apricots, as regular ones have sulphur dioxide added to make them orange.

For 6:
125g dried apricots (ideally organic, unsulphured)
125g dried mango
250ml home-pressed apple juice (or organic, cloudy apple juice)
Finely grated zest and juice of 1 lemon
3 medium eggs, separated
300g live Greek yoghurt

To serve
2 tbsp flaked almonds, dry-fried
2 tbsp hazelnuts, dry-fried and chopped
Seeds of 2 passion fruit (optional)

Soak the apricots and mango overnight in the apple juice with the lemon zest and juice. Put into a pan and cook over a low heat for 15 minutes until softened. Drain, reserving the juice, and allow to cool. Put the fruit into a food processor and purée until smooth, then place in a large bowl.

Put the egg yolks and juice from the fruit into another bowl, and whisk for 3–4 minutes until creamy. Add to the mango and apricot purée. In yet another bowl, whisk the egg whites until properly stiff. Fold the yoghurt into the fruit mixture, then the egg whites.

Chill in the fridge for an hour or so, or if you want it semi-freddo, pour into glasses and freeze until firm (about 1 hour; remove from the freezer 10 minutes before serving). Sprinkle with the toasted nuts and, if you like, the passion fruit seeds.

» 254 calories per serving

More on » lemons *p346* » eggs *p61* » yoghurt *p44* » hazelnuts *p50*

Pomegranate rice pudding

A no-sugar rice pudding, which is perfect autumn and winter comfort food, particularly with the added benefit of pomegranate – both the sharp sweetness of the pomegranate molasses and the crunch of the seeds. Unlike most rice puddings, this is very quick to make, and it's also good for breakfast.

You can make this dairy-free using almond milk (see page 347). Nielsen Massey rosewater is a great one to choose, as it has an intense flavour.

For 6:
1 litre full-fat milk
180g arborio risotto rice, or round-grain pudding rice
1 tsp ground cinnamon
½ tsp freshly grated nutmeg
1 star anise
1 tsp rosewater (to taste)
Seeds of 1 pomegranate (see p46)
Pomegranate molasses (to taste), to serve

Put the milk, rice, cinnamon, nutmeg and star anise into a large pan. Bring to the boil then reduce the heat and simmer gently for 15 minutes, stirring occasionally. Once the rice is tender and the milk has been absorbed, take off the heat.

Add the rosewater and the pomegranate seeds and stir in.

Serve the rice pudding in bowls and drizzle with a little pomegranate molasses.

» 244 calories for 6 servings

More on » milk *p252* » rice *p224* » cinnamon *p22* » pomegranates *p46*

Orange and almond cake

A classic cake you can either serve whole as a pudding, or as mini, muffin-like cakes. It is free of sugar, dairy and gluten, and is one of my favourite cakes; it's particularly delicious with blood oranges when in season. You use the fruit whole, peel and all, which adds to the flavour and goodness, as a lot of citrus vitamins and minerals are in the peel. The oil in the almonds means the cake keeps for at least a week in the fridge, and it also freezes well.

The cake is packed full of protein – from the almonds – so a little goes a long way.

For 12 muffin-sized cakes or 1 whole cake for 12–15:
A little melted set coconut oil or organic unsalted butter, for greasing the tin
2 large or 3 small oranges
220g sultanas or stoned dates
1 large sprig of rosemary, leaves picked
250g ground almonds
5 medium eggs
1 tsp gluten-free baking powder

Line a muffin tray with muffin cases (if you use a silicone muffin mould, you don't need to line it). Or grease and line a 25cm cake tin.

Put the whole oranges into a medium saucepan. Cover with cold water and bring to the boil. Reduce the heat and simmer for about 45 minutes to an hour (depending on size), until the skins feel soft when poked with a sharp knife. Remove the oranges from the water and leave to cool.

Cut the cooled, boiled oranges in half. Flick out any pips. Put the orange halves into a food processor with the sultanas or dates and the rosemary. Blitz until a smooth paste is achieved.

Add the ground almonds, eggs and baking powder and pulse until combined.

Preheat the oven to 180°C/gas mark 4.

Fill the muffin tins or cake tin with the mixture. Bake the muffins in the oven for 30 minutes until the tops are golden and domed and a skewer inserted in the centre comes out clean. If cooked as a whole cake, it will need 1 hour – test to see if it is done in the same way.

Remove from the oven and leave to cool, then remove from the tin. Serve with live natural yoghurt (see page 44).

» 213 calories for 12 servings, 170 for 15

More on » oranges *p49* » almonds *p347* » eggs *p61*

Coconut oil is high in **medium-chain triglycerides** (MCTs), healthy fats that may help reduce the risk of heart disease. There is some research to show that MCTs can help with weight loss by reducing appetite, boosting metabolism and increasing fat cell activity.

Always buy organic coconut oil to avoid oil that is chemically treated. Coconut oil is solid at room temperature and can be substituted for butter in many baking recipes. You can substitute any liquid oil with coconut oil: 1 tbsp set coconut oil is equivalent to 25ml liquid oil. As it has a high smoke point, coconut oil is also ideal for frying (see page 14).

Beetroot brownie

Very rich, sustaining and simple to make, this gluten-, dairy- and sugar-free brownie tastes like a soft, rich chocolate orange, and can either be served for a mid-morning treat or afternoon tea, or as a pudding with yoghurt or cream. It freezes well, and the beetroot makes it slow to stale.

For about 18 small pieces:
2 or 3 (200g) beetroots
200g best-quality dark chocolate (at least 70% cocoa solids)
200g stoned dates, chopped
100g ground almonds
Finely grated zest and juice of 1 orange
2 medium eggs, beaten
½ tsp gluten-free baking powder

Cook the beetroots in a large pan of boiling water for 30–40 minutes until soft. Peel and coarsely chop.

Preheat the oven to 180°C/gas mark 4. Line a small baking tin or dish (about 20 x 30cm) with baking parchment.

Break up and melt the chocolate in a heatproof bowl set over a pan of gently simmering water (the base of the bowl must not touch the water), stirring occasionally. Allow to cool slightly.

Put the cooked beetroot into a food processor with the dates and whizz until you achieve a smooth pink paste. Add the almonds, orange zest and juice, eggs and baking powder. Pulse a couple of times until combined. Then add the melted chocolate and blitz again. Spoon the mixture into the lined tin, and bake for 25–35 minutes.

Remove from the oven, then allow to cool in the tin. Cut into 18 pieces.

» 143 calories per piece

More on » beetroot *p85* » chocolate *p291*
» almonds *p347* » oranges *p49* » eggs *p61*

Spicy ginger cake

Stem ginger in syrup is crammed with cane sugar, so if you have time, make your own version for this.

For 9 pieces:
100g wholemeal flour
2 tsp ground ginger
1 tsp ground mixed spice
1½ tsp ground cinnamon
½ tsp ground cloves
60g stem ginger in syrup (see page 45), chopped
1 heaped tsp baking powder
2 tbsp blackstrap molasses
50g organic unsalted butter
50g coconut palm sugar
1 medium egg, beaten

Preheat the oven to 180°C/gas mark 4. Line a square 21cm cake tin with baking parchment (or grease with butter). Sift the flour into a large bowl. Add the spices, ginger and baking powder. Heat the molasses, butter and coconut sugar in a saucepan until melted, then pour into the dry ingredients. Mix well. Make a well in the centre and add the egg. Beat to combine. Pour the mixture into the tin and bake for 20–25 minutes, until firm. Remove from the oven and leave in the tin until cold.

Turn out, cut into squares and serve with live natural yoghurt (see page 44) or Frozen stem ginger and cardamom yoghurt (see page 306).

» 136 calories per piece

More on » ginger *p200* » cinnamon *p22* » butter *p104* » coconut palm sugar *p316* » eggs *p61*

Blackstrap molasses Molasses is the syrup produced when sugar cane is processed to make sugar. It is highly nutritious, and blackstrap molasses – rich in copper for improving hair quality, iron for anaemia, calcium and magnesium for bone development, and the **antioxidant** mineral, selenium – is superior to any other.

Summer berry jelly

This summer pudding contains no bread, and is light on the jelly. It's made the day before serving and the rather precise amount of gelatine will give a nice soft, not rubbery, set. It's tempting to buy the apple juice; if you do, choose cloudy and ideally organic. Fresh home-pressed juice contains much more goodness than any commercially extracted juice – so, if you have a juicer, make your own.

For 8:
4 x 1.6g leaves of gelatine
450g strawberries, hulled (and halved if large)
250g raspberries
250g blueberries, plus extra to decorate
200g blackcurrants or redcurrants
600ml home-pressed apple juice (or organic, cloudy apple juice)
A few lemon verbena or mint leaves

Put the gelatine leaves into a bowl of cold water. Put the fruit into a 2 litre summer pudding bowl, alternating handfuls of berries.

Warm the apple juice in a pan. Squeeze the water from the gelatine leaves and add to the juice. Stir to dissolve over a gentle heat. Allow to cool slightly, then pour over the fruit. Chill overnight until set.

Dip the bowl into warm water and turn the jelly out onto a plate. Decorate with the extra blueberries and a few leaves of lemon verbena or mint.

» 92 calories per serving

More on » raspberries *p326* » blueberries *p328* » blackcurrants *p294* » mint *p326*

Variation

Apple, blackberry and pelargonium jelly Replace the same weight of fruit with apples and blackberries in equal measure. Stew for 10 minutes with 5–6 leaves of scented pelargoniums (Mabel Grey, Attar of Roses or Lady Plymouth). Make as above.
» 91 calories per serving

Blackcurrant and almond cake

This gluten-free cake makes a good pudding, served warm with live Greek yoghurt. You can make it in advance and reheat it gently, covered with a piece of foil.

Blackcurrants are increasingly emerging as one of our top superfoods, with higher phytonutrient levels than even blueberries. They're also excellent brain food, so we should include them in our diet as often as we can.

For 6–8:
200g organic unsalted butter, plus extra for greasing
200g coconut palm sugar
3 medium eggs
200g ground almonds
1 tsp vanilla extract
200g blackcurrants

Preheat the oven to 180°C/gas mark 4. Butter a 25cm loose-bottomed flan tin, and line the base with a circle of baking parchment.

Cream the butter and sugar together in a food processor or with a hand beater until the mixture is pale. Add the eggs, one at a time, beating well. After each addition, fold in some of the ground almonds and a few drops of vanilla extract. Repeat until everything is well combined.

Put the mixture into the flan tin and scatter over the blackcurrants. Their flavour is intense, so don't be tempted to use more fruit.

Bake for 30 minutes until golden and just firm. Remove from the oven and allow to cool, or serve warm, with live Greek yoghurt.

» 619 calories for 6 servings, 465 for 8

More on » butter *p104* » coconut palm sugar *p316* » eggs *p61* » almonds *p347* » blackcurrants *p244*

Light cheesecake with marinated strawberries

Best served in a glass rather than on a plate, this pudding has a fraction of the fat of a standard cheesecake, and uses honey and maple syrup rather than sugar. The cheesecake filling is best prepared the day before so it can set in the fridge overnight, then the whole thing can be quickly assembled when you're ready to eat.

You can serve this all year round with whatever fruit is in season. Frozen berries work fine, and in the autumn I love this cheesecake made with Blackberry and elderberry compote (see page 319) instead of the marinated strawberries.

For 6–8:

For the crumble topping
60g wholemeal flour (or ground almonds for gluten-free)
60g hazelnuts, roughly chopped
20g rolled oats (or quinoa flakes for gluten-free)
Pinch of ground cinnamon
40g coconut palm sugar (or soft brown sugar)
40g cold organic unsalted butter, cut into chunks

For the cheesecake filling
400g quark
Finely grated zest of 1 lemon
Juice of ½ lemon
1 tsp vanilla extract
1 tbsp poppy seeds, dry-fried
60ml clear honey
60ml maple syrup
250g live Greek yoghurt

For the marinated strawberries
1kg strawberries
Juice of 1 orange
Juice of 1 lemon
A little coconut palm sugar

Preheat the oven to 180°C/gas mark 4.

Put the crumble topping ingredients into a bowl and, with your fingers, rub in the butter. Spread the mix over a baking tray and cook in the middle of the oven for 7–9 minutes, stirring halfway through. Take out and leave to cool.

Put all the cheesecake ingredients into a food processor and blend until combined. Pour into a bowl and chill overnight to firm up.

Hull the strawberries and slice them in half. Drizzle with the orange and lemon juice, and enough sugar to taste. Chill for an hour or until you are ready to serve, stirring from time to time.

To assemble, spoon some strawberries into a glass, pour in some of the cheesecake filling and sprinkle over the crumble topping. Repeat the layers if there is room.

» 402 calories for 6 servings, 302 for 8

More on » almonds *p347* » hazelnuts *p50* » oats *p25* » quinoa *p140* » cinnamon *p22* » coconut palm sugar *p316* » butter *p104* » lemons *p346* » honey *p334* » maple syrup *p27* » yoghurt *p44* » oranges *p49*

Coconut pannacotta

Here is a proper pudding for when you feel you need one. It's low-fat, using yoghurt and coconut milk instead of cream, yet you wouldn't know it – there's nothing hair-shirt about this pannacotta. Make it the day before, so the caramel is absorbed overnight, and serve with orange segments, or any fruit in season.

For 6:

For the caramel
140g coconut palm sugar

For the pannacotta
20g gelatine leaves
400ml tin of coconut milk
2 tbsp coconut palm sugar
1 tsp vanilla extract
1 vanilla pod, split and seeds scraped out
400g live Greek yoghurt
4 oranges (blood oranges when in season), peeled and
   segmented (see p49), to serve

Start by making the caramel. Put the sugar and 5 tablespoons water into a heavy-based saucepan over a low heat. Stir slowly until the sugar has dissolved, then allow the syrup to boil without stirring. Take off the heat when it starts to turn brown – take care not to burn it. Divide the caramel between six ramekins. Set aside.

Now start the pannacotta. First, in a small bowl, soak the gelatine leaves in cold water to cover.

Meanwhile, put the coconut milk into a pan over a low heat, adding the sugar, vanilla extract, vanilla pod and seeds. Stir until the sugar has dissolved and the mixture is gently simmering.

Squeeze the water out of the gelatine leaves and add them to the coconut milk pan, still over a gentle heat. Stir until the gelatine has dissolved. Take the pan off the heat and allow the mixture to cool slightly, then stir in the yoghurt.

Ladle the mixture into the ramekins, and when cool transfer to the fridge to set.

To serve, loosen the sides of each pannacotta with a small knife. Put a small plate on top of each one, and carefully invert to turn out. If the pannacotta is reluctant to come out of the ramekin, dip the base briefly into a bowl of hot water.

Serve with blood orange segments.

» 308 calories per serving

More on » coconut milk *p235* » yoghurt *p44*
» oranges *p49*

Coconut palm sugar comes from the buds of coconut palm tree flowers. It has the same amount of calories but is more nutritious than table sugar, and it's sweeter, so you can get away with using less. It also contains tiny amounts of the **minerals** iron, zinc, calcium and potassium, along with some short-chain fatty acids, **polyphenols** and **antioxidants**. Coconut palm sugar also contains the **prebiotic fibre**, inulin, which may slow glucose absorption and gives it a lower **Glycaemic Index** then regular sugar.
   It's worth knowing that coconut palm sugar is the same as coconut sugar, with a consistency like soft brown sugar. Palm sugar is different – it is made from the sap of the sugar palm tree (also called the date palm); it is highly processed and, like table sugar, should be avoided or restricted.

Blackberry and apple crumble

This is a no-flour, no-sugar, no-butter crumble topping, which sounds very unpromising! However, it makes a light and delicious pudding, and it's just as good cold for breakfast. It's also gluten-free. For a fragrant flavour, add scented pelargonium leaves to the fruit mix if you have any in your garden.

For 4–6:
4 Granny Smith apples
400g blackberries
1 tbsp set coconut oil, melted
2 tbsp maple syrup
½ tsp ground cinnamon

For the topping
100g stoned dates
50g hazelnuts
50g almond flakes
20g coconut flakes
50g oat flakes
2 tbsp set coconut oil, melted

Preheat the oven to 180°C/gas mark 4.

Peel, core and cut the apples into chunks. Put into a pan with the blackberries, melted coconut oil, maple syrup and cinnamon and heat gently for 10 minutes, stirring occasionally.

Meanwhile, whizz the dates and hazelnuts together for 30 seconds in a food processor. Add the almond, coconut and oat flakes and the melted coconut oil, and whizz for about a minute until the mixture is even, stopping before it gets too fine and dusty.

Pour the stewed fruit into a pie dish (about 18cm in diameter). Add the topping. Bake for 15 minutes, then serve with live natural yoghurt (see page 44).

» 489 calories for 4 servings, 326 for 6

More on » apples *p288* » coconut oil *p309* » maple syrup *p27* » cinnamon *p22* » hazelnuts *p50* » almonds *p37* » oats *p25*

Blackberry and elderberry compote

Eat this compote by itself, or with an ice cream or sorbet; you can also use it in the cheesecake on page 314, substituting the compote for the strawberries.

Elderberries are extremely high in vitamin C and many plant nutrients; they are the superfruit to prevent and combat flu. In early autumn they are readily available almost anywhere, in both town and countryside. Be careful, though, with berries growing close to busy roads.

For 6–8:
300g blackberries
300g elderberries
100g sultanas
1 tbsp clear honey
2 tbsp coconut palm sugar
2 star anise

Put all the ingredients into a saucepan and heat gently for 8-10 minutes, stirring occasionally.

Pour into a bowl, allow to cool, then store in the fridge.

» 122 calories for 6 servings, 92 for 8

More on » honey *p334* » coconut palm sugar *p316*

Healthy mincemeat

You have to have a mince pie at Christmas, so here is a crunchy, lower-fat and lower-sugar version of mincemeat. There are plenty of natural sugars in the dried fruit, so you don't need any extra. This recipe makes enough mincemeat for 16 mincemeat baskets (see right) or 50 mini canapé cases.

For about 1kg:
100g dried figs
100g dates, ideally Medjool
75g dried apple
75g raisins
100g dried apricots
50g good-quality candied citrus peel
50g sultanas
75g currants
50g dried cranberries
50g dried cherries
50g almonds
30g stem ginger in syrup (see p45)
200g dessert apples, peeled, cored and chopped into 1cm cubes
Finely grated zest and juice of 1 orange
½ tsp ground cinnamon
Finely grated zest and juice of ½ lemon
Good grating of nutmeg

Soak the dried fruit in boiling water for 20 minutes, then blitz the figs and dates in a food processor until a smooth paste is formed. Add the dried apple, raisins and apricots and pulse until roughly chopped and combined. Pour into a large bowl. Add the rest of the ingredients and stir. Put into jars.

Keep in the fridge and use within 3 days – or stir in 3 tablespoons brandy and then it will keep for a couple of months, also stored in the fridge.

» About 140 calories per serving if divided into 16 portions

More on » figs *p307* » apples *p288* » cranberries *p242* » almonds *p347* » ginger *p200* » oranges *p49* » cinnamon *p22* » lemons *p346*

Filo mincemeat baskets with pomegranate

You'll need a 16-hole muffin tin to make these light mince pies, which have a good crunch to them from the filo pastry. Serve them as a pudding, with some pomegranate and lime yoghurt, or make mini ones and serve them at a Christmas party.

For 16:
8 sheets of filo pastry
Cold-pressed rapeseed oil or walnut oil, for brushing
1 quantity mincemeat (see left)
Seeds from ½ pomegranate (see p46), to serve

For the pomegranate and lime yoghurt
Seeds from ½ pomegranate (see p46)
Finely grated zest of 1 lime
200g live Greek yoghurt

Preheat the oven to 180°C/gas mark 4.

Mix together the pomegranate and lime yoghurt ingredients.

Each mince pie is made up of two layers of pastry so brush one sheet of filo pastry lightly with oil. Place another sheet on top and brush with a little more oil. Then cut the oiled pastry into four squares and gently place each one into a muffin tin. Repeat with the remaining filo pastry sheets until you have 16 lined muffin tins in total. Dollop a heaped tablespoon of mincemeat into each pastry cup.

Bake in the oven for 20 minutes, until the pastry is golden and, when lifted out of the tin, the bottom is crisp.

Serve the little mincemeat baskets warm, with pomegranate seeds scattered on top and some pomegranate yoghurt alongside.

» 229 calories per basket

More on » pomegranate *p46* » yoghurt *p44*

Drinks

EVERY DAY, FOR our health, we need to drink plenty of liquid, and straight pure water is the best of all. The usual daily guidelines are 1.6 litres for women and 2 for men, and more if you are active. I, for one, often don't drink nearly enough water. Where I live, the tap water is heavily chlorinated and not very nice, so I'm rarely tempted to fill a glass, unless the water is filtered. (Filtering tap water at home is a good idea: it improves the taste and removes most of the chemicals.) In fact, the only way I manage to drink enough is to have a bottle or jug of filtered water on my desk, then I can gauge the amount I've drunk, and there is something physical in front of me to remind me.

If you get bored with plain tap or filtered water, you can add fruit and herb flavourings for a hint of taste and virtually no sugar. Water with chopped cucumber and fresh mint is refreshing and simple, and there are plenty of other, more unusual, ideas here. If you like your water or other drinks sweet, strawberries make an excellent sweetener. Frozen are cheaper than fresh, and they're almost as good for us as freshly picked. Coconut water is excellent, particularly when diluted 50/50 with straight water. Its natural electrolytes help to hydrate the body at a cellular level.

In my cookery school, we make lots of cordials to be diluted with water, but even these have too much sugar to be really healthy. Despite this, they are better than canned drinks such as cola, ginger beer, fizzy elderflower or cloudy lemonade, which have anything from nine to 13 teaspoons of sugar in a single glass. The World Health Organisation set a guideline in 2002 that sugar should make up less than 10 per cent of our total energy intake, with a recommendation in 2015 to get it down as low as 5 per cent (the equivalent of 25g – or six teaspoons – of sugar per day). So with just one glass of any of these canned drinks, you've shot through your daily limit; and recent advice is to cut this even further, to just 15g per day.

Also to be avoided are most bought fruit juices. Micronutrients are likely to be more available in fresh home-made juice than juice that has been stored for any length of time. Even home-juiced fruit juices should not be drunk regularly, as you still get a big dose of sugar with little fibre to balance it. Look at what you leave behind in your juicer and you'll see what I mean. That's where much of the goodness lies – in the peel and fibre, which also helps to slow sugar absorption, a very good thing. And, to boot, depending on the variety, size and ripeness, four apples yield approximately 350ml of juice – which equates to a lot of sugar in each glass that you drink.

Don't turn to the sweeter veg like beetroot and carrots for every day either. I love beetroot juice: it's hugely nutritious and good for cardiovascular and brain health. But be aware that beetroots have the highest sugar content of any vegetable, with carrots close behind. We need to be wary of 'free' sugars that are released when vegetables are juiced – not sugars that are intrinsic to the veg. Tomato juice is still sweet but has a lower sugar content, and many health benefits. If you are going to home-juice, pears and berries are the best fruits

to use, containing less sugar than all the others, and they too are full of beneficial phytonutrients.

Several recipes here include pears and berries, but they are always combined with vegetables in a so-called smoothie. With smoothies, you whizz the whole vegetable or de-cored fruit, so nothing is lost. These are great health drinks, often giving you two or three of your veg/fruit quota a day in one small glass. There's enough fibre to balance the sugar in the fruit too. For optimum nutrition, aim for at least 3:2 veg to fruit.

Staying with the more earthy stuff, there has been a widespread fashion for small shots of the juice of wheatgrass and blue-green algae, such as spirulina. Wheatgrass shots are generally thought to be therapeutic and have been used for ulcerative colitis, cancer, liver and skin problems, although there have been very few robust clinical studies. It is known that the juice must be fresh and drunk on an empty stomach for the best results. Spirulina can have serious side-effects including liver damage, so always check with your GP or a nutritionist before drinking lots of shots of spirulina.

In colder weather when you'll want more hot drinks, don't always reach for coffee and black tea out of habit. They can dehydrate you, so don't count them as part of your liquid intake. Caffeine is one of the things – like alcohol – that is fine in small quantities, but few of us leave it at that. More than two to three espressos (or strong cups of black tea) a day is potentially not good for you.

Instead, the best thing to start the day on – whether the weather is cold or hot – is a mug of hot water with a slice of lemon. Your body is at its most acid in the morning, and paradoxically, lemon juice, once metabolised, releases minerals that are alkalising to the body and counteract the effects of too many acid-forming foods in our diet. Dentists will tell you to rinse your mouth with fresh water or clean your teeth after this – to protect the enamel on your teeth from the acidity of the lemon.

Green tea is also full of goodness. The leaves are steamed, rolled and dried after picking (not fermented like black tea), which preserves the key antioxidants. You can add a range of flavours and have it hot or cold. Green tea is generally less caffeinated than black tea but do be aware of how much you're drinking, and think about re-using the leaves, which decreases the caffeine content each time (although this also lowers the beneficial phytonutrient content). This is also a way of making expensive loose green teas go further!

Lots of nutritionists are also big fans of chai tea. Chai is black, green or rooibos tea with added spices (including cinnamon, ginger, star anise and even black pepper). You can buy ready-blended tea bags or make your own. The spices help to improve digestion and support the immune system, as well as having anti-inflammatory and antioxidant properties.

Drinking alcohol is part of many people's lives, and is a pleasure and a relaxant. Red wine contains phytonutrients that may have health benefits, so as long as you stick to one small glass a day, it can be a good thing. If you do drink alcohol on a regular basis, it is advisable to have no more than one small glass of wine a day, and to have at least two alcohol-free days each week. Drinking alcohol affects how the whole body works – including your brain, heart, liver and pancreas. It can affect blood-sugar regulation and of course is calorific, so can cause you to gain unnecessary weight. And if your immune system is low, or you are fighting a disease like cancer, all alcohol is best avoided.

So what are the guidelines for drinks?
» Make sure you are drinking enough.
» Best of all is water.
» Be aware of how much sugar there is in canned and bottled sweet drinks – read the labels and swap them for my healthier alternatives.
» Fruit juices are only for the odd occasion – otherwise, eat the straight fruit instead.
» Limit your coffee and black tea intake.
» Swap black tea for green tea to benefit from its extra phytonutrients.
» Drink alcohol in moderation.

The main thing to understand is that what you drink is as important to your health as what you eat.

Cucumber, melon and raspberry flavoured water

This is my favourite flavoured water, with a gentle sweetness from the melon and raspberries, and a freshness from the cucumber. It looks good too, layered up in a wide-necked bottle or jug, the chunks of melon, strands of cucumber and the brilliance of the red berries. Sometimes I also add a few sprigs of mint.

For 1.5–2 litres:
½ cucumber
1 small ripe Galia (or other sweet) melon, peeled and cubed
1 small punnet of raspberries (30 or so)
1.5 litres filtered water
Ice (optional)

You'll need a large (1.5–2 litre) jug, wide-necked jar or bottle.

Cut the cucumber into long strips with a vegetable peeler, stopping when you reach the seeds.

In the jug, jar or bottle, create layers of melon and cucumber, alternating with a layer of raspberries. Pour over the water, filling to the top, and put in the fridge. Leave to infuse, ideally overnight, or for at least 3 hours.

Strain as you pour into glasses with ice (if using). If serving at a party, you could add a raspberry or two and a ribbon of cucumber to each glass.

As you drink, top up the water in the bottle or jar a few times until the flavour becomes too dilute.

» The calories in flavoured waters are not possible to calculate exactly, but they are very low.

More on » cucumber *p148*

Raspberries grow brilliantly in the UK, are truly delicious and, for their size, pack a huge punch in terms of nutrition. They are the **fibre** winners in the berry clan. Cup your hands together and fill them with raspberries: you'll be holding about 125g, which will give you a huge 8g of dietary fibre. Nutritionists and doctors recommend 25–35g of fibre a day, whereas our average daily intake is a paltry 13g for women and only 15g for men. Raspberries – like all berries – should be eaten within 48 hours of picking otherwise their vitamin C and **antioxidant** content perishes. When frozen, they retain better levels of these compounds than fresh raspberries that have been flown from the other side of the world and spent time in a cold store (and frozen are often half the price). Organic are best.

Drinks

Pomegranate and berry flavoured water

This flavoured water is the colour of a light rosé wine, and it's good and tangy. Lightly crush half the pomegranate seeds and whichever berries you use to release the flavour; leave some whole, so they're like jewels in the water. If you grow blackcurrants, it's well worth harvesting the leaves to flavour almost any drink. They have a sharp, strong, blackcurrant flavour, and are ideal in the mix here.

For 1.5–2 litres:
Seeds of 1 pomegranate (see p46)
100g blackcurrants or blueberries
1.5 litres filtered water
1 lime, peeled, all white pith removed, sliced
10 mint leaves
3 blackcurrant leaves (if available)
Ice (optional)

You'll need a large (1.5–2 litre) jug, wide-necked jar or bottle with a lid.

Put half the pomegranate seeds and half the berries in the jar or bottle, and crush them a little with the end of a rolling pin.

Pour over the water, then add the remaining pomegranate seeds and berries, the lime, mint and blackcurrant leaves (if using). Put in the fridge and leave to infuse, ideally overnight, or for at least 3 hours.

Strain as you pour into glasses with ice (if using). If serving at a party, you could add a sprig of mint to each glass.

As you drink, top up the water in the bottle or jar a few times until the flavour becomes too dilute. After drinking the water, add the fruit to a smoothie.

» The calories in flavoured waters are not possible to calculate exactly, but they are very low.

More on » pomegranate *p46* » blackcurrants *p294* » mint *p326*

Blueberries Like all berries, blueberries are a good source of **fibre** and vitamin C, but it's the **anthocyanins** they contain that give them their colour and potent health benefits. These **phytonutrients** can help to improve heart health, prevent cancer and boost memory. According to a study by Harvard Medical School, elderly people who eat plenty of blueberries are less likely to suffer from cognitive decline. And the plant **polyphenols** in berries such as blueberries also help protect against neurodegenerative diseases such as Parkinson's and dementia. It's likely that many of these benefits apply to all berries, but to date blueberries have had the most research and clinical trials done on them – which is why they fill our supermarket shelves. Local and ideally organic are best, and frozen berries have more nutrients in them (and are cheaper) than those flown in from other parts of the world.

Cucumber and kiwi flavoured water

This summery drink looks and tastes so good that you won't miss canned drinks or cordials. The cucumber and mint add freshness, with a hint of sweetness from the kiwi. Any mint variety will do, but I love the flavour of apple mint here. When the flavour has gone from your water, start a fresh jar, eating the kiwis from the bottom of the first jar (or adding them to a smoothie).

For 1.5–2 litres:
½ cucumber
2 ripe kiwi fruits, peeled and sliced
1.5 litres filtered water
10 mint leaves
Ice (optional)

You'll need a large (1.5–2 litre) jug, wide-necked jar or bottle with a lid.

Cut the cucumber into long strips with a vegetable peeler, stopping when you reach the seeds.

Fill the bottom of the jar or bottle with the slices of kiwi, pour over the water, add the cucumber and mint leaves and put in the fridge. Leave to infuse, ideally overnight, or for at least 3 hours.

Strain as you pour into glasses with ice (if using). If serving at a party, you could add a sprig of mint and ribbon of cucumber to each one.

As you drink, top up the water in the bottle or jar a few times until the flavour becomes too dilute.

» The calories in flavoured waters are not possible to calculate exactly, but they are very low.

More on » cucumber *p148* » mint *p326*

Citrus flavoured water

The grapefruit and scented-leaf pelargonium give this water a depth of flavour, the lime and mint a bright sharpness. Attar of Roses or Lemon Fizz are my two favourite scented-leaf pelargoniums to use for drinks, and it's well worth keeping a plant or two in pots near the kitchen so you can harvest them from late spring until Christmas. Over winter, keep them somewhere light but frost-free until the leaves start to grow again in the spring.

For 2 litres:
1 pink grapefruit
1 orange
1 lemon
2 limes
1.5 litres filtered water
10 mint leaves
10 scented-leaf pelargonium leaves (if available)
Ice (optional)

You'll need a large (at least 2 litre) jug, wide-necked jar or bottle with a lid.

Remove the peel and as much of the white bitter pith as you can from all the citrus fruits, then slice thinly into cartwheels. (If you slice the fruit with the peel and pith still on, the water will be bitter.) Place the citrus slices in the jar or bottle, and pour over the water. Add the mint and pelargonium leaves (if using) and put in the fridge. Leave to infuse, ideally overnight, or for at least 3 hours.

Strain as you pour into glasses with ice (if using). If serving at a party, you could add a sprig of mint or pelargonium leaf to each glass.

As you drink, top up the water in the bottle or jar a few times until the flavour becomes too dilute.

» The calories in flavoured waters are not possible to calculate exactly, but they are very low.

More on » grapefruit *p340* » oranges *p49*
» lemons *p346* » mint *p326*

Strawberry and orange tea

Simple, summery and sweet, this tea is best if you first put the orange zest and strawberries into boiling water to extract the flavour, then top up with hot or cold water and ice. Once you've got the strength of flavour from the heated base, add fresh strawberries to make it look fresh and pretty. I also like this tea with added rhubarb, which the strawberries and star anise sweeten enough that you don't need sugar.

For 1 litre (diluted):
1 orange
1 litre filtered water
200g strawberries, fresh or frozen, roughly chopped
1 rhubarb stalk, finely sliced (optional)
2 star anise (optional)
Ice (optional)

You'll need a large (at least 1 litre), wide-necked jar or bottle with a lid. If the orange has been waxed, de-wax it first by dropping into a bowl of boiling water for 30 seconds. Remove from the water, then slice off ribbons of zest using a very sharp knife or veg peeler, aiming to remove as little of the bitter pith as possible.

Bring 400ml of the filtered water to the boil, and pour into a saucepan. Add the orange zest to the boiled water, then add the strawberries (and rhubarb and star anise if using), and bring back to the boil for 3–4 minutes. Leave to infuse for 15 minutes then strain. You can eat the jam-like strawberries and rhubarb – and the zested orange.

This is nice drunk hot, diluted with a little boiling water. Or you can pour some into a glass of ice, with some fresh sliced strawberries. And you could dilute it with the remaining 600ml filtered water.

» The calories here, like in flavoured waters, are not possible to calculate exactly, but they are very low.

More on » oranges p49

Rhubarb and strawberry cordial

The addition of strawberries enables you to cut the sugar content of this by half compared to most home-made cordial recipes. This has a strong flavour, so dilute 1:5.

For 1.8 litres (36 x 50ml servings, diluted with 250ml water):
800g rhubarb, cut into chunks
1.2kg strawberries
8 cardamom pods, crushed, or star anise (optional)
1 litre filtered water
600g sugar

Put the rhubarb, strawberries and cardamom or star anise (if using) into a large pan and add the filtered water. Bring up to the boil, then turn down the heat and simmer gently until the fruit is soft. Take off the heat, and allow to cool and for the flavours to infuse for 15 minutes or so.

Once cooled, pour the fruit and juice into a large jelly bag (hanging over a large bowl) and allow the juice to drip through overnight.

Now pour the collected juice into a pan over a low heat and add the sugar, stirring until dissolved. Allow to cool, then pour into sterilised bottles and store in the fridge. Use within a week. This also freezes well.

» 77 calories per 50ml

Triple lemon green tea

This drink is made with super-healthy green tea, flavoured with three delicious varieties of citrus: a peeled and de-pithed lemon, a stalk or two of lemongrass and some leaves of lemon verbena. Add a fourth citrus flavour of lemon or lime leaves (available from Asian supermarkets) if you can find them. This is good served hot – or cold, in glasses over ice, with a sprig of lemon verbena.

For about 1.2 litres:
2 green tea bags
1.2 litres filtered water, brought to the boil
1 lemon, peeled, all white pith removed, finely sliced
10 lemon verbena leaves, fresh or dried
2 lemongrass stalks, outer leaves removed, finely sliced
4 lemon or lime leaves (optional)
Ice (optional)

Make a jug of green tea with the tea bags and boiling water.

Add the sliced lemon, the verbena leaves, lemongrass stalks and lemon or lime leaves (if using). Leave to infuse for 5 minutes and serve hot, straining as you pour.

Or, to serve cold, remove the tea bags, but leave the rest to steep overnight, or for a minimum of 3 hours, putting in the fridge once cool.

Strain as you pour over glasses with ice (if using). If serving at a party, you could add a sprig of lemon verbena to each glass.

» 24 calories per 1.2 litres

More on » lemons *p346*

Variations
Ginger and lemon tea Finely slice a thumb-sized piece of fresh root ginger (there's no need to peel) and add to the mixture above.
» 42 calories per 1.2 litres
Ginger, turmeric and lemon tea You can also add a thumb-sized piece of the spicy, powerfully anti-inflammatory turmeric root to a green tea. When you peel turmeric (as with ginger, this is best done with a teaspoon), it will stain your hands nicotine yellow – but happily it's not really necessary to peel it for this tea.
» 67 calories per 1.2 litres

Green tea For green tea, the harvested leaves are just steamed, rolled and dried after picking. They are not fermented like black tea leaves, and have a gentler flavour. This steaming preserves the key **antioxidants** and so the leaves, when soaked in boiling water for several minutes and strained, produce a drink that is full of goodness. You can add a range of flavours and have it hot or cold.

Many people think that green teas contain less caffeine than black teas, but this is not always the case: in fact, green tea made from the same leaves as black tea will have a marginally higher caffeine content.

There have been numerous studies into the benefits of drinking green tea regularly, and it is considered protective against cardiovascular disease, diabetes and obesity. It is also thought that green tea stimulates brain function and so may help to protect the brain in old age. It's a good all-round tea to drink.

Kombucha

This is an ancient fermented tea drink which requires a so-called 'mother' or SCOBY (a Symbiotic Culture Of Bacteria and Yeast, similar to a vinegar mother, containing one or more species of bacteria and yeasts) to get the ferment going. The SCOBY needs caffeine and sugar to thrive, and does not like being moved around too much. It will eat up any sugar, so you don't need to worry that you're consuming it. You can order a SCOBY online, cultivate one from a bottle of kombucha, find them in good health-food shops, or get one from a friend. The fermentation gives the drink a characteristic tangy flavour and makes it extremely beneficial for digestion. Full of probiotics, it can be particularly good for syndromes such as IBS, but is also excellent for the general immune system.

You can buy kombucha in health-food shops, or brew it yourself (see below) – this takes time and some getting used to, but it's worth it.

You will need a large storage jar with a wide neck that holds at least 4 litres, and is food grade and sterilised (see below). You will also need a piece of sterilised muslin and a large elastic band to fit round the neck of the jar, and several sterilised drinks bottles with screw-top lids.

For 4 litres:

Stage 1
10 normal black tea bags
At least 3 litres mineral water – hot, not boiling
6 tbsp organic soft brown sugar
1 SCOBY

Stage 2
Fruit to flavour (e.g. strawberries, raspberries, melon, blueberries, lemon, crystallised ginger)

To start off a kombucha Sterilise the jar and the bottles by putting them through a very hot dishwasher cycle or boiling them in a pan of water for 10 minutes instead. Leave to cool, covered.

Put the tea bags in the hot, not boiling, mineral water in a clean heatproof jug. Add the sugar and stir. Remove the bags after 5 minutes. Allow to cool to room temperature and then pour into the sterilised jar. Add the SCOBY. Wipe the lip of the jar carefully, cover with the piece of muslin and secure with an elastic band. Put in a cool place where it won't be disturbed, and leave for a week.

A new SCOBY will have grown on the liquid surface. Taste the liquid with a straw. It's ready when the sugar has all been used up by the SCOBY and the taste is sour, not sweet. Remove the SCOBY – old and new – from the jar and put it in a bowl, scooping out a little kombucha to keep it hydrated. It's easy to remove as it will be floating on the top of the liquid. Put to one side, ready to start the next.

Pour the rest of the kombucha into individual bottles, filling to within 3cm or so of the top. It's too vinegary at this stage to drink. The next fermentation, with added flavourings, will carbonate it, and make it milder and less vinegary in flavour. Add a small handful of raspberries, blueberries or strawberries, chunks of mango flesh, a segment of lemon, or some crystallised ginger to flavour and feed each bottle, and seal. Leave for at least 4 days in a cool dark place for the second ferment. The fruit will supply the sugars for this next stage. Move the kombucha to the fridge for a few more days, then strain through a sieve and drink.

To continue a kombucha When you fill your bottles with the kombucha, wash and sterilise your glass kombucha jar. Put your SCOBY, which you have kept hydrated, in the clean jar. Fill it up with a new brew of cooled sugary tea and continue from the beginning again. You can double the quantities once you've got your SCOBY well established.

» The calories are minimal, as the sugar will have been used up by the SCOBY.

Rose geranium and lemon tea

At the cookery school, we make tisanes every day to serve as a caffeine-free drink. These are often made with a handful of lemon verbena leaves or lemon basil, mint (black spearmint is the best), chamomile flowers, or the green or black seed pods of sweet cicely. Our favourite, though, is scented-leaf pelargonium, and we now grow big blocks of the pelargonium varieties, Attar of Roses and Lemon Fizz, especially for tea. (We also add the fragrant leaves to blackberry and apple pies and crumbles, which they transform, adding a distinctive and delicious flavour.)

Rose geranium essential oil is anti-fungal, anti-depressant, antiseptic, anti-spasmodic, anti-inflammatory and astringent, and this tea is traditionally used to soothe anxiety and stress.

For 1 litre:
5 or 6 pelargonium Attar of Roses or Lemon Fizz leaves
Lemon or lime zest (optional)
1 litre boiling water

Simply infuse the pelargonium leaves and lemon or lime zest (if using) in boiling water in your largest teapot. Leave to stand for 5–10 minutes.

Pour and serve immediately – warm, without milk or sugar. You could also allow it to cool, then serve with plenty of ice and a squeeze of fresh lemon.

» 3 calories for the whole teapot

More on » lemons *p346*

Honeygar

Honeygar – honey and organic cider vinegar – is a powerful immuno-stimulant, which I drank, first thing in the morning, when I was a doctor on the wards. People around me were collapsing with colds and flu, but not me, as it gave my immune system a major boost. The apple cider vinegar is also good for those suffering from arthritis.

For 1 (350–400ml):
350–400ml boiling water
1 tsp clear or set honey, ideally unpasteurised
1 tbsp organic apple cider vinegar

Pour the boiling water into a mug and stir around a little to cool.

Spoon in the honey and vinegar and stir until the honey has dissolved. This method, rather than pouring water over the honey and vinegar, retains the most nutrition.

» 20 calories

More on » apple cider vinegar *p63*

Honey has been used by numerous cultures for its medicinal properties, particularly its ability to heal wounds – its anti-bacterial and anti-fungal properties mean it acts as a natural antiseptic. Although it is still sweet, honey does not provoke the same blood-glucose response as sugar, and it provides additional nutrients. The quality of honey is important, and raw is best, whether clear or set. Try and buy local and untreated honey, rather than pasteurised.

Watercress, kiwi and cucumber smoothie

A delicate and refreshing summer smoothie made with super-healthy watercress, which we should all eat as much of as we can. If you want something a little sweet, this one is excellent with a teaspoon of honey. Also try the Watercress gazpacho on page 63.

For 2 (600ml):
½ large cucumber
Large bunch of mint
50g watercress
2 kiwi fruits, peeled
1 tbsp milled organic flaxseeds
250ml coconut water
Ice (optional)

Coarsely chop the cucumber. Strip the mint leaves off their stalks and coarsely chop them.

Blend the mint, watercress, cucumber, kiwi fruits and flaxseeds with the coconut water in a food processor or blender.

Pour into two glasses, with or without ice, and drink straightaway.

» 136 calories per serving

More on » cucumber *p148* » watercress *p70* » flaxseeds *p30*

Mint tea is excellent at soothing an upset stomach and aiding digestion; it is ideal for drinking at the end of a meal, as it calms the muscles of the stomach and improves the flow of the digestive juices and bile secretions. Several studies support the use of mint for indigestion and irritable bowel syndrome, since it has been shown to ease the pain and bloating.

Avocado and apple smoothie

If you like a smoothie, it's always best in terms of health for the fruit and veg to be simply chopped and blitzed, not juiced, so it's packed with fibre. Made with coconut water, it's also dairy-free. A whole avocado equals two of your recommended portions a day, with another from the spinach (or kale), as well as the apple. The celery stick, basil and lemon combined give one more, adding up to five portions. If you drink the whole thing yourself during the day, you'll also get your recommended daily amount of omega-3s in the flaxseeds. Have a few of these a week and you'll notice the difference.

For 2 (600ml):
1 dessert apple, cored
1 avocado, peeled
1 celery stick
1–2 kale leaves, de-stemmed (or a small handful of washed spinach)
10g fresh ginger
12 basil leaves
1 tbsp milled organic flaxseeds
Grated zest and juice of 1 lemon
200ml coconut water
Ice (optional)

Coarsely chop the fruit, veg, ginger and basil leaves.

Put all the ingredients (apart from the ice) with 100ml water into a blender and blitz.

Pour into two glasses, with or without ice, and drink straightaway.

» 258 calories per serving

More on » apples *p228* » avocado *p119* » kale *p117* » spinach *p54* » ginger *p200* » flaxseeds *p30* » lemons *p346*

Asparagus, pea and mint smoothie

This smoothie is really rich and creamy, more like a soup in a glass than a drink. It feels like comfort food and yet it's packed full of goodness, with four veg units from the asparagus alone, plus two from the peas and another two from the cucumber. This is nicest ice-cold, so use the peas straight out of the freezer. Frozen peas have been picked from the field, briefly blanched and frozen, so they retain maximum sweetness and nutrition.

Split this with someone and you've already consumed four of your daily portions of veg and half your recommended amount of omega-3s.

For 2 (550ml):
125g asparagus spears
½ cucumber
15 mint leaves
100g frozen peas
20 sugarsnap peas, topped, tailed and de-stringed
1 tbsp milled organic flaxseeds
150ml coconut water
Pinch of sea salt
Ice (optional)

Asparagus spears break at a natural point where the tender tissue becomes more fibrous, so just bend and break each spear. Discard the bases of the stalks, and coarsely chop the rest, including the tips. Coarsely chop the cucumber and the mint leaves.

Put all the ingredients (apart from the ice) into a blender, making sure the cucumber is in the layer nearest the blades, and blitz. Pour into two glasses, with or without ice, and drink straightaway.

» 138 calories per serving

More on » asparagus *p126* » cucumber *p148* » peas *p74* » flaxseeds *p30*

Variation
Almond green smoothie To make this even more sustaining, add a small handful of raw almonds or cashews, which have been soaking in a bowl of filtered water overnight. Rinse the almonds well before adding to the smoothie when blitzing.
» 267 calories per serving

Coconut water is the juice found inside young, green coconuts and has been used as a medicinal food in Asia for centuries. Thinner in consistency than coconut milk (which is extracted from the coconut's flesh), each serving of coconut water has four to five times less sugar than fruit juice, so it is both an excellent drink and a perfect base for smoothies. Coconut water is full of **electrolytes**, which are vital for bodily functions such as muscle movement, brain function and the transmission of nerve signals. It is fabulous for rehydration, but do be aware that coconut water has a certain amount of natural sugars in it, so don't overdo it. Coconut water also provides lauric acid and another group of nutrients called **cytokines**, a group of **plant hormones** that regulate cell division and influence the rate at which plants age – it is thought that these may be able to play a similar role in human health by slowing the ageing process and lowering the risk of dementia and cancer.

Strawberry, basil and almond smoothie

Strawberries are brilliant for drinks – refreshing and fragrant. However, when conventionally grown, strawberries are high on the list of fruits contaminated with pesticide residues, so buy organic if you can.

This is made with almond milk, which you can buy ready-made – but check the sugar content – or, better still, make it yourself (see page 347). This smoothie is a real favourite of mine.

For 1–2 (400ml):
200g strawberries, hulled and chopped
8–10 basil leaves
250ml almond milk (see p347)
1 tbsp ground almonds or milled organic flaxseeds
Grated zest of 1 lime
Black pepper
Clear honey (optional, to taste)
Ice (optional)

Blitz the first five ingredients in a blender until smooth.

Add a good grinding of black pepper to taste, and honey if required – this will depend on the strawberry variety. Blitz again briefly.

Pour into one or two glasses, with or without ice, and serve straightaway.

» Without honey, 189 calories for 1 serving, 95 for 2
» With honey, 209 calories for 1 serving, 105 for 2

More on » almonds *p347* » flaxseeds *p30*
» honey *p334*

Tomato, herb and red pepper smoothie

This is a bright, fresh and zingy smoothie which is at its best when tomatoes, peppers and cucumbers are at their tastiest in summer. The tomatoes here give you two of your recommended portions of veg a day, with two more coming from the pepper, another from the apple. The celery stick, herbs and lime add up to six. You've got flaxseeds here too, for your all-important daily intake of omega-3s. The oil in the seeds helps with vitamin absorption.

For 2 (500ml):
200g cherry or small tomatoes, plus a few slices
   of tomato to serve
1 celery stick
1 red pepper, deseeded
½ cucumber
Grated zest and juice of 1 lime
1 tbsp milled organic flaxseeds
15g flat-leaf parsley leaves
15g coriander leaves
Ice (optional)

Halve the tomatoes. Coarsely chop the celery, red pepper and cucumber.

Place the tomatoes in a blender in the layer nearest the blades, as they will provide the liquid to get the blending process going. Add all the other ingredients (apart from the ice) and blitz.

Pour into two glasses, with or without ice. Place a couple of tomato slices on top and drink straightaway.

» 114 calories per serving

More on » tomatoes *p142* » cucumber *p148*
» flaxseeds *p30* » parsley *p136* » coriander *p204*

Carrot, beetroot, apple and ginger smoothie

This smoothie uses fresh turmeric root, as well as the more traditional ginger; the fresh root is particularly nutritious, but if you can't find it, you can add a half teaspoon of ground turmeric instead.

I like this smoothie made with grapefruit juice, which gives a rich and distinctive after-taste. But be aware that grapefruit juice interacts with many medications and some disorders, so if any of these apply to you, use lemon or orange juice instead. The olive oil here helps with the absorption of vitamin A, which is fat-soluble.

For 2 (500ml):
100g organic carrots
1 small (120g) dessert apple
100g beetroot
1 pink grapefruit (or lemon or orange)
5g piece of fresh turmeric root
5g piece of fresh ginger root
1 tbsp milled organic flaxseeds
100ml coconut water
Drop of olive oil
Handful of ice cubes

Wash and trim the carrots. Core the apple. Coarsely chop the carrots, beetroot and apple.

Zest and juice the grapefruit. Chop the turmeric and ginger.

Put all the ingredients into a blender and blitz. This one is nice super-cold, so include ice when you blitz. You can serve it with even more ice in the glass.

Pour into two tall glasses and serve straightaway.

» 200 calories per serving

More on » carrots *p121* » apples *p288* » beetroot *p85* » turmeric *p87* » ginger *p200* » flaxseeds *p30* » coconut water *p337*

Grapefruit is ideal to eat and drink for breakfast. Your body is at its most acid in the morning, so first thing is just the time to put this right – and, paradoxically, acidic fruit actually stimulates the production of alkaline substances in the body. Grapefruit is low in calories and high in **fibre**, so will fill you up, and research is currently being carried out regarding its impact on insulin levels and weight loss. High in vitamin C and potassium, grapefruit appears to lower **cholesterol** and may have some anti-cancer benefits; pink grapefruit also contain the valuable orange pigment **beta-carotene**, which is good for the eyes.

However, be aware that grapefruit juice affects the way the body metabolises many medications, so you should consult your doctor if you are taking prescription medicine.

Pear and beetroot smoothie

You wouldn't think you could drink raw, blitzed beetroot, but it's delicious – earthy and sweet. Beetroot contains the most sugar of any veg, so it's good to combine with pears, which are low in sugar (and good for sugar balance), instead of apples. The lemons and mint give this smoothie a lovely bright flavour. I sometimes add a splash of organic cider vinegar, which makes this smoothie not just good for cardiovascular and brain health, but excellent for joint health and arthritis too. Try it as well with a grating of super-healthy horseradish.

There are five portions of fruit and veg in here (two from the beetroot, two from the pear and at least one from the lemon and mint), so if you drink this yourself through the day, you're sorted on your fruit/veg count as well as your omega-3s.

For 2 (500ml):
2 pears (about 200g)
200g beetroots
30 mint leaves
Grated zest and juice of 1–2 lemons (to taste)
1 tbsp milled organic flaxseeds
200ml coconut water
Ice (optional)

Core and chop the pears. Wash and chop the beetroot.

Place the pear in a blender in the layer nearest the blades, as it – along with the coconut water – will provide the liquid to get the blending process going. Add all the other ingredients (apart from the ice) and blitz.

Pour into two glasses, with or without ice, and drink straightaway.

» 150 calories per serving

More on » pears *p162* » beetroot *p85* » mint *p326* » lemons *p346* » flaxseeds *p30* » coconut water *p337*

Kale with berries, pear and apple smoothie

With a good portion of kale to enrich it and boost the nutrition, this smoothie is based on fruit. Apart from deepening the colour, you won't notice the kale, as it doesn't affect the flavour. There are at least five portions of fruit and veg here if you drink it all yourself (one each from the apple, pear, kale and two from the berries), as well as your daily requirement of omega-3s. You can also add a banana, straight from the freezer, if you want extra sweetness.

For 2 (400ml):
1 pear
1 dessert apple
1 large leaf of kale or cavolo nero, de-stemmed
100g berries (blackcurrants, redcurrants, blueberries, raspberries and/or strawberries, fresh or frozen)
20 mint leaves
1 tbsp milled organic flaxseeds
100ml coconut water
Ice (optional)

Core and chop the pear and the apple.

Put all the ingredients (apart from the ice) into a blender and blitz, with the pear and berries in the layer nearest the blades, as they – along with the coconut water – will provide the necessary liquid to get the blending process going.

Pour into two glasses, with or without ice, and drink straightaway.

» 112 calories per serving

More on » pears *p162* » apples *p288* » kale *p117* » mixed berries *p343* » mint *p326* » flaxseeds *p30* » coconut water *p337*

Protein berry smoothie

Here berries are mixed with beans. This may sound off-putting, but the beans, along with the yoghurt and flaxseeds, add valuable protein and substance, as well as all-important omega-3s, making the smoothie much more filling and sustaining. Cannellini beans have such a gentle flavour that I promise you won't know they're there, and they're a great aid to lowering 'bad' cholesterol.

Adjust the number of dates according to your preferred level of sweetness.

For 3 (750ml):
250g summer fruits (blackberries, blackcurrants, blueberries, redcurrants, strawberries and raspberries; out of season, frozen is fine), plus extra to serve
200g live natural yoghurt (see p44)
300ml coconut water
1 heaped tbsp tinned cannellini beans, rinsed and drained
Grated zest and juice of 1 lime
1 tbsp milled organic flaxseeds
2–4 stoned dates
1 tsp grated fresh root ginger
Ice (optional)

Put all the ingredients (apart from the ice) into a blender and blitz.

Pour into three glasses, with or without ice, topped with extra berries, and serve.

» With 2 dates, 182 calories per serving
» With 4 dates, 226 calories per serving

More on » blackcurrants *p294* » blueberries *p328* » raspberries *p326* » yoghurt *p44* » coconut water *p337* » flaxseeds *p30* » ginger *p200*

Variation
Chocolate berry smoothie Add 2 teaspoons raw cacao powder and float a few cacao nibs on the top with a berry or two.
» With 2 dates, 199 calories per serving
» With 4 dates, 243 calories per serving

Mixed berries Berries – blueberries, strawberries, raspberries and blackberries – are high in **fibre** and have a low sugar content compared to other fruit, so they're low in calories. They have also been shown, as part of a healthy diet, to help protect against cardiovascular disease by lowering **cholesterol** and preventing clogging of the arteries, and may help to stave off certain cancers (particularly of the cervix, breast, colon and liver). Berries are firmly established as memory-protecting foods, and are anti-ageing. They are good for our eyes, helping to protect against glaucoma and cataracts; new research suggests they may also help to prevent macular degeneration, the commonest cause of blindness in those aged over 65.

Those bags of frozen mixed berries (ideally organic) are fine and are generally cheaper. Two studies have even found that they have more nutrients in them, as they are picked and frozen straightaway – so much better than those 'fresh' ones on the supermarket shelves that have been harvested several days previously.

Cocoloco

Based on a recipe from the Kamalaya health resort in Thailand, this has bananas, coconut, cinnamon and tahini – four good ingredients together in a glass. With the banana and sesame seeds in the tahini, this smoothie keeps you feeling full for ages. The liquid in this smoothie is coconut water, which has been used for centuries as a medicinal food in Asia. Here I've used frozen grapes as extra-delicious ice cubes.

For 2 (500ml):
350ml coconut water
100g peeled banana
50g fresh coconut flesh (see p212; from brown or green coconuts)
1 tbsp milled organic flaxseeds
2 tsp tahini
Pinch of ground cinnamon
Ice or sliced frozen grapes (optional)

Blitz all the ingredients (apart from the ice) in a blender until smooth and creamy.

Pour into two glasses, with or without ice and grapes, and serve immediately.

» 206 calories per serving

More on » coconut water *p337* » flaxseeds *p30* » tahini *p184* » cinnamon *p22* » grapes *p298*

Variation
Chocolate cocoloco Add 2 teaspoons raw cacao powder to the mix in the blender, and float a few cacao nibs on the top.
» 231 calories per serving

Bananas are fibre-rich (3–4g per fruit, and nutritionists and doctors recommend 25g–35g of fibre a day), and contain small amounts of a particular fibre called inulin. We don't digest the inulin in our stomach. Instead, it acts as a **prebiotic**, feeding our beneficial intestinal bacteria as it passes through the gut. As with the **probiotic** foods – fermented yoghurt, sauerkraut and traditionally prepared olives – this is very good for us and boosts our whole immune system.

Bananas are a famously good source of potassium: this helps maintain our fluid and **electrolyte** balance and, with that, healthy hydrated cells. Potassium is a crucial nutrient, and has an important role in muscle and nerve function and heart health; low levels of potassium are associated with heart arrhythmias, muscle cramps and weakness. It also helps to control blood pressure. People who consume a lot of processed foods, which are laden with sodium (salt), can become deficient in potassium. The body needs a healthy balance of these two **minerals**, and low intake of potassium-rich foods, especially when linked with a high intake of sodium, can lead to hypertension and contribute to poor bone health. Eating bananas regularly is one of the things you can do to help correct this.

Ginger lassi

This is one of my favourite summer drinks: bright, sharp and very thirst-quenching. Lassis are traditionally drunk with a curry – the yoghurt helps calm the burning sensation from the chilli – but I like to drink them without food.

For 2 (500ml):
Seeds of 4 cardamom pods
1 tbsp milled organic flaxseeds
200g live natural yoghurt (see p44)
200ml coconut water
1 heaped tbsp peeled and finely grated fresh root ginger
1 tbsp maple syrup
Handful of ice

Dry-fry the cardamom seeds in a small frying pan then crush with a pestle and mortar. Blitz all the ingredients in a blender. Serve in two tall glasses.

» 127 calories per serving

More on » flaxseeds *p30* » yoghurt *p44* » coconut water *p337* » ginger *p200* » maple syrup *p27*

Lemons are a rich source of **vitamins**, **minerals** and dietary **fibre**, all of which enhance overall well-being. Recent research also shows that the **phytochemicals** in lemons can reduce the risk of many chronic diseases. They're bursting with **antioxidants**, in the form of vitamin C and **flavonoids**. These flavonoids have been shown to inhibit the growth of cancer cells, prevent the spread of tumours and protect against cardiovascular disease. Vitamin C is excellent for healthy skin and wound healing, and is needed for the metabolism of stress hormones. Its anti-viral and anti-bacterial properties help fight colds, flu and viral infections, and boost immunity. Vitamin C is also used in detoxification in the body.

If using the zest of a lemon, try to buy unwaxed fruit, or drop them into boiling water for 30 seconds to remove the coating of wax.

Lemon, cardamom and poppy seed lassi

Poppy seeds give a delicious nutty flavour – without the calories of nuts – and the cardamom goes well with yoghurt too. This is a drink you want to serve super-cold, so it's blended with ice.

This mixture also makes an excellent semi-freddo or frozen yoghurt. To make these, simply pour the mix into an ice-cream maker, if you have one, and remove it when it is semi-solid. If you don't have an ice-cream maker, pour the mix into a suitable freezer container and freeze for an hour before forking it through and eating.

For 2 (500ml):
1 tsp poppy seeds
Seeds from 4 cardamom pods (or ½ tsp ground cardamom)
200g live natural yoghurt (see p44)
Grated zest and juice of ½–1 lemon (to taste)
1 tbsp milled organic flaxseeds
200ml coconut water
1 tsp maple syrup
Handful of ice

Put the poppy seeds in a frying pan and dry-fry briefly until they start to pop and turn grey.

Dry-fry the cardamom seeds until fragrant, then crush in a pestle and mortar.

Pour the yoghurt into a blender, add all the remaining ingredients, and blitz.

Pour into two tall glasses and serve immediately.

» 156 calories per serving

More on » yoghurt *p44* » flaxseeds *p30* » coconut water *p337* » maple syrup *p27*

Almond milk

Nut milks are good drinks in themselves – you can make lots of different flavours – and they're ideal for dairy-free porridge, smoothies, pancakes and soups. You can use nut milk in tea or coffee, but it does tend to separate.

Lots of the almond milks sold in cartons contain sugar and preservatives so, if you have time, make your own. If you have a strong blender, it's simple to do. I sometimes like mine sweetened with raisins (or dates work well), but for lower calories, you can leave these out. You can also use this recipe to make hazelnut or cashew milk, neither of which need any extra sweetness from dried fruit.

As a general rule, use a ratio of 1:4 nuts to water. If you want a quicker result, use flaked almonds, and then you can just soak for an hour or two, or use whole almonds and leave to soak overnight.

For about 750ml:
250g almonds
100g raisins (optional)
1 litre filtered water or mineral water

Soak the almonds and raisins (if using) in a bowl of water for up to 12 hours or overnight (it will start to ferment if left for longer). Drain and rinse well.

Put the almonds and raisins (if using) into a strong blender, along with the measured water, and blitz at the highest speed for 1 minute. (You can use it like this for a thick, smooth rich base for smoothies.) For a more milk-like consistency to make flavoured 'milk-shakes' as below, pour into a sieve lined with muslin and set over a bowl or jar. Allow to drip for 45 minutes. If you're in a hurry, you can squeeze the liquid through, but you will get some of the pulp and this will thicken the milk. Discard the pulp, or store in the fridge to use in a smoothie.

Store the nut milk in the fridge for two to three days. If it tastes at all sour, it's past its best.

» 191 calories per 100ml with raisins, 161 without

Variations
Chocolate almond milk shake Add 2 tablespoons dark cocoa powder, or raw cacao nibs, and blitz briefly in a blender.
» 201 calories per 100ml with raisins, 171 without
Vanilla almond milk shake Add 1 teaspoon pure vanilla extract (or the seeds from a vanilla pod) and blitz briefly in a blender.
» 192 calories per 100ml with raisins, 162 without
Cinnamon milk shake Add 1 teaspoon ground cinnamon to the vanilla almond milk recipe above, plus a grating of nutmeg, and blitz briefly in a blender.
» 192 calories per 100ml with raisins, 162 without

Almonds are lower in calories than other nuts and are highly nutritious, giving us plenty of heart-healthy **monounsaturated fats**, which can help to improve our blood **lipid** profile. They also contain plenty of **fibre** (3g of dietary fibre per 28g), lots of **vitamins** and **minerals**, in particular magnesium and vitamin B2 – two nutrients needed for energy production. If you want to make your own almond milk, you should soak the nuts first, as they have substances in them to prevent them being destroyed by insects and microbes. These act as **enzyme** inhibitors in our digestive systems. Soaking increases the availability of their nutrients, activating beneficial enzymes and making the nuts more digestible and easily utilised by our bodies.

Broccoli, apple and ginger juice

With this, we move away from smoothie-type drinks, where the whole vegetable and cored fruit are used, to juices. It always seems a waste to eat broccoli florets and then chuck the central stalk. The stalk has the same level of super-healthy antioxidant glucosinolates, but is almost never eaten, so that's where this juice comes in. You may not find the idea of a broccoli juice very tempting, but mixed with apple, ginger and lemon, you don't taste it – yet it's there, setting you up with plenty of antioxidants for the day.

You can swap the broccoli for kale to get a similar level of goodness. Add a few oats to make this more sustaining.

For 2 (500ml):
1 lemon
500g broccoli, stalks and all
500g apples (sweet or sharp, depending on preference)
25–50g fresh root ginger (to taste)
Handful of mint leaves (optional)
1 tbsp rolled oats (optional)
Ice (optional)

Pare the zest off the lemon using a peeler or zester. Keep to one side for garnish. Chop the lemon flesh into pieces.

Cut the broccoli, apple and ginger into pieces that will fit into the juicer feed, and juice them, along with the chopped lemon and mint.

Blitz the oats (if using) in a food processor until you have a *really* fine powder, then add to the green zingy juice.

Stir well, pour into two glasses, with or without ice, and top with lemon zest.

» 253 calories per serving

More on » lemons *p346* » broccoli *p151* » apples *p288* » ginger *p200* » mint *p326* » oats *p25*

Kamalaya detox juice

This is a delicious drink based on coconut water, which is very good for us. This detox juice has a great balance of nutrients to keep the body well hydrated, and includes pineapple, a fruit that is super-rich in vitamins, minerals and enzymes.

For 2 (500ml, or 1 litre with ice):
500g fresh pineapple
10g bunch of basil (mint's good too)
400ml coconut water
A few ice cubes
Crushed ice (optional)

Slice the bottom off the pineapple, and slice off the bunch of leaves at the top. Stand the pineapple on its base and cut off the skin all round, from top to bottom. Cut the pineapple in half, then quarters, lengthways. Retain the tough core in the middle (it has the most nutrients), and roughly chop all the flesh and core.

Use a juicer to extract the juice from the pineapple, mixed with the bunch of basil, leaves and stalks.

Pour the extracted juice into a blender and add the coconut water with some ice cubes. Blend on a medium speed for about 30 seconds.

Pour into two glasses, along with some crushed ice (if using).

» 162 calories per serving

More on » coconut water *p337*

Blackcurrant shrub

Blackcurrant syrups are usually full of sugar, but here is a healthy, delicious and invigoratingly sharp version – a traditional vinegar drink the Americans call 'shrub'. Pre-refrigeration, shrubs were made as a way of preserving soft fruit in hot summers. Regular vinegar and sugar are replaced here with honey and apple cider vinegar.

For 300ml:
500g blackcurrants (or other soft fruit such as gooseberries, raspberries, redcurrants, elderberries, pomegranates and cranberries, or blackberries or bluberries mixed with fresh ginger)
2 heaped tbsp set honey
125ml organic apple cider vinegar

You will need a 500ml storage jar with a lid, as well as a 350ml bottle with a screw-top. Sterilise these by putting through the hot cycle of the dishwasher. Put the fruit in the bottom of the storage jar.

In a pan, warm the honey with the vinegar, just so the honey melts but not to boiling point (as this will decrease the goodness). Pour into the jar so it just covers the fruit and, with the end of a rolling pin, crush to mix. Put the lid on the jar and shake well. Leave somewhere cool for three or four days (or longer if you put it in the fridge), and shake once a day, or whenever you remember.

Strain through a jelly bag set over a bowl, allowing the juice to drip through overnight. Then, using a funnel, pour the juice into your sterilised bottle. You can now store this in the fridge for months. To serve, use the shrub as a cordial. Mix with sparkling mineral water and pour into glasses full of ice, with a slice of lemon and a sprinkling of lemon zest – or use for a cocktail.

» The calories are negligible as the fruit isn't used: about 15 calories per glass of diluted shrub.

More on » blackcurrants *p294* » honey *p334*
» apple cider vinegar *p63*

Pomegranate bellinis

This is an ideal drink at Christmas – partyish, easy to make and delicious. Pomegranates are at their sweetest and best from late autumn through early winter, so make the most of them. Ideally make the pomegranate juice yourself, or buy it – but make sure it has no added sugar. Mixed, this has a deep amber colour, with a bright, not too sweet taste.

For 8 (about 1.5 litres):
2 pomegranates or 250ml shop-bought pomegranate juice, chilled
Juice of 2 oranges, freshly squeezed
5 cardamom pods, lightly crushed
3 tbsp Cointreau (or Grand Marnier or any other orange-flavoured liqueur)
2 x 750ml bottles of prosecco

First make the pomegranate juice as described on page 352. Or use shop-bought juice.

Put the pomegranate and orange juices in a medium pan with the cardamom pods and Cointreau, and simmer for 6–7 minutes, until reduced to about 300ml.

Allow to cool, then strain into a jug, discarding the cardamom pods.

Divide the syrup equally between eight glasses, and top up with the prosecco.

» 182 calories per serving

More on » pomegranates *p46* » oranges *p49*

Sangria

The danger with a classic Sangria is the sugar-packed lemonade, but this recipe uses sparkling water instead. If you don't want to juice your own pomegranates, you can buy good juice, but check the ingredients on the carton to make sure it's pure. Even the best brands are usually made from concentrate, and will have fewer nutrients than your own home-made.

This is a much more delicious alternative to Pimms, with a slightly sour tang, which is light and yet summery for a hot day. With the red wine diluted by half with juice and sparkling water, it is also lower in alcohol.

Freeze grapes to use as ice-cubes – they're a good thing for many of the drinks in this chapter.

For 6 (about 2 litres):
2 pomegranates or 250ml shop-bought pomegranate juice
About 200ml still mineral or filtered water
1 x 750ml bottle of fruity red wine (Rioja or Beaujolais), chilled
250ml home-squeezed orange juice
1 orange, thinly sliced
2 limes, thinly sliced
Finely grated zest and juice of 2 limes

To serve
500ml sparkling mineral water
Ice (optional)
Good bunch of mint, separated into small sprigs or leaves
250g red seedless grapes, frozen (instead of ice-cubes)

First start to make the pomegranate juice. To extract the seeds, gently roll the fruit around a few times on the bench, then slice them in half over a bowl to collect the juice. Holding one half of the fruit cut-side down over the bowl, tap the skin with a wooden spoon. The seeds will drop into the bowl without their bitter cream-coloured pith.

Put the seeds of both pomegranates (and any juices) into a blender or food processor, and add enough of the 200ml water to just cover the seeds. Blitz for a good minute and then strain into a large glass jug (this must hold at least 1.5 litres). Chill the juice, whether home-made or shop-bought.

Mix all the ingredients into the pomegranate juice in the jug. Put this back in the fridge for an hour for the flavours to infuse.

When ready to serve, stir in the sparkling water. Pour into ice-filled glasses (if using) with some mint, and add the grape ice-cubes.

» 200 calories per serving

More on » pomegranates *p46* » oranges *p49* » mint *p326* » grapes *p298*

Red wine Resveratrol, the powerful **antioxidant** in red wine, may protect against memory loss and Alzheimer's. In combination with other **polyphenols**, resveratrol is thought to be one of the factors behind the 'French paradox', whereby those in Mediterranean countries such as France have a low risk of heart disease, despite their relatively high consumption of **saturated fats** and red wine. Resveratrol is also found in peanuts and blueberries, as well as the skin of red grapes. Remember that red wine should be drunk in moderation for any health benefits to be felt!

Healthy ginger ale

Here is a sparkly, spicy ginger ale, without the usual massive dose of sugar. Apples provide the sweetness here, and although they contain a lot of sugar, it's nothing like the quantity in commercial ginger ale, which tops the charts in terms of sugar per can. I sometimes add a beetroot or two to this as well.

The ginger ale is delicious straight, but to lengthen the glass and cut down the sugar per glass, dilute with sparkling mineral water.

For 1 (300ml):
2 small green dessert apples (should make about
    120ml juice)
50g fresh root ginger (should make about 30ml juice)
Ice
150ml sparkling mineral water

Juice the apples and ginger together. You don't need to prepare either in any way: just chop and juice them straight, core, peel and all.

Pour into a long glass, with a few ice cubes, top with the sparkling mineral water and stir.

» 83 calories

More on » apples p288 » ginger p200

Horseradish is a member of the brassica family, and one of the plants richest in **glucosinolates**, powerful **antioxidants** which appear to protect against cancer. Anti-bacterial and anti-viral, horseradish has a very strong flavour – you can tell how ferocious it is when you peel and grate it fresh, as it makes your eyes water, and you'll soon understand why it's traditionally used for clearing the sinuses!

Crimson Mary

A healthy version of a classic Bloody Mary, using beetroot juice as the base. Beetroot juice is very easy to make yourself, super-fresh and nutrient-rich, or you can now buy it by the carton.

This is delicious with a salt and pepper rim. Rub the juiced lime halves around the rim of the glasses and then put the rim of the upside-down glass onto a saucer of cracked pepper and flaky salt. Top it with freshly grated horseradish: this can be kept ready-peeled in the freezer, and grated from frozen with a microplane.

If you are juicing your own beetroots, add a little fresh root ginger – and you could, of course, add 200ml vodka (8 x 25ml shots)...

For 8 (1 litre):
1.6kg smallish beetroots, or 1 litre shop-bought
    beetroot juice
Juice of 4 limes
1 tsp celery salt
1 tsp Tabasco sauce (or to taste)
Black pepper
1 tsp Worcestershire sauce (or to taste)

To serve
Ice (optional)
Fresh horseradish, grated (to taste)
Stalks of lovage, or celery sticks
Lime quarters

Wash the beetroots, and cut off the leaves. Chop and juice. Small beetroots tend to give a milder flavour.

Mix all the ingredients together in a large jug, then chill in the fridge.

Pour into tall tumblers with ice (if using). Add grated horseradish and serve with a lovage or celery stick stirrer and some lime quarters.

» 53 calories per serving

More on » beetroot p85

Glossary

ALA (Alpha Linolenic acid) A type of omega-3 fatty acid found in plants such as flaxseeds, rapeseed and walnuts and their oils. It can be converted in the body to EPA and DHA (see right), or can be used as an energy source.

Amino acids There are 22 nitrogen-containing amino acids which, in different combinations, form proteins.

Anthocyanin A type of phytonutrient, called a flavonoid. Anthocyanins typically give plants their red to blue colours, e.g. blueberries, blackcurrants, red grapes and cherries.

Anti-inflammatory A substance that acts to reduce inflammation in the body.

Antioxidant A substance that prevents damage from free radicals and oxidative stress.

Apoptosis Programmed cell death in response to signals from within the body – the cell effectively commits suicide.

Bacterium Single-celled organism. Millions of bacteria live in harmony in the body; however if this balance is disrupted, or foreign bacteria access the body, ill health can follow.

Beta-carotene Known as pro-vitamin A, this is a plant carotene that can be converted to vitamin A in the body.

Carbohydrate Sugars and starches mostly found in plants. The body can convert these sugars to energy or energy stores.

Carotenoid A type of phytonutrient that gives plants their yellow, orange and red colours, e.g. carrots, sweet potatoes, kale, mangoes, apricots and peaches.

Cholesterol Made by the body in the liver and also found in some foods, this is important for cellular function, formation of bile, certain hormones and vitamin D. There are different types of cholesterol: HDL (high-density lipoprotein) is considered protective, while LDL (low-density lipoprotein) in excess is considered unhealthy.

Cytokine A protein that is produced by cells in the immune system which regulate the body's immune response by sending through messages to other cells.

DHA (Docosahexaenoic acid) A type of omega-3 fatty acid found in cold-water 'oily' fish and, in small amounts, in seaweed. It is required for the development and proper function of the brain and nervous system.

DNA A cell's genetic blueprint, found within its nucleus.

Electrolytes The form that minerals take when dissolved in the body, electrolytes can conduct electrical impulses.

Enzyme A protein that acts as a catalyst to speed chemical reactions in the body.

EPA (Eicosapentaenoic acid) A type of omega-3 fatty acid found in cold-water 'oily' fish and, in small amounts, in seaweed. It generally has an anti-inflammatory effect within the body.

Fermentation A process in which an organism, such as bacteria or yeast, converts sugars and starches into an alcohol or acid.

Fibre The indigestible part of plant-based food. Soluble fibre dissolves in water and is beneficial for blood-sugar balance and satiety amongst other things. Insoluble fibre does not dissolve in water and is able to increase stool bulk and transit time.

Flavonoids A large group of polyphenols that provide colour to plants and have many beneficial actions in the human body.

Free radicals Any atom or group of atoms with an unpaired electron that can cause damage to cells.

Glycaemic Index (GI) A measure of the rate at which a carbohydrate causes a rise in blood sugar.

Glucosinolates Sulphur-rich compounds found in cruciferous vegetables such as broccoli, cabbage, kale, Brussels sprouts, cauliflower and mustard.

Gluten A protein in many grains such as wheat, rye and barley that gives elasticity to dough. It should be avoided by those with coeliac disease.

Inflammation The body's reaction to injury, illness and other sources of stress.

Lipids Hydrocarbons that form part of the structure of cells. These are insoluble in water, but soluble in alcohol. Some are used as a source of energy.

MCT (Medium-chain Triglyceride) A type of fatty acid that is soluble in water and known for its health benefits. It is typically found in coconut oil and olive oil.

Micronutrients Vitamins and minerals found in plant- and animal-based food that are needed by the body in small amounts.

Minerals Inorganic substances with a definite chemical arrangement that are needed by the body in small amounts.

Monounsaturated fats Plant fatty acids with one double bond, e.g. olive oil and avocado oil.

Nitrate An inorganic compound made of nitrogen and oxygen, found in several foods as an additive or preservative, e.g. in cured meats.

Omega-3 and omega-6 fatty acids Polyunsaturated fatty acids needed for various functions within the body.

Oxalates Organic acids made by plants, animals and humans.

PCBs (Polychlorinated Biphenyls) Organic compounds that are highly resistant to breakdown by biological or chemical means. They are toxic to all living organisms and are lipid-soluble, so can accumulate in body fat.

Pectin A carbohydrate that is a soluble dietary fibre.

Peptides Short chains of two or more amino acids.

Phytoestrogens Compounds found in plants that can have an oestrogen-like effect on the body.

Phytonutrients (Phytochemicals) A large group of naturally occurring substances found in plants.

Phytosterols These are sterols found in plants that are similar in make-up to cholesterol but are generally not absorbed into the bloodstream. They may have a cholesterol-lowering effect.

Plant hormones Chemicals that regulate plant-growth processes.

Polyacetylenes Bioactive compounds found in Apiaceae food plants such as carrots, celery and parsley.

Polyphenols Largest family of phytochemicals found in plants.

Polyunsaturated fats These are found in plant- and animal-based foods (e.g. in salmon, vegetable oils, and some nuts and seeds) and contain two or more double bonds.

Prebiotic A non-digestible plant fibre, e.g. in chicory, artichokes, leeks and bananas, that acts as food for probiotics (see below).

Proanthocyanidins A flavonoid mainly found in the skin and seeds of grapes and is also present in cocoa and apples, amongst other foods. They are powerful antioxidants.

Probiotic A substance that helps the growth of beneficial bacteria in the gut.

Protein Various combinations of amino acids that form complex nitrogen-based organic compounds. Proteins can be animal- or plant-based and are needed for growth and repair, and to form enzymes and hormones.

Punicalagins Complex polyphenol compounds found in pomegranates, with high levels of antioxidant activity.

RDA (Recommended Dietary Allowance) The daily amount of a nutrient needed by the body to prevent nutritional deficiency.

Saturated fats These are mostly of animal origin, but some are vegetable fats that are solid at room temperature.

Trans fats Processed fats that cause damage in the body.

Unsaturated fats Vegetable fats that are liquid at room temperature.

Vitamins Organic substances, most of which cannot be made in the body, but all of which are needed in small amounts. Vitamins are either fat-soluble or water-soluble.

Useful websites

American Journal of Clinical Nutrition
ajcn.nutrition.org
This top-rated journal publishes original research on nutrition topics that underpins government and health organisation reports.

Authority Nutrition
authoritynutrition.com
Accessible health, nutrition and weight-loss content based on scientific evidence.

British Nutrition Foundation
nutrition.org.uk/healthyliving
This registered charity delivers authoritative information about nutrition science, healthy eating and food in schools.

Huffington Post
huffingtonpost.com/healthy-living
Articles and entertaining lists on the theme of healthy living.

The Institute for Functional Medicine
functionalmedicine.org
Patient-centred approach to medical research on current issues, including the role of diet in the development of disease.

Institute of Food Research (IFR)
ifr.ac.uk
Based in Norwich, this is a publicly funded UK research institute that addresses challenges of food security, diet and health, healthy ageing and food waste.

John Innes Centre
jic.ac.uk
An independent, international centre based in Norwich, UK, that specialises in plant science and microbiology.

Linus Pauling Institute
lpi.oregonstate.edu
A Nobel Prize-winning institute that promotes optimal health and lifespan through research into the biology of ageing, age-related diseases and healthy ageing.

Nutritional Research Foundation
nutritionalresearch.org/research
Provides up-to-date information, advice and research about plant-based diets.

The Nutrition Society
nutritionsociety.org/yournutrition
Europe's largest society for nutrition, this website offers insights about current issues from researchers.

The Nutrition Source
hsph.harvard.edu/nutritionsource
From the experts at the Harvard School of Public Health, this website provides current information on scientific breakthroughs, and advice for leading a healthy, sustainable lifestyle.

PubMed
ncbi.nlm.nih.gov/pubmed
A free resource with more than 25 million citations from biomedical literature, life science journals and online books.

Scientific Advisory Committee on Nutrition
gov.uk/government/collections/sacn-reports-and-position-statements
UK government reports and recommendations on nutrition issues: most recently, a study of the link between consumption of carbohydrates, sugars, starch and fibre and a range of health outcomes.

SELF Nutrition Data
nutritiondata.self.com
Dietary advice, interactive tools for diet analysis and healthy recipes.

Telegraph
telegraph.co.uk/food-and-drink
Regular features on food trends and healthy eating.

The World's Healthiest Foods
whfoods.com
A popular healthy food website with articles on various nutrition topics, recipes and lifestyle advice.

World Cancer Research Fund
wcrf-uk.org
The WCRF supports scientific research into cancer prevention, and advises on dietary changes to reduce the risk of cancer.

Further reading

Bowden, J., *The 150 Healthiest Foods on Earth: The Surprising, Unbiased Truth About What You Should Eat and Why* (Fair Winds Press, 2007)

Food Standards Agency and Public Health England, *McCance and Widdowson's The Composition of Foods*, 7th edition (Royal Society of Chemistry, 2014)

Katz, S. E., *Wild Fermentation* (Chelsea Green Publishing, 2003)

Kurihara, H., *Everyday Harumi* (Conran, 2009)

Murray, M. T. and Pizzorno, J. E., *The Encyclopedia of Natural Medicine*, 3rd edition (Simon & Schuster, 2012)

Osiecki, H., *The Nutrient Bible*, 9th edition (Bioconcepts, 2014)

Ottolenghi, Y. and Tamimi, S., *Jerusalem* (Ebury Press, 2012)

Steel, S. (ed), *Neal's Yard Remedies: Healing Foods* (Dorling Kindersley, 2013)

Index

Acknowledgements

I had lots of help on recipe testing and food shoots. Huge thanks to the whole Perch Hill team, particularly Sorrel Scott Blackmore who had so many brilliant ideas, as well as helping with endless recipe testing, and writing up recipes for months on end. And Jo Clark, who was there at the first food shoot and at the last, and did the final invaluable read-through of every recipe. I could not have done the book without them. Thanks too to Debbie Waters, Shenley Moore, Lily Canetty-Clarke, Anna Canetty-Clarke, Melanie Todd, Connie Booth and Sophie Kusel. My daughter Molly Nicolson helped testing on occasions too, as did Esther Palmer and my sister, Jane, as well as friends, Sofka Zinovieff, Flora McDonnell and Carien van Boxtel, all at different times over the many years of this book's evolution.

Tessa Bishop worked out the calorie counts for every single one of the 250-plus recipes, as well as patiently proofreading each chapter as I fed them through to her. Colin Pilbeam grew most of the veg, and Josie Lewis, Mary Pocock and Josh Asson the herbs and edible flowers we used from the garden.

My friend Kate Hubbard smoothed out the language of the most important parts of the book, making the chapter introductions in particular easier to read, and friends Lucinda Fraser, Aurea Carpenter and Rebecca Nicolson all read parts and gave me advice too.

At Bloomsbury, Natalie Bellos was always there with truly book-changing advice and I'm really grateful for her clear-thinking realism and belief, and with her Alison Cowan, Alison Glossop, Xa Shaw Stewart and Marina Asenjo. Thank you so much for your support – and to Caroline Michel, my agent. Thank you to Susan Fleming, who was a joy to work with, for her brilliant editing and lightness of touch. Lawrence Morton has done a beautiful job in terms of design, with this book in the same family as my previous cookbooks, but simpler, cleaner and somehow healthier in its feel. I also want to thank Susie Smith and Alison Walker, the editor and food editor at *Country Living* magazine.

I wrote quite a few of these recipes first for them.

I stayed in various places to write – Alexandra Henderson's house on Hydra on many occasions, as well as Martin and Miranda Thomas's house in Cornwall. That made the job so much nicer to do.

Enormous thanks to the nutritionists and nutritional experts – Alice Lyon, Juliet Norman (julietnormannutrition.com) and Lisa Smith (nutriology.co.uk), as well as the medical doctor/nutritional therapist, Sarah Macdermott. This book had a steep learning curve. I felt like I was learning or to an extent re-learning a whole new language and they were, all four, incredibly patient with my basic questions, as well as hugely generous with their knowledge and expertise. Alice worked on it with me for well over a year, and Lisa helped me with ideas for the Eat yourself healthy section. I am so grateful to you all.

My business partner and friend, Lou Farman, and my family really did have to put up with more on this book than any other. It has been a vastly long haul, and that was hard and oppressive at times. Adam, Rosie, Molly and Lou all put up with the stress and odd bout of tears. Thank you.

I have dedicated this book to Jonathan Buckley – the photographer I have worked with for a long time now. We have shot gardens, plants, wild flowers and food together – and together we evolve a style for each book that we both love. It's Jonathan more than anyone who has moulded the look of this book. Massive, heart-felt thanks.

Recipes

Many thanks for specific recipes go to Tom Wolff for the Bircher muesli (see page 20); Francis Hamel-Cooke for Frank's granola (page 21); Esther Palmer for Esther's spelt and orange porridge (page 25); Dina Hermelin for Swedish crispbread (page 32); Alice Lyon for Buckwheat pancakes (page 34); Jeni Cook for Healthy breakfast 'crumble' (page 42); Jane Raven for Eggs with shrimps (page 55), Kale and chickpea curry (page 235) and Super-simple fruit bullets (page 290); Sorrel Scott Blackmore for A more virtuous full English (page 60), Warm Asian vegetable noodle salad (page 132), Cucumber and wakame salad (page 154) and Black bean and chicken burritos (page 231); Jo Clark for Sweet potato, carrot and peanut butter soup (page 72), Lemon chicken and herb salad (page 153) and Perry pears with Parma ham and goats' cheese (page 162); Harumi Kurihara for Miso soup with konjac noodles (page 97) and Watercress with a light peanut dressing (page 251); Sophie Burnside for the Spiced beetroot soda bread (page 102); Lily Canetty-Clarke for the Wilted kale, avocado and pomegranate salad (page 116) and Vietnamese summer rolls (page 210); Sally Edwards for the Asparagus, pea and broad bean salad (page 126); Kamalaya health resort for Green pawpaw, carrot and cashew salad (page 128) and Steam-stirred pak choi with ginger and lemongrass (page 200); Sue Thompson for Roast roots with walnut oil dressing (page 134); Hugh Fearnley-Whittingstall for Parsnip, rocket and lentil salad (page 138); Gartine's Restaurant, Amsterdam, for the Wild salmon tartare (page 148); Debbie Waters for the Smoked chicken, mango and spring herb salad (page 156), Peanut and sesame noodle dressing (page 226) and Tomato and poppy seed tart (page 282); Tony Dasent for Marinated olives (page 179); Lisa Smith for Seed and nut protein bread (page 191) and Protein berry smoothie (page 343); Hiroe Kaji for Fried peppers Japanese style (page 199); Sofka Zinovieff for Patmos chickpeas (page 201); Teresa Wallace for the Courgette 'meatballs' (page 206); Laura Gatacre for the Raw herring plate (page 216); Ivan Samarine for the Provençal squid stew (page 246); Lawrence Malinson for Smoked haddock and beetroot gratin (page 252); Alison MacDonald for Sweet potato, coconut and lime 'dauphinoise' (page 273); Rosanna James for Snooker ball nectarines (page 294); and Yotam Ottolenghi for the Grilled figs (page 306).

About the author

Sarah Raven worked as a doctor at the Royal Sussex County Hospital in Brighton before becoming a broadcaster, teacher and writer. She has cooked all her life for family and friends with an emphasis and commitment to goodness, healthiness and general wellbeing. Sarah runs her own cookery and gardening school at Perch Hill in East Sussex, and has established a mail order gardening company with 80,000 active customers. She has made regular appearances on the BBC's *Great British Garden Revival* and *Gardeners' World*; and she is the author of *Sarah Raven's Food for Friends and Family*, *Sarah Raven's Complete Christmas*, *Sarah Raven's Garden Cookbook* (which was the Guild of Food Writers' Cookery Book of the Year 2008) and *The Cutting Garden*.

About the photographer

Jonathan Buckley is a specialist garden and food photographer who has been collaborating with Sarah Raven for many years. His work has been widely published in books, magazines and newspapers worldwide. His awards have included the Garden Media Guild Garden Photographer of the Year, Feature Photographer of the Year and Single Image of the Year.

Bloomsbury Publishing
An imprint of Bloomsbury Publishing Plc

50 Bedford Square	1385 Broadway
London	New York
WC1B 3DP	NY 10018
UK	USA

bloomsbury.com

BLOOMSBURY and the Diana logo are trademarks of Bloomsbury Publishing Plc

First published in Great Britain 2016
Text © Sarah Raven's Cutting Garden Limited, 2016
Photography © Jonathan Buckley, 2016

Sauerkraut recipe (page 194) reprinted from *Wild Fermentation* © 2003 by Sandor Ellix Katz,
used with permission from Chelsea Green Publishing (chelseagreen.com).

British Library Cataloguing-in-Publication Data
A catalogue record for this book is available from the British Library.

ISBN: HB: 978-1-4088-3555-5
              ePub: 978-1-4088-7269-7

2 4 6 8 10 9 7 5 3 1

Designer: Lawrence Morton
Photographer: Jonathan Buckley
Indexer: Vicki Robinson

Printed and bound in China by RR Donnelly

To find out more about our authors and books visit www.bloomsbury.com. Here you will find extracts,
author interviews, details of forthcoming events and the option to sign up for our newsletters.